Ayşe Erkmen & Mona Hatoum
Displacements / Entortungen

Museum der bildenden Künste Leipzig

Ayşe Erkmen
Mona Hatoum
Displacements
Entortungen

Inhalt / Contents

Grußwort der Kulturstiftung des Bundes

»Wir müssen«, so sagte die mit dem Bauhaus aus Deutschland vertriebene Textilkünstlerin Anni Albers, »aus dem Wolkenreich, das wir in aller Unbestimmtheit bewohnen, zur Erde zurückkehren und das Wahrhaftigste erfahren, das es gibt: Material.« Die – wie es im Ausstellungstitel heißt – »Entortung«, mit der Anni Albers ihre unfreiwilligen Erfahrungen machen musste, verleiht ihrer Wahrnehmung der Dinge im Raum eine ganz eigene Dringlichkeit. Ein vergleichbarer Perspektivwechsel lässt sich auch bei den in dieser Leipziger Doppelausstellung präsentierten Künstlerinnen Ayşe Erkmen und Mona Hatoum erkennen. Für beide bilden Erfahrungen des Wandelns zwischen verschiedenen räumlichen und kulturellen Bezügen einen breiten Vorrat an Material, mit dem sie sich in großer Sensibilität und in überaus konkreter, ›irdischer‹ Weise auseinandersetzen. Aber weder in den Skulpturen noch in den Rauminstallationen kommt das einmal verwendete Material je zu sich selbst. Immer sind es semantische Störungen und irritierende Bedeutungsverschiebungen, die die Arbeiten beider Künstlerinnen auslösen: Mona Hatoums filigran verfremdete Reproduktion einer Handgranate in kostbarstem venezianischem Muranoglas versteht sich als ironische Nobilitierung eines Tötungsinstruments ebenso wie als Kommentar zur Globalisierung von Kunst- und Waffenhandel. Auch Ayşe Erkmen greift in der in grüne Keramik gefassten Landminen-Edition das Thema Waffen auf. Ihre Leipziger Raumintervention *Half of* kommentiert dagegen eine Museumsarchitektur, deren monumentale Zentralkubatur sie – Schritt für Schritt für Schritt – in eine im Raum schwebende Serie stetig verkleinerter Stoffkörper transformiert. Eine minimalistische ›Luftnummer‹ ist das – und zugleich das subtile Durchkreuzen der architektonischen Rhetorik eines der wichtigsten deutschen Kunstmuseen.

Am Ende ist es weniger die Wahrhaftigkeit als vielmehr die Genauigkeit, mit der sowohl Ayşe Erkmens wie auch Mona Hatoums Verfremdungen einem konkreten Ort oder einem Thema gerecht zu werden versuchen. Es ist ein Glücksfall, diese Versuche im Museum der bildenden Künste Leipzig in einer Doppelausstellung erfahren zu können, die Hauptwerke beider Künstlerinnen ebenso zeigt wie neue Interventionen vor Ort. Die Kulturstiftung des Bundes dankt daher dem Museumsdirektor Dr. Alfred Weidinger sowie dem gesamten Ausstellungsteam unter der Leitung von Dr. Frédéric Bußmann mit Elizabeth Youngman und insbesondere den Künstlerinnen Ayşe Erkmen und Mona Hatoum für ein Ausstellungsprojekt, dem wir ein großes Publikum und eine positive Resonanz weit über Leipzig hinaus wünschen.

Hortensia Völckers
Vorstand / Künstlerische Direktorin

Alexander Farenholtz
Vorstand / Verwaltungsdirektor

Greetings from the German Federal Cultural Foundation

The textile artist Anni Albers, who together with the Bauhaus was expelled from Germany, declared, 'We must return to the earth from the realm of clouds that we inhabit in utmost uncertainty and experience the most truthful thing that exists: material.' The 'displacement' – as it is called in the exhibition title – which Anni Albers had to involuntarily experience, gives her spatial perception of things an immediacy of its own. A comparable change of perspective can also be seen in the work of the two artists presented in the double exhibition in Leipzig, Ayşe Erkmen and Mona Hatoum. For both artists, experiences of transformation between different spatial and cultural references provide a broad supply of material with which they work with great sensitivity in an exceedingly 'earthly' way. However, the material used never comes into its own in the sculptures or installations. The works of both artists are always semantically disruptive and provoke disturbing shifts of meaning. Mona Hatoum's delicately altered reproduction of a hand grenade in the most opulent Venetian glass from Murano can be understood as an ironic ennoblement of an instrument of death as well as also a commentary on the globalisation of art and weapon trades. Ayşe Erkmen also takes up the subject of weapons in her green ceramic landmine edition, while her spatial intervention in Leipzig, *Half of,* comments on the monumental architecture of the museum that she transforms – step by step – into a soaring series of fabric bodies that increasingly decrease in size. It is a minimalistic 'aerial act' – and simultaneously the subtle thwarting of the architectonic rhetoric of one of the most important German art museums.

Ultimately it is less the truthfulness than the precision with which both Ayşe Erkmen's and Mona Hatoum's disassociations aim to do justice to a specific place or a subject. It is a stroke of luck to be able to experience these attempts in the Leipzig Museum of Fine Arts in a double exhibition that shows major works by both artists as well as new interventions created in situ. The German Federal Cultural Foundation extends its thanks to the museum's director Dr Alfred Weidinger and his whole exhibition team under Dr Frédéric Bußmann with Elizabeth Youngman and especially the artists Ayşe Erkmen and Mona Hatoum for an exhibition project that we hope reaches a large audience and receives a positive reception that extends beyond Leipzig.

Hortensia Völckers
Executive Board / Artistic Director

Alexander Farenholtz
Executive Board / Administration Director

Grußwort der Peter und Irene Ludwig Stiftung

Ayşe Erkmen und Mona Hatoum in einer Ausstellung einander gegenüber zu stellen rückt zwei Künstlerinnen in den Mittelpunkt, die jede für sich in den letzten Jahrzehnten ein bemerkenswertes und international höchst anerkanntes und wahrgenommenes Werk geschaffen haben.

Beide verbindet – bei aller Unterschiedlichkeit und Eigenheit – eine spezifische Konzentration auf Fragestellungen von politischer und gesellschaftlicher Tragweite, ohne je vordergründig eine ›Kunst über Politik‹ zu machen. Beide arbeiten konzeptuell, installativ und raumbezogen. Ayşe Erkmen insbesondere auch für den sogenannten öffentlichen Raum, Mona Hatoum mit einer spezifischen Konzentration auf prekäre Räume und gewaltbestimmte Situationen. Die Ausstellung *Displacements / Entortungen* zu betiteln folgt daher einer inneren Logik, die sich aus den Werken der beiden Künstlerinnen ableiten lässt.

In einer heutigen Welt gilt es die Aktivitäten der parlamentarischen und der außerparlamentarischen Politik im Auge zu behalten. Die Themen, die bis vor kurzem in der Bundesrepublik insbesondere unter Opposition und Alternative verstanden wurden, oder – bezogen auf die APO der ausgehenden 1960er Jahre – zu einem historischen Begriff geworden sind, lassen sich im Zeitalter der Globalisierung nur in der Mehrzahl und auch nur durch mehrere Begriffe charakterisieren: Klimawandel, Freihandel, Verschwinden des öffentlichen Raumes, Verschwinden der Institutionen, Ende der Kunst, Skulptur versus Performance, Kunst und Politik, Ort, Un-Ort, Post-Kolonialismus, Neo-Liberalismus, asymmetrische Kriege, Fluchtbewegungen, Diktaturen, Demokratien, Dystopien, Freiheiten, Märkte und Macht sind nur einige davon. Das Verhandeln und die Verschiebung von Identitäten stehen dabei immer wieder im Fokus.

KünstlerInnen sind als kritische DenkerInnen über unsere Zeit und in unserer Zeit Teil dieser gesamten Entwicklungen. Sie reflektieren und kommentieren und entziehen sich den Diskursen nicht, sondern machen sie nutzbar für ihr Werk. Eine Ausstellung zu fördern, die Arbeiten von Erkmen und Hatoum gemeinsam zeigt und sie unter den Aspekten der Entortung, der Verschiebungen, eben des Displacement präsentiert, lag für die Peter und Irene Ludwig Stiftung aufgrund der Aktualität gewissermaßen auf der Hand.

Dass für dieses Projekt nicht nur bereits bestehende Arbeiten versammelt und neu präsentiert werden, sondern auch eigene Werke entstanden sind, freut uns umso mehr, zeigt das doch auch den anregenden Charakter des inhaltlichen Ausstellungsansatzes für die beiden Künstlerinnen.

Die Ludwig Stiftung dankt den Künstlerinnen und den Kuratoren Dr. Frédéric Bußmann und Elizabeth Youngman sehr herzlich für ihr Engagement sowie die Ausstellungsidee und -konzeption. Dem neuen Museumsdirektor Dr. Alfred Weidinger gratulieren wir herzlich zum Start in Leipzig und freuen uns auf die kommende Zusammenarbeit. Das Museum der bildenden Künste Leipzig zu fördern und zu unterstützen, dort zukunftsweisende Projekte für Leipzig und darüber hinaus realisieren zu helfen, ist für uns Ansporn und Motivation zugleich. Wir wünschen dem Museum und der Ausstellung die verdiente Aufmerksamkeit und den BesucherInnen neue Einsichten und ungewohnte Seherfahrungen.

Dr. Brigitte Franzen
Vorstand

Greetings from the Peter and Irene Ludwig Foundation

The comparison of Ayşe Erkmen and Mona Hatoum in an exhibition focuses on two artists, each of which have created a body of noteworthy works that have received the highest recognition all over the world over the past decades.

In spite of their differences and distinctiveness, they both share an intrinsic concentration on issues of political and social significance, without the overt intention of making 'art about politics' their main objective. Both create works embracing conceptual approaches, installations and site-specific modes. Ayşe Erkmen is especially concerned with so-called public space, while Mona Hatoum concentrates on precarious spaces and situations that are defined by violence. There is an inherent logic to the exhibition's title, *Displacements / Entortungen,* which is derived from the works of both artists.

In today's world it is important to keep an eye on the activities of parliamentary and extra-parliamentary politics. The topics, which until just recently were considered oppositional or alternative in the Federal Republic of Germany or – as is the case with the Extra-Parliamentary Opposition, known as APO, of the late 1960s – have become historical terms, can only be characterised in the age of globalisation by referring to them in the plural or by using multiple terms: climate change, free trade, disappearance of public space, disappearance of institutions, the end of art, sculpture versus performance, art and politics, sites, non-sites, postcolonialism, neoliberalism, asymmetrical wars, refugee movements, dictatorships, democracies, dystopias, freedom, markets and power are only a few of them. The terms are always focused on the negotiation and displacement of identities.

As critical thinkers about our time and in our time, artists are part of this whole development. They reflect and comment and do not shy away from the discourse, appropriating it in their work. It seems obvious that the Peter and Irene Ludwig Foundation would support an exhibition that presents the work of Erkmen and Hatoum together under the issue of displacement due to the currency of this topic.

We are pleased that this project has also resulted in the creation of new works, instead of only presenting already existing works, thus showing that the exhibition content also had a stimulating effect on both artists.

The Ludwig Foundation would like to thank the artists and the curators Dr Frédéric Bußmann and Elizabeth Youngman for their commitment as well as for the idea and conception of the exhibition. Congratulations and a very warm welcome are also extended to the new director of the museum, Dr Alfred Weidinger, with whom we look forward to many exciting future projects. Our incentive and motivation is to promote and support the Leipzig Museum of Fine Arts in its implementation of forward-looking projects in Leipzig and beyond. We hope that both the museum and the exhibition will receive the attention they deserve, and we wish the visitors new insights and extraordinary visual experiences.

Dr Brigitte Franzen
Chairwoman

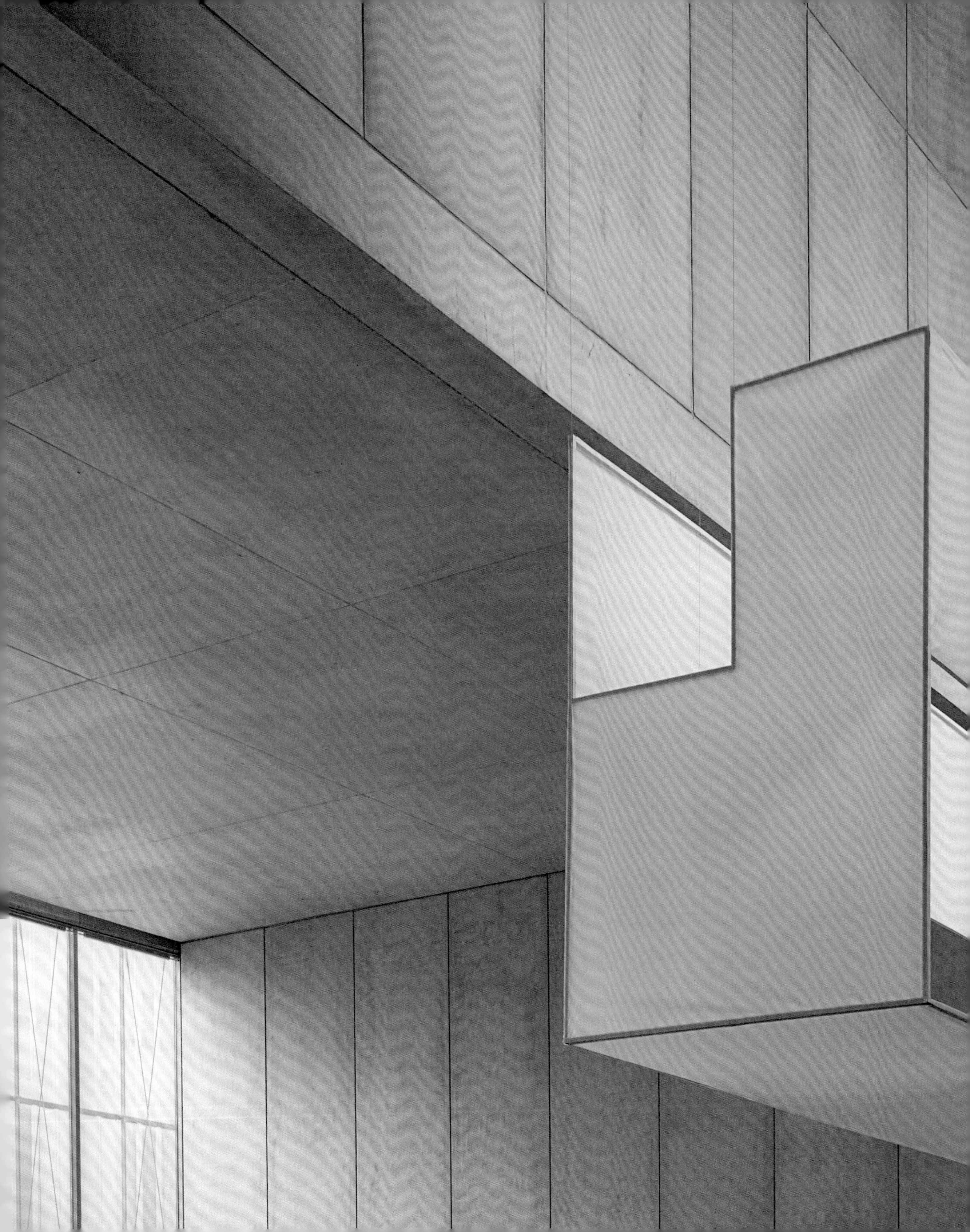

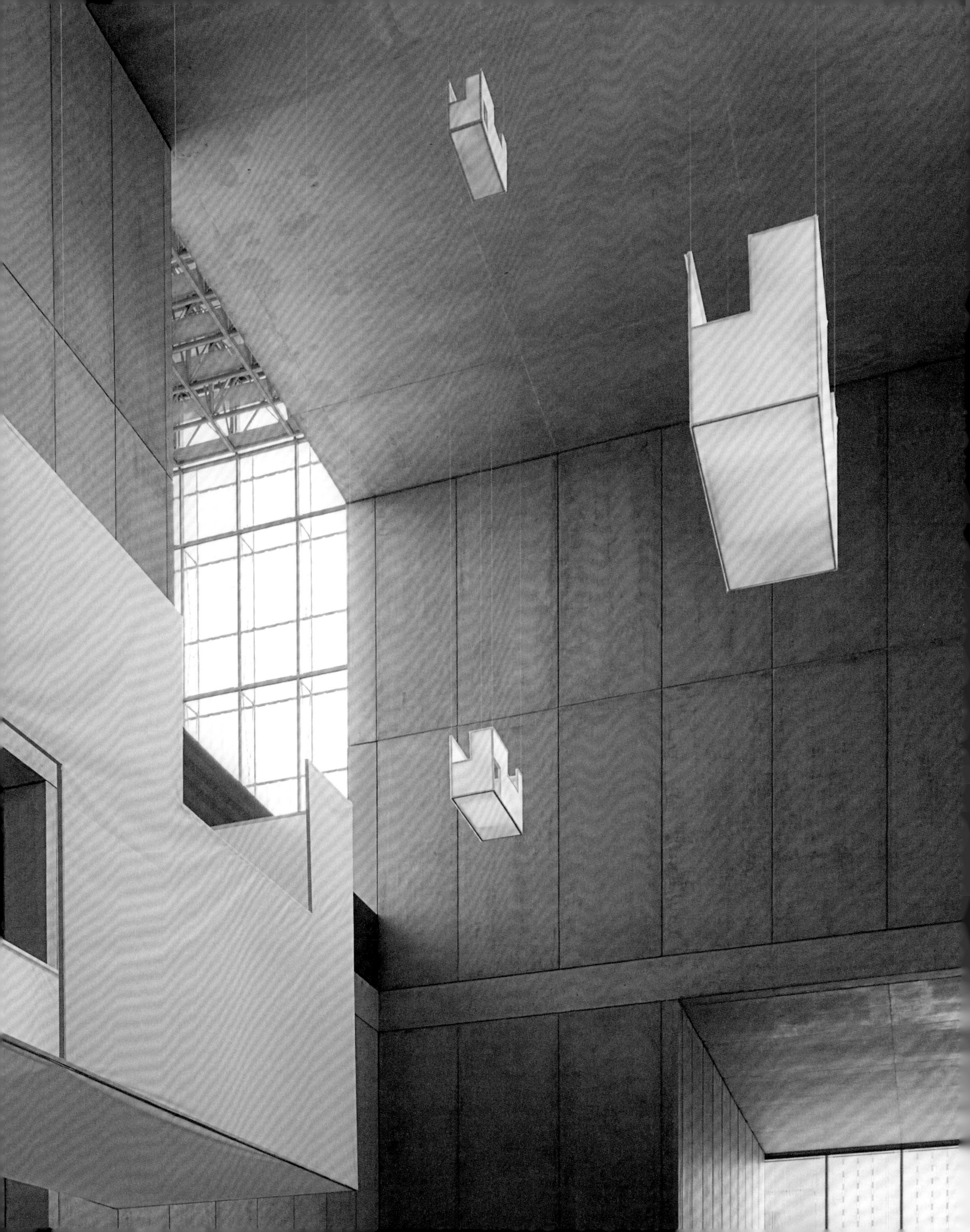

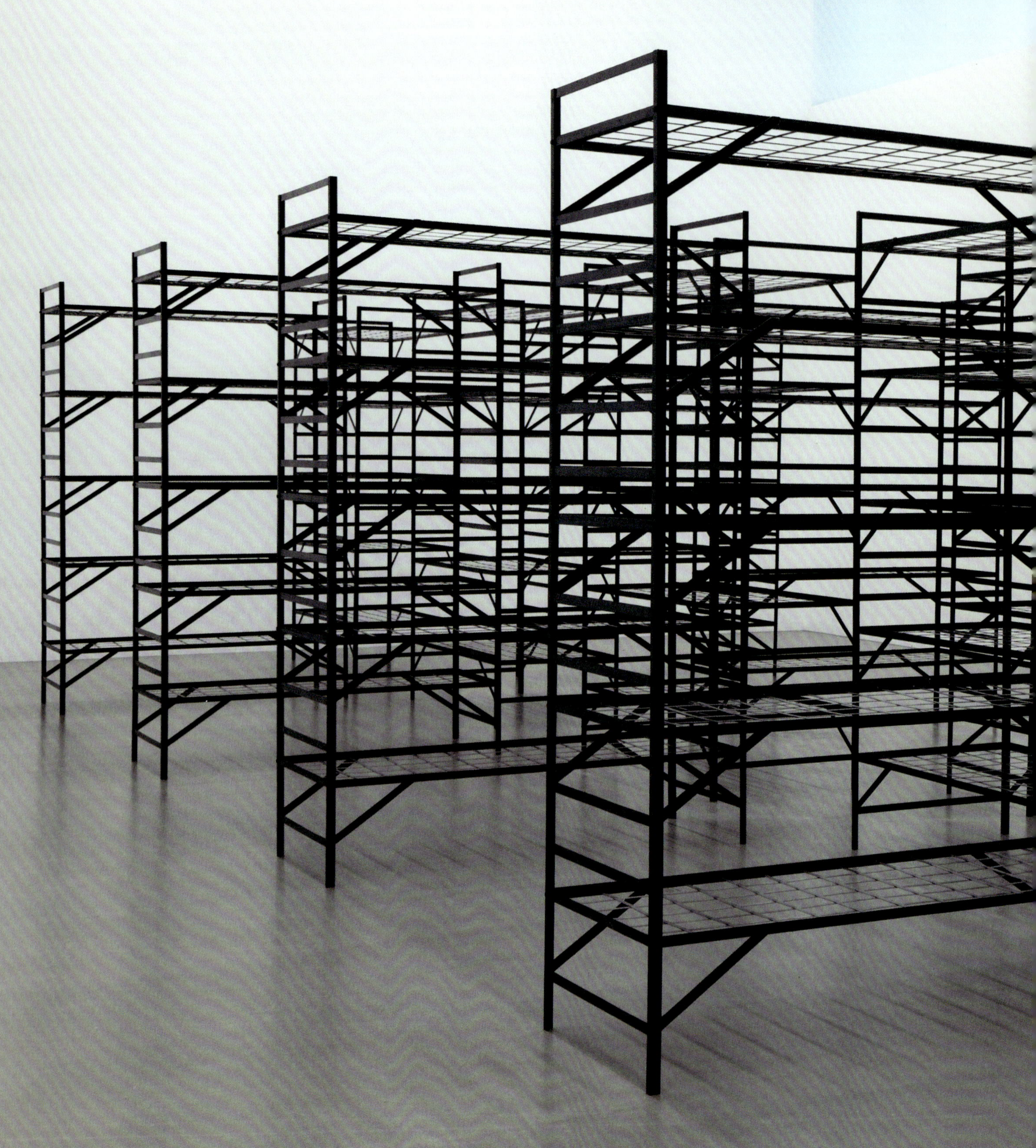

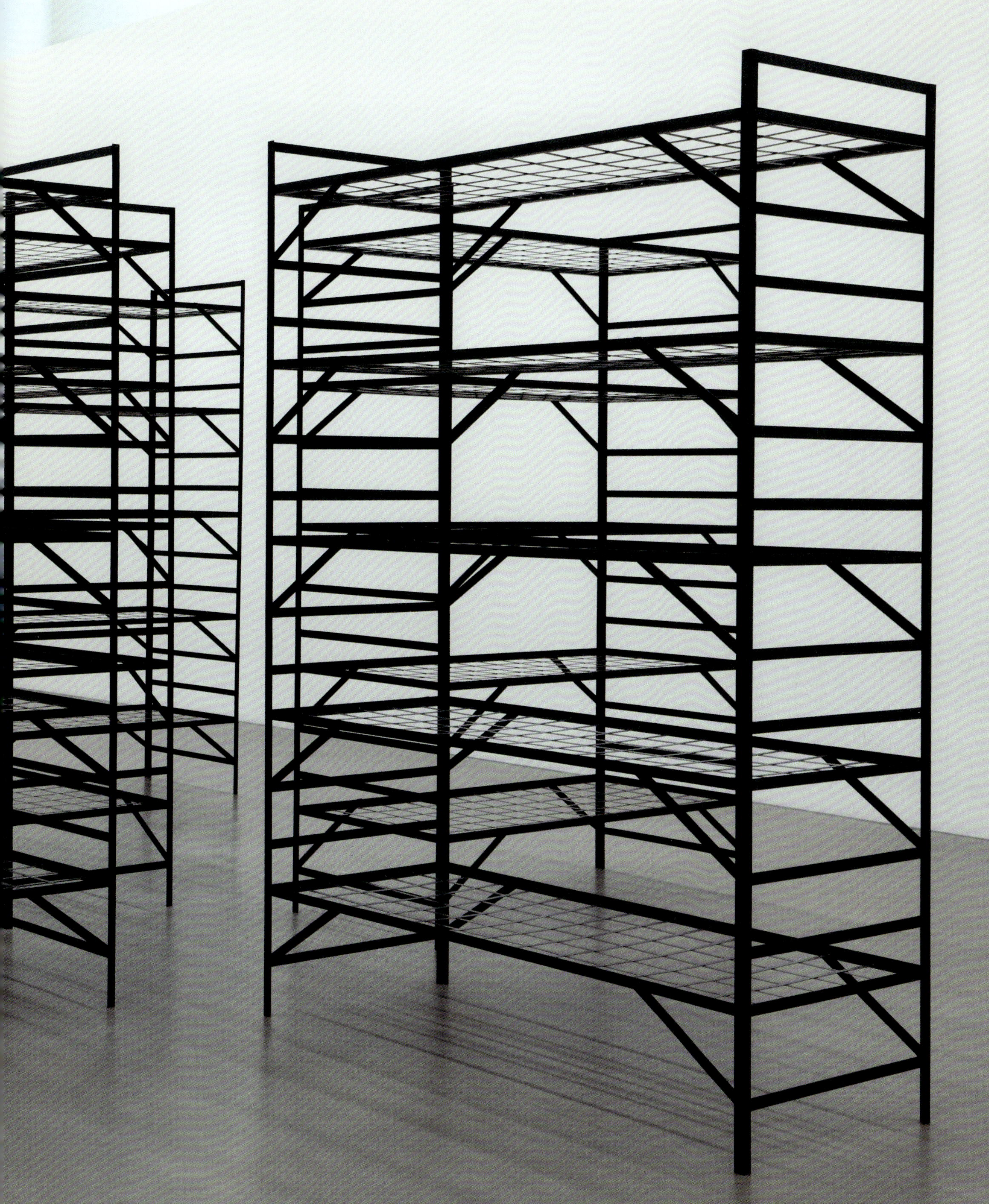

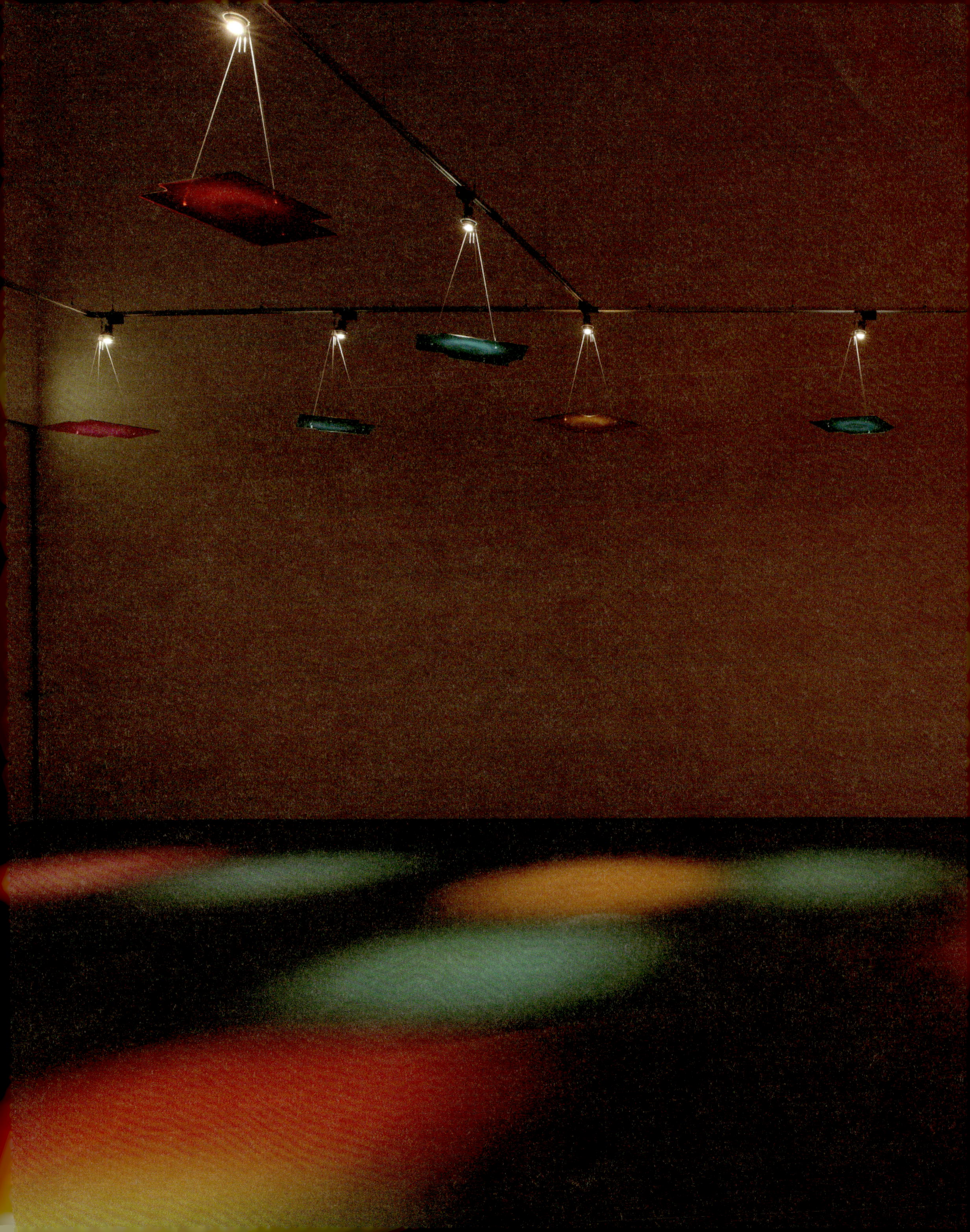

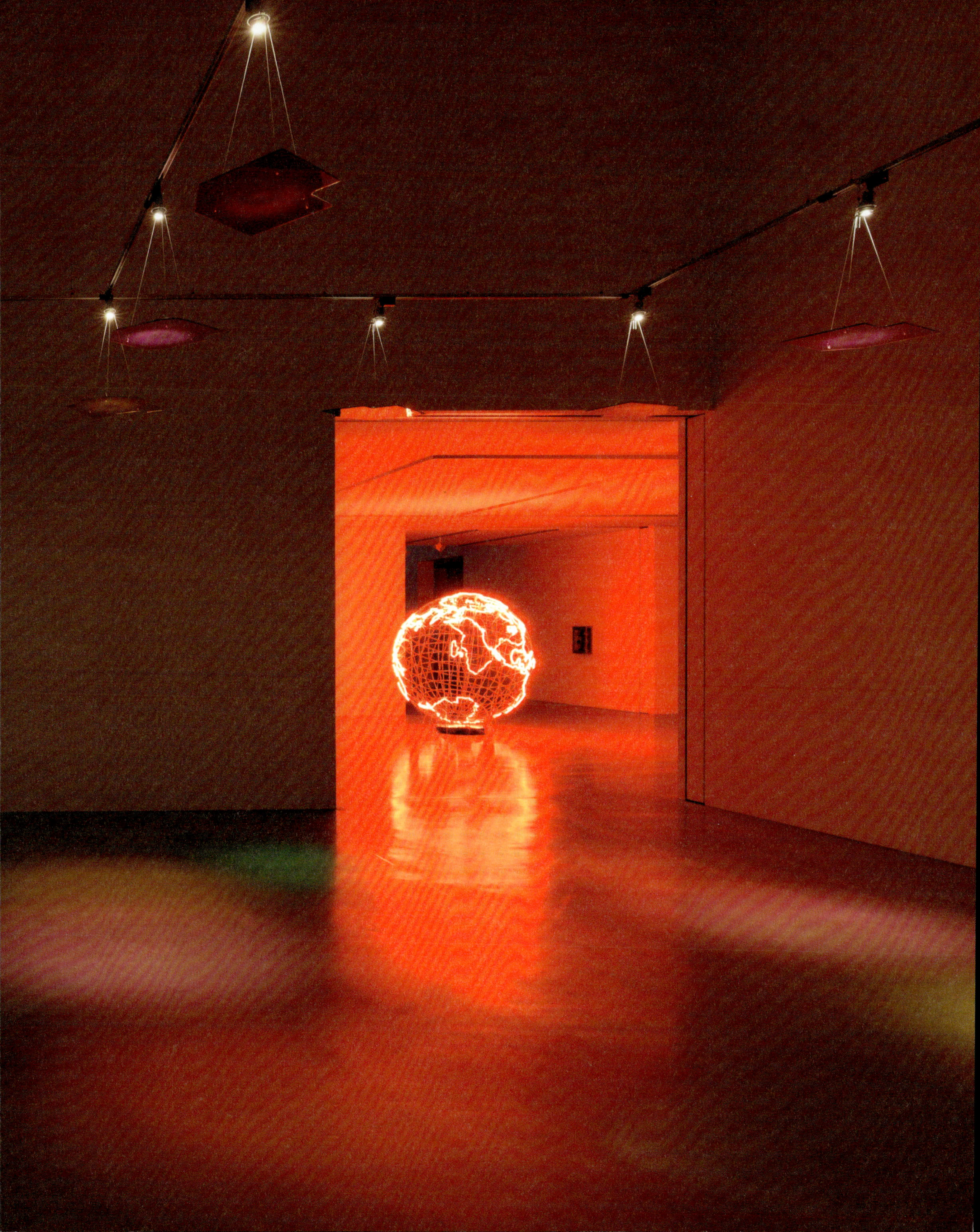

Ayşe Erkmen
Mona Hatoum

Displacements
Entortungen

Frédéric Bußmann & Elizabeth Youngman

Zur Kunst der Verschiebung

Unter dem Titel *The Art of Displacement: Mona Hatoum's Logic of Irreconcilables* veröffentlichte der palästinensisch-amerikanische Literaturkritiker und postkoloniale Theoretiker Edward Said im Jahr 2000 einen Essay über Mona Hatoum, in dem er mit dem englischen Begriff ›displacement‹ das Unvereinbare und Unversöhnliche in den Werken der Künstlerin beschreibt: »Vertrautheit und Fremdheit sind in seltsamster Weise miteinander verbunden, nah beieinander und unversöhnlich zugleich.«[1] Hatoum unterwandere das Gefühl emotionaler, intellektueller und auch physischer Sicherheit, entfremde Bekanntes und lasse Fremdes sich annähern. Diese Idee des Displacement, der Verschiebung oder wörtlich der Entortung, dient als Leitmotiv für die Ausstellung *Displacements / Entortungen,* für die Mona Hatoum und Ayşe Erkmen zu einer gemeinsamen Präsentation in das Museum der bildenden Künste Leipzig eingeladen wurden. Denn sowohl Hatoum als auch Erkmen haben künstlerische Positionen zwischen individueller Erfahrung und globaler Praxis entwickelt, in denen die Reflexion über die Spezifität eines Ortes und damit verbunden über künstlerische, aber auch über gesellschaftliche und politische Fragen eine bedeutende Rolle spielt.

Displacements wird als Inbegriff eines entgrenzten Verständnisses von Identität und Kunst, von Politik und Gesellschaft im Zeichen von Globalität und eines »global turn« verstanden,[2] wie es in Deutschland mit der *documenta X* (1997) von Catherine David zum ersten Mal in Diskurs und Praxis einer Ausstellung umgesetzt und in Okwui Enwezors *Documenta11* (2002) konsequent weltumfassend und in postkolonialer Sichtweise erweitert wurde.

Displacements (und die Freiheit des Denkens)

Das pluralistische Leitmotiv *Displacements* kann als offene Denkfigur verstanden werden, die psychologische, politische ebenso wie künstlerische Felder umfasst. Mit dem Begriff können Verschiebungen, Verdrängungen oder Entortungen bezeichnet werden. Er beschreibt also keine festen Zustände, sondern Prozesse, Transitorisches oder Bewegungen.[3] Ziel der damit in Verbindung gebrachten Kunstwerke ist nicht die Etablierung neuer Wahrheiten oder die Propagierung von Überzeugungen, sondern die Infragestellung von Gewissheiten und die Verschiebung fester Standpunkte.

Affektverschiebung

Mit dem Terminus ›Affektverschiebung‹ – im Englischen: ›displacement‹ –, der von Sigmund Freud in der *Traumdeutung* (1900) eingeführt und von seiner Tochter Anna weiterentwickelt wurde, wird in der Psy-

[1] »Familiarity and strangeness are locked together in the oddest way, adjacent and irreconcilable at the same time.« (Said 2000, 15.)

[2] Vgl. Casid / D'Souza 2014; vgl. stellvertretend für die Vielzahl von Publikationen zum Thema Global Art ferner Belting / Buddensieg 2016; vgl. zum Thema der Entgrenzung und Grenzüberschreitung im ästhetischen und philosophischen Feld Wenzel 2011.

[3] Displacement wird häufig auch mit ›Verschiebung‹ übersetzt. Der Begriff ›Entortung‹ verweist jedoch auch auf das von Robert Smithson geprägte Begriffspaar *site / non-site,* das für die künstlerische Strategie des Displacement wie auch der *dislocation* in den 1990er Jahren von zentraler Bedeutung war (vgl. Brohl 2003); Smithson setzte seine Vorstellung von Displacement in verschiedenen Werken wie etwa in *Chalk-Mirror Displacement* (1969, Art Institute of Chicago) oder in der Serie der *Yucatan Mirror Displacements* (1969, New York,

On the Art of Displacement

The Palestinian-American literary critic and postcolonial theorist Edward Said wrote an essay on Mona Hatoum entitled *The Art of Displacement: Mona Hatoum's Logic of Irreconcilables* in 2000 using the term *displacement* to describe the incongruous and irreconcilable aspects of the artist's works: 'Familiarity and strangeness are locked together in the oddest way, adjacent and irreconcilable at the same time.'[1] Said states that Hatoum undercuts the feeling of emotional, intellectual and physical safety, alienating the known and making the unknown more familiar. This idea of displacement is the leitmotif of *Displacements / Entortungen,* for which Mona Hatoum and Ayşe Erkmen were invited to present a joint exhibition of their works at the Leipzig Museum of Fine Arts. Hatoum and Erkmen have both developed artistic positions that link individual experience and global practice, in which reflection on the specifics of place as well as the related questions of art, society and politics play a central role.

Displacement is a byword for the borderless understanding of identity and art, and of politics and society in the name of globality and 'in the wake of the global turn', as it was presented in Germany for the first time in theory and practice of an exhibition by Catherine David at *documenta X* (1997) and then logically expanded to embrace the world from a postcolonial perspective by Okwui Enwezor at *Documenta11* (2002).[2]

Displacements (and Freedom of Thinking)

The pluralistic leitmotif of displacements – translated in German as *Entortungen*[3] – is to be understood as an open intellectual idea that encompasses psychological and political as well as artistic fields. The term does not describe a permanent condition, but rather processes, transitory states and movements. The aim of associating works of art in this way is not to establish new realities or promote convictions, but rather to question certainties and displace established positions.

Displacement in Psychology

The term *displacement* (*Verschiebung* or *Affektverschiebung*), which was introduced by Sigmund Freud in *The Interpretation of Dreams* (1900) and later refined by his daughter Anna, describes the process of displacing mental energy or emotion. The process includes the displacement of the original cause of a deeply felt or disquieting compulsion or feeling, such as the experience of fear or humiliation, onto an object or another person. This happens in the form of a substitution of ambiguous imagery: 'Displacement usually occurs in such a way that a colourless and abstract

[1] Said 2000, 15.

[2] See Casid / D'Souza 2014; in lieu of the many publications on global art, see especially Belting / Buddensieg 2016; on the subject of blurred and crossed borders in aesthetic and philosophical fields see Wenzel 2011.

[3] *Entortung* has been used as the German translation of the term *displacement* due to its reference to Robert Smithson's dichotomy *site / non-site,* which was of central importance for the artistic strategy of displacement as well as dislocation in the 1990s (see Brohl 2003); Smithson explored his idea of displacement in various works, including *Chalk-Mirror Displacement* (1969, Art Institute of Chicago) or in the series of *Yukatan Mirror Displacements* (1969, Solomon R. Guggenheim Museum, New York). The unwieldiness of the term *Entortung* is reminiscent of Theodor W. Adorno's term *Entkunstung,* or the de-aestheticisation of art.

4 Freud 1900/2000, 335; vgl. zur Verschiebungsarbeit ebd., 305–308.

5 Vgl. Kuhlmann 2014, 12. »Exilierte begreifen sich als Ausgegrenzte im doppelten Sinne: Sie sind ausgeschlossen vom Leben in ihrer Ursprungsgemeinschaft im Heimatland und sie gehören nicht zur Gesellschaft, in der sie leben (müssen).« (Ebd.)

6 Adorno 1951/2014, 35. »Jeder Intellektuelle in der Emigration, ohne alle Ausnahme, ist beschädigt und tut gut daran, es selber zu erkennen, wenn er nicht hinter den dicht geschlossenen Türen seiner Selbstachtung grausam darüber belehrt werden will.« (Ebd.)

7 Arendt 1943, 69.

Solomon R. Guggenheim Museum) um. In seiner Sperrigkeit erinnert ›Entortung‹ zudem an den von Theodor W. Adorno geprägten Begriff der ›Entkunstung‹.

chologie der Vorgang der Verschiebung einer seelischen Energie oder einer Emotion beschrieben. Dieser Prozess umfasst die Verschiebung vom ursprünglichen Auslöser eines tief empfundenen oder verstörenden Triebes oder Gefühls, etwa der Erfahrung von Angst oder Erniedrigung, auf ein Objekt oder eine andere Person. Dies geschieht in Form einer Substitution hin zu einer mehrdeutigen Bildlichkeit: »Die Verschiebung erfolgt in der Regel nach der Richtung, daß ein farbloser und abstrakter Ausdruck des Traumgedankens gegen einen bildlichen und konkreten eingetauscht wird.« 4 Solche Vorgänge sind in der künstlerischen Praxis durchaus gängig und stehen der Sublimierung nahe, nach Sigmund Freud eine der Ursachen kulturellen Schaffens. So ist das psychologische Konzept der Verschiebung auf eine künstlerische Ebene übertragbar: Künstlerinnen und Künstlern können Werke als Objekte dienen, auf die sie ihre Empfindungen, Ängste oder Aggressionen projizieren oder verschieben. Zugleich kann ein Objekt oder ein Reiz auch Ausbrüche von Emotionen hervorrufen, die bis dahin im Inneren des Menschen verschlossen waren, und so bisweilen auch die Auseinandersetzung mit einer einschneidenden, auch verletzenden Erfahrung ermöglichen.

Migration, Flucht, Exil
Mit ›Vertreibung‹ übersetzt, verweist Displacement auf individuelle Schicksale von Migrantinnen und Migranten sowie auf politische, religiöse und wirtschaftliche Konflikte oder auch ökologische Katastrophen, die zur Flucht und Vertreibung größerer Gruppen in einem globalen Kontext führen. Die Betroffenen sind gezwungen, ihre Heimat, ihren Wohnort und damit eventuell auch eine identitätsstiftende Gemeinschaft zu verlassen. Die verschiedenen Entortungszustände im Exil, in der Diaspora oder im Immigrationsland unterscheiden sich dabei in Bezug auf Dauer, Rückkehrmöglichkeiten, Integrationsbereitschaft sowie in Bezug auf das Gefühl der Zugehörigkeit zur alten Heimat.5 Verbindend ist dabei die Erfahrung einer destabilisierten Existenz; die Betroffenen können sich nicht in einem gleichbleibenden, vertrauten Umfeld bewegen, sondern müssen dieses in Abhängigkeit von äußeren Faktoren erst neu erkunden und besetzen. Vertreibung und Exil bedeuten Leid und Entbehrung – Theodor W. Adorno bezeichnet diese Erfahrung im Untertitel seiner *Minima Moralia* als »das beschädigte Leben« und spricht weiter von einer »scheinhaften und irrealen Existenz«.6 Durch die in den letzten Jahren steigende Zuwanderung von Geflüchteten – oder von »Newcomern«,7 wie Hannah Arendt sich selbst und andere Flüchtlinge in ihrem 1943 veröffentlichten

19

expression in the dream-thought is exchanged for one that is visual and concrete.' 4 Such processes are quite common in artistic practice and are close to the sublimation that according to Freud is one of the sources of cultural creativity. The psychological concept of displacement can thus be transferred to an artistic level: works can serve artists as objects on which they project or displace their feelings, fears or aggressions. At the same time, an object or a stimulus can cause an eruption of emotions that until then had been held inside the person, and thus make the confrontation with a dramatic or even painful experience possible.

Migration, Displacement and Exile
Displacement can also refer to the individual destinies of migrants and to the political, religious, economic conflicts, or even ecological disasters that result in the displacement of larger groups in a global context. Those affected are forced to leave their home country, their place of residence and also the community that gives them their identity. The different states of displacement in exile – in the diaspora or in the country of immigration – vary in terms of length, possibility of return, readiness for cultural assimilation and continued feeling of belonging to the former home country. 5 The experience of a destabilised existence is unifying; those affected cannot act within a constant, familiar environment, but instead have to investigate and occupy it while dependent on external factors. Displacement and exile stand for suffering and hardship – Theodor W. Adorno refers to this experience in the subtitle of his book *Minima Moralia* as 'a damaged life' and goes on to speak of an 'illusory and unreal existence'. 6 In the past few years due to the increasing immigration of refugees – or 'newcomers' as Hannah Arendt preferred to call herself and other refugees in her 1943 essay *We Refugees* 7 – involuntary displacement has gained public awareness and is also increasingly the subject of art.

The painful experience of displacement and migration can also contribute to the intellectual overcoming of borders, as Vilém Flusser stresses that the migrant is 'a window through which those who have been left behind may see the world.' 8 Displacement and exile can lead to a larger inner freedom, to an intellectual independence that feeds on the experience of different perspectives and cultures as well as foreignness and exclusion. Edward Said describes the antinomies between inner and outer borders, and homeland and exile as follows: 'The exile knows that in a secular and contingent world, homes are always provisional. Borders and barriers, which enclose us within the safety of familiar territory, can also become prisons, and are often defended beyond reason or necessity. Exiles

4 Freud 1900/2015, 283; on displacement, see ibid., 258–59.

5 See Kuhlmann 2014, 12. 'Exiles see themselves as excluded in a double sense: they are excluded from life in their original community, and they are not part of the society in which they (have to) live.' (Ibid.)

6 'Every intellectual in emigration is, without exception, damaged, and if one does not wish to be taught a cruel lesson behind the airtight doors of one's self-esteem, would do well to recognise this.' (Adorno 1951/2005, aphorism no. 13).

7 Arendt 1943, 69.

8 Flusser 1994/2003, 14.

8 Flusser 1994, 8.

9 »The exile knows that in a secular and contingent world, homes are always provisional. Borders and barriers, which enclose us within the safety of familiar territory, can also become prisons, and are often defended beyond reason or necessity. Exiles cross borders, break barriers of thought and experience.« (Said 1984/ 1991, 365.)

10 Vgl. Vogel 2014a, 40.

11 Ebd., 56.

Text *We Refugees* lieber genannt wissen wollte – tritt die unfreiwillige Entortung im Sinne von Vertreibung verstärkt ins öffentliche Bewusstsein und wird vermehrt zum künstlerischen Verhandlungsgegenstand.

Die schmerzhafte Erfahrung von Vertreibung und Migration kann auch zur intellektuellen Überwindung von Grenzen führen, wie Vilém Flusser betont: »Wir Migranten sind die Fenster, durch welche die Einheimischen die Welt sehen können.«[8] Vertreibung und Exil können zu einer größeren inneren Freiheit führen, zu einer intellektuellen Unabhängigkeit, die aus der Erfahrung unterschiedlicher Sichtweisen und Kulturen, aus Fremdheit und Exklusion gespeist wird. »Der Exilierte weiß, dass in einer säkularen und ungewissen Welt das Zuhause stets provisorisch ist. Grenzen und Barrieren, die uns innerhalb der Sicherheit vertrauter Territorien eingrenzen, können ebenso zu Gefängnissen werden, und werden häufig jenseits von Vernunft und Verstand verteidigt«, beschreibt Edward Said die Antinomien zwischen inneren und äußeren Grenzen, Heimat und Exil. »Exilierte überschreiten Grenzen, durchbrechen Barrieren, die ihre Gedanken und Erfahrungen einschränken.«[9] Neue Sichtweisen, Perspektivwechsel, Infragestellungen von festen Glaubensgrundsätzen und Überzeugungen werden befördert, nicht der Glaube an kulturelle und politische Einheitlichkeit oder gar an eine homo-gene nationale Gemeinschaft. Das Fremdsein wird zur *condition humaine*.

Künstlerische Verschiebungen

Im Bereich der Kunst können mit Displacement auf formaler und inhaltlicher Ebene Praktiken der Aneignung des Fremden und der Verfremdung des Bekannten bezeichnet werden, die über das In-Beziehung-Setzen von künstlerischen mit außerkünstlerischen Diskursen ebenjene neu verhandeln. So können etwa Veränderungen der Raumwahrnehmung, ob sie nun durch Eingriffe in die bestehende Architektur, durch den Einsatz von Licht und akustischen Reizen oder durch Installationen im Ausstellungsraum erfolgen, zu den Praktiken des Displacement gezählt werden.[10] Das Publikum ist in diesen Fällen gezwungen, sich den veränderten Raum visuell oder physisch zu erschließen, muss sich selbst neu darin verorten. Mit Displacement lassen sich neben der Erweiterung der Raumerfahrung ferner Praktiken und Prozesse beschreiben, die über die Rekontextualisierung einzelner Objekte zu Denkanstößen führen. Durch die Umnutzung von Bekanntem wird eine »Neubewertung von Dingen und Prozessen des täglichen Lebens« erreicht.[11] Werden alltägliche Gegenstände oder Materialien in veränderter Form in einen neuen Kontext transferiert – solche Strategien sind bekannt seit Dada,

20

cross borders, break barriers of thought and experience.'[9] New ways of seeing, changes in perspective, reconsiderations of strong principles of faith and convictions are advanced, not the belief in cultural and political unity or even in a homogenous national community. Not belonging becomes a *condition humaine*.

Artistic Displacements

The term *displacement* is used in art to describe practices in form and content that appropriate the foreign and alienate the familiar, which in addition to merely correlating artistic and non-artistic discourse also deal with them anew. Practices of displacement include changes in the perception of space, whether they are interventions in existing architecture, involve the use of light and acoustical stimuli or consist of installations in the exhibition space.[10] In these cases the audience is forced to visually or physically explore the altered space and re-position itself within it.

In addition to describing the extension of spatial experience the term *displacement* can also be used to describe practices and processes that give thought-provoking impulses by re-contextualising individual objects. Re-purposing familiar things brings about a 're-evaluation of things and processes from everyday life.'[11] When everyday objects or materials are transferred to a new context in a changed form – such strategies have been familiar since Dada, Surrealism and Pop Art – this can be disconcerting. Such disturbing moments have the potential to provoke changes in perception, for 'whether they are colours, objects or fabric, these materials are set pieces that convey everyday stories, evoke memories and in part become new stories, not mimicking but creating branched connections.'[12] Elements of one's own culture or other cultures are taken up, both in the form of appropriation or alienation. In this way, artists reflect on their own identity, on culturally prescribed gender roles, and existing global structures. The works do not only refer to their original context, but also enter into a dialogue with the visitors who are challenged to reconsider their own position and to question contradictions.

Displacements / Entortungen
Ayşe Erkmen & Mona Hatoum

The leitmotif of displacements surfaces in the work of Ayşe Erkmen and Mona Hatoum in, for example, their artistic approach to the displacement of meanings or contexts. Both artists view places and institutional, historical and social contexts as a part of the realm of artistic reflection. They both deal in their own particular way with questions of identity, autonomy and control, and with the power and dominance of institutional,

9 Said 1984/1991, 365.

10 See Vogel 2014a, 40.

11 Ibid., 56.

12 Ibid., 54.

12 Ebd., 54.

13 Foucault 1967/1992, 39.

Surrealismus oder Pop Art –, kann dies zu irritierenden Momenten führen. Diese tragen das Potenzial in sich, Wahrnehmungsveränderungen hervorzurufen, denn »ob Farben, Objekte oder Stoffe, die Materialien sind Versatzstücke, die Alltagsgeschichten tragen, die Erinnerungen wecken und zum Teil neuer Erzählungen werden, nicht nachahmen, sondern verzweigte [...] Verbindungen erstellen«.[12] Elemente eigener oder fremder Kulturen werden aufgegriffen, sei es im Modus der Aneignung oder der Verfremdung. Künstlerinnen und Künstler reflektieren so ihre eigene Identität sowie kulturell vorgeschriebene Geschlechterrollen und hinterfragen bestehende globale Ordnungen. Die Arbeiten verweisen nicht nur auf ihren jeweiligen Ursprungskontext, sondern treten in einen Dialog mit dem Publikum, das dazu aufgefordert wird, seinen Standpunkt zu überdenken und Antagonismen zu hinterfragen.

Displacements / Entortungen
Ayşe Erkmen & Mona Hatoum

Das Leitmotiv Displacements weist mit Blick auf den künstlerischen Ansatz der Verschiebung etwa von Bedeutungen oder Kontexten Berührungspunkte zu den Werken von Ayşe Erkmen und Mona Hatoum auf. Beide Künstlerinnen begreifen Orte und institutionelle, historische und gesellschaftliche Kontexte als Teil der künstlerischen Reflexion. Auf je eigene Art setzen sie sich mit Fragen der Identität, Selbstbestimmung und Kontrolle, der Macht und Dominanz im institutionellen und künstlerischen ebenso wie im politischen Bereich auseinander. Formal greifen beide Künstlerinnen Überlegungen der Konzeptkunst, der Minimal und Postminimal Art auf, überwinden aber deren Selbstreferenzialität; besonders Mona Hatoum ergänzt die modernistische Formensprache um persönliche Narrationen und politische Metaphern. Beide Künstlerinnen richten ihr Augenmerk häufig auf die Identitäten und Konnotationen von Orten. Gemein ist ihnen die Verwendung scheinbar vertrauter Formen und Ausdrucksmittel, die neu konnotiert, verfremdet und in ihrer Bedeutung verschoben werden, um vom Publikum Reaktionen und Positionierungen einzufordern. Hatoum und Erkmen verweisen dabei nicht auf Utopien, sondern schaffen eher »Gegenplatzierungen oder Widerlager« zu gängigen Vorstellungen von Kunst und Gesellschaft – »Heterotopien«, wie Michel Foucault 1967 Orte und Institutionen bezeichnet hatte, die den Normen zuwiderlaufende Bedeutungsverschiebungen erfahren haben.[13]

Ayşe Erkmen

Die in Istanbul geborene Ayşe Erkmen studierte in den 1970er Jahren Bildhauerei an der Staatlichen Kunst-

21

artistic and political contexts. In formal terms they are both informed by Conceptual, Minimal and Post-Minimal Art, but they go beyond the self-referentiality of those movements; Hatoum, especially, combines a modern language of forms with personal narratives and political metaphors. Both artists focus on the identities and connotations of place. They share the use of seemingly familiar forms and means of expression to which they give new complexity, through alienation and shifts in meaning, thus demanding reactions and stances from their audience. Hatoum and Erkmen do not refer to utopias but instead create 'counter-sites or abutments' to commonplace ideas of art and society – 'heterotopias', to use the term coined by Michel Foucault in 1967 to describe places and institutions that have experienced changes in meaning that are contrary to the norm.[13]

Ayşe Erkmen

Born in Istanbul, Ayşe Erkmen studied sculpture at the Istanbul State Academy of Fine Arts in the 1970s. She does not follow a fixed formal concept in her artistic work; instead she allows herself in each new work to engage in the qualities inherent in each place or context. The artist explained her overall approach in a 1997 interview: 'I search for what the place and situation require of me. You always work with givens. No space is neutral. Each city is different, which in turn influences the conditions of reception. There is always a context. I take that into account and make it as visible as possible.'[14] Her references can be topographical, historical or social in nature, and they can involve the collection of an institution or even the architecture. Undermining certain expectations is also part of her artistic strategy. She admits, 'Confusion and misunderstandings are welcome, as I see them as a result of the layered complexity of a work.'[15] Erkmen's work is characteristically temporary, created in situ and lasting only for the length of an exhibition. She reacts to the special features of a place or an institution, and thus creates new constellations.

Although Erkmen's conceptually based oeuvre is not defined by formal constants, she often re-uses ideas from older projects, which gives her work coherence. Erkmen applies concepts and ideas to new contexts, using them as tools to develop interventions that are the offshoots of a central idea,[16] showing not only the continuities of her artistic idea but also the special features of each situation. Over the years, she weaves an artistic and intellectual network – a system of reference – that reflects her own work as well as the sites in question in a mode of constant renewal. Her works refer to and withdraw from places, they are displaced and re-located. This sort of re-contex-

13 Foucault 1967/1986, 24.

14 Ayşe Erkmen in Herbstreuth 1997, 279; see also Volk 2008.

15 Ayşe Erkmen in Senova 2011.

16 'Maybe it can be said that I use locations as a tool to inform my work, playing with what belongs and what I bring in and the tension I try to achieve from this encounter.' (Ayşe Erkmen in ibid.; see Schaschke 2008 on the question of repetition and imitation.)

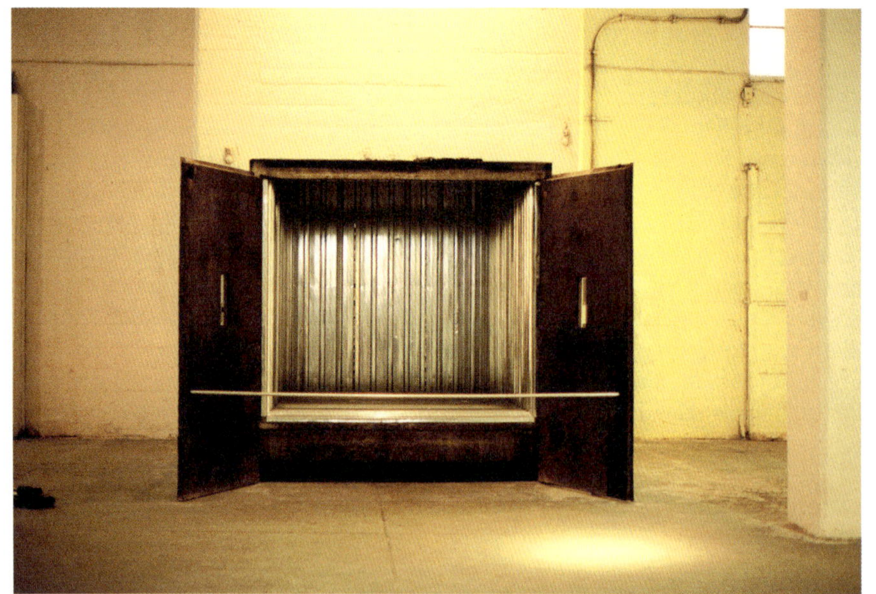

Ayşe Erkmen
Wertheim ACUU, 1995
Installationsansicht /
installation view, 4th
Istanbul Biennale 1995

22

tualisation of central questions can also be seen as a technique of displacement.[17]

Many of Erkmen's works deal with questions of material, space and form (such as *Wertheim ACUU,* 1995). ⟶ **22** Although it is difficult to compare her way of working with that of other artists, in many ways her approach is reminiscent of Robert Smithson's. With his theory of site and non-site and the related idea of art as a reflection and a material, with his artistic consideration of *displacement* and *dislocation*, Smithson provided important impulses for contemporary art as aesthetic research.

Erkmen's interventions are open in their interaction with visitors, whose movements and experience of the space are integrated into the artistic reflexion. The works take on a discursive dimension through unexpected or even random references and thus avoid a clear-cut, didactic or authoritarian position. In her contribution to the Turkish pavilion at the Venice Biennale (*Plan B,* 2011), she confronted the audience with a construction of pipes of various colours, which at first glance seemed like a postmodern reaction to Minimalism, but turned out to be a device for the purification of water from the Venetian canals. This unexpected twist referred *en passant* to the responsibility of artists to take a stance on ecological and thus also economic questions, and to indirectly influence debates relevant to society today. Decisive in the creation of this piece was the fact that Venice, like Erkmen's home city Istanbul, is a city that is defined by water, and that the Turkish pavilion is one of the few rooms in the Arsenale that has a window facing a canal.

Erkmen's works frequently consist of subtle interventions in space. They are discreet gestures that unfold their potency with a certain hesitation. A good example is *Portiport* (1996), a security gate of the sort that one finds in airports and other public places, which the artist built at the entrance to Portikus in Frankfurt am Main. The security gates were not immediately recognisable as artistic interventions and provoked various reactions on the subject of control and power, trust and security. *On Water* (2017), Erkmen's most recent intervention at the *Skulptur Projekte Münster 2017,* is subliminal and barely visible, only finally materialising through the participation of the visitors in a sort of border-crossing. ⟶ **24** Just under the surface of the water at the harbour basin, the artist had a walkway built that is usable although not immediately visible. Visitors are invited to cross the walkway to reach the other side of the harbour where they are rewarded with an expansion of their own scope of experience. Erkmen's basic ideas for interventions are often based on strategies of displacement, movement, shifting or

17 Ayşe Erkmen wrote the following in reference to her participation in the *Skulptur. Projekte in Münster,* 1997 (*Sculptures on the Air*) and 2017 (*On Water*): 'From *Air* to *Water* is simply a shift in this exhibition project, which is constantly developing, that makes the work of art essential and imperative.' (*Out of Place* [Spring 2017], publication in preparation for the *Skulptur Projekte Münster 2017;* see too Münster 2017, 181–186.)

14 Ayşe Erkmen in
Herbstreuth 1997, 279;
vgl. Volk 2008.

15 »Confusions and misun-
derstandings are welcome, as
I see them as the result of the
layered complexity of a work.«
(Ayşe Erkmen in Senova 2011.)

16 »Maybe it can be said
that I use locations as a tool to
inform my work, playing with
what belongs and what I bring
in and the tension I try to
achieve from this encounter.«
(»Vielleicht kann man sagen,
dass ich Orte als ein Werkzeug
nutze, das meiner Arbeit zugrunde liegt, dabei spiele ich
mit dem Vorhandenen und
dem von mir Eingebrachten sowie der Spannung, die ich
durch diese Begegnung zu erzeugen versuche.« Ayşe
Erkmen in ebd.; vgl. zur Frage
der Wiederholung und Nachahmung Schaschke 2008.)

akademie Istanbul. Sie folgt in ihrer Kunst keinem un-
veränderlichen formalen Konzept, sondern lässt sich
bei jedem neuen Werk ganz auf die spezifischen Eigenheiten eines Ortes, auf den Kontext ein. »Ich suche
danach, was der Ort und die Situation von mir verlangen«, so beschreibt die Künstlerin ihre Herangehensweise 1997 in einem Interview, »man arbeitet immer
mit Vorgaben. Kein Raum ist neutral. Jede Stadt ist
anders, was wiederum die Rezeptionsbedingungen
beeinflusst. Es gibt immer eine Umgebung der Arbeit.
Das beziehe ich ein und mache es so weit wie möglich sichtbar.«[14] Ihre Bezugnahmen können topog-
rafischer, historischer oder sozialer Natur sein, können
die Sammlung einer Institution oder auch die Architektur betreffen, wobei auch das Unterlaufen bestimmter Erwartungshaltungen Teil ihrer künstlerischen Strategie ist: »Verwirrungen und Missverständnisse sind
willkommen«, so die Künstlerin, »da ich diese als Ergebnis der vielschichtigen Komplexität eines Werkes
verstehe.«[15] Die temporäre, auf die Dauer einer Ausstellung angelegte Arbeit *in situ* gehört zu den Charak-
teristika der künstlerischen Vorgehensweise Erkmens.
In ihren Werken reagiert sie auf die Besonderheiten
eines Ortes oder einer Institution und schafft neue
Konstellationen.

Das konzeptionell angelegte Gesamtwerk
Ayşe Erkmens zeichnet sich zwar nicht durch formale
Konstanten aus, der Rückgriff auf ältere Projektideen
allerdings verleiht ihrem Œuvre Kohärenz. Erkmen
wendet Konzeptionen und Ideen gleich Werkzeugen
auf neue Kontexte an,[16] um Interventionen zu entwickeln, die wie Filiationen einer zentralen Idee sowohl
die Kontinuitäten des künstlerischen Denkens als auch
die Besonderheiten der jeweiligen Situation aufzeigen.
So webt sie über die Jahre hinweg ein künstlerisch-in-
tellektuelles Geflecht, ein Referenzsystem, das sowohl
die eigene Arbeit als auch die in Frage kommenden
Orte in einem Modus der konstanten Erneuerung
reflektiert. Ihre Werke beziehen sich auf Orte und
entziehen sich ihnen wieder, sie werden entortet und
wieder neu geortet – auch diese Neukontextualisie-
rung von zentralen Fragestellungen kann als Technik des Displacement und der Entortung verstanden
werden.[17]

Viele Werke Erkmens offenbaren die Auseinandersetzung mit Material-, Raum- und Formfragen
(etwa die Arbeit *Wertheim ACUU,* 1995). ⟶ **22** Auch
wenn Erkmens Arbeitsweise nur schwer mit der von
anderen Künstlerinnen und Künstlern vergleichbar ist,
erinnert sie in mancher Hinsicht an den Ansatz von
Robert Smithson. Mit seiner Theorie von *site* und *non-
site* und der damit zusammenhängenden Idee von
Kunst als Reflexion und Material, mit seinen künstlerischen Überlegungen zu *displacement* und *disloca-*

23

re-locating. This does not only apply to the movement
of the visitors, but also to existing works of art that
are transferred into a new context and therefore given
new meaning. Her spectacular idea of suspending
sculptures belonging to the Westfälisches Landesmuseum from a helicopter that circled the city and the
cathedral of Münster (*Sculptures on the Air,* 1997), after the cathedral chapter had rejected her proposals
for artistic interventions on the outside of the building,
received much attention at the *Skulptur. Projekte in
Münster* in 1997. ⟶ **74** She also referred to a technique of displacement here: the historic sculptures
from the city, which had been heavily damaged during the Second World War, had been put into storage
at the Landesmuseum for conservational reasons;
Erkmen returned them to their original location, at
least as an idea, for a short moment. *Kuckuck* (Cuckoo,
2003) at Kunstmuseum St. Gallen consisted of putting
taxidermic animals from the natural-history collection
on already existing tracks and moving them around,
in a precise schedule, within the art-historical part of
the museum; with this local displacement she put
them in a new context referring to Swiss precision
and gave them new 'life'.

Strategies of displacement are often used
when Erkmen intervenes in spatial contexts with reduced means and works with found objects and situations. For example, she lowered the ceiling lights
of a gallery space to modify the visitors' experience
of the space (*Das Haus* [The House], 1993–94). Parallel
to this intervention she created perhaps her most
popular permanent work in public space, *Am Haus*
(On the House) in the Kreuzberg 36 district of Berlin
in 1994. ⟶ **26** By applying the endings of the con-
jugation of a Turkish verb form (reported past using
the ending *miş*), which expresses possibility and hear-
say in Turkish oral traditions, onto a building façade
on Oranienstraße, she draws attention to the perma-
nently provisional existence of Turkish migrants and
Turkish culture in the area. One of her most well-known
projects, *Shipped Ships* (2001), for which she had
three passenger ferry ships from Istanbul, Shingū and
Venice brought with their crews to Frankfurt am Main,
where they offered scheduled excursions on the Main
river, also bears the leitmotif of displacement, reloca-
tion and contextual shift. ⟶ **28** Occasionally Erkmen
gives her work a personal narrative, such as in *İki
kardeş* (Two Siblings, 2007), which was installed on
Taksim Square in Istanbul and addresses the Armenian
Genocide that affected her own family's history.

Ayşe Erkmen in Leipzig
Erkmen's participation in the exhibition *Displacements /
Entortungen* in Leipzig extends from the exhibition

17 So schreibt Ayşe Erkmen mit Blick auf ihre Teilnahme an den *Skulptur. Projekten in Münster* 1997 (*Sculptures on the Air* – Luft) und 2017 (*On Water* – Wasser): »Von Luft zu Wasser ist einfach eine Verschiebung in diesem sich kontinuierlich weiterentwickelnden Ausstellungsprojekt, die das Kunstwerk an dieser Stelle unverzichtbar und zwingend macht.« (*Out of Place* (Frühling 2017), Publikation in Vorbereitung der *Skulptur Projekte Münster 2017*; vgl. auch Münster 2017, 181–186.)

tion lieferte Smithson wichtige Impulse für die zeitgenössische Kunst als ästhetische Forschung.

Erkmens Interventionen sind offen im Umgang mit den Betrachterinnen und Betrachtern, deren Bewegung und Erfahrung im Raum in die künstlerische Reflexion integriert werden. Die Werke entwickeln durch unerwartete oder auch beiläufige Bezüge eine diskursive Dimension, die eine eindeutige, didaktische oder gar autoritäre Haltung meidet. In ihrem Beitrag zum türkischen Pavillon auf der Biennale in Venedig (*Plan B,* 2011) etwa konfrontierte sie das Publikum mit einer in unterschiedlichen Farbtönen gehaltenen Rohrkonstruktion, die als Einrichtung zur Reinigung des venezianischen Kanalwassers diente. Die Funktion des Werks verwies nebenbei auf die Verantwortung von Künstlerinnen und Künstlern, sich zu ökologischen und damit auch zu ökonomischen Fragen zu positionieren und indirekt auch auf gesellschaftliche Debatten einzuwirken. Ausschlaggebend bei der Entwicklung dieser Arbeit war, dass Venedig wie Erkmens Heimatstadt Istanbul eine durch das Wasser bestimmte Stadt ist und der türkische Pavillon als einer der wenigen Räume im Arsenale ein Fenster zum Kanal aufweist.

Erkmens Interventionen bestehen häufig aus subtilen Eingriffen in den Raum. Es sind zurückhaltende Gesten, die erst mit einer gewissen Verzögerung

ihre Wirkmächtigkeit entfalten. Als Beispiel kann die Arbeit *Portiport* (1996) dienen: Erkmen baute am Eingang des Portikus in Frankfurt am Main Sicherheitsschleusen auf, wie man sie auf Flughäfen und an anderen öffentlichen Orten findet; sie waren nicht sofort als künstlerische Intervention zu erkennen und provozierten unterschiedliche Haltungen zum Themenkomplex von Kontrolle und Macht, Vertrauen und Sicherheit. Zurückhaltung und Unterschwelligkeit, aber auch die partizipierende Bewegung des Publikums in einer Form der Grenzüberschreitung prägen ebenfalls die jüngste Intervention Erkmens bei den *Skulptur Projekten Münster* 2017 (*On Water,* 2017). ⟶ **24** Die Künstlerin ließ knapp unterhalb der Wasseroberfläche einen Steg durch das Hafenbecken anlegen, der somit zwar benutzbar, aber nicht sofort sichtbar war. Das Publikum war eingeladen, über den Steg auf die andere Hafenseite zu gehen und eine Erweiterung des eigenen Erfahrungsraums zu erleben.

Erkmens Grundideen für Interventionen beruhen also häufig auf Strategien des Displacement, der Bewegung, der Verschiebung oder Verlagerung. Diese betreffen nicht nur die Bewegung des Publikums, sondern auch bestehende Kunstwerke, die in einen neuen Kontext überführt und damit in neue Bedeutungsnetze eingespannt werden. Schon 1997 hatte sie bei den *Skulptur. Projekten in Münster* mit der spekta-

24

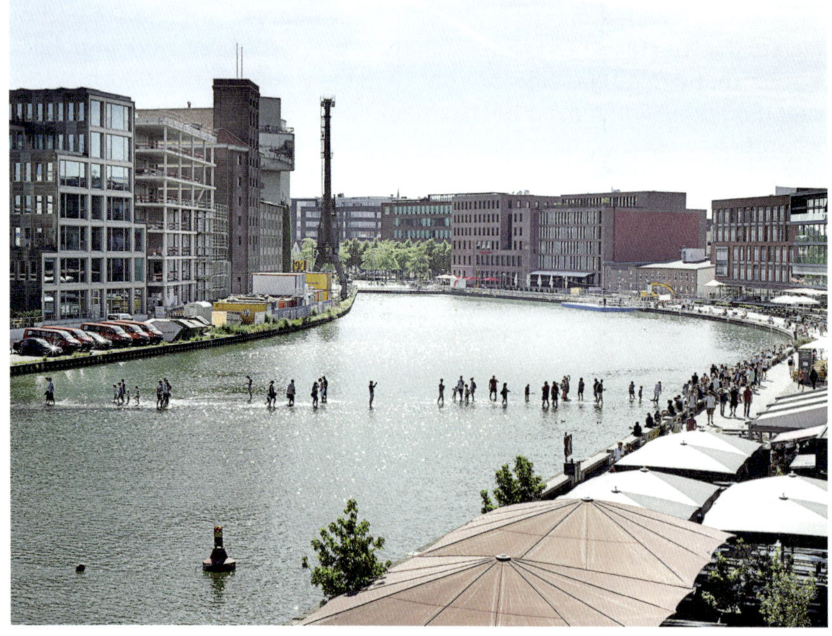

Ayşe Erkmen
On Water, 2017
Installationsansicht /
installation view, *Skulptur Projekte Münster 2017*

kulären Idee Aufmerksamkeit erregt, Skulpturen aus der Sammlung des Westfälischen Landesmuseums, befestigt an einem Hubschrauber, über dem Dom kreisen zu lassen (*Sculptures on the Air*, 1997), nachdem das Domkapitel ihr jegliche künstlerische Intervention an der Kathedrale untersagt hatte. ⟶ **74** Auch hier griff sie auf eine Technik des Displacement zurück: Die historischen Skulpturen aus der Stadt, die im Zweiten Weltkrieg zu großen Teilen zerstört wurde, werden aus konservatorischen Gründen im Depot des gegenüberliegenden Landesmuseums magaziniert; Erkmen versetzte sie zumindest ideell für einen kurzen Moment zurück an ihren ursprünglichen Bestimmungsort. Auf konzeptionell ähnliche Weise ging Erkmen bei der Arbeit *Kuckuck* (2003) im Kunstmuseum St. Gallen vor, in der sie naturhistorische Tierpräparate der Sammlung auf Schienen nach einem exakten Zeitplan regelmäßig durch den kunsthistorischen Teil des Museums fahren ließ. Durch diese örtliche Verschiebung rekontextualisierte sie die Objekte unter Anspielung auf die Präzision eines Schweizer Uhrwerks und erweckte sie zu neuem ›Leben‹.

Strategien des Displacement finden ebenso häufig Anwendung, wenn Erkmen mit reduzierten Mitteln in räumliche Kontexte interveniert und mit vorgefundenen Objekten und Situationen arbeitet. So hat sie etwa die Deckenbeleuchtung eines Galerieraums tiefer gehängt, um die Raumerfahrung der Besucher zu modifizieren (*Das Haus,* 1993–1994). Parallel zu dieser Intervention hat sie 1994 ihre vielleicht bekannteste dauerhafte Arbeit im öffentlichen Raum geschaffen, *Am Haus* im Berliner Bezirk Kreuzberg 36. ⟶ **26** Mit der Anbringung von Endungen der Konjugation einer erzählerischen Vergangenheitsform des Türkischen (›miş‹-Vergangenheit), die als Ausdruck der Möglichkeit und des Hörensagens auf orale Traditionen in der türkischen Kultur verweist, an einer Hausfassade der Oranienstraße erinnert sie an die Präsenz eines permanenten Provisoriums türkischer Migranten und türkischer Kultur in Kreuzberg. Auch eines ihrer mittlerweile bekanntesten Projekte, *Shipped Ships* (2001) in Frankfurt am Main, für das sie drei Passagierschiffe inklusive ihrer Besatzung aus Istanbul, Shingū und Venedig an den Main transportieren ließ, wo sie regelmäßig Flussrundfahrten anboten, trägt in sich das Leitmotiv des Displacement, der örtlichen Verlagerung und kontextuellen Verschiebung. ⟶ **28** Bisweilen versieht Erkmen ihre Arbeiten auch mit einem persönlichen Narrativ, wie etwa in der Arbeit *İki kardeş* (2007), die auf dem Taksim-Platz in Istanbul realisiert wurde und in der sie anhand ihrer eigenen Familiengeschichte den Völkermord an den Armeniern thematisierte.

25

rooms on the lower floor to the rooms housing the museum's permanent collection on the upper floors, and also into the public space of the city. Three rooms on the lower floor are devoted to her works – two large exhibition rooms and a smaller cabinet – in direct proximity to the works of Hatoum, which are also shown in two large rooms and a cabinet. The presentation of Hatoum's objects and installations aims to show them within the space in a balanced and optimal manner; Erkmen contrasts this presentation by creating an arc of tension between complete emptiness in one room and brimming abundance in the other. With these extremes she exposes the style of exhibition display that is typical in museums of contemporary art while simultaneously entering into a creative dialogue with Hatoum.

The ceramic edition that was produced in 2013 based on anti-personnel landmines is an important feature of Erkmen's first room, which is literally 'brimming' with art. The models for these ceramic mines had been first produced in wood in 1997 and presented on pedestals, illuminated by spotlights, in a display window of Galeries Lafayette in Berlin with the title *Objects of Mine.* ⟶ **46** The artist is presenting this ninety-part series along with the computer animation *PFM-1 and others* (1997) ⟶ **48** and a frieze of ceramic tiles (*Alkoven* [Alcove], 1997/2016) ⟶ **50**, both of which have landmines as their subject. These works are unusual in Erkmen's oeuvre for their direct criticism[18] and can be associated with the political dimension of displacement, war and expulsion. They dominate the overall impression of the exhibition room due to their diversity of media and sheer number, distributed throughout the room. The colour green, which was originally assigned to mines as a way to camouflage them, is a common element to all of the objects, along with the thematic reference to anti-personnel mines, which are shaped like everyday objects and toys in order to kill people – especially children – most effectively. The other works in this room also have different shades of green, such as *Imitating Lines* (1985/2008) ⟶ **42**, the objects *M* and *5* from the series *Die Farben der Buchstaben* (Colours of Letters, 2006) ⟶ **52**, *Netz* (Net, 2006/2008) ⟶ **60**, *Row-row* (2012) ⟶ **62**, *Großes grünes Pompon* (Large green pompon, 2012) ⟶ **58** and *Kleines grünes Pompon* (Small green pompon, 2012) ⟶ **56** and the three bronzes from the series *not the color it is* (2014). ⟶ **64** The seven *Jalousien* (Blinds, 2007) ⟶ **54** that cover the high windows cast a faint green light into the museum space, and in the installation *Imitation / Taklit* (1987/2017) ⟶ **44**, which consists of bricks and a neon tube and is based on an existing street situation in Istanbul, the neon tube would glow with the same colour. The green

18   Asked in 1999 what the function of contemporary art is, Ayşe Erkmen gave the wry response: 'Not knowing the answers, not answering questions, not asking questions that have already been answered.' (Ayşe Erkmen in Matzner 1999, 182.) On her view of the political effectiveness of art Erkmen replied in an interview in 2008: 'I find it more effective and more forceful for the political message to be hidden or to be conveyed in a circuitous manner rather than directly […].' (Üstek / Erkmen 2008, 102.)

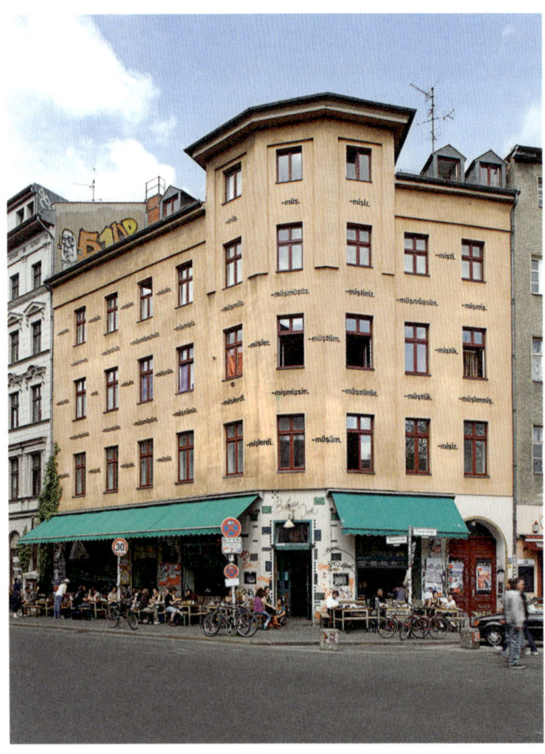

Ayşe Erkmen
Am Haus, 1994
dauerhafte Installation /
permanent installation Berlin,
Oranienstraße

26

unites the various works and softens their individual impact. Erkmen weaves a network of references to unite the brimming diversity of the various works and uses colour, with which she creates a soothing atmosphere in stark contrast to the usual 'white cube', as a technique of perceptual displacement.

The other two rooms devoted to Erkmen on the lower floor are characterised by a restraint of means – but do not lose any of their impact. Four videos from the series *Bronze Acid* (2014), which are presented in the cabinet, document the process of producing coloured bronze sculptures, three of which are in the first room. ⟶ **92** Shown simultaneously, the four videos dominate the space with the colours ochre, blue, green and yellow. These multiple colours are repeated and intensified in Erkmen's second large room in the museum, in which the artist intervenes with *Shutters* (2017) and *Glassworks* (2015 / 2017). ⟶ **90** *Shutters* is the most minimal form of artistic intervention: working with the existing museum technology, Erkmen programmed the shutters of the high windows to open and close every five minutes. This causes a change in light conditions: sometimes the exhibition space is artificially illuminated, and sometimes artificial light mixes with natural light; sometimes the space opens to the outside, and sometimes it remains totally closed. Visitors will not immediately recognise this form of

subtle interference with technical processes as an artistic act. This delayed effect heightens the impact of the intervention, raising questions about the essence of art, about materiality, visibility and concept and about the relationship of form and content. With *Shutters,* Erkmen also influences the effect of the second piece in this room, which is also practically 'objectless'. *Glassworks* consists of twenty-two glass plates of different colours and shapes that are mounted under spotlights, casting the entire room, which is otherwise empty, in a sea of colour. The piece is phenomenologically based; the perception of the different coloured lights creates a space that is open to association, in which fantasy and emotions, thought and reflection are given free rein. Similar to a Gothic cathedral or a mosque, the coloured light glows with a spiritual aura, which has to be experienced in the space by visitors in motion. The almost immaterial Leipzig intervention is part of a web of artistic analyses of the effects of colour that Erkmen has already explored with her light interventions *Glassworks* at Halle Verrière, Meisenthal (2015) ⟶ **86** or with coloured panels of cloth in *Busy Colors* at SculptureCenter, Long Island City, New York (2005) ⟶ **31**, *Hausgenossen* (Housemates) at K21, Düsseldorf (2008) or *Bluish* at Kunstverein Freiburg (2008).

The second central aspect of Erkmen's contribution to the exhibition in Leipzig is her artistic ques-

18 Auf die Frage, welche Funktion zeitgenössische Kunst habe, hat Ayşe Erkmen 1999 ironisch geantwortet: »Die Antworten nicht kennen, Fragen nicht beantworten, Fragen nicht stellen, auf die es Antworten gibt.« (Ayşe Erkmen in Matzner 1999, 182.) Zu ihrer Auffassung von politischer Wirksamkeit von Kunst sagte Erkmen im Interview 2008: »I find it more effective and more forceful for the political message to be hidden or to be conveyed in a circuitous manner rather than directly […]« (»Eine politische Botschaft ist meiner Ansicht nach effektiver und zwingender, wenn sie versteckt ist oder auf Umwegen transportiert wird, als wenn sie unmittelbar überbracht wird […] « Üstek / Erkmen 2008, 102.)

Ayşe Erkmen in Leipzig
Ayşe Erkmens Beteiligung an der Ausstellung *Displacements / Entortungen* in Leipzig erstreckt sich sowohl auf die Ausstellungssäle im Souterrain und die Räume der ständigen Sammlung des Museums in den oberen Etagen als auch auf den städtischen Raum. Im Souterrain stehen die drei von ihr bespielten Räume – zwei größere Ausstellungssäle und ein Kabinett – in unmittelbarer Nachbarschaft zu den Werken von Mona Hatoum, die in gleicher Raumabfolge gezeigt werden. Die Präsentation von Hatoums Objekten und Installationen zielt auf Ausgewogenheit und optimale Wirkung im Raum ab; Erkmen kommentiert diese Präsentationsweise, indem sie zwischen ihren beiden Ausstellungssälen einen Spannungsbogen zieht, der von völliger Leere im einen Raum hin zu einer überbordenden Fülle im anderen reicht. Mit diesen beiden Extremen des Ausstellungsdisplays thematisiert sie die in Museen zeitgenössischer Kunst üblichen Präsentationsmechanismen und tritt in einen kreativen Dialog mit den Werken Mona Hatoums.

Eine wichtige Gruppe in Erkmens erstem, vor Kunstwerken ›überbordenden‹ Raum bildet die 2013 produzierte Keramik-Edition nach Antipersonenminen. ⟶ **46** Die Modelle dazu hatte sie 1997 in Holz produzieren lassen und diese dann auf Sockeln stehend und von Spots beleuchtet unter dem Titel *Objects of Mine* in einem Schaufenster der Berliner Galeries Lafayette präsentiert. Die Künstlerin zeigt die 90-teilige Serie zusammen mit der ebenfalls auf das Minenmotiv zurückgehenden Computeranimation *PFM-1 and others* (1997) ⟶ **48** und einem Tisch mit Keramikfliesen mit derselben Thematik (*Alkoven*, 1997/2016). ⟶ **50** Diese für Erkmen in ihrer offenen Kritik ungewöhnlichen Arbeiten, [18] die mit der politischen Dimension des Displacement, mit Krieg und Vertreibung in Verbindung gebracht werden können, dominieren durch die Vielfalt unterschiedlicher Medien, durch Anzahl und Verteilung im Raum den Gesamteindruck des Ausstellungssaals. Gemeinsames Element dieser Werke ist neben dem inhaltlichen Bezug auf Antipersonenminen – die nach Alltagsobjekten und Spielzeugen geformt sind, um möglichst effektiv Menschen und vor allem Kinder zu töten – die Farbe Grün, die die Minen ursprünglich als Tarnfarbe erhalten haben. Unterschiedliche Grünabstufungen weisen auch die anderen Werke Erkmens in diesem Raum auf, wie etwa die *Imitating Lines* (1985/2008) ⟶ **42**, die Objekte *M* und *5* aus der Reihe *Die Farben der Buchstaben* (2006) ⟶ **52**, das *Netz* (2006/2008) ⟶ **60**, *Rowrow* (2012) ⟶ **62**, *Großes grünes Pompon* ⟶ **58** und *Kleines grünes Pompon* (beide 2012) ⟶ **56** oder die drei Bronzen aus der Reihe *not the color it is* (2014) ⟶ **64**. Die sieben *Jalousien* (2007) ⟶ **54** vor den

27

tioning of space, both its architectonic quality with reference to its perception by visitors and the question of its publicness and use. With *Gemütliche Ecken* (Cosy Corners, 2009) – variously shaped, monochromatically painted metal panels of different sizes, which she had originally created for *steirischer herbst* in Graz in 2009 – Erkmen intervenes in selected cultural institutions as well as in the city centre of Leipzig which is marked by commerce, monuments and services. ⟶ **100** Placed seemingly at random and with forms and colours that give absolutely no points of reference, the works call attention to the use of public space and to public art's role in providing possible meaning, conceived as rebellious or like 'a counterweight' to this cultivated and history-conscious city. Erkmen's installation *By Nature* (2015/2017), which is in a transitional room on the third floor, also creates a connection between urban space and art space. ⟶ **98** The artist displaces everyday objects – this time in the form of miniature porcelain figures of penguins that she has found at flea markets – into the museum context. These knick-knacks enter into a dialogue with a series of six penguin sculptures by August Gaul (ca 1919) that seem to gaze out into the urban space. At the interface between inside and outside – Erkmen places the animal figures in front of the only window in the permanent collection (apart from the terraces) through which the city can be seen –

the work comments in a cryptic, ironic manner on the museum's strategies of presentation and the different valuation of art and crafts. In the *Beethoven* room on the first floor, the largest room of the permanent collection in the museum, Erkmen intervened with the sound installation *Ewig Dein* (Forever Yours, 2011). ⟶ **96** The slight disharmony of the soprano performing Ludwig van Beethoven's three-voice canon *Ewig Dein* disturbs the sacred presentation of Max Klinger's sculpture of the composer. The pathos of the inflated, godlike representation of Beethoven is accompanied by female intonation. At the same time this intervention is an artistic confrontation with the space – in this case, the acoustic space.

With her main contribution to the exhibition, *Half of* (2017), installed next to *Ewig Dein,* Erkmen refers to the largest open space inside the museum, the airspace over the terrace on the first floor. ⟶ **94** The subject of the piece is the architecture of the museum, which was designed by the former Berlin architectural office Hufnagel, Pütz, Rafaelian and inaugurated in 2004, and its perception by the public. In a sort of architectural *mise en abyme* Erkmen repeats the dimensions of the rooms and the openings of the hall on the first floor in five scaled-down fabric cubes. These mimetically based objects reproduce the space in which they are exhibited. The first object measures about

Oberlichtern tauchen den Museumsraum in leichtes Grün, und auch bei der aus Ziegelsteinen und einer Neonröhre bestehenden Installation *Imitation / Taklit* (1987 / 2017), die ursprünglich auf eine vorgefundene Straßensituation in Istanbul zurückgeht, würde das Neon in diesem Farbton leuchten. ⟶ **44** Das Grün verbindet die verschiedenen Arbeiten und lässt sie in ihrer jeweiligen Wirkung etwas zurücktreten. So webt Erkmen innerhalb der überbordenden Vielfalt unterschiedlicher Werke ein Geflecht von Bezügen. Sie nutzt die Farbgebung als Technik der Wahrnehmungsverschiebung, um eine beruhigende Raumstimmung zu erzeugen, die sich von der üblichen Atmosphäre eines White Cube absetzt.

Die beiden anderen von Erkmen bespielten Ausstellungsräume im Souterrain hingegen sind durch Zurückhaltung der Mittel – aber nicht der Wirkung – geprägt. Im Kabinett werden vier Videoarbeiten der Serie *Bronze Acid* (2014) präsentiert, in welchen Erkmen den Produktionsprozess farbiger Bronzeplastiken zeigt, von denen drei im ersten Saal zu sehen sind. ⟶ **92** Die vier simultan ablaufenden Videoarbeiten dominieren den Raum mit den Farben Ocker, Blau, Grün und Gelb. Diese Mehrfarbigkeit wird in Erkmens zweitem großen Ausstellungssaal, in dem die Künstlerin mit den Arbeiten *Shutters* (2017) und *Glassworks* (2015 / 2017) interveniert, wieder aufge-

nommen und intensiviert. ⟶ **90** *Shutters* ist die denkbar minimalistischste Form einer künstlerischen Intervention. Die künstlerische Praxis beschränkt sich hier darauf, vorhandene Museumstechnik, in diesem Fall die Fensterblenden der Oberlichter, so programmieren zu lassen, dass sie sich im Intervall von fünf Minuten öffnen und schließen. So wechseln im Ausstellungsraum die Lichtverhältnisse: Mal herrscht reines Kunstlicht, mal mischt sich künstliches mit natürlichem Licht, mal öffnet sich der Raum nach außen, mal bleibt er völlig abgeschlossen. Für das Publikum wird diese Form der subtilen Einmischung in technische Abläufe nicht sofort als künstlerischer Akt einsichtig. Dieser Verzögerungseffekt steigert die Wirkung der Intervention, wirft er doch Fragen nach dem Wesen von Kunstwerken, nach Materialität, Sichtbarkeit und Konzeptionalität, nach dem Verhältnis von Form und Inhalt auf. Mit *Shutters* beeinflusst Erkmen auch die Wirkung der zweiten, ebenso fast ›objektlosen‹ Arbeit in diesem Raum, *Glassworks*: 22 Glasscheiben in verschiedenen Farben und Formen, die unter den Ausstellungsstrahlern angebracht wurden, tauchen den gesamten, ansonsten leeren Raum in ein Farbenmeer. Das Werk ist phänomenologisch ausgerichtet; die Wahrnehmung unterschiedlicher Farblichter schafft einen offenen Assoziationsraum, in dem Fantasie und Emotionen, Gedanken und Reflexionen freier Raum

28

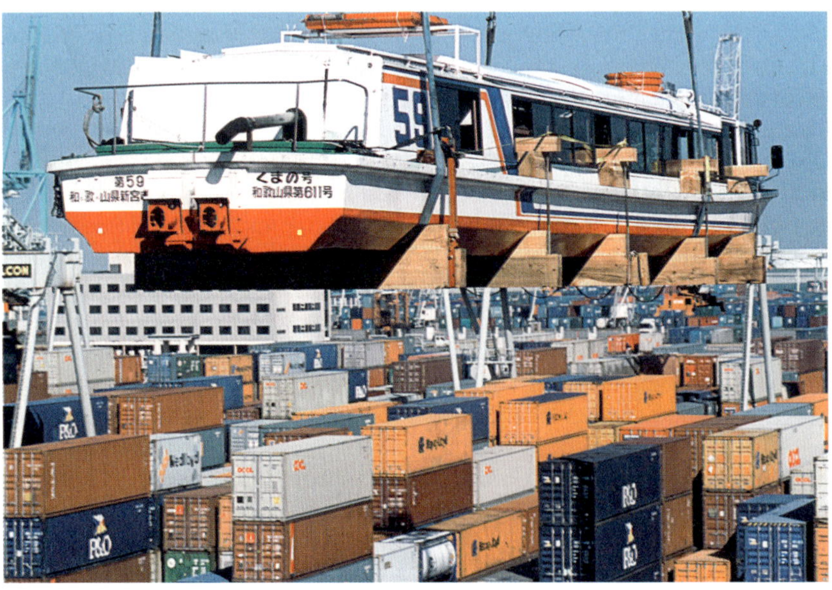

Ayşe Erkmen
Shipped Ships, 2001

gelassen wird. Wie in gotischen Kathedralen oder auch in Moscheen strahlt hier das farbige Licht eine vergeistigte Aura aus, die durch das Publikum in der Bewegung im Raum erfahren werden muss. Erkmen verwebt diese fast immaterielle Leipziger Intervention in ihr Geflecht künstlerischer Analysen von Farbwirkungen, die sie zuvor schon mit ihrer Lichtintervention *Glassworks* in der Halle Verrière, Meisenthal (2015) ⟶ **86** oder mit farbigen Stoffbahnen etwa in *Busy Colors* im SculptureCenter, Long Island City, New York (2005) ⟶ **31**, in *Hausgenossen* im K21, Düsseldorf (2008) oder in *Bluish* im Kunstverein Freiburg (2008) betrieben hat.

Der zweite zentrale Aspekt des Beitrags Erkmens zur Leipziger Ausstellung ist die künstlerische Befragung des Raumes, seiner architektonischen Qualität mit Blick auf seine Wahrnehmung durch den Menschen, aber auch die Frage seiner Öffentlichkeit und Nutzung. Mit ihren *Gemütlichen Ecken* (2009) – unterschiedlich geformten, einfarbig gefassten Metallplatten verschiedener Größen, die sie ursprünglich für den *steirischen herbst* 2009 in Graz geschaffen hatte – interveniert Erkmen in verschiedenen kulturellen Institutionen und in der Leipziger Innenstadt, die von Erinnerungsorten und Kommerz, von Denkmälern und Dienstleistungen geprägt ist. ⟶ **100** Die wie zufällig abgestellten Arbeiten, deren Form und Farbgebung sich jeder Aussage verweigern, lenken den Blick auf die Nutzung des öffentlichen Raumes und auf etwaige Sinnstiftung durch öffentliche Kunstwerke, wirken sie doch wie Störenfriede oder ›Gegenlager‹ in dieser kultur- und geschichtsbewussten Stadt. Im Museum stellt Erkmens Installation *By Nature* (2015/2017) in einem Durchgangsraum der dritten Etage ebenfalls eine Verbindung von Stadt- und Kunstraum her. ⟶ **98** Die Künstlerin verschiebt auch hier Alltagsgegenstände – diesmal in Form von verkleinerten, auf Flohmärkten gefundenen Pinguinen aus Porzellan – in den Museumskontext. Die wie Nippes wirkenden Figuren treten in Dialog mit einer Reihe von sechs in den städtischen Raum blickenden Pinguin-Plastiken von August Gaul (um 1919). An der Nahtstelle zwischen Innen und Außen – Erkmen platziert die Tierfiguren vor dem einzigen Fenster, durch das man im Bereich der ständigen Sammlung (mit Ausnahme der Terrassen) auf die Stadt sehen kann – kommentiert die Künstlerin auf hintersinnig-ironische Weise museale Präsentationsstrategien und die damit verbundenen unterschiedlichen Wertigkeiten künstlerischer und handwerklicher Produktion. Im *Beethoven-Saal* der ersten Etage, dem größten Galerieraum im Museum, interveniert Erkmen mit der Toninstallation *Ewig Dein* (2011). ⟶ **96** Der leicht disharmonisch wirkende Gesang einer Sopranistin nach Ludwig van

29

half the original space, and the four other cubes are each reduced again by half. Erkmen draws attention to the distinctiveness of the monumental and sculpturally conceived museum architecture. In this way, the artist highlights the specifics of the architecture and simultaneously, in an almost playful manner, breaks with the grand aura of the space and the institution of the museum.

Mona Hatoum

Mona Hatoum was born and raised in cosmopolitan Beirut, where she attended Beirut University College from 1970 to 1972. She has lived in London since 1975, when it was impossible for her to return home due to the outbreak of the Lebanese Civil War. In London she studied at the Byam Shaw School of Art from 1975 to 1979 and at the Slade School of Fine Art from 1979 to 1981. The experience of exile and constant questioning have marked her early work: '[…] the fact that I grew up in a war-torn country, the fact that my family was displaced, a Palestinian family that ended up living in exile in Lebanon, has obviously shaped the way I perceive the world', said the artist in an interview in 1996. 'It comes into my work as a feeling of unsettledness. The feeling of not being able to take anything for granted, even doubting the solidity of the ground you walk on.'[19]

In her performances and videos of the 1980s she dealt with the themes of surveillance, social control, conflict and war. The body is central as a 'metaphor for society' and as an object in dealing with political and feminist subjects (such as in *So much I want to say*, 1983 ⟶ **32**; *Roadworks*, 1985; *Corps étranger,* 1994). Michel Foucault's view of 'biopolitics' as a technique of power in government comes through in these works.[20] In the late 1980s Hatoum gradually moved from time-based video and performance works to site-specific installations and sculptures, which nevertheless often retained certain characteristics of performance in their staging and in their interaction with the audience. Influenced by a phenomenological approach, the physical and sensual experience of the artwork increasingly took centre stage in Hatoum's considerations during this period. 'I wanted to explore the phenomenology of the space and materials to create a direct physical interaction – a kind of gut reaction,'[21] said the artist about the change in her way of working in the 1990s. Reacting to the artistic heritage of Minimalism and Conceptual Art, she began creating larger installations with political and social connotations (such as *Light Sentence,* 1992; *Current Disturbance,* 1996). Hatoum relied on the strategies of Minimalism in terms of the relationships of space, object and spectator and on the use and repetition of geometrical forms, expand-

19 Mona Hatoum in Spinelli 1996/2016, 128.

20 See Hatoum 2015a; Mansoor 2010.

21 Mona Hatoum in Spinelli 1996/2016, 128.

19   Mona Hatoum in Spinelli 1996, 16.

Beethovens dreistimmigem Kanon *Ewig Dein* bricht mit der sakral anmutenden Präsentation der Skulptur Max Klingers von Beethoven. Das Pathos der überhöhenden, gottgleichen Darstellung des Komponisten wird durch diese doppeldeutige Form der weiblichen Intonation begleitet. Zugleich ist auch diese Intervention eine künstlerische Auseinandersetzung mit dem Raum – in diesem Falle mit dem akustischen Raum.

Mit ihrem zentralen Ausstellungsbeitrag *Half of* (2017) in unmittelbarer Nachbarschaft zu *Ewig Dein* bezieht sich Ayşe Erkmen schließlich auf den größten freien Luftraum innerhalb des Museums, den Luftraum über der Terrasse der ersten Etage. ⟶ **94** Gegenstand der Arbeit ist die Architektur des 2004 eröffneten Hauses, konzipiert vom damaligen Berliner Architekturbüro Hufnagel, Pütz, Rafaelian, und deren Wahrnehmung durch das Publikum. In einer Art architektonischer *mise en abyme* wiederholt Erkmen die Raummaße und Öffnungen der Halle der ersten Etage in fünf verkleinerten Stoffkuben. Die mimetisch angelegten Objekte reproduzieren den sie beherbergenden Raum, wobei das erste Objekt etwa die Hälfte des Originalraums misst und die vier weiteren jeweils um die Hälfte des vorhergehenden verkleinert werden. Erkmen macht auf die Besonderheiten der monumentalen und skulptural gedachten Museumsarchitektur aufmerksam. So unterstreicht die Künstlerin die Spezifika der Architektur und bricht zugleich fast spielerisch mit der herrschaftlichen Aura des Raumes und der Institution Museum.

Mona Hatoum
Mona Hatoum wurde geboren und wuchs auf im kosmopolitischen Beirut, wo sie von 1970 bis 1972 am Beirut University College studierte. Während eines London-Urlaubs im Jahr 1975 brach im Libanon der Bürgerkrieg aus, wodurch ihre Rückkehr nach Beirut unmöglich wurde. Seitdem lebt sie in der englischen Hauptstadt. Dort studierte sie von 1975 bis 1979 an der Byam Shaw School of Art und von 1979 bis 1981 an der Slade School of Fine Art. Die Erfahrung des Exils, das konstante Infragestellen, prägen Mona Hatoum und ihre künstlerische Arbeit: »Die Tatsache, dass ich in einem kriegszerrissenen Land aufwuchs, dass meine Familie schließlich im libanesischen Exil landete, hat ganz offensichtlich meine Wahrnehmung geprägt«, so die Künstlerin im Interview 1996. »Dies spielt in Form eines Gefühls der Unsicherheit in mein Werk hinein. Das Gefühl, nichts als gegeben hinzunehmen und sogar die Festigkeit des Bodens anzuzweifeln.«[19]

In ihren Performances und Videoarbeiten der 1980er Jahre werden die Themen Überwachung, soziale Kontrolle, Konflikte und Krieg verhandelt. Der Körper spielt dabei als »Metapher für die Gesellschaft« und

30

ing this further with a narrative and critical layer of meaning. The professed neutrality of Minimalism, which Rosalind Krauss described as a 'resistance to meaning' using the example of Dan Flavin,[22] was greatly criticised in the 1990s: the works of such artists as Robert Morris, Dan Flavin, Carl Andre and Donald Judd, whose forms were far from neutral and whose subjects were hardly immanent in the artworks themselves, were deemed proponents of an inherently male discourse of power and accused of a 'domineering, sometimes brutal rhetoric'.[23] Hatoum expanded the devices of Minimalism by offering material for interpretations ranging from feminist and postcolonial critiques to references to precarious living conditions all over the world as well as to war, violence and oppression (*Cube*, 2006). ⟶ **35** The artist stated in 2015: 'In the large installations I used the grid, the geometry of the cube, seriality and repetition, all of which are formal minimal devices. But when the cube turns into a cage and the grid becomes a barrier, they cease to be abstract since they bring in references to containment, control and ultimately the architecture of the prison.'[24]

Hatoum shares an interest in material with one of the independent 'protagonists' of modern art – Piero Manzoni – as well as a certain sense of humour, making direct reference to him with the work *Socle du Monde* (1992–93). There are also references in her work to women artists such as Eva Hesse, whose use of the body as a site for Post-Minimal Art was one of Hatoum's important early influences, as well as to Arte Povera artists, which is evident in Hatoum's use of industrial and organic materials such as glass, steel, soap and cloth. In several works of the 1980s and 1990s, Hatoum uses her own body along with her own blood, skin, nails or hair as materials, thereby placing herself within a feminist tradition of art that was initiated in the 1970s by Carolee Schneemann, Hannah Wilke and others. Another recurring element in her installations is the use of fluctuating lights (for instance *Undercurrent (red)*, 2008). ⟶ **33** The abstract formal language of the 1960s and 1970s is expanded by Hatoum to include a further layer of social and political narrative similar to that seen in the work of artists such as Félix González-Torres or Doris Salcedo from the 1990s. Some of Hatoum's works deal with issues related to her own Palestinian background (for example *Measures of Distance*, 1988). Also, she frequently addresses the specific context of an exhibition, referring to the architecture, the institution, the social mechanisms or other aspects of the venue (for instance *Present Tense*, 1996; *Bourj*, 2010–11). Another example of this is *Twelve Windows*, a work created in collaboration with Inaash, a Lebanese non-governmental organisation that provides employment to women in Palestinian refugee

22   Krauss 1977/1998, 245.

23   Chave 1990/1992, 265; see New York 1994; Schlenzka 2008.

24   Hatoum 2015b.

20 Vgl. Hatoum 2015a; Mansoor 2010.

21 Mona Hatoum in Spinelli 1996, 17.

22 »The resistance to meaning [...]« (Krauss 1977/1998, 245.)

23 Chave 1990/1998, 648; vgl. New York 1994; Schlenzka 2008.

24 »In the large installations I used the grid, the geometry of the cube, seriality and repetition, all of which are formal minimal devices. But when the cube turns into a cage and the grid becomes a barrier, they cease to be abstract since they bring in references to containment, control and ultimately the architecture of the prison.« (Hatoum 2015b.)

Objekt der Auseinandersetzung mit politischen und feministischen Themen eine zentrale Rolle (etwa in *So much I want to say,* 1983 ⟶ **32**; *Roadworks,* 1985; *Corps étranger,* 1994) – die Lektüre Michel Foucaults und dessen Auffassung von »Biopolitik« als Machttechnik von Gouvernementalität scheint hier durch. [20] In den späten 1980er Jahren wechselt Hatoum allmählich von der zeitbasierten Kunst der Performances und Videos hin zu einer ortsspezifischen Kunst, wobei diese in ihrer Inszenierung und ihrer Interaktion mit dem Publikum häufig bestimmte Elemente der Performancekunst beibehält. Unter dem Einfluss phänomenologischer Ansätze gerät zunehmend die körperliche und sinnliche Erfassung der Kunstwerke durch das Publikum ins Zentrum von Hatoums Überlegungen. »Ich wollte die Phänomenologie des Raumes und der Oberfläche untersuchen, um einen direkten physischen Austausch, eine Art unmittelbare Reaktion der Eingeweide zu provozieren«, [21] so die Künstlerin über den Wechsel ihrer Arbeitsweise in den 1990er Jahren. In Auseinandersetzung mit dem künstlerischen Erbe der Minimal Art und der Konzeptkunst wendet sie sich nun unter politischen und gesellschaftskritischen Vorzeichen großformatigeren Installationen zu (etwa in *Light Sentence,* 1992; *Current Disturbance,* 1996). Hatoum greift die Strategien der Minimal Art etwa mit Blick auf das Verhältnis von Raum, Objekt und Betrachter oder auf die Verwendung und Wiederholung geometrischer Formen und Raster auf. Doch erweitert sie diese um eine narrative und zumeist kritische Bedeutungsebene. Die vorgebliche Neutralität der Minimal Art, die Rosalind Krauss am Beispiel Dan Flavins mit der Formulierung »Widerstand gegen Bedeutung« charakterisiert hat, [22] wurde in den 1990er Jahren scharfer Kritik unterzogen: Den Werken von Robert Morris, Dan Flavin, Carl Andre, Donald Judd und anderen, deren Form man keineswegs als neutral, deren Thematik man keineswegs als rein kunstimmanent wahrnahm, wurde ein inhärenter männlicher Machtdiskurs, ja eine »despotisch-arrogante, manchmal brutale Rhetorik« unterstellt. [23] Mona Hatoum erweitert die Dispositive der Minimal Art um ein Interpretationsangebot (etwa *Cube,* 2006), das feministische und postkoloniale Kritiken aufnimmt und auf prekäre Lebensverhältnisse weltweit, auf Krieg, Gewalt und Unterdrückung verweist. ⟶ **35** »In den großen Installationen habe ich auf Raster, auf die Geometrie des Kubus ebenso wie auf Serialität und Wiederholungen, auf die Mittel der Minimal Art, zurückgegriffen«, so die Künstlerin 2015, »aber wenn sich der Kubus in einen Käfig verwandelt und wenn das Gitter zur Barriere wird, hören sie auf, abstrakt zu sein: Sie verweisen auf Grenzen, auf Kontrolle, und schließlich auf die Gefängnisarchitektur.« [24] Das Interesse am Material als einem in der modernen

31

Ayşe Erkmen
Busy Colors, 2005
Installationsansicht /
installation view,
SculptureCenter,
New York

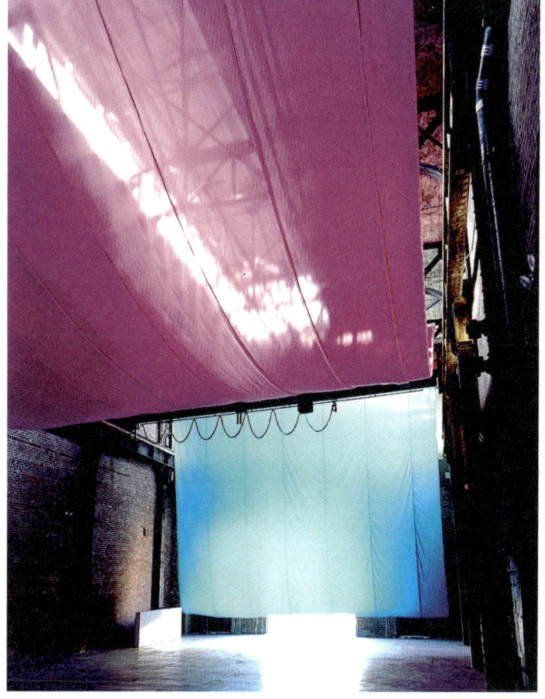

Kunst eigenständigen ›Akteur‹ und einen gewissen Witz teilt sie mit Künstlern wie Piero Manzoni, auf den sie mit ihrem *Socle du Monde* (1992–1993) direkt Bezug nimmt. Auch finden sich in ihrem Œuvre Verweise auf Künstlerinnen wie Eva Hesse, die als Protagonistin der Post-Minimal Art und in ihrer Betonung des Körperlichen zu Hatoums wichtigen frühen Referenzen zählt, sowie zu Künstlern der Arte Povera, etwa in der Verwendung von Materialien sowohl industrieller als auch organischer Natur wie Glas, Stahl, Seife, Stoff. In einigen Werken vor allem der 1990er Jahre nutzt Hatoum auch ihren eigenen Körper, nutzt Blut, Haut, Nägel oder Haare als Materialien und verortet sich damit in einer feministischen Kunsttradition, die in den 1970er Jahren von Carolee Schneemann, Hannah Wilke und anderen angestoßen wurde. Auch spielt bewegtes Licht immer wieder eine große Rolle in ihren Installationen (etwa bei *Undercurrent (red)*, 2008). ⟶ 33 Die abstrakte Formensprache der Kunst der 1960er und 1970er Jahre erweitert Hatoum um eine soziale und politische narrative Ebene, wie es seit den 1990er Jahren auch bei vergleichbaren Künstlerinnen und Künstlern wie Félix González-Torres oder auch Doris Salcedo gebräuchlich ist. In einigen ihrer Arbeiten thematisiert Hatoum ihren eigenen biografischen Hintergrund (beispielsweise in *The Negotiating Table*, 1983; *Measures of Distance*, 1988). Häufig wendet sie sich aber auch dem spezifischen Kontext einer Ausstellung zu, bezieht sich auf die Architektur, die Institution, die sozialen Mechanismen oder andere Aspekte eines Ortes (wie etwa bei *Present Tense*, 1996 / 2011; *Bourj*, 2010–2011). Zu nennen ist hier auch *Twelve Windows*, eine Installation, die Mona Hatoum zusammen mit Frauen der libanesischen Nichtregierungsorganisation Inaash hergestellt hat, die sich für die Verbesserung der Arbeitssituation von Frauen in palästinensischen Flüchtlingscamps im Libanon einsetzt. Zwischen 2012 und 2013 wurden mit traditionellen palästinensischen Motiven zwölf Tücher bestickt, die Hatoum an einem kreuz und quer durch den Raum verlaufenden Stahlseil hängend ausgestellt hat.

Hatoums Werke verbinden komplexe konzeptionelle Reflexionen mit sinnlich ansprechenden Mitteln, Formen und Materialien. Die ästhetische, ja bisweilen haptische Qualität dieser Materialien steht häufig in einem gegensätzlichen Verhältnis zum Inhalt. In Hatoums Arbeiten leuchten Hoffnungsschimmer und Glücksversprechen auf, um hinter einer dunklen Ahnung von Gewalt und Unterdrückung wieder zu verblassen; Verführung und Sinnlichkeit können zu Gefahrenquellen und Bedrohungsszenarien werden.[25] Eine These der Ausstellung ist es, dass sich Mona Hatoum dabei Techniken des Displacement bedient, Techniken der Verschiebung im Sinne einer Verfremdung,

32

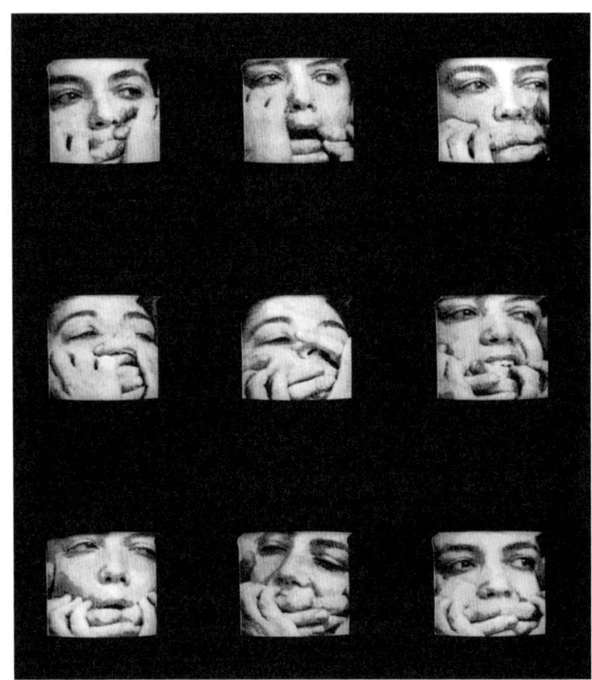

Mona Hatoum
So much I want to say, 1983

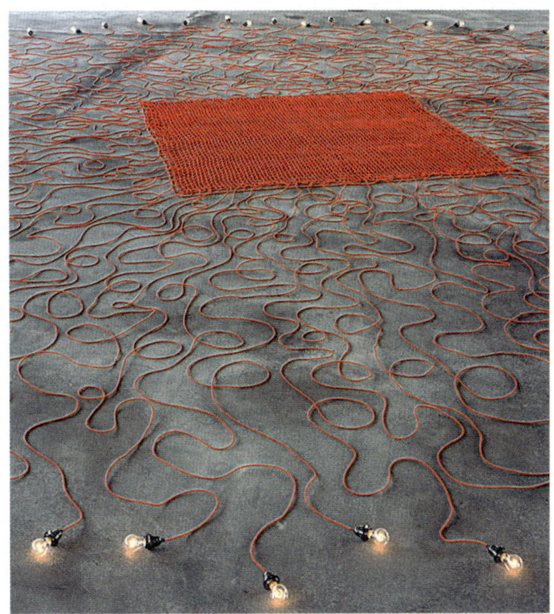

33

camps in Lebanon. Between 2012 and 2013, using traditional Palestinian motifs, they embroidered twelve pieces of fabric that Hatoum displayed pegged to a steel cable which criss-crossed the exhibition space.

Hatoum's works link complex conceptual reflections with exceptionally sensual means, forms and materials. The aesthetic, even haptic qualities of these materials often stand in stark contrast with the artwork's content. In Hatoum's works there is a glimmer of hope and a promise of happiness that fades behind a dark suggestion of violence and oppression, where temptation and sensuality can become sources of danger and threatening scenarios.[25] One hypothesis of this exhibition is that Hatoum uses the techniques of unsettling, alienating displacement to redefine spaces and objects. A strategy of re-classification using the psychological techniques of Surrealism, similar to those used by Meret Oppenheim or René Magritte, can be discerned in Hatoum's way of altering scale and re-interpreting everyday objects such as household appliances. Her approach might be understood as a form of psychological displacement. Through alteration of dimensions and alienating combinations of materials, Hatoum creates unexpected, threatening scenarios whose visual reception leads to an intense, physical experience (for example, *La grande broyeuse (Mouli-Julienne ×17)*, 1999 ⟶ **36**;

Paravent, 2008; *Daybed,* 2008). 'I like to engage people in a visual and physical way at first so that the associations or interpretations emerge out of that initial physical encounter with the work,' said the artist in connection with her exhibition that opened in June 2015 at the Centre Pompidou in Paris. 'I wanted my own body to be replaced by that of the viewer. In the large installations, which can be quite enveloping, the viewer becomes enmeshed in the phenomenology of the space and the formal elements of the work to experience for themselves a feeling of instability or threat, for instance.'[26] The works become surfaces onto which the audience projects its fears and uncertainties. One might be reminded of an experience one has had, or be seduced and wooed, and at other times rejected and alienated. Hatoum's works physically confront the spectator with confinement, danger or even imagined pain (*Hot Spot III*, 2009; *Impenetrable*, 2009). Conversely the artist tempts the audience with the superficial beauty of objects that seem elegant or formal (*A Bigger Splash*, 2009; *Natura morta*, 2009), but on second glance are revealed to be a source of danger for body and soul – this too is an effect of displacement on the level of reception and meaning. Exhibitions, on the other hand, go through a functional displacement with Hatoum's sculptures and interventions: places where meaning

25 'I like it when the work pushes and pulls us in opposite directions, when you are seduced by the beauty of the work, before perceiving the totally opposing or perhaps even dangerous implications contained in it.' (Mona Hatoum in Vogel 2014b, 163, translated from German.)

26 Hatoum 2015b.

26 »I like to engage people in a visual and physical way at first so that the associations or interpretations emerge out of that initial physical encounter with the work. I wanted my own body to be replaced by that of the viewer. In the large installations, which can be quite enveloping, the viewer becomes enmeshed in the phenomenology of the space and the formal elements of the work to experience for themselves a feeling of instability or threat, for instance.« (Hatoum 2015b.)

die verunsichern und Räume wie Objekte neu definieren wollen. So kann man in der Strategie der Maßstabsverschiebung und in den Umdeutungen von Alltagsgegenständen, etwa von Haushaltsgeräten, eine künstlerische Umwidmung durch Aneignung von psychologischen Techniken des Surrealismus erkennen, die etwa Meret Oppenheim oder René Magritte angewandt haben. Hatoums Vorgehensweise könnte auch als eine Form der Affektverschiebung verstanden werden. Hatoum erzeugt durch maßstäbliche Verschiebungen und befremdliche Materialkombinationen unerwartete, bedrohliche Szenarien, deren visuelle Rezeption zu einem intensiven, körperlichen Erleben führt (etwa *La grande broyeuse (Mouli-Julienne ×17)*, 1999 ⟶ **36**; *Paravent*, 2008; *Daybed*, 2008). »Ich verleite die Leute gerne zu einer visuellen und körperlichen Herangehensweise, so dass sich aus dieser direkten physischen Begegnung mit dem Werk die Assoziationen und Interpretationen ergeben«, so die Künstlerin im Rahmen ihrer im Juni 2015 im Pariser Centre Pompidou eröffneten Ausstellung. »Ich wollte, dass der Körper des Betrachters meinen eigenen ersetzt. In den großen Installationen wird der Betrachter allmählich eins mit dem Raum und den formalen Bestandteilen des Werkes, um schließlich die Erfahrung etwa von Instabilität oder Bedrohung zu machen.« **26** Die Werke können als Projektionsflächen der Ängste

und Unsicherheiten des Publikums dienen. Man mag sich an eigene Erfahrungen erinnert fühlen, wird mal verführt und angezogen, mal befremdet abgestoßen. Hatoums Werke konfrontieren die Betrachterinnen und Betrachter physisch mit Enge, Gefahr oder auch mit der Vorstellung eines drohenden Schmerzes (etwa *Hot Spot III,* 2009; *Impenetrable,* 2009). Umgekehrt lockt die Künstlerin das Publikum mit der oberflächlichen Schönheit von Objekten (*A Bigger Splash,* 2009; *Natura morta,* 2009), die etwas Edles oder Ursprüngliches ausstrahlen, um auf den zweiten Blick als Gefahrenquelle für Leib und Seele erkannt zu werden – auch dies ein Verschiebungseffekt auf der Rezeptions- und Bedeutungsebene. Ausstellungen wiederum erfahren durch Mona Hatoums Objekte und Interventionen eine funktionale Verschiebung: Aus Orten der Bedeutungsproduktion und Selbstvergewisserung werden Orte der Anteilnahme und Selbstreflexion.

Mona Hatoum in Leipzig
Die Ausstellung in Leipzig konzentriert sich auf Werke, die Mona Hatoum in den letzten 15 Jahren geschaffen hat, zeigt aber auch Videoarbeiten und Arbeiten auf Papier aus den 1980er Jahren. Einige fokussieren den Themenkomplex von Konflikten, Krieg, Gewalt, Vertreibung, Unterdrückung und Zerstörung, forcieren also eine politische Lesart des Begriffs ›Displacement‹.

34

and self-reassurance are produced become places of compassion and self-reflection.

Mona Hatoum in Leipzig
The exhibition in Leipzig focuses on works that Hatoum has produced in the last fifteen years and includes some videos and works on paper from the 1980s. Several works revolve around the subject of conflict, war, violence, displacement, oppression and destruction, calling for a political reading of the term *displacement*. Others have a more personal charge and handle the emotional and psychological side of displacement and the themes of threat and fear. Among the early works are videos from the 1980s (*Changing Parts,* 1984 ⟶ **126**; *Measures of Distance,* 1988 ⟶ **130**) and a video documentation of a performance (*Roadworks,* 1985 ⟶ **128**) as well as the billboard-like work *Over my dead body* (1988 / 2002). ⟶ **132** They reveal Hatoum's analysis of themes that range from surveillance and social control to marginalisation and stereotyping, as well as war and expulsion. In her performance and video works, she negotiates larger political and social questions of identity and the hegemonic relationship of the 'West' to the 'Third World' directly in front of (and with) an audience: 'My awareness of political social issues came, I suppose partly, from analysing and reflecting on my position and daily reality of existing in

a Western culture that is not my own […]. I saw myself as a marginal person and I saw performance as a kind of intervention from the margins of the art world.' **27**

Along with Hatoum's growing success in the early 1990s, which moved her away from the 'margins' and more into the centre of the global art world, came an increased interest in sculpture and installations. *Quarters* (2017) is a good example. ⟶ **134** Here Hatoum has revisited a work that was originally made in 1996 with twelve bunk bed units that were subsequently separated to create three installations with four bunk bed units each. For the installation in Leipzig, Hatoum created a slightly larger version of this work, filling the whole room. The original piece from 1996 was inspired by a visit to the Eastern State Penitentiary Prison in Philadelphia in 1995, where she came across a similar kind of prison bunk beds. The dark, metal bed frames dominate both the room and the visitors, who are free to walk around them; the audience is at the mercy of the piece, and they experience a feeling of hidden control and threat. Hatoum nods to the general tendency of modernism to use grid structures, which refer to strategies of rationalisation and surveillance, culminating in Minimalism.

Hatoum's installations in the central hall of the lower level relate to the term *displacement* in two ways. In one sense they refer to the aesthetic recep-

27 Mona Hatoum in Spinelli 1996 / 2016, 128; see also the essay by Kelly Baum in this publication.

27 Mona Hatoum in
Spinelli 1996, 16; vgl. den
Aufsatz von Kelly Baum
in dieser Publikation.

Andere sind stärker persönlich aufgeladen und verhandeln die emotionale und psychologische Seite der Affektverschiebung sowie die Themen Bedrohung und Angst.

Zu den früheren Werken zählen die Videoarbeiten (*Changing Parts,* 1984 ⟶ **126**; *Measures of Distance,* 1988 ⟶ **130**) und die Dokumentation von Performances aus den 1980er Jahren (*Roadworks,* 1985 ⟶ **128**) sowie das plakatartige *Over my dead body* (1988/2002 ⟶ **132**). Sie offenbaren Hatoums Beschäftigung mit Themenkomplexen, die von Überwachung und sozialer Kontrolle über Ausgrenzung und Stereotype bis hin zu Krieg und Vertreibung reichen. In ihrer Performance und den Videoarbeiten verhandelt Hatoum größere politische und soziale Fragen zur Identitätspolitik und zum hegemonialen Verhältnis des ›Westens‹ zur ›Dritten Welt‹ direkt vor (und mit) dem Publikum: »Mein Interesse an politischen und sozialen Themen resultiert zumindest teilweise aus der Analyse meiner Position in einer westlichen Kultur, die nicht meine eigene ist. […] Ich verstand mich selbst als marginale Person. Performance schien mir eine Intervention, die aus einer Randzone in die Kunstwelt eingriff.« [27]

Hatoums zunehmender Erfolg in den frühen 1990er Jahren, als sie von den ›Randzonen‹ mehr und mehr ins Zentrum der globalen Kunstwelt rückte, ging einher mit der verstärkten Hinwendung zu Objekten und Rauminstallationen. Als Beispiel hierfür kann in der Ausstellung *Quarters* (2017) dienen. ⟶ **134** Hatoum hat eine Arbeit aus dem Jahr 1996 mit zwölf Etagenbetten aufgegriffen, die in der Folge auf drei einzelne Installationen mit je vier Betten aufgeteilt wurde. Für Leipzig hat sie die Installation in etwas größerem Umfang neu produzieren lassen, so dass sie einen ganzen Ausstellungssaal füllt. Ihren Ausgangspunkt findet die Arbeit, deren Titel mit ›Quartiere‹ oder ›Lager‹ übersetzt werden kann, in einem Besuch Hatoums im Gefängnis Eastern State Penitentiary 1995 in Philadelphia, wo sie ähnliche Gefängnisbetten vorfand. Die dunkel-metallenen Bettgestelle dominieren den Raum und damit auch die Betrachterinnen und Betrachter. Das Publikum ist dem Werk ausgeliefert, kann am eigenen Leib ein Gefühl von Fremdbestimmung und Bedrohung empfinden. Hatoum bezieht sich hier auf die allgemeine Tendenz der künstlerischen Moderne zur Verwendung von Gitterstrukturen, die sich auch auf gesellschaftliche Rationalisierungs- und Überwachungsstrategien beziehen lässt und die in der Minimal Art kulminierte.

Hatoums in der zentralen Halle im Untergeschoss gezeigte Installationen können auf zwei Ebenen mit dem Begriff ›Displacements‹ in Beziehung gesetzt werden. Sie verweisen zum einen auf dessen

35

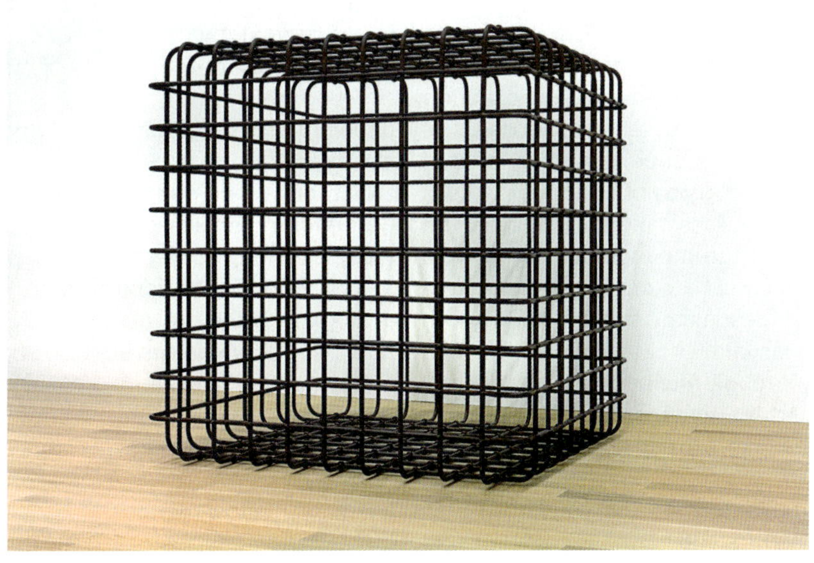

Mona Hatoum
Cube, 2006

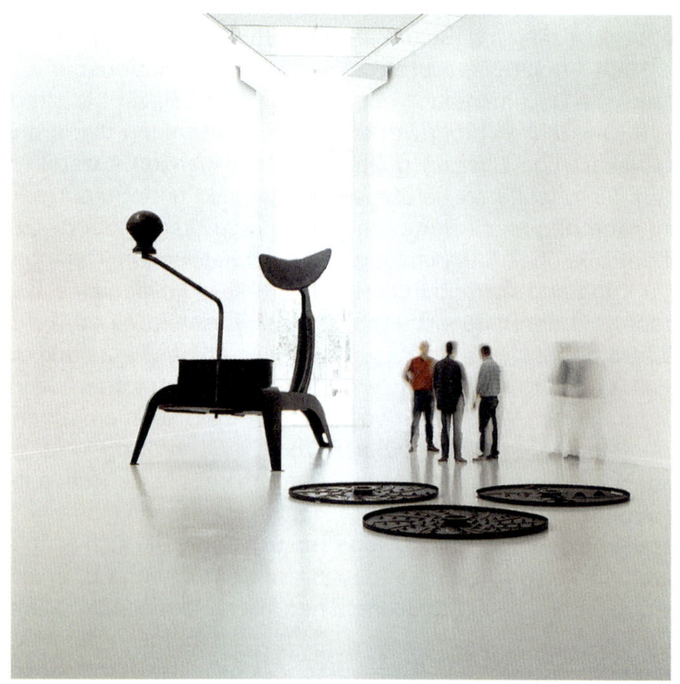

36

tion of displacement, which develops as the visitors move through and experience the installations and objects in the room. Simultaneously, displacement is shown through the subjects of war, crisis and the blurring of borders. This becomes clear in the installations *Impenetrable* and *Hot Spot III* (both 2009). ⟶ **158 +164** On one side of the room, *Hot Spot III,* a globe of steel and neon, could be seen as a symbol of the current, worldwide humanitarian and political crisis, while on the other, *Impenetrable,* which consists of barbed wire rods that form a cube, refers to restricted movement. The 'burning' globe of *Hot Spot III* serves as a warning and symbolises danger, while the cube of barbed wire refers to the impenetrability of barriers and borders. As in many of Hatoum's installations there is clearly a formal dependence on Minimalism, and in this case also the visual techniques of Op Art. This critical alienation through reference to material and forms of Minimal Art is also apparent in Hatoum's series of *Bourj* (2011) works, a group of sculptures made from stacked square steel tubes, which resemble models of modernist buildings. ⟶ **166** The steel tubes have been subjected to cutting and burning making the buildings seem scarred by war. These 'wounds' contrast greatly with the appearance and hardness of the material. The installation *Remains of the Day (s version)* (2016), which was created especially for the

exhibition in Leipzig, also refers to destroyed cityscapes. ⟶ **162** A larger version of this work was first as a contribution to Hatoum's 10th Hiroshima Art Prize exhibition in 2017. ⟶ **37** Although in Hiroshima the installation could be seen as a direct reference to the aftermath of the nuclear bomb, when shown in a different context it takes on a more universal meaning as a metaphor for the fragility of human existence in situations of war and crisis. Simultaneously it can be understood as an artistic and domestic visualisation of a historical catastrophe that otherwise remains abstract for certain people – perhaps inspired by the desire for a humanisation of political discourse and the questioning of Western concepts of humanity.

Following the idea of spatial displacement and analogous to the presentation of Erkmen's interventions, works by Hatoum are also shown in the rooms of the permanent exhibition. On the second-floor terrace of the museum, within view of Erkmen's intervention *Half of,* Hatoum presents her installation *Cellules* (2012–13). ⟶ **174** These cage-like structures, which are made of steel reinforcing bars, contain deep red, bulbous glass shapes that nestle up to the metal rods as if trying to escape from their prison. Although they are cold and hard, the glass shapes have the aura of imaginary warmth and softness in their form, colour and material appearance that is in stark contrast to

rezeptionsästhetische Dimension, die sich in der Bewegung des Publikums, das die Installationen und Objekte im Raum erfahren soll, entfaltet. Zugleich thematisieren sie Krieg und Krisen, Entgrenzungen und Entortungen. Das wird deutlich etwa an den Installationen *Impenetrable* und *Hot Spot III* (beide 2009). ⟶ **158** + **164** Auf der einen Seite wird der Stahl- und Neonglobus *Hot Spot III* als Symbol der gegenwärtigen globalen humanitären Krisen und politischen Konflikte gezeigt, auf der anderen die aus Stacheldraht bestehende Arbeit *Impenetrable,* die auf die Einschränkung von Bewegungsfreiheit Bezug nimmt. Der ›brennende‹ Globus dient als Warnung und symbolisiert Gefahr, der Stacheldrahtkubus verweist auf die Undurchdringlichkeit von Barrieren und Grenzen. Wie in vielen anderen Objekten ist die formale Anlehnung an die Minimal Art, hier auch an visuelle Techniken der Op Art, deutlich zu spüren. Diese kritische Verfremdung durch Rückgriff auf Material und Formen der Minimal Art ist auch in Hatoums Reihe der *Bourj* (2011) erkennbar, einer Gruppe von aufeinander gesetzten, aus Baustahlrohren geformten Strukturen, die Assoziationen an Modelle modernistischer Gebäude wecken. ⟶ **166** Durch die Behandlung mit Feuer und Einschnitten wirken die Stahlrohre, als seien sie vom Krieg beschädigt worden. Diese ›Verletzungen‹ stehen im Kontrast zu Erscheinung und Härte des

Materials. Auf zerstörte Stadtlandschaften verweist auch die Installation *Remains of the Day (s version)* (2016), die für die Ausstellung in Leipzig neu produziert wurde. ⟶ **162** Eine größere Fassung hatte Hatoum als Beitrag zum 10. Hiroshima Art Prize entwickelt. ⟶ **37** Auch wenn die Installation zunächst als Referenz an die nuklear verbrannte Lebenswelt Hiroshimas gesehen werden kann, erhält sie im veränderten Kontext eine universellere Bedeutung als Metapher für die Verletzlichkeit der menschlichen Existenz in Kriegs- und Krisensituationen. Zugleich kann die Arbeit als künstlerisch-häusliche Visualisierung einer historischen und für viele Menschen abstrakt erscheinenden Katastrophe verstanden werden, die vielleicht auch den Wunsch nach einer Vermenschlichung politischer Diskurse und die Infragestellung westlicher Humanitätskonzepte auslöst.

Der Idee des Displacement im Sinne einer räumlichen Verschiebung folgend sind analog zu den Interventionen von Ayşe Erkmen auch von Mona Hatoum Werke in den Räumen der Dauerausstellung zu sehen. Auf einer Terrasse in der zweiten Etage des Museums, in Sichtweite zu Erkmens Intervention *Half of,* präsentiert die Künstlerin die Installation *Cellules* (2012 / 2013). ⟶ **174** Die käfigartigen Strukturen aus Stahlarmierungen beherbergen dunkelrote, bauchige Glasformen, die sich an die Gitterstäbe schmiegen,

37

Mona Hatoum
Remains of the Day, 2017
Installationsansicht /
installation view,
Hiroshima City Museum
of Contemporary Art

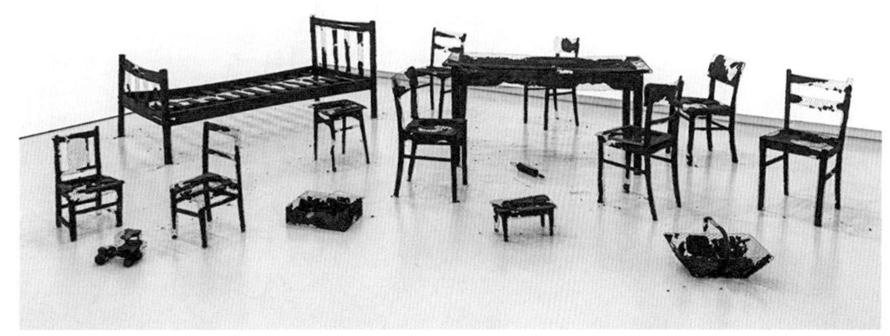

ihrem Gefängnis aber nicht entkommen können. Obwohl erkaltet und erhärtet, strahlen die Glasobjekte, die in Form, Farbe und materieller Erscheinung im Kontrast zum Baustahlgitter stehen, imaginäre Wärme und Weichheit aus. Die Materialität von Metall und Glas, aber auch die Serialität der Gitterstruktur werden hier in Beziehung gesetzt zur architektonischen Hülle des Museums, die aus Glas und Metall besteht. Hatoums Strukturen korrespondieren mit der Museumsarchitektur, die im Innenraum und nach außen von strengen Rastern, einer spezifischen Materialsprache und von offenen und geschlossenen Räumen bestimmt wird.

In der zweiten Etage des Hauses zeigt Hatoum ebenfalls die beiden Skulpturen *Daybed* und *Paravent* (beide 2008) ⟶ **170**, begleitet von einer Gruppe von Frottagen auf Wachspapier (1999) ⟶ **168**, die durch Küchenutensilien erzeugt wurden. *Daybed* und *Paravent* bieten ein bedrohliches Szenario: Auf übermenschliches Maß vergrößert, strahlen die beiden Haushaltsgeräte – Küchenreiben – in dunklem und schwerem Metall etwas Beunruhigendes oder Unheimliches aus. Hatoum kehrt Größenverhältnisse um, der Mensch fühlt sich angesichts der Utensilien klein und unterlegen; durch die perforierten, scharfkantigen Oberflächen scheint Gefahr von den Werken auszugehen. Hatoums dunkle Objekte aus dem Bereich des Häuslichen können als Resultate einer Affektverschiebung verstanden werden; legt man ihnen eine psychologische Verständnisebene von Displacement zugrunde, erscheinen sie wie Projektionsflächen erlittener Traumata und können aus feministischer Perspektive als Kritik an herrschenden Rollenbildern und als Ablehnung von Identitätszuschreibungen verstanden werden. Die Werke beherrschen den Galerieraum und treten unweigerlich in ein Interpretationsverhältnis zu den dort dauerhaft gezeigten Kunstwerken.

Wahrnehmungsverschiebungen

Die Leipziger Ausstellung *Ayşe Erkmen & Mona Hatoum. Displacements / Entortungen* eröffnet die Möglichkeit, Arbeiten und Interventionen dieser beiden wichtigen zeitgenössischen Künstlerinnen im Dialog zu erleben und dabei auch die eigenen Standpunkte zu überdenken. Die Werke sind bedeutungsoffen und kontrovers. Gerade die Widersprüchlichkeiten, die einigen der Arbeiten zu eigen sind oder die aus deren Rezeption erwachsen können, ermöglichen Perspektivwechsel und Diskussionen. So werden in der Ausstellung Objekte, Installationen und Interventionen gezeigt, die bestehende Überzeugungen und Sehgewohnheiten in Frage stellen, vielleicht auch Unsicherheiten auslösen. Über das ästhetische Erleben wird eine Reflexion der aufgeworfenen künstlerischen, aber auch

38

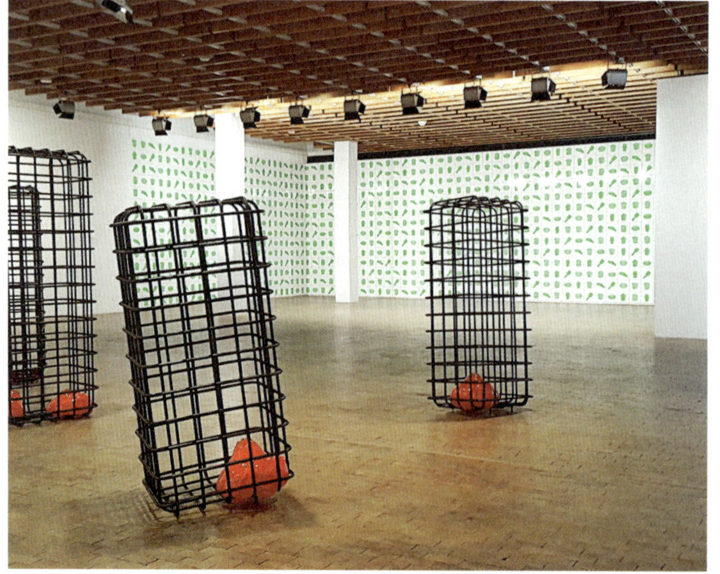

Ayşe Erkmen
Alkoven (Detail / detail),
1997 / 2016

Mona Hatoum
Kapan iki (Detail / detail), 2012

Installationsansicht /
installation view, Akademie
der Künste, Berlin 2016

28 In der Ausstellungsvermittlung wird auf die These von Christiane Brohl Bezug genommen, die 2003 im Rahmen ihrer Untersuchung *Displacement als kunstpädagogische Strategie* schrieb: »Displacement stellt eine Strategie von Gegenwartskunst dar, die eine Denk- und Arbeitsweise mit implizit kunstpädagogischem Impetus aufweist, weil sie eine diskursive ästhetische Forschungspraxis ist, die eine eben solche auf Seiten der Rezipienten auslöst.« (Brohl 2003, 10.)

29 Rancière 2008/2009, 33.

gesellschaftlichen und politischen Fragen angeregt. Dabei werden die Besucherinnen und Besucher mit unterschiedlichen Hintergründen und unterschiedlichem Vorwissen in ihrer sinnlichen Rezeption als eigenständige Akteure in der Wissens- und Bedeutungsproduktion wahrgenommen. [28] Denn: »Es bedarf der Zuschauer«, so Jacques Rancière über das Verhältnis von künstlerischer Arbeit und konstruktiver Rezeption durch das Publikum, »die die Rolle aktiver Interpreten spielen, die ihre eigene Übersetzung ausarbeiten, um sich die ›Geschichte‹ anzueignen und daraus ihre eigene Geschichte zu machen. Eine emanzipierte Gemeinschaft ist eine Gemeinschaft von Erzählern und von Übersetzern.« [29]

39

the steel grids. Both the materiality of metal and glass, and the seriality of the grid structure complement the architectural shell of the museum, which is built of glass and metal. Hatoum's structures correspond with the museum architecture, which is characterised inside and out by severe grids, a specific material language and both open and closed spaces.

Hatoum's sculptures *Daybed* and *Paravent* (both 2008) ⟶ **170** are accompanied by a group of frottages on wax paper (1999) that were made using kitchen utensils. ⟶ **168** *Daybed* and *Paravent* present a threatening scenario: bigger than a person, these enlargements of kitchen utensils – both graters – cast in dark and heavy metal emanate an uncanny, disturbing quality. Hatoum has scaled up everyday kitchen tools to the size of a room divider and a bed, making visitors feel small and inferior in comparison with the utensils, whose perforated, sharp-edged surfaces render them dangerous. Hatoum's dark domestic objects can be understood as the result of displacement; in terms of a psychological understanding of displacement, they seem to be surfaces for the projection of trauma and, from a feminist point of view, can be seen as a critique of prevailing gender roles and identity stereotypes. These works dominate the gallery space, inevitably interacting with the paintings from the permanent collection.

Displacement of Perception

The exhibition *Ayşe Erkmen & Mona Hatoum: Displacements / Entortungen* enables visitors to experience works and interventions by these two significant contemporary artists in dialogue and to re-consider their own positions. The works are controversial and open to interpretation. This contradictory nature, which is inherent in some of the works or can arise from their reception, makes discussion and a change of perspective possible. Some of the sculptures, installations and interventions in the exhibition are bound to call existing convictions and conventions of viewing into question and perhaps even cause discomfort. This aesthetic experience encourages us to reflect upon artistic, social and political issues. Visitors from different backgrounds and levels of knowledge could be considered independent actors in the production of knowledge and meaning. [28] For, as Jacques Rancière wrote on the relationship of artistic work and constructive reception, it 'requires spectators who play the role of active interpreters, who develop their own translation in order to appropriate the "story" and make it their own story. An emancipated community is a community of narrators and translators.' [29]

Translated from German by Tas Skorupa

28 The educational programme accompanying the exhibition will use this thesis by Christiane Brohl, who wrote in her examination of displacement as a strategy in art pedagogy, 'Displacement represents a strategy of contemporary art that has a way of thinking and working with an implicitly pedagogical impulse because it is a discursive aesthetic practice of research that causes another such impulse in the recipient.' (Brohl 2003, 10.)

29 Rancière 2008/2011, 22.

Ayşe Erkmen
Jalousie, 2007
Imitating Lines, 1985/2008
Alkoven, 1997/2017

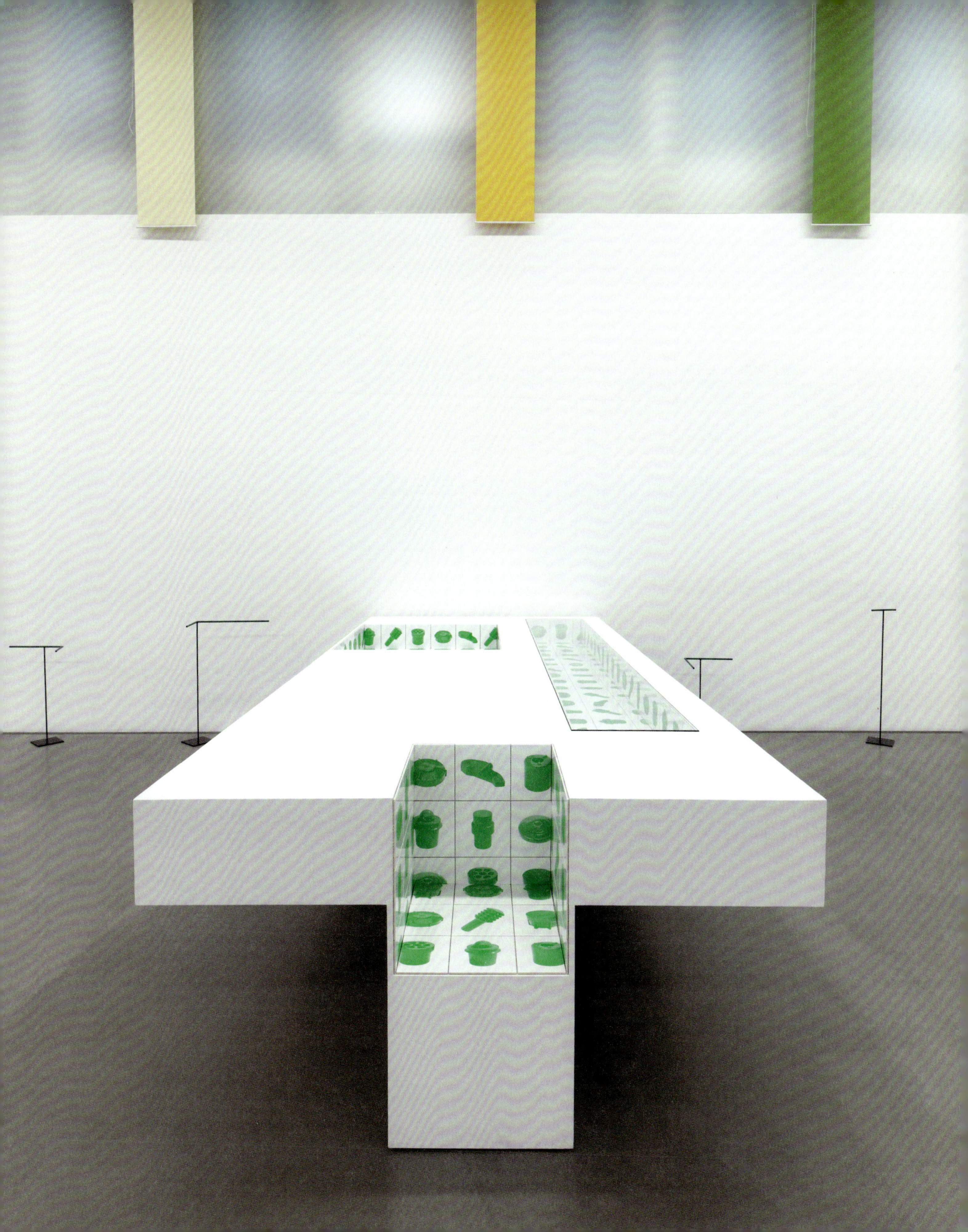

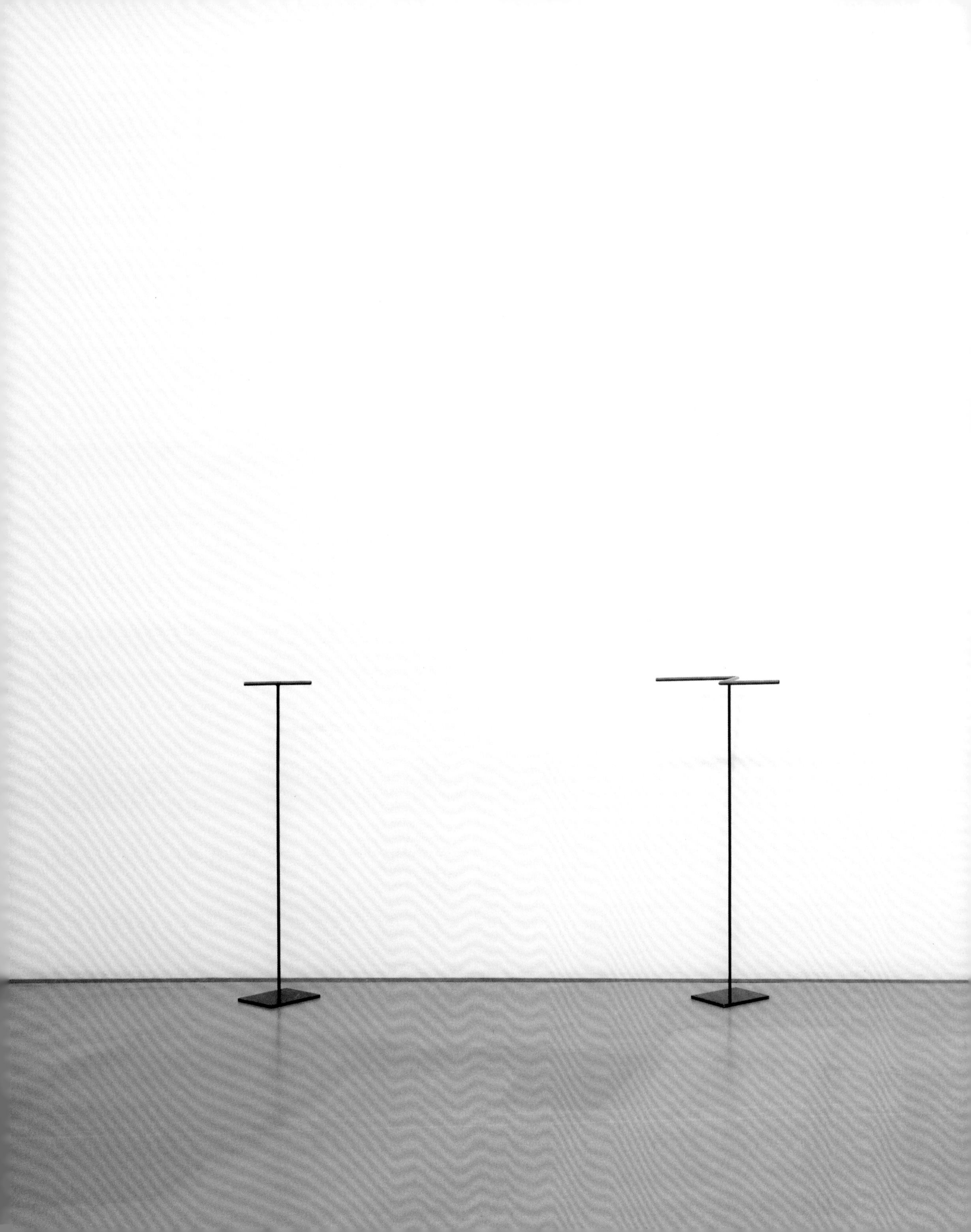

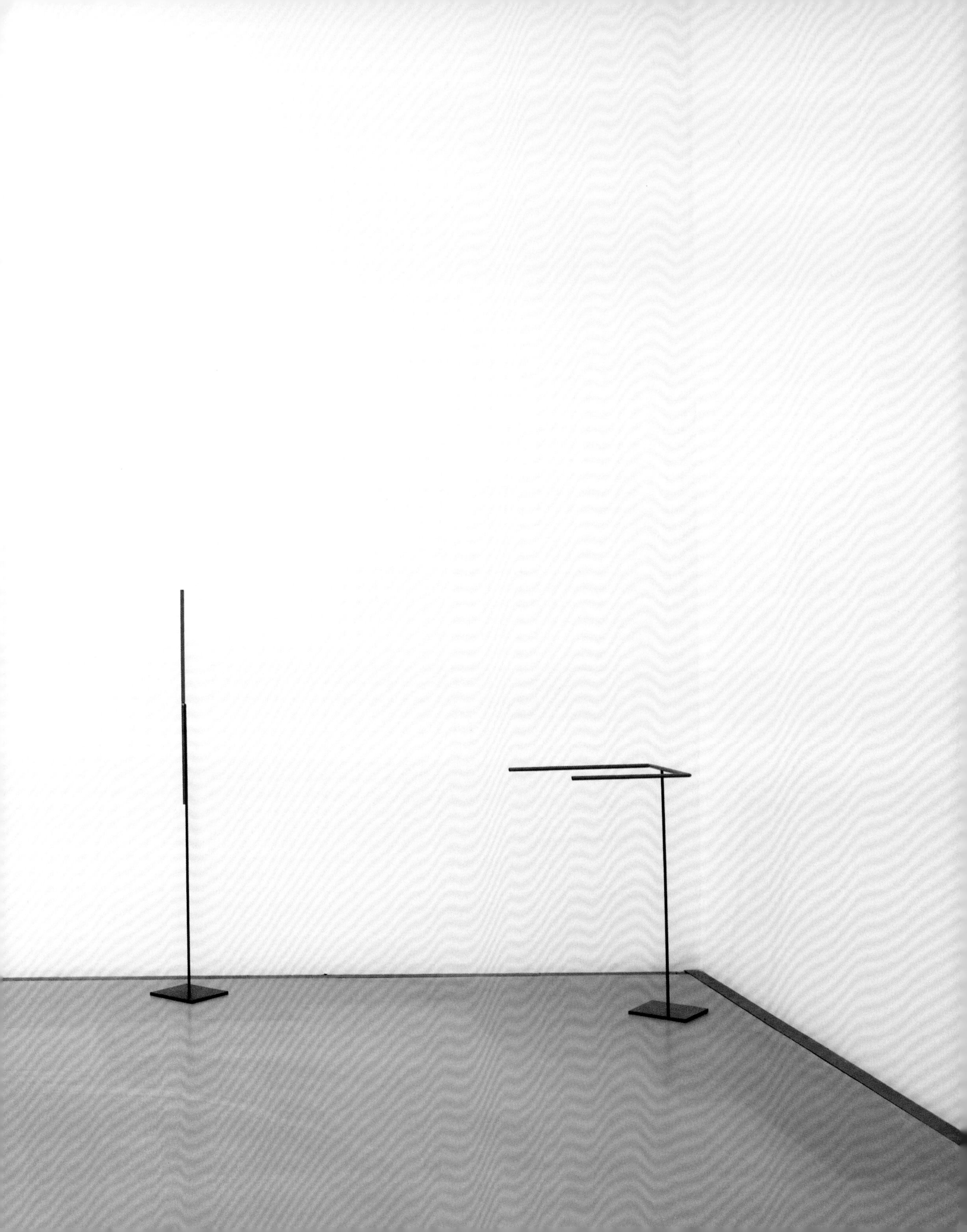

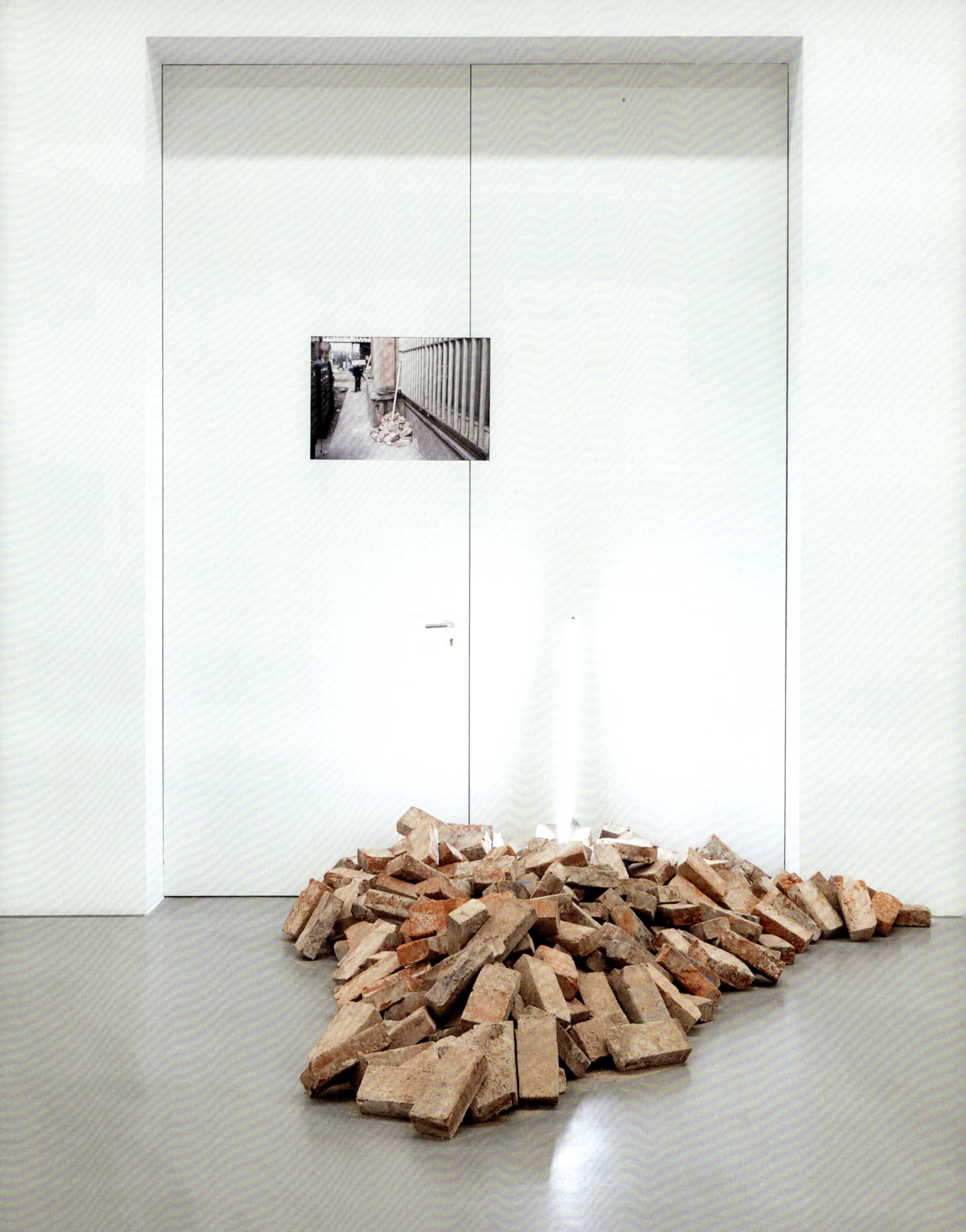

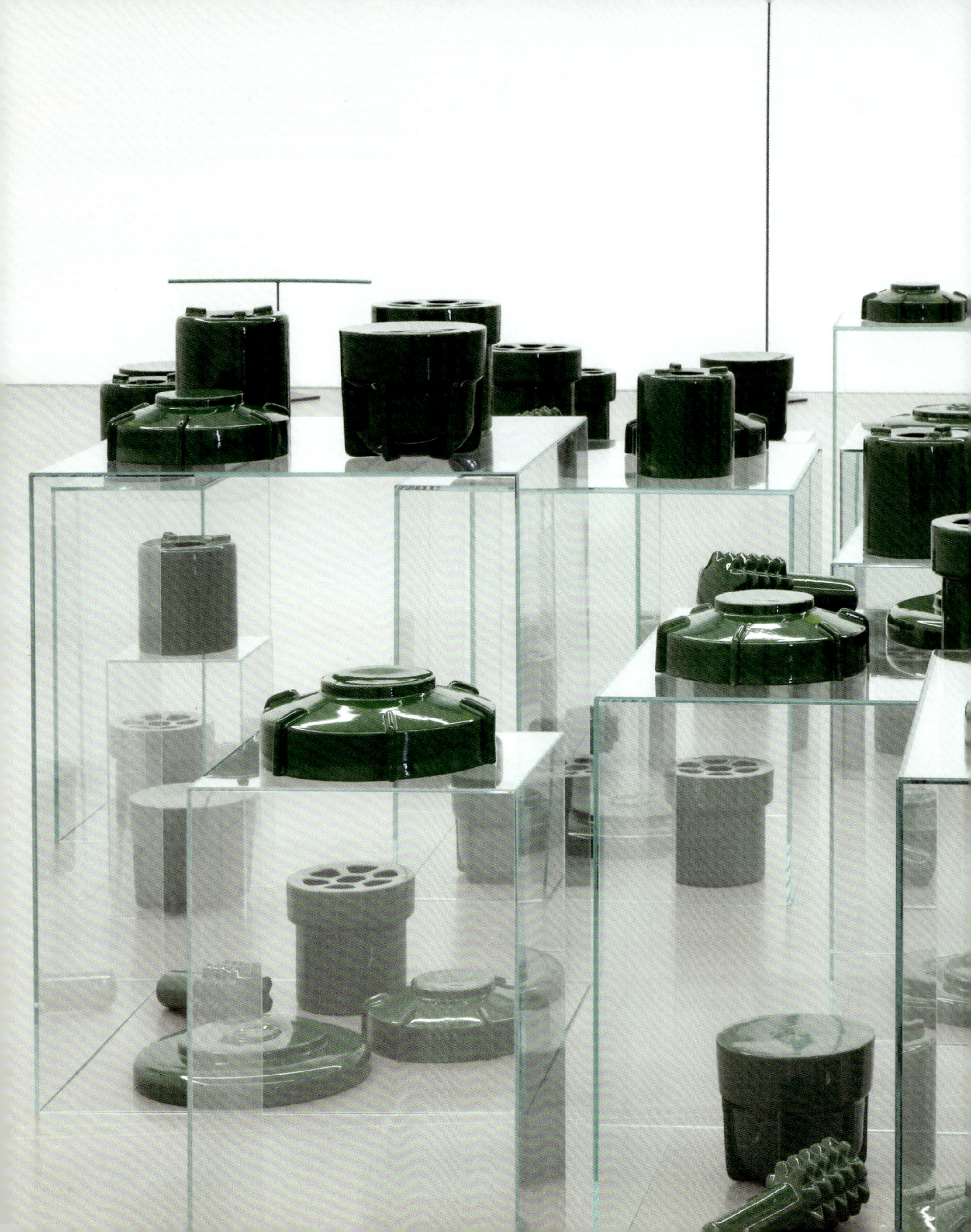

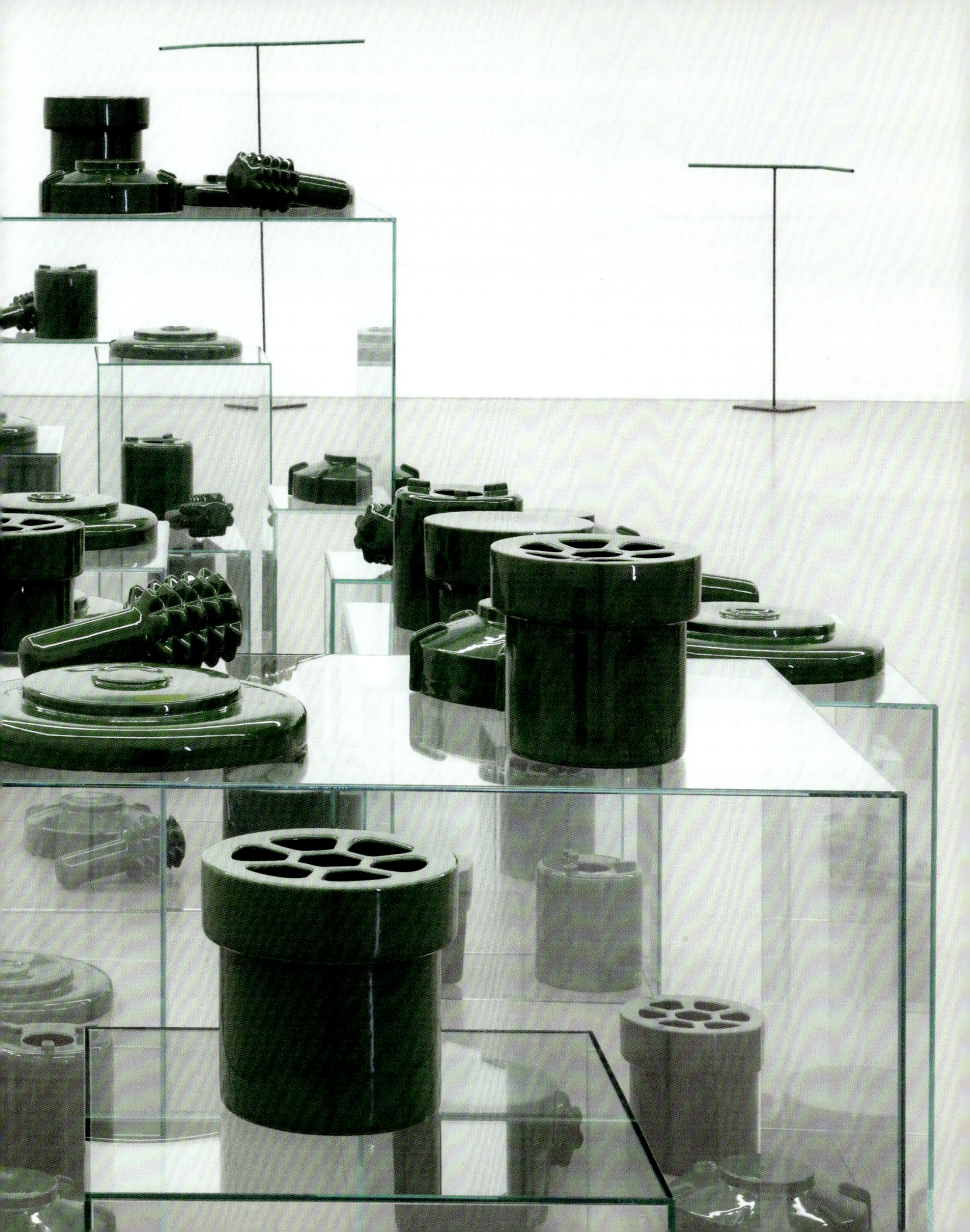

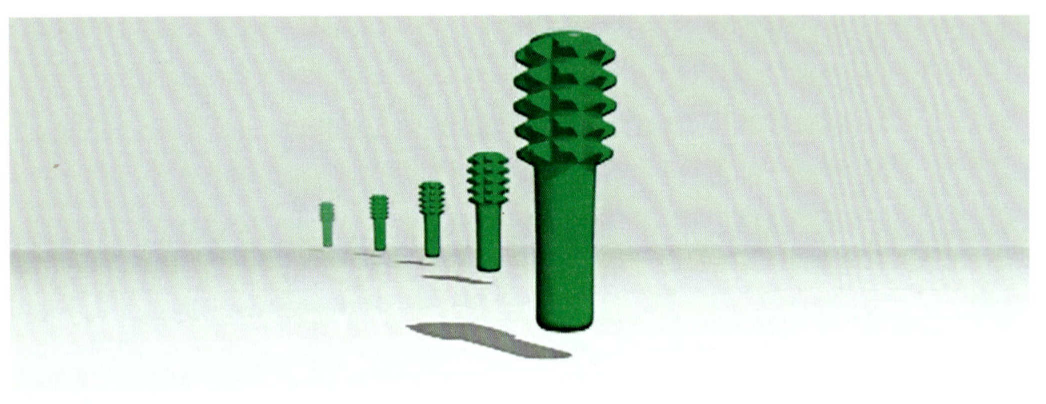
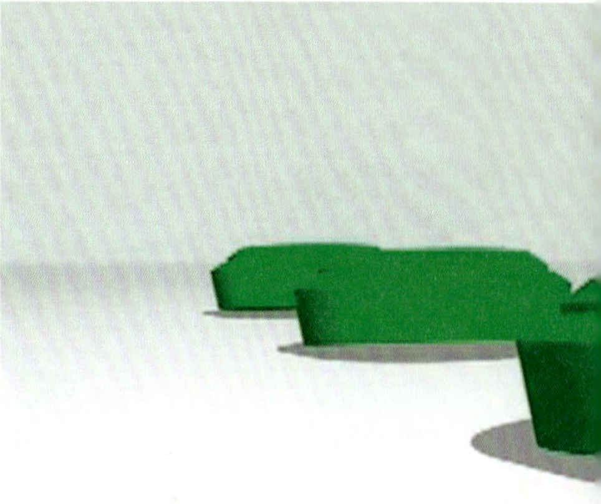
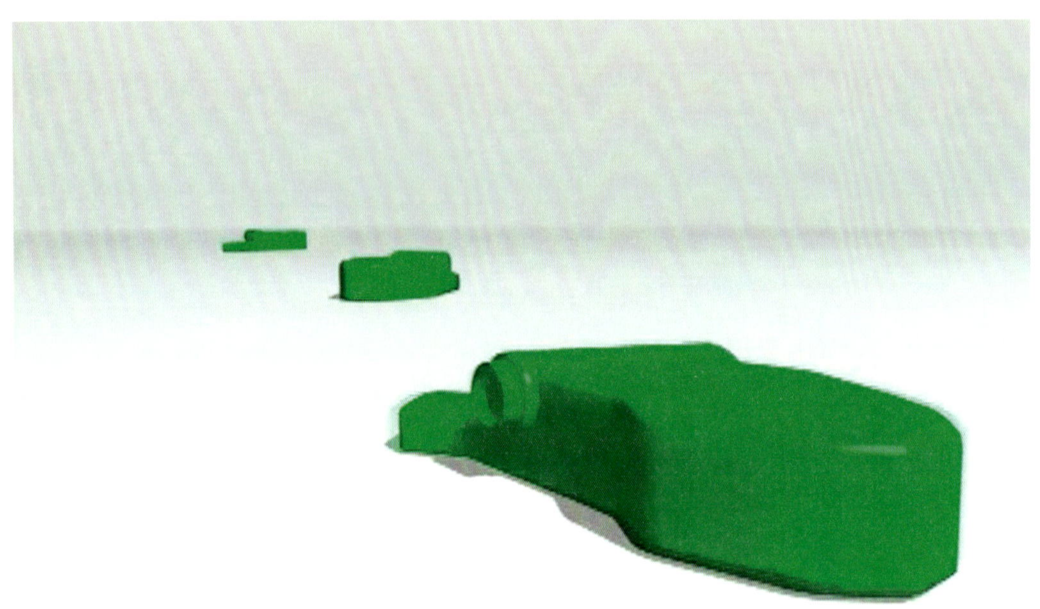
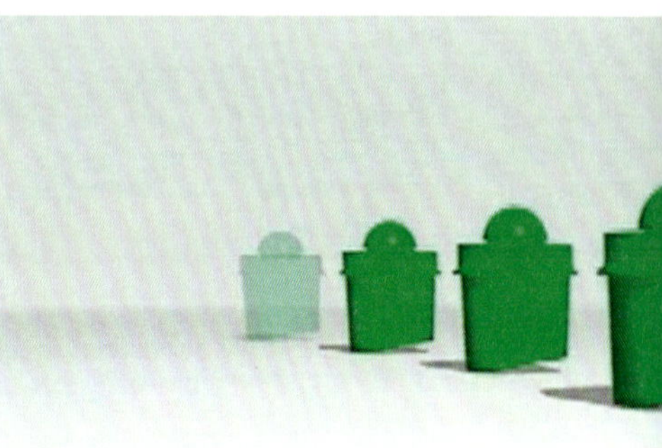

Ayşe Erkmen
PFM-1 and others, 1997 / 2013

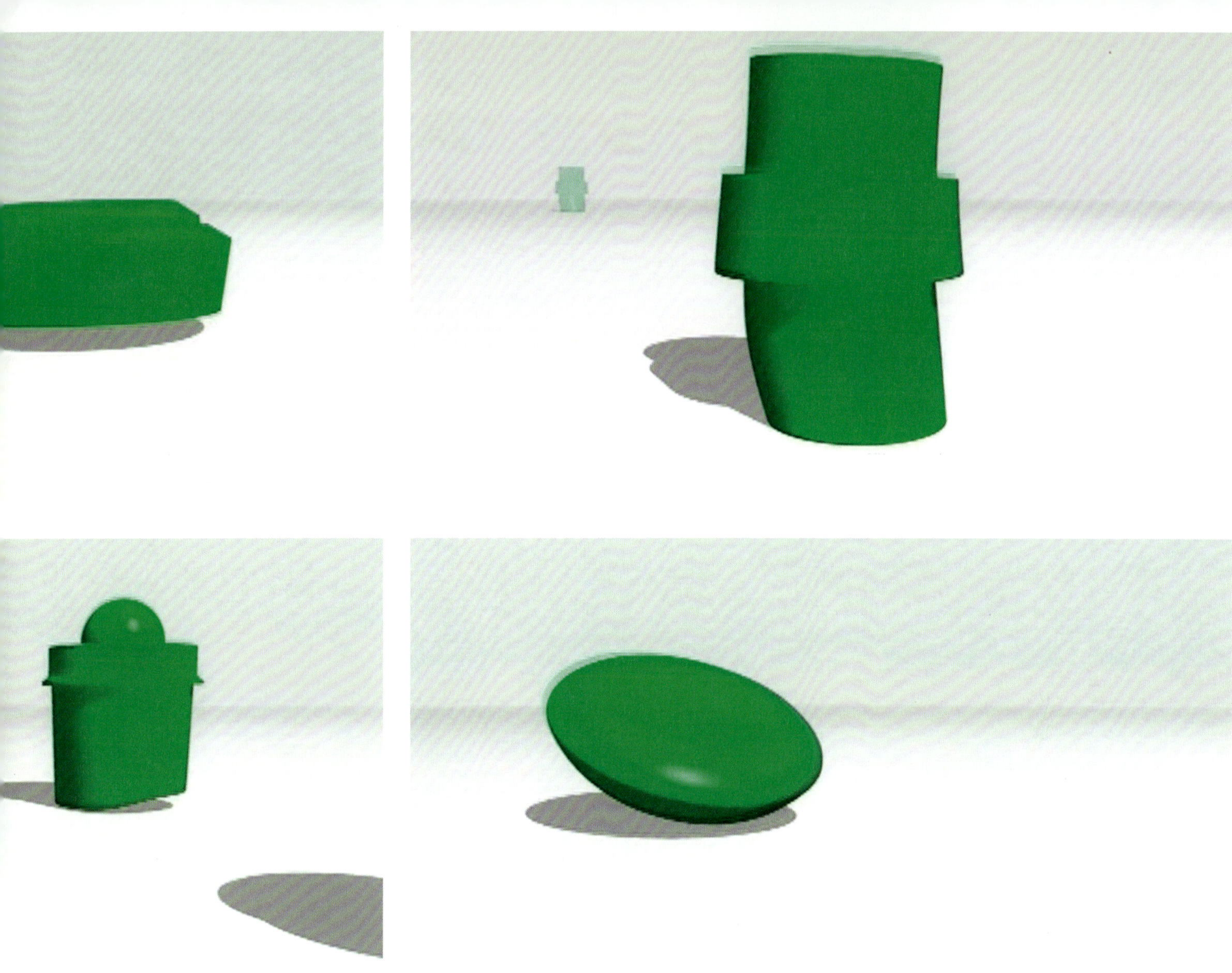

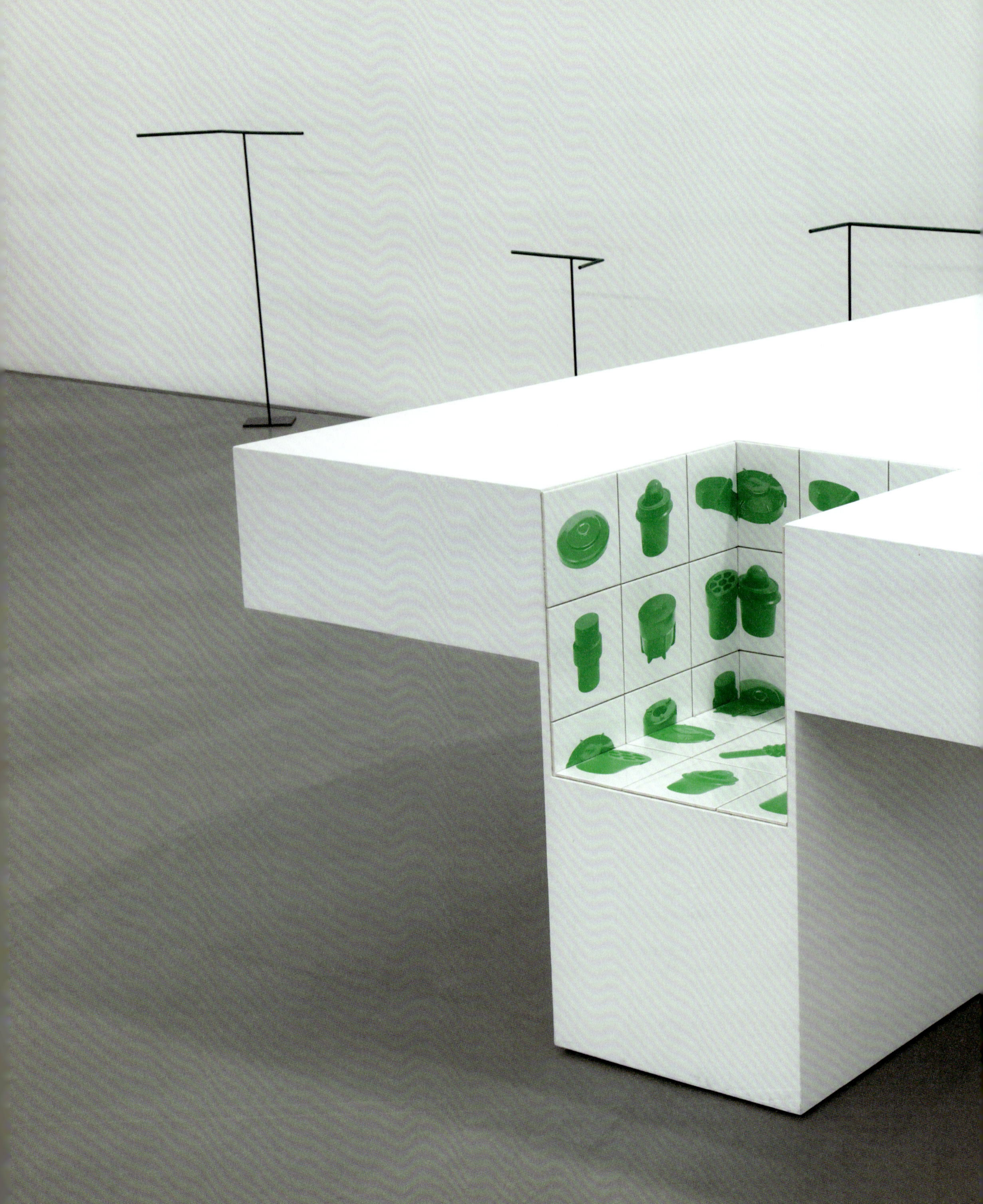

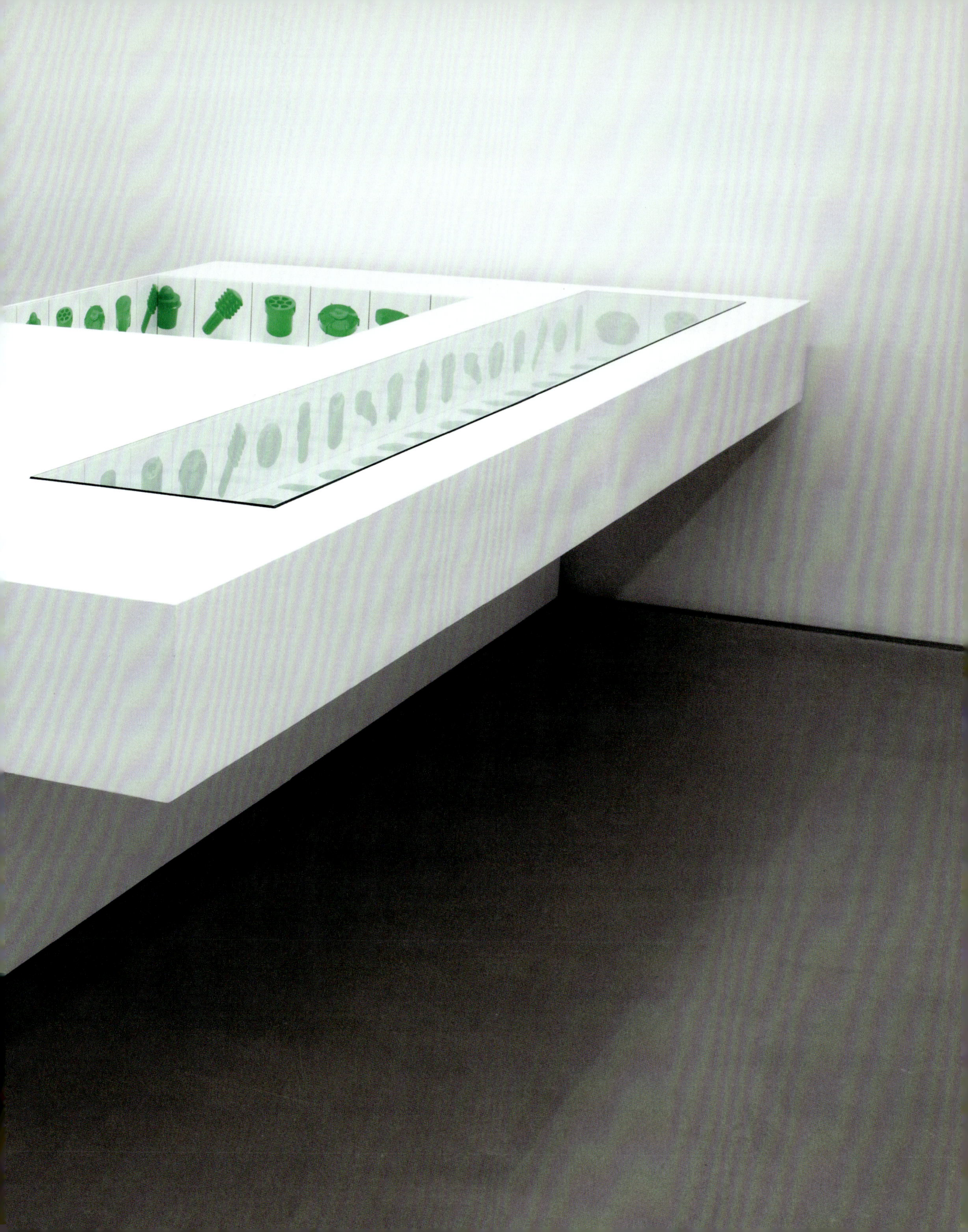

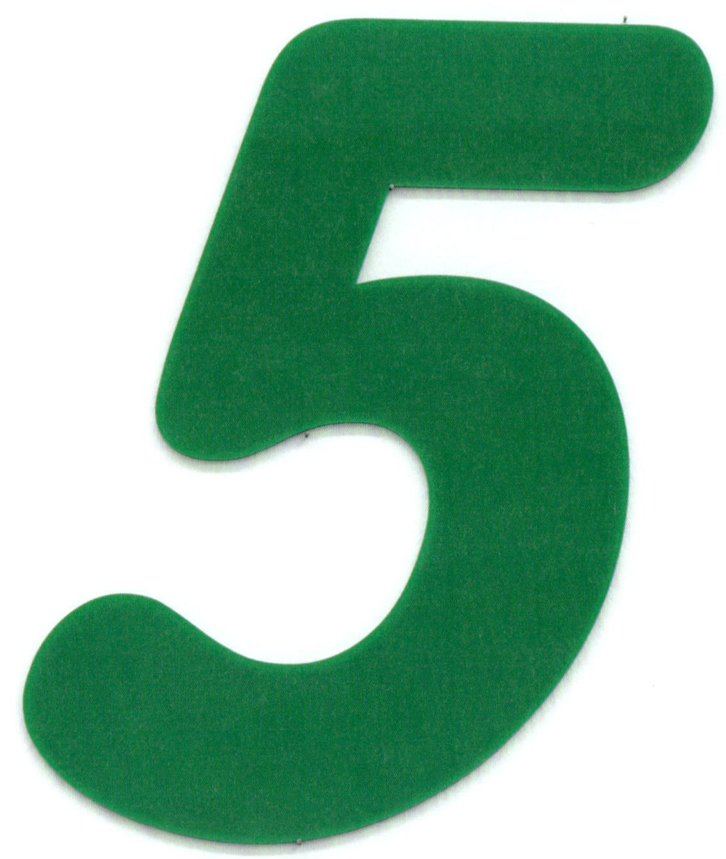

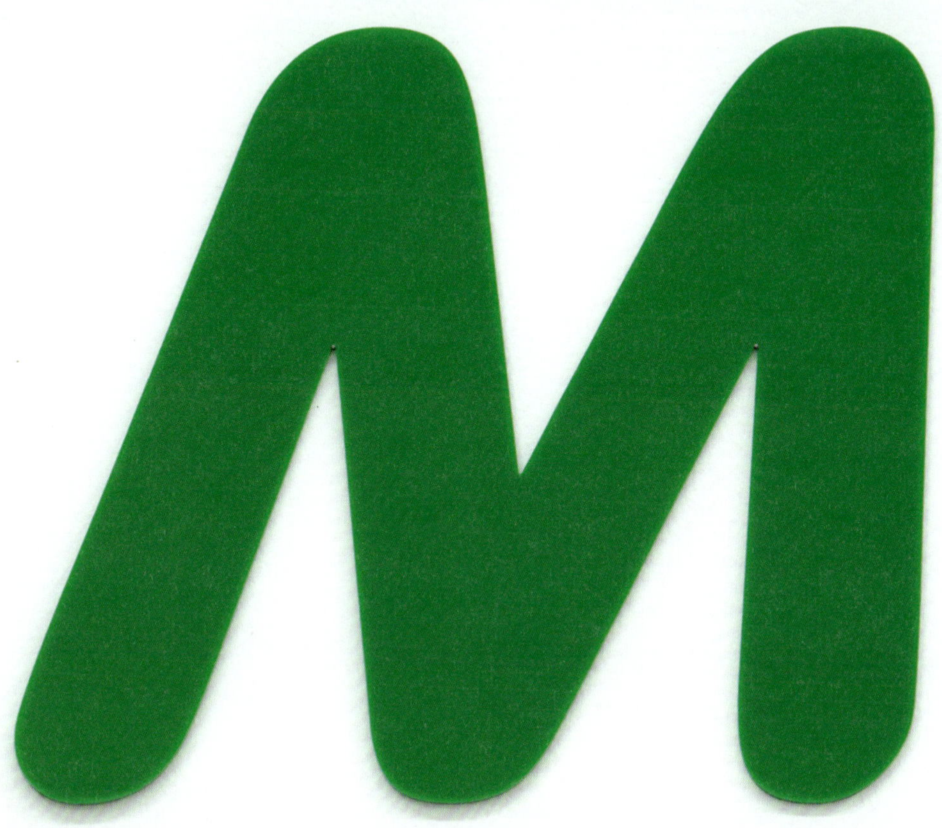

Ayşe Erkmen
Die Farben der Buchstaben (M), 2006

⟶ Ayşe Erkmen
Jalousie, 2007

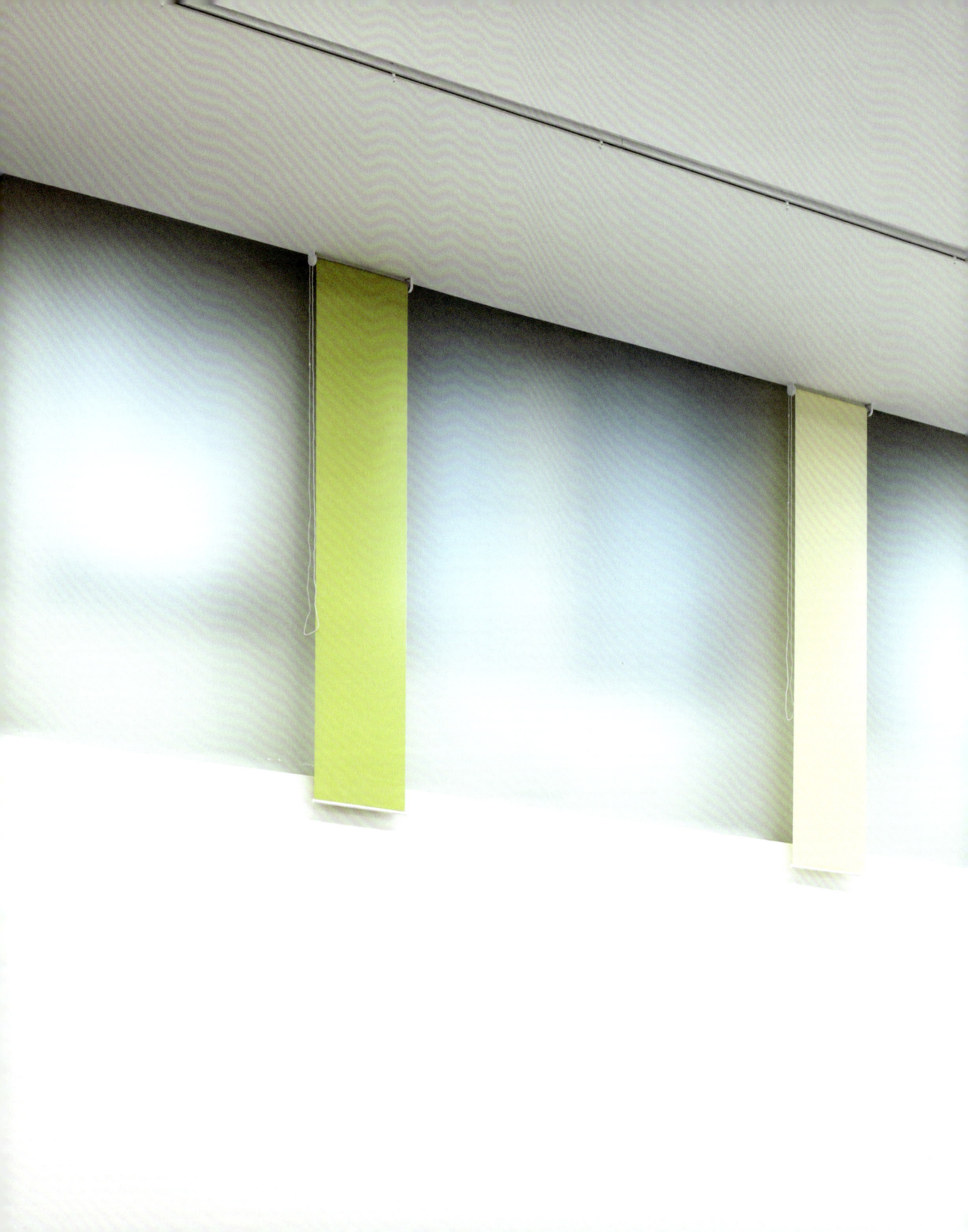

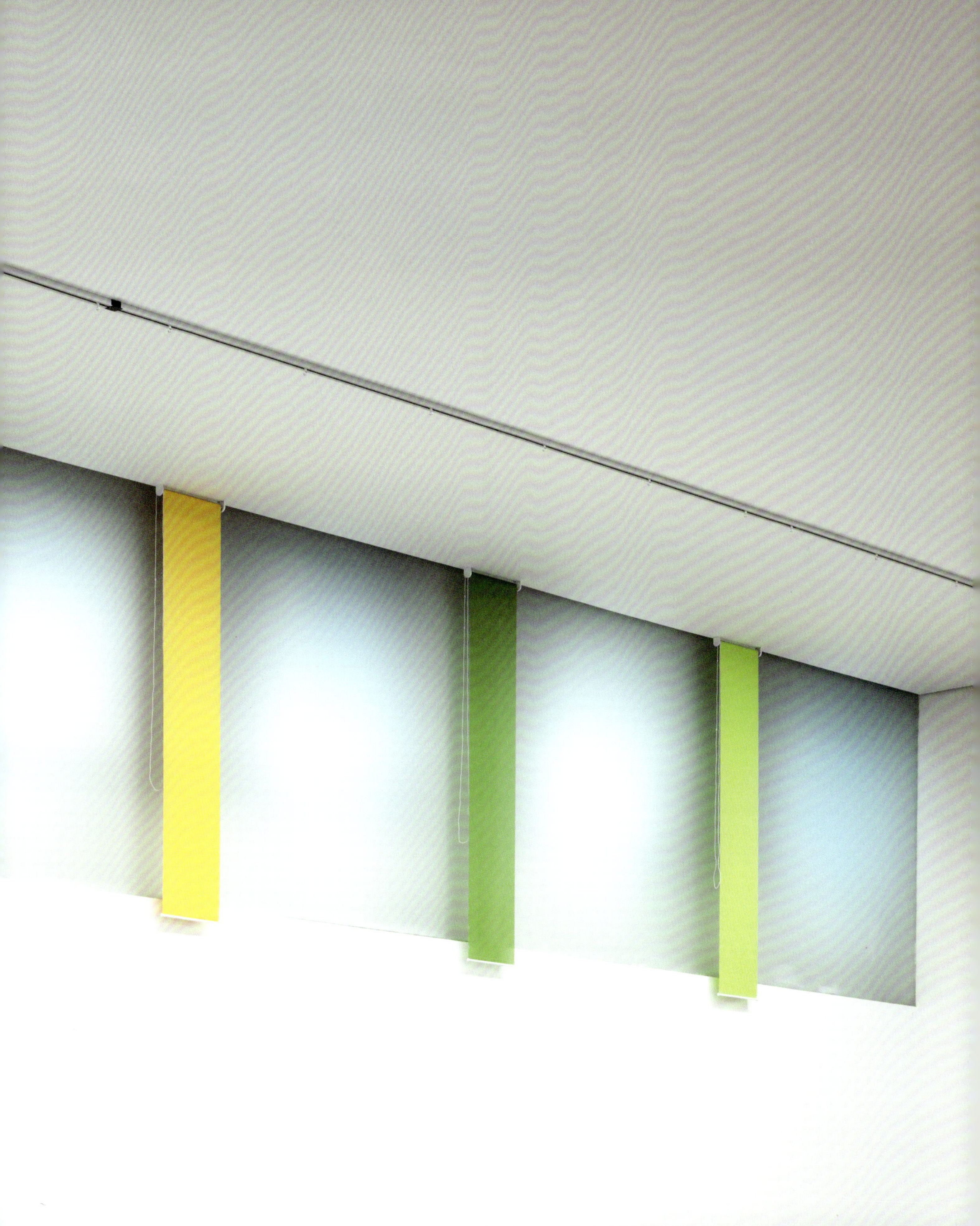

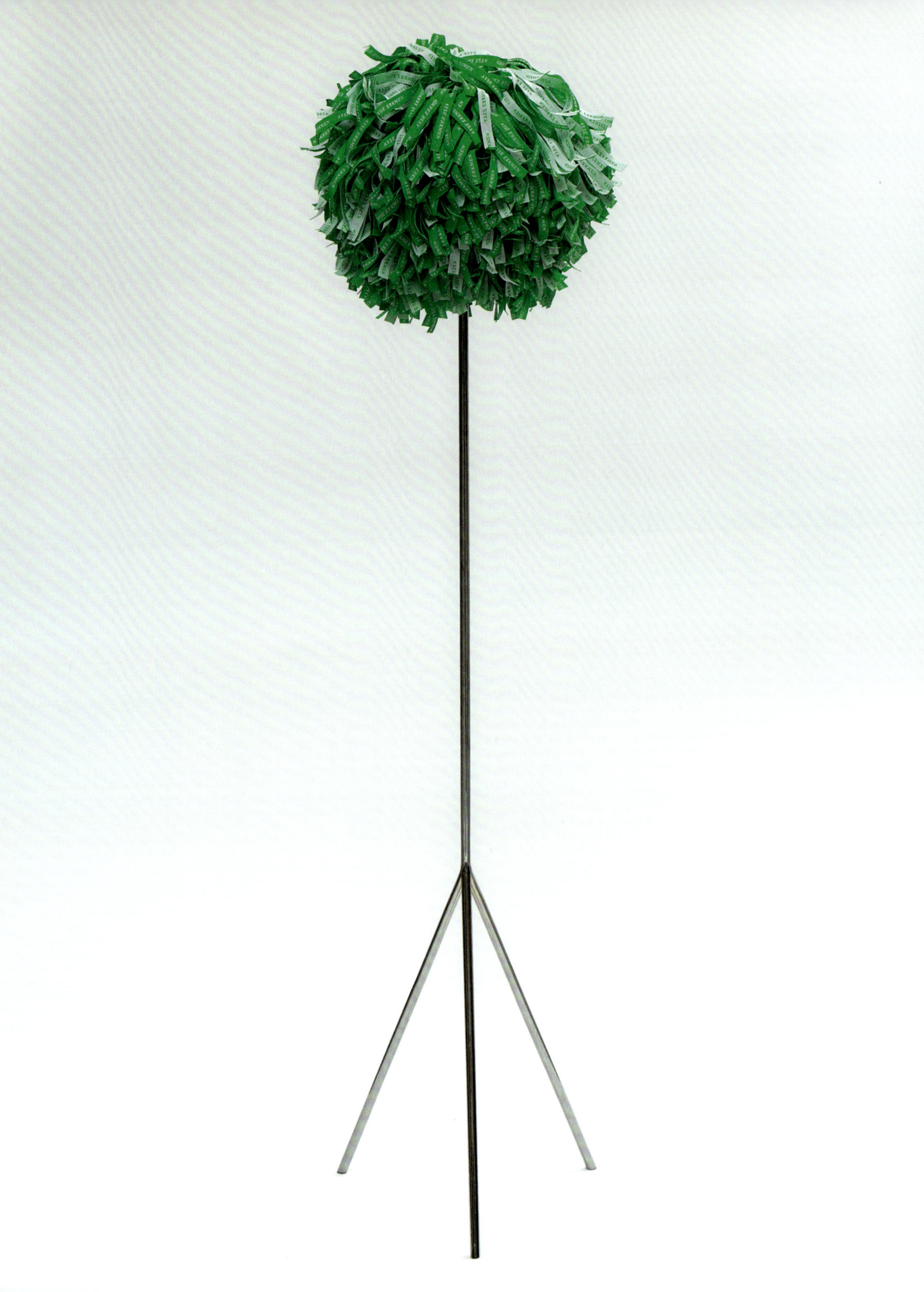

Ayşe Erkmen
Kleines grünes Pompon, 2012

Ayşe Erkmen
Großes grünes Pompon,
(Detail / detail), 2012

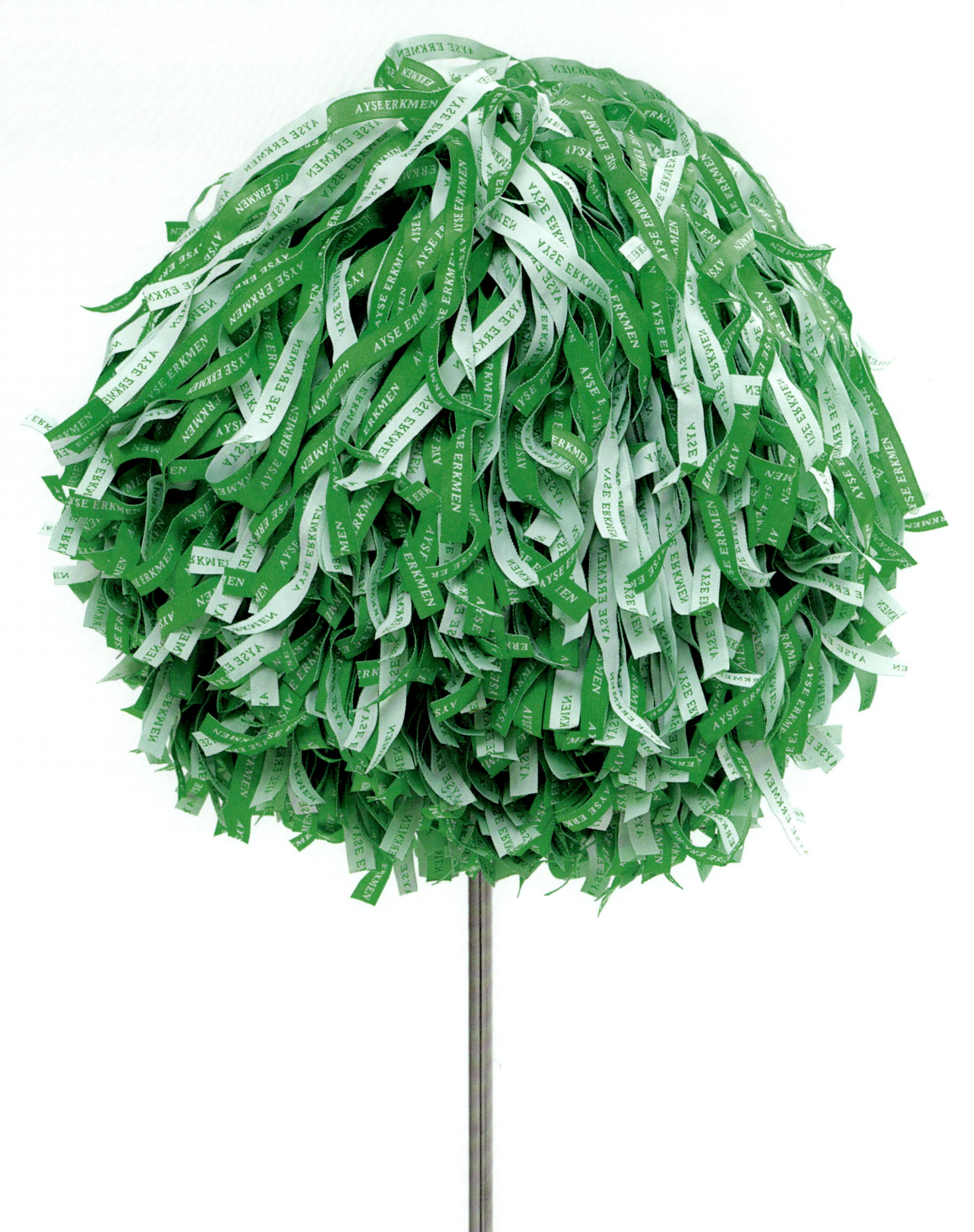

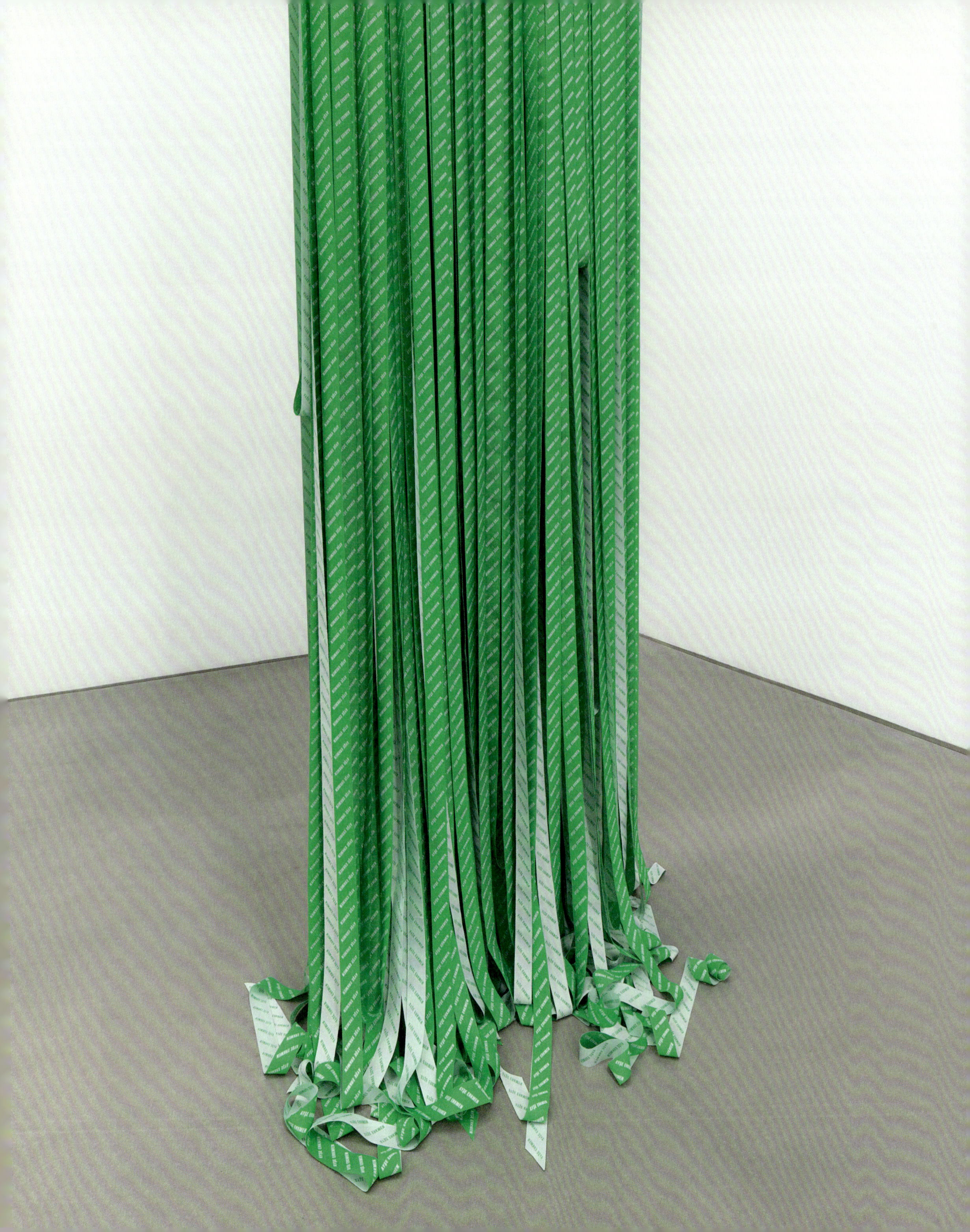

⟶ Ayşe Erkmen
Row-row, 2012

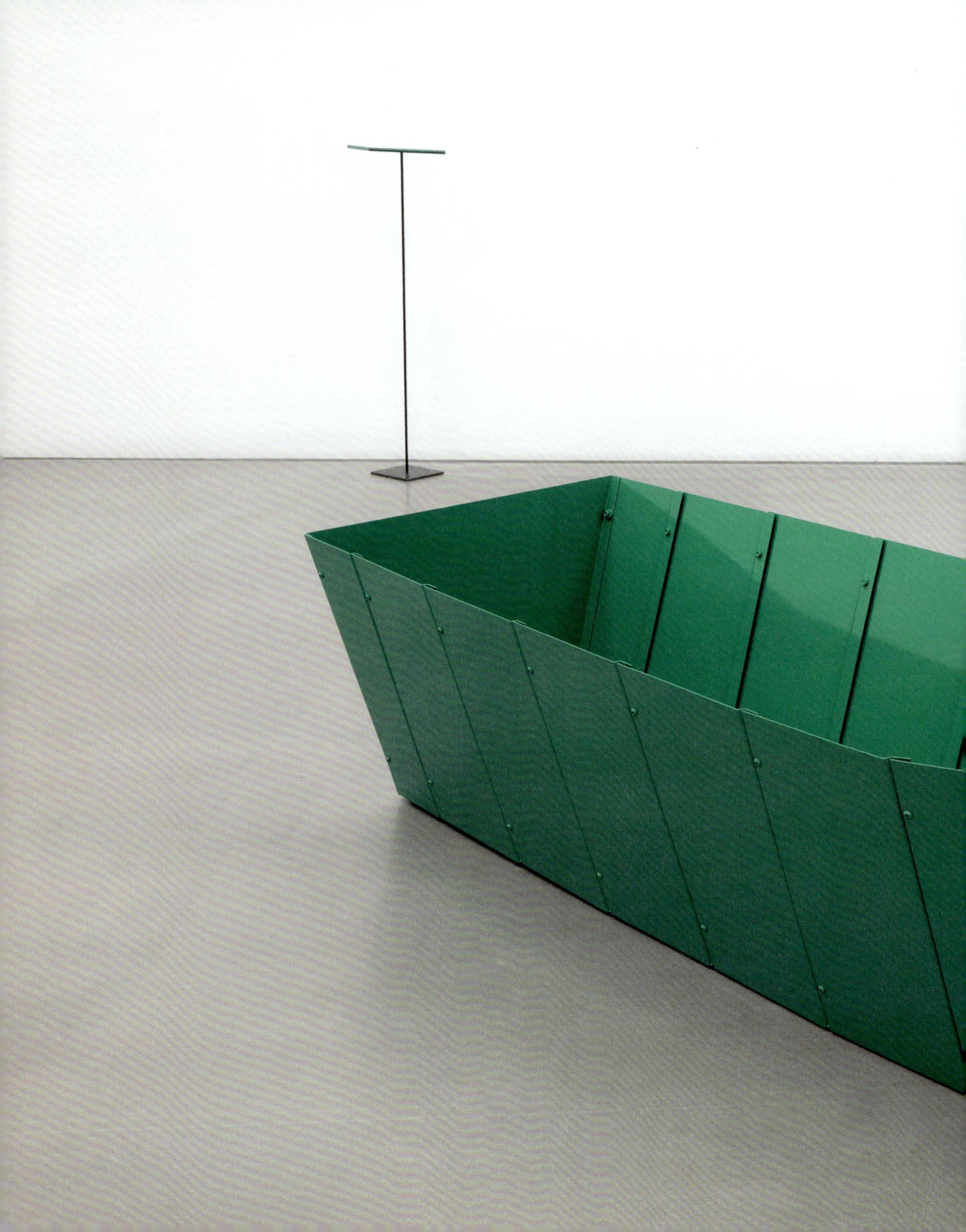

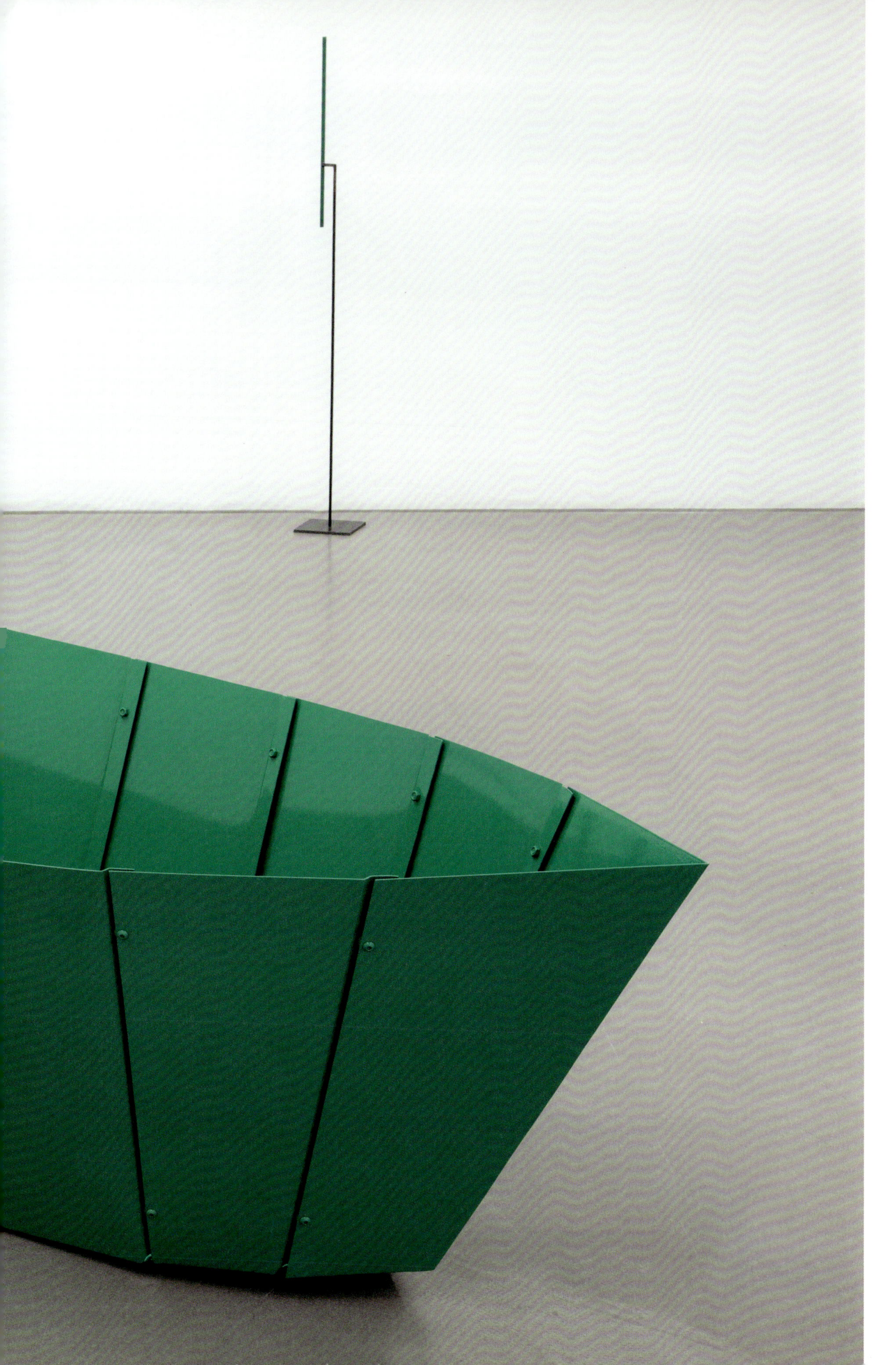

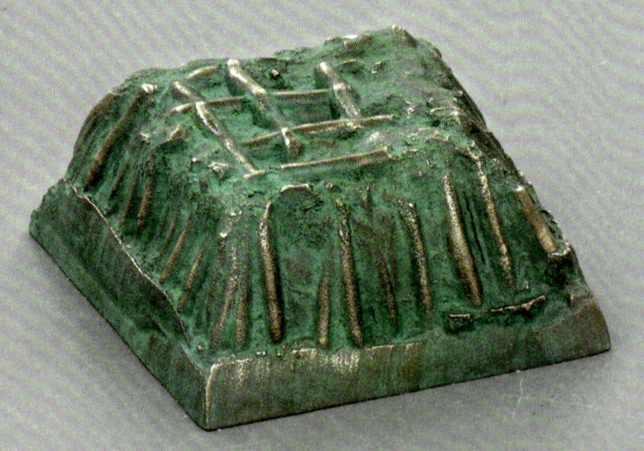
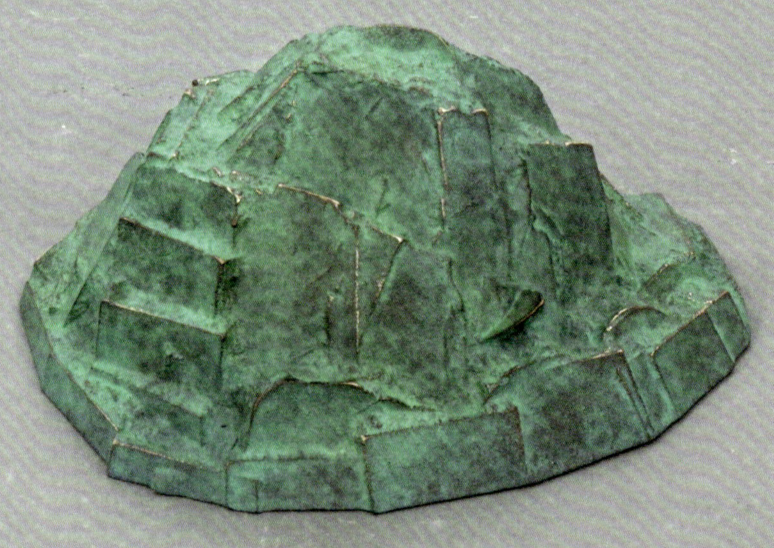

←—— Ayşe Erkmen
green / not the color it is, 2014
grass green / not the color it is, 2014
light green / not the color it is, 2014

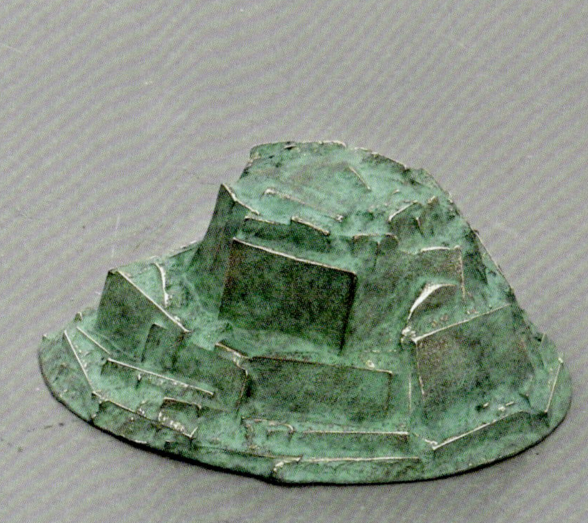

65

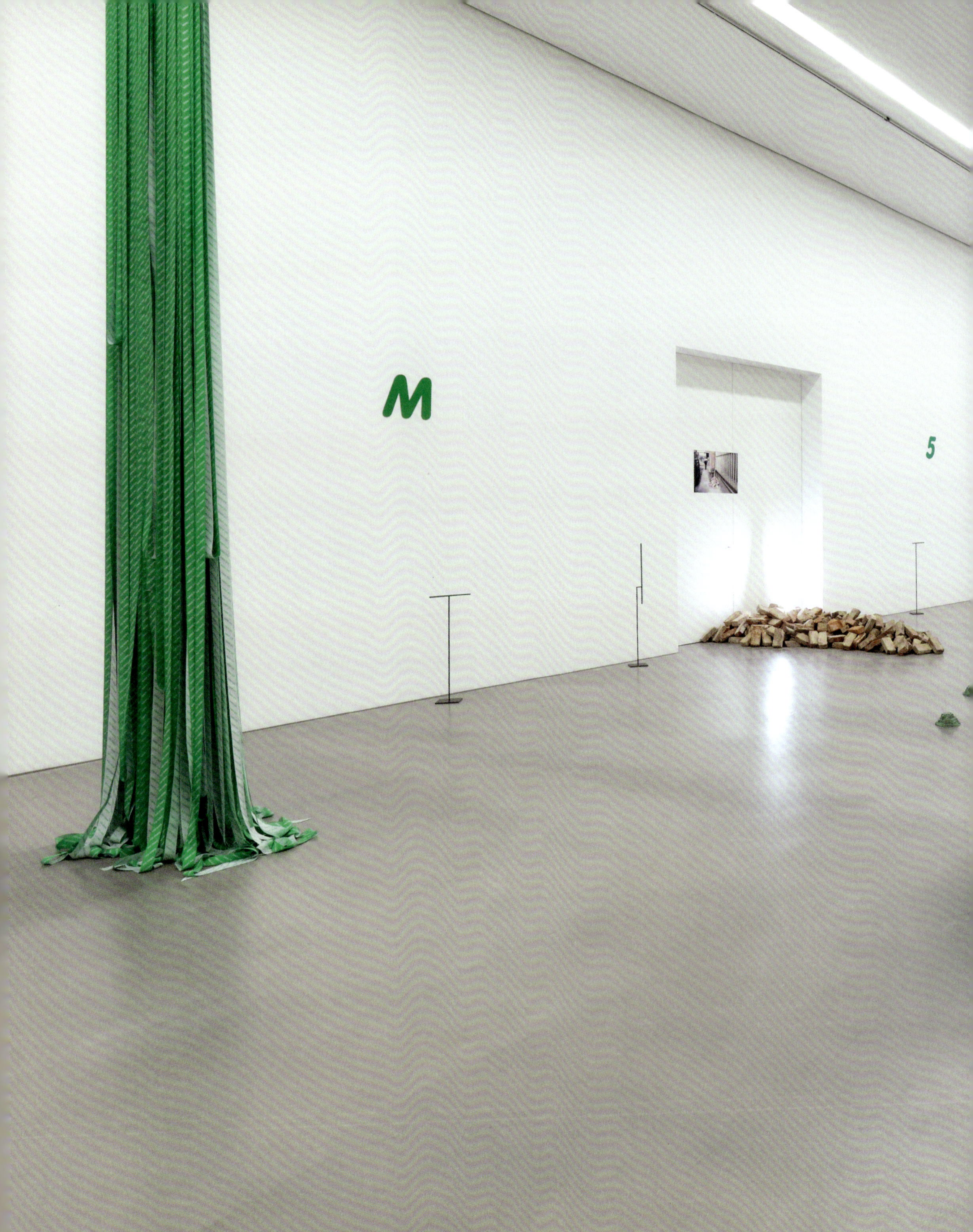

M
5

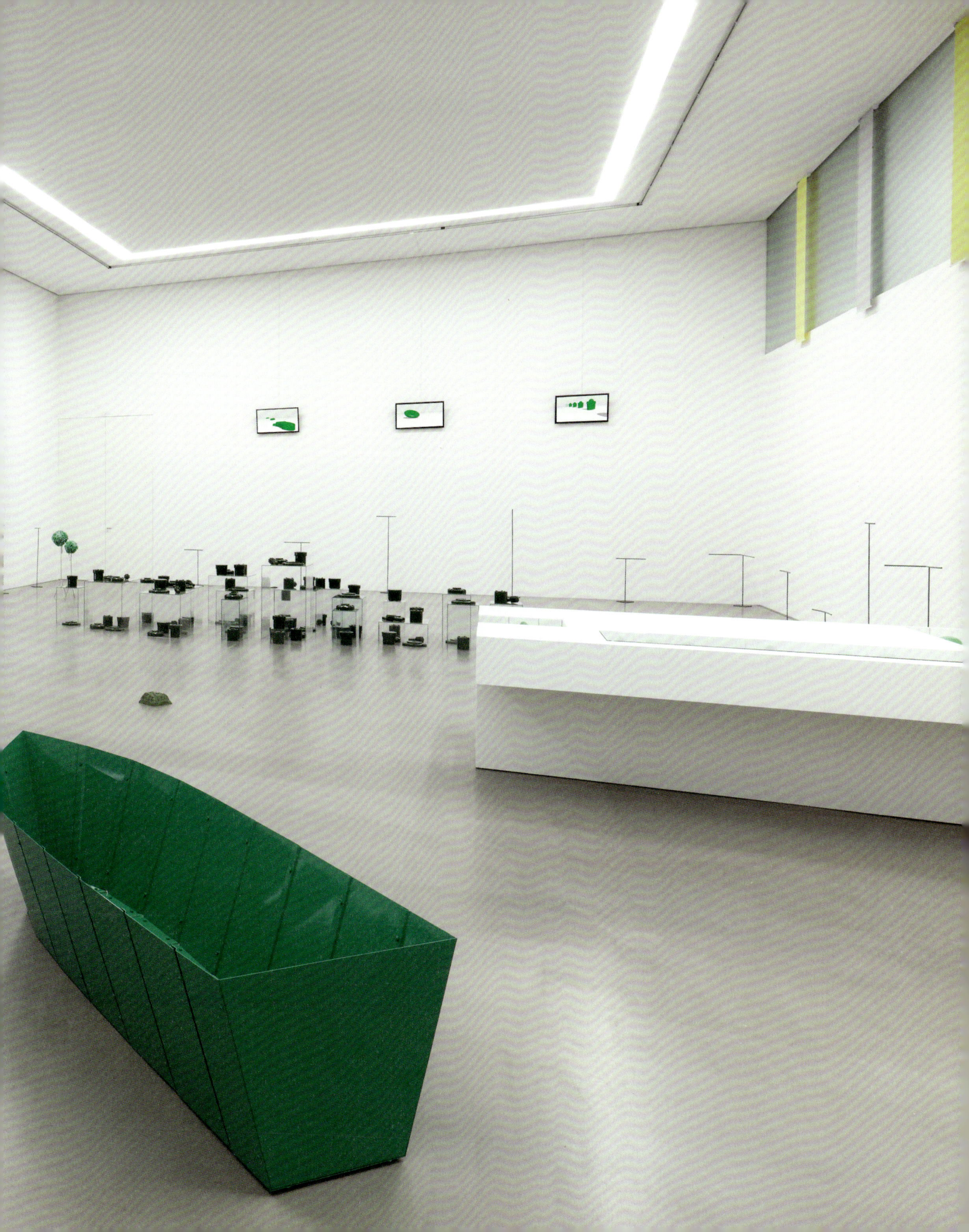

<—— Ausstellungsansicht mit
Objekten und Installationen von/
exhibition view with objects
and installations by Ayşe Erkmen

Verschiebung, Verdrängung, Entortung

Displacements im Werk von Ayşe Erkmen

Displacements in the Work of Ayşe Erkmen

Kassandra Nakas

1 Vgl. etwa Dogramaci 2013b.

Wohl kaum ein thematischer Überbegriff erscheint für das künstlerische Schaffen von Ayşe Erkmen so passend wie ›Displacements‹ – ›Entortungen‹. An der staatlichen Kunstakademie in Istanbul zur Bildhauerin ausgebildet, hat Erkmen seit den späten 1970er Jahren ein äußerst vielfältiges skulpturales und installatives Œuvre entwickelt, das sich stets auf den jeweiligen Ausstellungsort einlässt und meist temporären Charakter hat. Der Terminus ›displacement‹, der sich ins Deutsche auch mit ›Ablösung‹, ›Verschiebung‹, ›Verdrängung‹, ›Umsiedlung‹ oder ›Vertreibung‹ übersetzen lässt, bezeichnet dabei eine konkrete Handlung oder Erfahrung, wobei in der jüngeren kulturwissenschaftlichen Forschung zu Migration und Transkulturalität insbesondere deren affektive Dimension hervorgehoben wurde.[1]

Aspekte des Displacement: Ortsveränderungen, Bedeutungsverschiebungen, Umsiedlungen und Vertreibungen

Im Werk Ayşe Erkmens wird dieser Bedeutungshorizont zunächst durch ihre eigene Biografie aufgerufen, pendelt sie doch seit den 1990er Jahren regelmäßig zwischen ihren Wohnsitzen in Istanbul und Berlin, internationalen Ausstellungsorten sowie den Werkstätten und Ateliers, mit denen sie zusammenarbeitet. Die stetige Ortsveränderung beim Reisen geht einher mit einer spezifischen Sensibilität in der Wahrnehmung von Orten und Räumen, die die Künstlerin seit vielen Jahren unter Beweis stellt. Manchmal spielt sie dabei ironisch auf die Geschichte der Bildhauerei an, etwa wenn sie durch spielerische Eingriffe monumentale Gesten der Großplastik konterkariert. In diesem Sinne könnte man die drei bunten Kugeln von *Three Eyes* (2015) interpretieren, die die Künstlerin in den Nischen des Burgfelsens von Uçhisar platzierte, heute ein beliebtes Tourismusziel in Kappadokien. → **71** Der weiche Tuffstein des Berges ist durchzogen von Rückzugsräumen und Gängen, in deren Öffnungen die großen Kugeln in Rot, Gelb und Blau wie Verschlusssteine liegen und signalartig an kriegerische Auseinandersetzungen der Vergangenheit erinnern. Zugleich lassen die halbkreisförmige Anordnung und die kopfähnliche Kugelgestalt entfernt an die vier Präsidentenköpfe des unvollendeten Mount Rushmore National Memorial in South Dakota denken – ebenfalls ein beliebtes Tourismusziel –, dessen weithin sichtbare Monumentalität nicht über seine umstrittene Entstehungsgeschichte im Gebiet der Lakota-Indianer hinwegtäuschen kann.

Von solchen Gesten eines dauerhaften territorialen Herrschaftsanspruchs sind Erkmens Interventionen freilich weit entfernt, ebenso wie ihr die weit ausholende, dekonstruierende Geste des erweiterten Skulpturbegriffs fremd ist, mithilfe derer seit den 1960er Jahren das Feld der Bildhauerei zwischen Werk

70

Probably no generic term is better suited to describe the works of Ayşe Erkmen than *displacement*. Trained as a sculptor at the Istanbul State Academy of Fine Arts, since the 1970s Erkmen has created a highly diverse oeuvre of sculpture and installations that are always linked to the exhibition space and are usually temporary. The term *displacement,* which can be translated into German in a number of ways, including *Ablösung* (detachment), *Verschiebung* (shift), *Verdrängung* (expulsion), *Umsiedlung* (translocation) or *Vertreibung* (expulsion), refers to a concrete activity or experience, and recent cultural-history research on migration and transculturalism has particularly focused on its psychological dimension.[1]

Aspects of Displacement: Translocation, Shifts of Meaning, Relocation and Expulsion

This range of meanings in the works of Ayşe Erkmen is initially suggested by her own biography. Since the 1990s Erkmen has regularly commuted between her residences in Istanbul and Berlin, between the venues of international exhibitions and between workshops and studios with which she collaborates. Her constant translocation due to travel is linked to her sensitive perception of places and spaces, as the artist has demonstrated for many years. She sometimes makes an ironic reference to the history of sculpture, for example, when she thwarts the intention of grand gestures in monumental sculpture with her playful interventions. This is how the three colourful balls in *Three Eyes* (2015) could be interpreted, which the artist placed in the niches of Uçhisar Castle, a popular tourist destination today in Cappadocia. → **71** The soft volcanic rock of the mountain outcrop is interspersed with places of refuge and tunnels with openings that are obstructed by the large red, yellow and blue balls, which are like beacons reminding of past military conflicts. At the same time, the semi-circular arrangement and head-like shapes of the balls are reminiscent of the heads of the four presidents in the unfinished Mount Rushmore National Memorial in South Dakota – also a popular tourist attraction – which in spite of its highly visible monumentality cannot repudiate its controversial history in the territory of the Lakota Indians.

This sort of indelible gesture of territorial claim is admittedly quite foreign to Erkmen's interventions; the sweeping, deconstructivist gesture of the expanded concept of sculpture, which has re-charted the field of sculpture between work and progress, place and space, landscape and object since the 1960s, is just as far from her intentions. Although her works are positioned in exactly this realm of tension, their aim is rather to subtly reveal or draw attention

1 See, for example, Dogramaci 2013b.

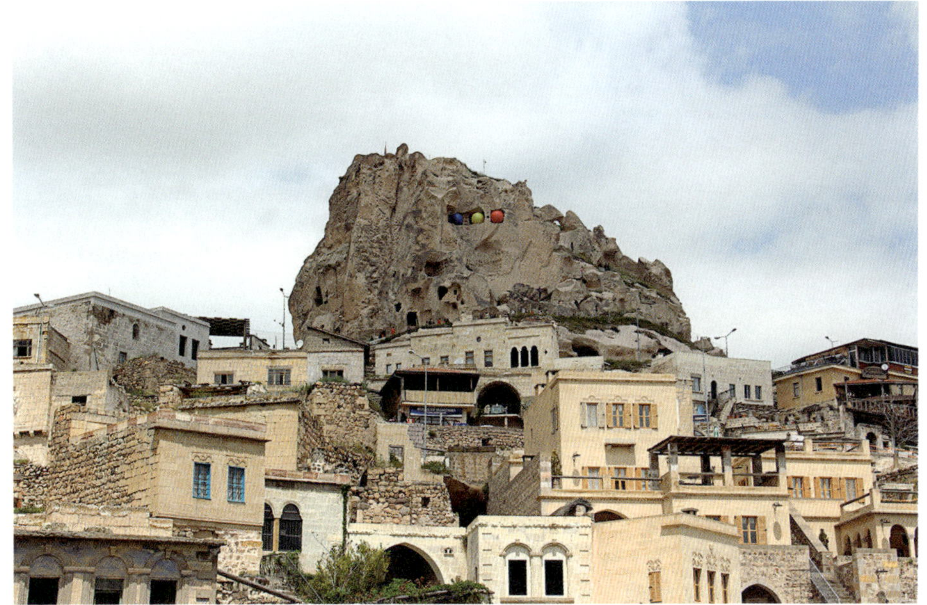

Ayşe Erkmen
Three Eyes, 2015
Burgfelsen von Uçhisar,
Kappadokien / Uçhisar
Castle, Cappadocia

71

to the specific properties of a place or space, its atmosphere or history, and its use or its psychological potential. Displacement can be observed when the artistic process negates the fiction of a tabula rasa in the mode and subject of destruction or deconstruction and instead focuses completely on creating an extended or heightened experience of that which is present in the situation. In the case of *bangbangbang,* Erkmen's contribution to the 13th Istanbul Biennial in 2013, one should say what is still present. Art critics took particular notice of the symbolic content of this work.[2] ⟶ **72** The artist parked a truck with a wrecking ball next to the Biennial's central exhibition hall, a former warehouse on the shore of the Bosporus that was used for the last time that year. However, the wrecking ball, as visitors quickly detected, did not have the power required to tear down a wall; the large green ball that was attached to the end of a long rope was made of plastic and thus reminiscent of a sport device or a buoy (it was in fact a buoy). Its thudding on the exterior wall of the hall, at a high altitude with little momentum, was more of a hesitant knock than a destructive process. The artistic gesture of protest that was characteristic of the deconstructivist acts of Gordon Matta-Clark, for example, was semantically displaced. Almost forty years earlier, and also on the occasion of a large exhibition – the Paris Biennial of

1975 – Matta-Clark had given his commentary on the gentrification processes in the centre of the French capital by cutting round, sculptural openings in two Baroque buildings that had been slated for demolition to make way for what was to become the Centre Pompidou (*Conical Intersect,* 1975). ⟶ **73** In comparison Ayşe Erkmen's *bangbangbang* is not a radical gesture but is reminiscent of the pendulum in a headstrong, manually driven chronometer clocking the time until demolition. In the context of the 13th Istanbul Biennial, which with the exhibitions held in Venice, São Paulo and Sydney is the most distinguished biennial and largely responsible for the growing international interest in contemporary Turkish art, Erkmen's intervention also raised awareness about the fact that urban processes of displacement are often the result of economic enhancement caused by the very movements of artistic exchange that eventually fall victim to these effects themselves. *bangbangbang* consciously left unanswered the question concerning adequate forms of artistic critique of such socio-economic developments and rather referred to another – historical – shift in dealing with contemporary art and the demands that are made of it: its relationship to institutions, city, and society today is acknowledged as too convoluted to actually be able to assert its critical potential (its 'criticality') in current discourse.

2   See, for example, Batty 2013.

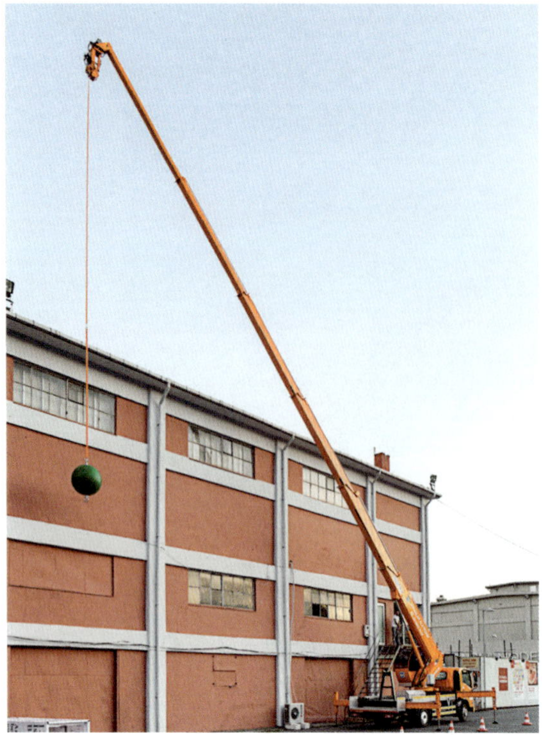

72

On another level, moments of displacement in Ayşe Erkmen's work are to be found in specific exhibition ideas; her iconic project *Sculptures on the Air* for *Skulptur. Projekte in Münster* in 1997 is probably the most famous example of this. Inspired by the opening scene of Federico Fellini's famous film *La Dolce Vita* (1960), the artist had several sandstone figures transported into the city by helicopter from the remote storage facilities of the Westfälisches Landesmuseum for the opening, flying over the roof of Münster's cathedral; the cathedral chapter had previously rejected several of the artist's proposals, in some instances with no reason provided.[3] ⟶ **74** As a kick-off to the exhibition, which takes place every ten years, this action of returning the historical sculptures temporarily to their original location referred to the act of making visible, which is likewise the core of both artistic and curatorial work. In this sense, Ayşe Erkmen's work repeatedly brings the everyday circulation of museum objects between storage, exhibition space of permanent collections and external loan places as forms of displacement into awareness. In 1999 in the context of the exhibition *Zeitenwenden* at the Kunstmuseum Bonn, in a restrained intervention (*More or Less [Az Çok]*, 1999), she had a hydraulic elevator element moving up and down in a continuous movement, thus making the architectural-technical infrastructure visible. ⟶ **76**

Displacements in Leipzig

For the exhibition in the Leipzig Museum of Fine Arts Ayşe Erkmen has conceived a series of spaces and spatial interventions. In the impressive central hall of the museum, which is over two stories tall, she created *Half of* (2017), which consists of hollow units of lightweight fabric of different sizes that all refer to the dimensions of the hall. ⟶ **94** The form of the five fabric units is based on the volume of the courtyard; the largest unit, which is 6.50 metres high, 4.50 metres wide, and 15 metres long, is roughly half the size of the courtyard. This large 'space within a space' is hung lengthwise at a height of over seven metres from the floor of the first level, and the other four units are grouped around it. Their dimensions are successively reduced by half; the largest thus measures 3.25 by 2.25 by 7.50 metres, and the smallest is 0.40 by 0.28 by 0.94 metres. Visitors can only fully appreciate the spatial and visual experience of *Half of* when they move vertically through the museum, by climbing the stairs to the terraces of the second floor. From the surrounding terraces they can look down on the five units that seem like a peaceful armada floating in the same direction.

Although these vessels thus also make remote reference to Erkmen's earlier work *Shipped Ships* (2001) ⟶ **28**, *Half of* is especially characterised by

3   A documentation of Erkmen's contribution to the *Skulptur. Projekte in Münster* in 1997 can be found online: <http://www.skulptur-projekte-archiv.de/en-us/1997/projects/77/> (accessed 19 September, 2017), and in Münster 1997, 142–49.

und Prozess, Ort und Raum, Landschaft und Objekt neu vermessen wurde. Zwar lassen sich ihre Arbeiten in genau diesem Spannungsfeld verorten, jedoch verfolgen sie das Ziel einer eher subtilen Sichtbar- oder Bewusstmachung der spezifischen Eigenschaften eines Ortes oder Raumes, seiner Atmosphäre oder Geschichte, seiner Nutzung oder seines affektiven Potenzials. Eine Verschiebung ist dann auch im Hinblick auf die künstlerische Handlung zu beobachten, die die Fiktion einer Tabula rasa im Modus und Motiv des Zerstörens oder Dekonstruierens negiert und sich stattdessen ganz auf die Erzeugung einer erweiterten oder gesteigerten Erfahrung des situativ Vorhandenen einlässt. Des *noch* Vorhandenen muss es im Fall von *bangbangbang* heißen, Erkmens Beitrag zur 13. Biennale von Istanbul 2013, dessen symbolischer Gehalt von der Kunstkritik seinerzeit aufmerksam registriert wurde.[2] ⟶ **72** An der in jenem Jahr letztmals genutzten zentralen Ausstellungshalle der Biennale, einem ehemaligen Lagerhaus am Ufer des Bosporus, stellte die Künstlerin einen Wagen mit einer Abrissbirne auf, welcher allerdings, wie den Besucherinnen und Besuchern schnell klar wurde, jede Durchschlagskraft fehlte; vielmehr bestand die große grüne, an einem langen Seil befestigte Kugel aus Kunststoff und erinnerte somit an eine Boje. Ihr Aufschlagen auf der Außenwand der Halle, in großer Höhe mit geringem Schwung vollzogen, war eher

ein zögerliches Pochen als ein destruktiver Vorgang. Semantisch verschoben wurde dabei die künstlerische Geste des Widerstands, die noch die dekonstruktivistischen Akte eines Gordon Matta-Clark gekennzeichnet hatte. Knapp vierzig Jahre zuvor und ebenfalls anlässlich einer Großausstellung – der Biennale von Paris 1975 – hatte Matta-Clark die Gentrifizierungsprozesse im Zentrum der französischen Hauptstadt durch kreisrunde skulpturale Einschnitte in zwei zum Abriss freigegebene barocke Stadtpalais kommentiert, die dem Areal des späteren Centre Pompidou weichen mussten (*Conical Intersect,* 1975). ⟶ **73** Ayşe Erkmens *bangbangbang* ist demgegenüber keine radikale Geste, sondern erinnert an das Pendel eines eigenwilligen, handgesteuerten Chronometers, das die Zeit bis zum Abriss misst. Im Rahmen der 13. Ausgabe der Istanbul Biennale, die neben den Großausstellungen von Venedig, São Paulo und Sydney inzwischen zu den profiliertesten Zweijahresschauen zählt und wesentlichen Anteil an der wachsenden internationalen Bedeutung der zeitgenössischen türkischen Kunst hatte, rückte Erkmens Intervention auch ins Bewusstsein, dass städtische Verdrängungsprozesse nicht selten Folge einer wirtschaftlichen Aufwertung durch eben jene künstlerischen Austauschbewegungen sind, die diesen Effekten schließlich selbst zum Opfer fallen. Die Frage nach einer adäquaten Form der künstlerischen

73

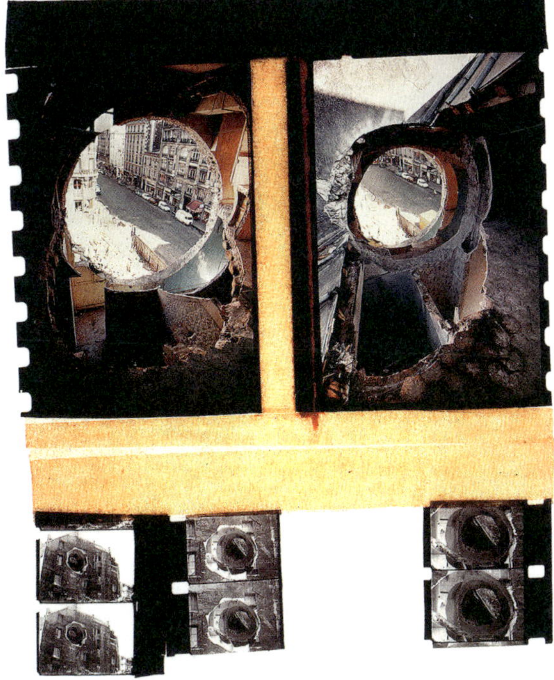

Gordon Matta-Clark
Conical Intersect, 1975

3   Eine Dokumentation zu Erkmens Beitrag zu den *Skulptur. Projekten in Münster* 1997 findet sich online unter: <http://skulptur-projekte-archiv.de/de-de/1997/projects/77/>, letzter Zugriff: 19.9.2017 und in Münster 1997, 142–149.

Kritik an solchen sozioökonomischen Entwicklungen ließ *bangbangbang* bewusst offen und verwies eher auf eine abermalige – historische – Verschiebung im Umgang mit zeitgenössischer Kunst und im Anspruch, der an diese gestellt wird. Deren Verhältnis zu Institutionen, Stadt und Gesellschaft wird heute als zu verwickelt anerkannt, als dass sie im aktuellen Diskurs widerspruchslos ein kritisches Potenzial (ihre *criticality*) behaupten könnte.

Auf einer weiteren Ebene lassen sich Anzeichen des Displacement im Werk Ayşe Erkmens in konkreten Ausstellungsideen verfolgen, wofür ihr ikonisch gewordenes Projekt *Sculptures on the Air* für die *Skulptur. Projekte in Münster* 1997 das vielleicht bekannteste Beispiel darstellt. Inspiriert von der Eingangsszene in Federico Fellinis berühmtem Film *La dolce vita* (1960), ließ die Künstlerin zur Eröffnung der großen Skulpturenschau per Helikopter mehrere Sandsteinfiguren aus dem entlegenen Depot des Westfälischen Landesmuseums in die Stadt und über das Dach des Münsteraner Doms transportieren, dessen Domkapitel zuvor mehrere Werkvorschläge der Künstlerin teils ohne Begründung abgelehnt hatte.[3] ⟶ **74** Als Auftakt der alle zehn Jahre stattfindenden Großschau führte die Aktion die historischen Plastiken vorübergehend an ihren ursprünglichen Bestimmungsort zurück und verwies so auf den Akt des Sichtbarmachens, der künstlerischem wie kuratorischem Handeln gleichermaßen zugrunde liegt. In diesem Sinne rückt Ayşe Erkmen auch immer wieder die alltägliche Zirkulation der musealen Exponate zwischen Depot, Schausälen und externen Leihorten als Formen des Displacement ins Bewusstsein. So ließ sie 1999 im Kunstmuseum Bonn im Rahmen der Ausstellung *Zeitenwenden* ein hydraulisch betriebenes Aufzugselement durchgehend aus dem Boden auf- und wieder absteigen und machte durch diesen zurückhaltenden Eingriff die architektonisch-technische Infrastruktur sichtbar (*More or Less (Az Çok)*, 1999). ⟶ **76**

Displacements in Leipzig

Für die Ausstellung im Museum der bildenden Künste Leipzig hat Ayşe Erkmen eine Reihe von Räumen und räumlichen Interventionen konzipiert. Im imposanten, sich über zwei hohe Geschosse erstreckenden zentralen Lichthof des Museumsbaus hat sie *Half of* (2017) realisiert, größenmäßig gestaffelte Hohlkörper aus leichtem weißem Textil, die auf die Dimensionen der Halle Bezug nehmen. ⟶ **94** Die Form der fünf textilen Hohlräume ist abgeleitet vom Volumen des Lichthofs, dessen Maße der größte Stoffkörper etwa zur Hälfte übernimmt. Er misst somit beeindruckende 6,50 Meter in der Höhe, 4,50 Meter in der Breite und 15 Meter in der Länge. In über sieben Metern lichter Höhe vom Bodenniveau des ersten Stocks aus und in Längsrichtung

74

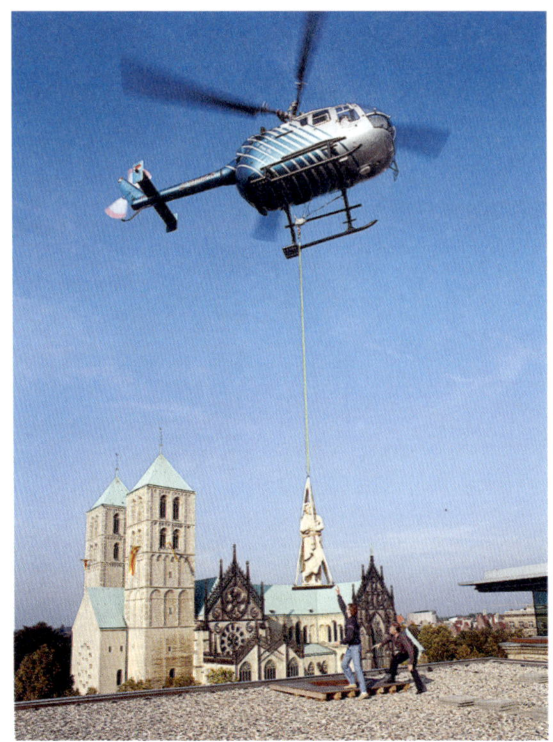

Ayşe Erkmen
Sculptures on the Air, 1997
Intervention / intervention
Skulptur. Projekte in Münster 1997

4 Zu den Ausstellungen *Raum.Prolog,* Berlin, Akademie der Künste 2005 und *Ayşe Erkmen – Half of,* Tokio, Galerie Deux 1999; vgl. den »Katalog ausgewählter Werke«, in Berlin 2008a, 23–142, hier 87–88, und die Chronologie ebd., 201 ff.

5 Vgl. Deleuze 1988/2000.

6 Die Begriffe finden sich auch im Untertitel von Pichler/Ubl 2009.

montiert, gruppieren sich um diesen großen Raum im Raum auf unterschiedlichen Höhenniveaus vier weitere Raumkörper, deren Kantenmaße jeweils sukzessive halbiert wurden; der größte ist somit 3,25 Meter hoch, 2,25 Meter breit und 7,50 Meter lang, der kleinste misst 0,40×0,28×0,94 Meter. Erst in der vertikalen Bewegung durch das Museum, im Emporsteigen der Treppen hinauf auf die Terrassen der zweiten Etage, lässt sich *Half of* von den Besucherinnen und Besuchern räumlich-visuell erfassen. Von den umliegenden Terrassen blicken sie auf die fünf Raumkörper, die wie eine friedliche Flotte in die gleiche Richtung zu schweben scheinen.

Entfernt nehmen diese ›Luftschiffe‹ somit auf Erkmens frühere Arbeit *Shipped Ships* (2001) —→ 28 Bezug, vor allem aber zeichnet *Half of* eine klare skulptural-architektonische Gestaltung aus.Vergleichbare frühere Umsetzungen des Konzepts in Berlin und Tokio resultierten in flacheren und offeneren abgehängten Stoffquadern, die wie überdimensionale Laternen den darunterliegenden Raum neu definierten.[4] Demgegenüber kennzeichnen in Leipzig die proportional veränderten Raummaße mit entsprechenden Wandöffnungen die schwebenden Quader als mimetische Objekte, die sich als gleichsam gefaltete Räume zu erkennen geben. Das Prinzip der Faltung, das sich in der ersten Realisierung der Arbeit in Tokio aus der originär japanischen Technik des Origami ergeben hatte, erfährt hier eine architektonische Wendung – wenngleich nicht im Sinne von Gilles Deleuze, bei dem die Figur der barocken Falte zu offenen und flexiblen Raumkontinuen führte, die sich in den fließenden Raumkonzeptionen der Architektur der 1990er Jahre niederschlugen.[5] Vielmehr wecken die über fragilen Fiberglaskonstruktionen gefalteten Stoffkuben Assoziationen zwischen dem White Cube des Ausstellungskontextes und anonymen Containern; in einer allgemeiner phänomenologischen Perspektive können sie als Raum-Materialisierungen begriffen werden, die den sonst leeren Luftraum des Lichthofs mit physisch greifbaren und zugleich körperlich unerreichbaren Einheiten markieren. Als topologische Setzung im euklidischen Raum sorgt *Half of* somit für eine Irritation in der Wahrnehmung der Betrachterinnen und Betrachter, spricht die Arbeit diese doch einerseits – auf Augenhöhe auf den Terrassen der zweiten Etage – in ihrer physischen Präsenz an und unterbricht doch andererseits das Kontinuum der räumlichen Bewegung durch den leeren Luftraum der Halle. Die textilen Raumkörper werden zu bildlichen Orten in einer diskontinuierlichen, instabilen Raumerfahrung.

Falten, Knoten, Netze und Stülpungen[6] sind Phänomene eines topologischen Denkens, eines Denkens in räumlichen Strukturen, das im Schaffen von

its clear sculptural and architectonic aspects. Earlier versions of this concept produced in Berlin and Tokyo consisted of fabric blocks that hung down in a flatter and more open way, redefining the space underneath like oversized lanterns.[4] In comparison to these, the floating cubes in Leipzig are mimetic objects that indicate the proportionally changed dimensions of the room along with the corresponding wall openings and are also folded spaces, so to speak. The principle of folding, which in the first version of the work in Tokyo was derived from the Japanese technique of origami, has an architectonic twist here – even if not exactly in the sense of Gilles Deleuze, who argued that the Baroque fold led to open and flexible spatial continua that were reflected in the flowing spatial concepts of the architecture of the 1990s.[5] The folded fabric cubes over their fragile fiberglass constructions evoke associations that range from the White Cube of the exhibition context to anonymous containers; from a general phenomenological perspective they are spatial materialisations that mark the airspace of the courtyard, which is otherwise empty, filling it with elements that are tangible and at the same time physically out of touch. As a topological element in Euclidian space, *Half of* causes a fair amount of confusion to viewers, since on the one hand the work addresses them – on eye level with the terraces of the second floor – in terms of its physical presence, while on the other hand the continuity of spatial movement is interrupted by the empty airspace of the hall. The textile units become a metaphorical space in a discontinuous, instable spatial experience.

Folds, knots, nets, and reversals[6] are phenomena of a topological way of thinking, a thinking in spatial structures that links, in the work of Ayşe Erkmen, the description of places with a reflection upon the institutional, social and psychological implications and potential of a given situation. The artist herself usually remains in the background, and only the formal minimalism of the intervention allows any conclusions to be drawn about her personal style. In a work such as *Netz* (Net, 2006–08), however, the letters of her name become a visible element and also a medium of contemplation on artistic processes of creation. —→ 60+77 The object consists of countless, interconnected ribbons with the artist's name on them. The unruly meshwork of these green-white ribbons[7] is mounted on the ceiling or wall and extends to the floor in a voluptuous mop. The ribbons are reminiscent of the fabric labels used in clothing to assign them a particular brand. The industrial production involved in their weaving process contrasts with the tedious work of manually knotting ribbons.

4 On the exhibitions *Raum.Prolog,* Berlin, Akademie der Künste 2005 and *Ayşe Erkmen – Half of,* Tokyo, Galerie Deux 1999, see the 'Katalog ausgewählter Werke,' in Berlin 2008a, 23–142, here: 87–88, and the chronology, ibid., 201ff.

5 Cf. Deleuze 1988/2000.

6 These terms also form the subtitle of Pichler/Ubl 2009.

7 A reduced version from 2006, *Turuncu,* consisted of orange-white ribbons; see Gent 2015, 30, with illustration.

7 Eine reduzierte Version von 2006, *Turuncu,* bestand aus orangefarben-weißen Bändern, vgl. Gent 2015, 30, Abb.

8 Boltanski / Chiapello 1999 / 2003.

9 Im Werkkatalog (Berlin 2008a) werden diese Verbindungen aufgezeigt.

Ayşe Erkmen die Beschreibung von Orten mit der Reflexion der institutionellen, sozialen und affektiven Implikationen und Potenziale der gegebenen Situation verbindet. Zumeist bleibt die Künstlerin selbst dabei im Hintergrund, nur der formale Minimalismus des Eingriffs lässt Rückschlüsse auf ihre ›Handschrift‹ zu. In einem Werk wie *Netz* (2006 / 2008) wird allerdings der Schriftzug ihres Namens zum sichtbaren Motiv und zum Medium des Nachdenkens über künstlerische Schaffensprozesse an sich. ⟶ **60 + 77** In dem Objekt sind unzählige, mit dem Namen der Künstlerin versehene Bänder aneinandergeknüpft. Als widerspenstiges Maschenwerk werden die grün-weißen Bänder an der Decke oder der Wand montiert und reichen in üppigem Bausch bis auf den Boden.[7] Die Bänder erinnern an Textiletiketten, wie sie in Kleidungsstücken verwendet werden, um diese einer konkreten Marke zuzuordnen. Der maschinelle Webprozess ihrer Herstellung kontrastiert dabei mit der mühseligen Arbeit des manuellen Verknotens zu langen Bahnen.

Wo man *Netz* allzu leichtfertig im Reich der standardisierten Reproduzierbarkeit und der Warenästhetik verorten mag, drängen sich so Assoziationen an manuelle und kollektive Produktionsweisen in den Vordergrund; und wo das Primat des Konzepts die Werkidee zu dominieren scheint, eröffnet das eigensinnige Material Verbindungslinien zur postminimalistischen Plastik eines Robert Morris oder einer Eva Hesse. In *Netz* sind somit die Sphären der traditionellen Handarbeit mit jenen der technologisch-kommunikativen Vernetzung und produktiven Auslagerung im Sinne eines »neuen Geists des Kapitalismus«[8] buchstäblich verknüpft. Im Motiv des Knotens ist der Arbeit überdies eine strukturelle Zeitlichkeit eingeschrieben, die über den Ausstellungszeitraum hinausreicht: Die netzartige Struktur bleibt für weitere Anknüpfungen offen, als Form fügt sie sich nicht zu einem abschließbaren Ganzen. In vertikaler Ausrichtung an der Wand oder an der Decke installiert, konfrontiert *Netz* die Betrachterinnen und Betrachter mit einer fragilen, vorläufigen Struktur, die durch die eingeschriebene Signatur die künstlerische Arbeit auktorial definiert und zugleich zum fortlaufenden, unabgeschlossenen und kollaborativen Prozess erklärt.

Entsprechend fand und findet *Netz* wie auch andere Arbeiten der Künstlerin in modifizierten Umsetzungen und unterschiedlichen Konstellationen Eingang in ihre Ausstellungen.[9] In Leipzig ist die Arbeit in einem Raum zusammen mit einer Reihe weiterer Werke installiert, die auf vergleichbare Weise Fragen der Autorschaft, der Wiedererkennbarkeit und des Brandings thematisieren, so die unterschiedlich großen Pompons aus grünen Kleideretiketten an Chromständern (*Großes grünes Pompon* und *Kleines grünes*

76

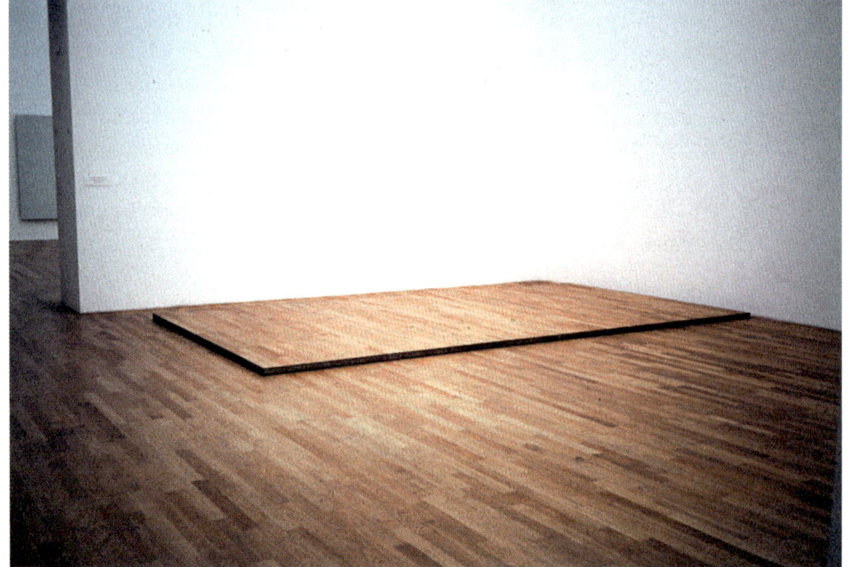

Ayşe Erkmen
More or Less (Az Çok), 1999
Installationsansicht / installation
view, Kunstmuseum Bonn

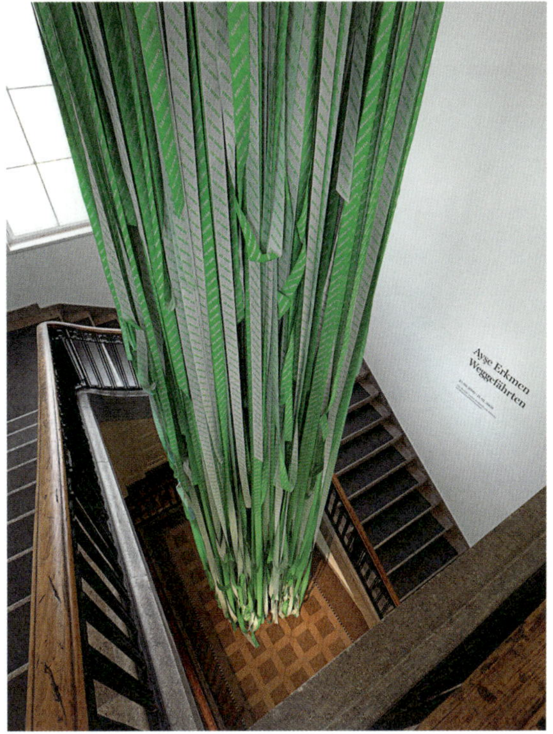

Ayşe Erkmen
Netz, 2006 / 2008
Ausstellungsansicht /
exhibition view,
Hamburger Bahnhof,
Berlin

77

Although one is tempted to put *Netz* into the category of standardised reproducibility and merchandise aesthetics, associations of manual and collective ways of production come to the forefront; and while the primacy of the concept seems to dominate the idea of the work, the stubborn material has connections to the Post-Minimalist sculpture of Robert Morris or Eva Hesse. In *Netz* the spheres of traditional handicrafts are literally linked with technological communication networks and product outsourcing following the 'new spirit of capitalism'.[8] The knot motif also gives the work a structural temporality that reaches beyond the duration of the exhibition: the net-like structure is open to additional applications, since the form resists becoming a completed whole. Installed vertically on a wall or from a ceiling, *Netz* confronts the viewer as a fragile, temporary structure. Its embroidered signature defines it as an artistic work and simultaneously declares it as a continuing, unfinished, and collaborative process.

Accordingly, *Netz* – as is the case with other works by the artist – was and is often included in her exhibitions in modified form and different constellations.[9] In Leipzig the work is installed in a room with a series of other works that question authorship, recognisability and branding in a similar way, such as the differently sized pompons made of green clothing labels on chrome stands (*Large green pompon* and *Small green pompon,* both 2012) ⟶ **56** or the die-cut numbers and letters made of green plexiglass (*Die Farben der Buchstaben (M)* [Colours of Letters (M)] and *Die Farben der Buchstaben (5)* [Colours of Letters (5)], both 2006). ⟶ **52** Green is the dominant colour in this room: due to the turquoise green cotton blinds (*Jalousie,* 2007) ⟶ **54** the room is bathed in a 'tinted' atmosphere, and the sculptural works – *Row-row* (2012) ⟶ **62**, a large boat-like form made of thin, green metal that seems to have been folded, and three small-sized bronze objects on the floor – are also coloured in varying shades of green.

These sculptures (*green / not the color it is; grass green / not the color it is; light green / not the color it is,* all from 2014) are stimulating due to their form and colours, which oscillate between naturalness and artificiality. ⟶ **64** Although the hill-like physiognomies seem strangely familiar on first glance, seen up close their brusque tectonics are surprising. Their forms are based on holes in the sand that now, in their inverted state, become flamboyant 'stumbling blocks'. The green colour that they share varies between light and more intense nuances, and it becomes apparent that these are not just a layer of paint that has been applied to the bronze. Instead the various hues result from a complicated patination process and are thus

8   Boltanski / Chiapello 1999 / 2003.

9   The catalogue of works (Berlin 2008a) shows these connections.

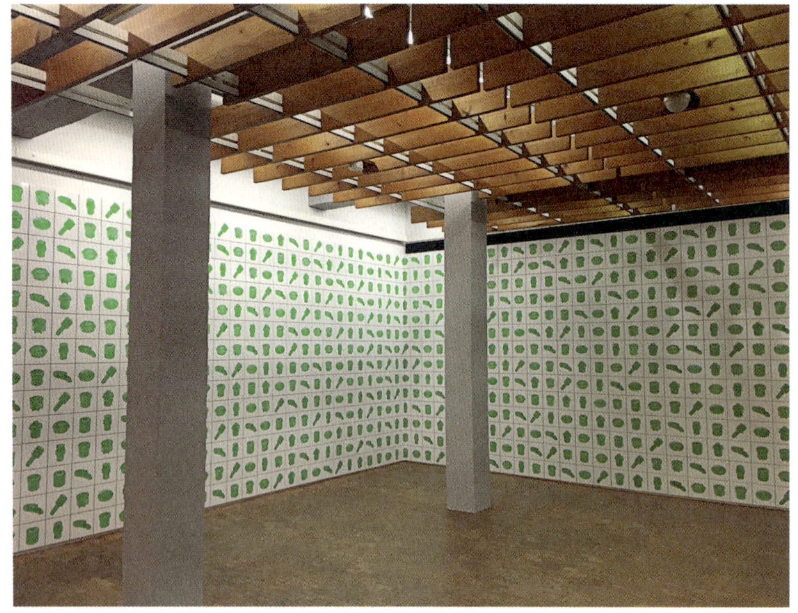

Ayşe Erkmen
Alkoven, 1997 / 2016
Installationsansicht /
installation view,
Akademie der Künste,
Berlin

78

Ayşe Erkmen
PFM-1 and others (Detail / detail),
1997 / 2013

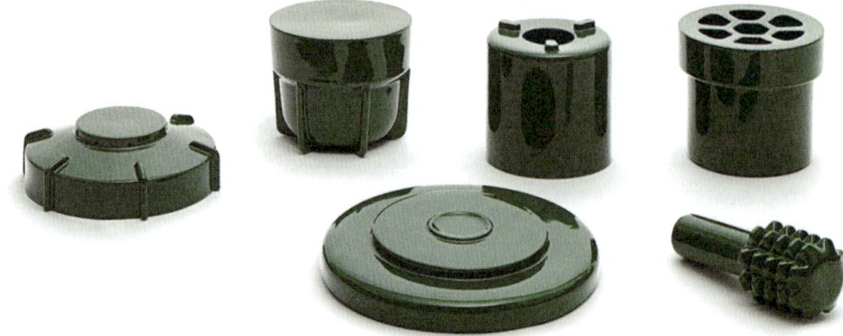

Pompon, beide 2012) ⟶ **56**, oder die ausgestanzten typografischen Ziffern und Lettern aus grünem Plexiglas (*Die Farben der Buchstaben (M)* und *Die Farben der Buchstaben (5)*, beide 2006). ⟶ **52** Grün ist in diesem Raum der dominierende Farbton: Durch türkisgrüne Baumwolljalousien (*Jalousie*, 2007) ⟶ **54** ist er in eine entsprechend ›gefärbte‹ Atmosphäre getaucht, und auch die skulpturalen Arbeiten – *Row-row* (2012) ⟶ **62**, eine wie gefaltet erscheinende große Bootsform aus dünnem grünem Metall sowie drei kleinformatige Bronzeobjekte auf dem Boden – weisen variierende Grüntöne auf.

Letztgenannte Plastiken (*green / not the color it is; grass green / not the color it is; light green / not the color it is,* jeweils 2014) irritieren durch ihre zwischen Natürlichkeit und Künstlichkeit schwankende Form- und Farbgebung: Seltsam vertraut scheint auf den ersten Blick die hügelartige Physiognomie, doch aus der Nähe überrascht die schroffe Tektonik. ⟶ **64** Ihre Form geht auf ausgehobene Sandlöcher zurück, die nunmehr als Inversionen zu auffälligen ›Stolpersteinen‹ werden. Der verbindende Farbton Grün variiert zwischen hellen und kräftigeren Nuancen, wobei deutlich wird, dass dieser nicht etwa als Farbschicht auf die Bronze aufgetragen wurde. Vielmehr resultieren die unterschiedlichen Färbungen aus einem aufwändigen Patinierungsprozess und sind auf diese Weise gleichsam wesenhaft mit der Form verbunden. (Der Farbgebungsprozess in einer Bronzegießerei ist Gegenstand der vierteiligen Videoinstallation *Bronze Acid Blue / Green / Ochre / Yellow*, 2014, die in einem separaten Raum gezeigt wird.)

Grün, die in der christlichen wie in der islamischen Religion gleichermaßen symbolträchtige Farbe, kennzeichnet auch die im gleichen Raum ausgestellten Werke *Alkoven* (1997/2017) und *PFM-1 and others* (1997/2013). *Alkoven* zeigt als Fries auf Keramikfliesen jene Motive, die auf der gegenüberliegenden Wand als handliche Objekte unter dem Titel *PFM-1 and others* auf Regalen positioniert sind: Nachbildungen realer Landminen, die trotz internationaler Ächtung weiterhin produziert und eingesetzt werden. ⟶ **46+50+78** Ayşe Erkmen hat diese Tod und Verstümmelung bringenden Waffen in dunkelgrün glasierte, minimalistisch anmutende Keramikobjekte transformiert. Die ästhetisierende Camouflage der Objekte, deren schiere Formenvielfalt die grausame Prosperität dieses Wirtschaftszweigs in Erinnerung ruft – über 600 verschiedene Minentypen sollen weltweit existieren –, führt auch vor Augen, dass die vermeintlich harmlose Unscheinbarkeit der Minen ihr Gefahrenpotenzial insbesondere für Kinder zusätzlich erhöht – ein Umstand, auf den auch Erkmens Videoarbeit *PFM-1 and others* (1997) anspielt, in der computeranimierte Minen-Objekte in unterschied-

79

integrally linked with the form. (The colouring process in a bronze foundry is the subject of the four-part video installation *Bronze Acid Blue / Green / Ochre / Yellow*, 2014, which is shown in a separate room.)

Green, the colour that has symbolic meaning in both Christianity and Islam, is also characteristic of the other works that are on display in the same room: *Alkoven* (Alcove, 1997/2017) and *PFM-1 and others* (1997/2013). ⟶ **46+50+78** *Alkoven* is a frieze of ceramic tiles using the same motifs as the objects that could be held in one's hands and that are displayed on the opposite wall: replicas of actual landmines, which in spite of international condemnation continue to be produced and used. Ayşe Erkmen has transformed these lethal and crippling weapons into minimalistic ceramic objects that are glazed dark green. The aesthetically appealing camouflage of these objects, which are available in such a variety of different forms – over six hundred different types of mines are thought to exist all over the world, calling to mind how gruesomely prosperous this economic branch is – shows that the apparently harmless inconspicuousness of these weapons has increased their potential for danger among children. Erkmen's video *PFM-1 and others* (1997) alludes to this fact, with computer-animated mine objects jumping around the screen in different sequences of motion. ⟶ **48**

The United Nations reported over fifteen thousand landmine victims and over five hundred thousand wounded in 2013; every year on 4 April the International Mine Awareness Day calls attention to the hidden dangers in the ground that in areas of war and civil war have developed their own perfidious logic of displacement and expulsion, making large areas of territory in the affected regions uninhabitable.

PFM-1 and others stands out among the dozen or so short videos that Ayşe Erkmen has produced over the past twenty years: due to its high profile and the fact that it has been shown often in exhibitions, but also due to its radical approach, which links the artistic imitation of everyday objects (even if they are unusual ones) with an anthropomorphic interpretation and staging (here in a film).[10] Erkmen has been concerned with the problem of imitation, simulation and mimesis since her earliest works, such as *Imitation / Taklit* (1987/2017), which she presented for the first time in 1987. ⟶ **80** Chancing upon a pile of bricks with a neon tube sticking out of it on the streets of Istanbul, she transferred it to the exhibition space of a Kunstverein, where the rubble was presented together with a photograph of the found situation and a journal-like description of the way she found it during a walk in the city.[11] Although the genesis of *Imitation / Taklit* is reminiscent of the phenomenologically inspired

10 On the aspect of anthropomorphisation see Nakas 2008, 24.

11 See Schaschke 2008, 170.

10 Zum Aspekt der Anthropomorphisierung vgl. Nakas 2008, 24.

11 Vgl. Schaschke 2008, 170.

lichen Bewegungsabläufen über den Bildschirm springen. ⟶ 48 Mehr als 15 000 Todesopfer von Landminen zählten die Vereinten Nationen im Jahr 2013 und über 500 000 Verletzte; alljährlich erinnert am 4. April ein Internationaler Tag der Minenaufklärung an die zumeist im Erdboden verborgene Gefahr, die in Kriegs- und Bürgerkriegsgebieten eine eigene perfide Logik der Verdrängung und Vertreibung entwickelt, macht sie doch weite Landstriche in den betroffenen Regionen unbewohnbar.

Aus dem etwa einen Dutzend kurzer Videofilme, die Ayşe Erkmen in den vergangenen 20 Jahren produziert hat, sticht die Videoarbeit *PFM-1 and others* heraus: einerseits durch ihre Bekanntheit und umfangreiche Ausstellungsgeschichte, andererseits durch die Radikalität ihres Ansatzes, der die künstlerische Nachahmung von (wenn auch ungewöhnlichen) Alltagsobjekten mit deren anthropomorphisierender Interpretation und (hier filmischen) Inszenierung verbindet.[10] Dabei beschäftigt Erkmen das Problem der Nachahmung, Imitation oder Mimesis seit ihren frühesten Werken, wie die Arbeit *Imitation / Taklit* (1987/2017) zeigt, die sie 1987 erstmals realisierte. ⟶ 80 Einen Zufallsfund in den Straßen von Istanbul, bestehend aus einem Haufen Ziegelsteinen und einer daraus emporragenden Neonröhre, transferierte sie seinerzeit in den Ausstellungsraum eines Kunst-

vereins, wo der Bauschutt zusammen mit einer Fotografie der vorgefundenen Situation sowie einer tagebuchartigen Beschreibung ihres Auffindens im Laufe eines Stadtspaziergangs präsentiert wurde.[11] Auch wenn die Genese von *Imitation / Taklit* an die phänomenologisch inspirierten Stadt- und Landerkundungen in Konzeptkunst und Land Art erinnert, unterscheidet sich Erkmens Ansatz doch grundlegend von diesen historischen Referenzen. Zwar hatte auch Robert Smithson in den 1960er Jahren in Natur und Industriebrachen vorgefundene Materialien wie Steine und Erde in den Ausstellungskontext transferiert: *A Nonsite (Franklin, New Jersey)* (1968) etwa besteht aus Gesteinsbrocken vom im Werktitel genannten Ort, einer konzeptuellen Fotografie sowie schriftlichen Notizen zur Arbeit ⟶ 82 Smithson verstand diese und vergleichbare Arbeiten als Nicht-Orte (*non-sites*) im Ausstellungsraum, wobei er die vorgefundenen Materialien in geometrischen Containern oder in verspiegelten Settings präsentierte und so den Bereich von Kunst und Kultur als topischen Gegenpol der entropischen Prozesse in der Natur definierte. Wesentlich war ihm dabei die Idee des *non-site* als eines Containers, der die natürlich-entropischen Prozesse zähmte und dauerhaft konservierte. Entsprechend finden sich seine *non-sites* heute als begehrte Ausstellungsobjekte in renommierten Museumssammlungen. Der synekdochische Transfer – das

80

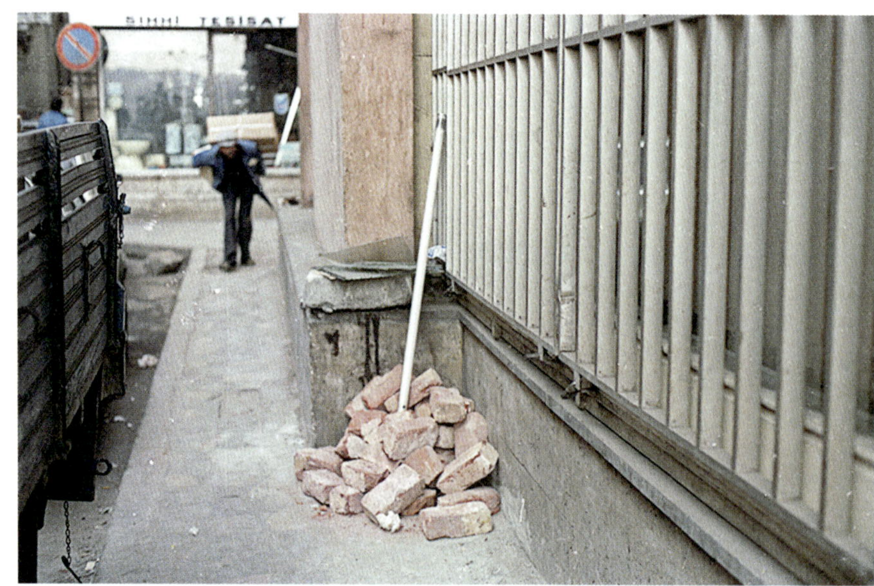

Ayşe Erkmen
Imitation / Taklit, 1987,
Istanbul

12 Vgl. Smithson 2000, 106–107.

Displacement – eines ›natürlichen‹ Ortes an einen anderen, kulturell determinierten Ort im Ausstellungskontext entsprach Smithsons theoretisch-künstlerischem Programm einer Neubestimmung der Skulptur, mit dem er die normative Fokussierung auf den Ort und einen engen, statischen Werkbegriff kritisierte.[12] Auch Ayşe Erkmens Schaffen kennzeichnet eine kontinuierliche Befragung der skulpturalen Mittel, ihr Interesse ist gleichwohl anders gelagert: Ihre Bezugnahme auf den konkreten Ausstellungsort speist sich gerade aus dessen – oftmals erst auf den zweiten Blick sich offenbarenden – räumlichen, sozialen und atmosphärischen Besonderheiten. Die Fertigung bleibender Objekte, in denen sich der Abstand zwischen natürlichen Formprozessen und ihrer symbolischen Fixierung öffnet, steht nicht im Vordergrund. Für die Leipziger Ausstellung wurde *Imitation / Taklit* denn auch mithilfe von Schutt aus einer städtischen Baustelle realisiert und verweist somit auf die umgebende Stadt als Ort aktueller urbaner Transformationsprozesse. ⟶ **44** Aushube, Bauschutt und industrielle Baumaterialien sind in der jüngsten Vergangenheit verstärkt ins Blickfeld einer jüngeren Generation von Künstlerinnen und Künstlern geraten – zu nennen wären etwa Lara Almarcegui und Oscar Tuazon –, die Architektur im Spannungsfeld von Konstruktion und Destruktion und auf das Verhältnis von öffentlichem Raum und privatem Handeln hin befragen. *Imitation / Taklit* lässt sich gegenüber diesen oft großmaßstäblichen Werken eher als ein zeichenhafter Verweis auf (zerstörte) Architektur beschreiben und behauptet zugleich ironisch-beharrlich ein Minimum an skulpturaler Konstruktion, ist doch in der Kombination von sockelartigem Bauschutt und aufragender, elektrisch leuchtender Neonröhre das Grundprinzip der klassischen Bildhauerei, ihre gleichsam zeitenthobene Statuarik, ins Bild gesetzt.

Die möglichen Assoziationen zur Geschichte der Skulptur ›im erweiterten Feld‹ (Rosalind Krauss) sind dabei vielfältig: Neben den *non-sites* erinnert die Materialität der Neonröhren ganz offenkundig an Dan Flavins ausschließliche Nutzung der Leuchtstofflampe seit den frühen 1960er Jahren, wohingegen deren Platzierung auf die *Barres de bois rond* anspielen mag, jene buntlackierten Holzstäbe, die André Cadere in den 1970er Jahren als Objekte an der Schnittstelle von Malerei, Skulptur und Performance gegen die Wand von Galerien und Ausstellungshäusern lehnte. ⟶ **83** Diese Lektüreangebote setzen die Vorstellung einer nachahmenden, mimetischen Bezugnahme in Gang, die *Imitation / Taklit* explizit im Titel trägt, lässt sich der Begriff doch im Deutschen mit ›Imitation‹, ›Nachahmung‹, ›Nacheiferung‹ und auch ›Fälschung‹ wiedergeben. Dabei bleibt bewusst offen, ob sich der mimetische Zugang eklektizistisch auf die skulpturalen

81

exploration of cities and countrysides in Conceptual Art and Land Art, Erkmen's approach differs fundamentally in comparison with these historical references. It is true that in the 1960s Robert Smithson had transferred materials such as stones and earth that he had found in nature and industrial wastelands to the exhibition context: *A Nonsite (Franklin, New Jersey)* (1968), for example, consists of pieces of rock from the place named in the title, a conceptual photograph and written notes on the piece. ⟶ **82** Smithson considered these and similar works to be 'non-sites' in the exhibition space; by presenting the found materials in geometric containers or in mirrored settings, he defined the area of art and culture as the topical opposite of the entropic processes in nature. The idea of the *non-site* was essential for him as a container that tamed the natural entropic processes of nature and preserved them. His *non-sites* are thus coveted exhibition objects in famous museum collections today. The synecdochic transferal – the displacement – of a 'natural' place to another culturally determined place in the exhibition context corresponded to Smithson's theoretical and artistic intention of redefining sculpture, with which he criticised the normative focus on place and a restricting, static concept of the work.[12] Ayşe Erkmen's work is also characterised by an uninterrupted questioning of sculptural means, although her interests have a different bias: her reference to the concrete exhibition space also feeds on its spatial, social and atmospheric qualities, which are often only revealed on second glance. The production of lasting objects that highlight the distance between natural forming processes and their symbolic fixation is not her priority. For the exhibition in Leipzig, *Imitation / Taklit* was created using rubble from a local construction site and thus refers to the surrounding city as a place of current urban transformation processes. ⟶ **44** Excavations, rubble, and industrial building materials have recently become the focus of a younger generation of artists – such as Lara Almarcegui and Oscar Tuazon, to name two – who question architecture in the interplay of construction and destruction and the relationship of public space and private actions. *Imitation / Taklit* can be described in opposition to these often large-scale works as a more willingly symbolic reference to (destroyed) architecture; simultaneously it displays a minimum of sculptural construction with ironic insistence: the combination of pedestal-like rubble and the illuminated neon tube that sticks out of it contains the basic principles of classical sculpture and showcases its timeless statuary qualities.

Many associations can be made regarding the history of sculpture 'in the Expanded Field' (Rosalind

12 See Smithson 2000, 106–07.

13   Vgl. Koch / Völher /
Voss 2010.

14   Vgl. das Teilprojekt *Min-
dere Mimesis* in der DFG-For-
schergruppe *Medien und
Mimesis* (FOR 1867), online:
<http://www.fg-mimesis.de/
teilprojekte/>, letzter
Zugriff: 20.3.2017.

Eigenheiten der genannten Künstler bezieht, oder auf die vorgefundene Situation in den Straßen Istanbuls sowie deren Foto-Dokumentation und materielle Rekonstruktion, oder schließlich auf die Nachstellung (*reenactment*) ebendieser Installation 30 Jahre später, im Leipzig des Jahres 2017. Die Nachahmung der Natur, ihre Mimesis, war ebenso wie das Streben nach einem Kunstideal (*imitatio*) jahrhundertelang ein zentrales Bezugskonzept im westlichen Kunstverständnis, insbesondere im dreidimensionalen Medium der vermeintlich realitätsnahen Gattung Skulptur. Mit dem Verzicht auf abbildhafte Darstellung in der Abstraktion der Moderne wurde die mimetische Nachahmung aus den Künsten nur scheinbar verabschiedet; demgegenüber setzte sich im jüngsten ästhetischen Diskurs eine erweiterte, handlungsorientierte Auffassung des Mimesis-Konzepts durch, der zufolge sich Mimesis im Wirklichkeitsbezug des Kunstschaffens vollziehe und die semantischen Bereiche von Darstellung, Ausdruck und sinnlicher Vergegenwärtigung umfasse.[13] Die aktuelle Mimesis-Forschung wendet sich dabei explizit jenen ästhetisch »minderen« Phänomenen zu, die bislang kulturell als nicht nachahmenswert oder nachahmbar übersehen wurden, und für die sich dennoch mimetische Darstellungstechniken – etwa im filmischen *reenactment* – etabliert haben.[14]

Imitation / Taklit fordert die Werthierarchie von Ur- / Vorbild und Nachahmung heraus. Mit dem zwischen Imitation, Nacheiferung und Fälschung oszillierenden Titel problematisiert die Arbeit die normative Entscheidung darüber, was kulturell überhaupt als nachahmenswert anerkannt wird und was nicht. Darüber hinaus reflektiert sie die Authentizität des Entorteten, und schließlich, in kunsthistorischer Perspektive, das eigene Schaffen innerhalb einer Genealogie der modernen Skulptur. Deutlich wird, dass Ayşe Erkmens Bezugnahmen auf Orte und Räume immer schon eine im weiteren Sinne mimetische, weil deren Erscheinung sinnlich vergegenwärtigende Dimension betonen, wovon die frühen, wie minimalistische, zeichnungsartige Raumstrukturen anmutenden *Imitating Lines* zeugen (*Uyumlu Çizgiler*, 1985). ⟶ **42 + 84** Die sinnlich-affektive Raumerfahrung steht in zwei weiteren Räumen des Leipziger Museums der bildenden Künste im Zentrum: *Glassworks* (2015 / 2017) taucht einen großen Eckraum im Untergeschoss in das bunte Licht einer Vielzahl gefärbter Glasscheiben, die unterhalb der Deckenstrahler montiert sind. ⟶ **86 + 90** Die Buntheit des raumfüllenden Lichts erinnert an die utopischen Architekturfantasien aus farbigem Glas zu Beginn des 20. Jahrhunderts – Bruno Tauts Glashaus für die Kölner Werkbundausstellung von 1914 ist das bekannteste Beispiel. Darüber hinaus eignet der Installation eine immersive Qualität, die den

82

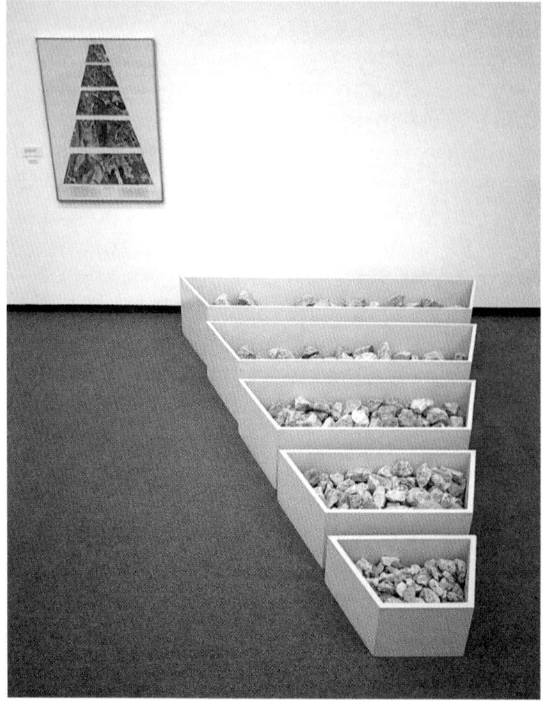

Robert Smithson
A Nonsite (Franklin, New Jersey),
1968

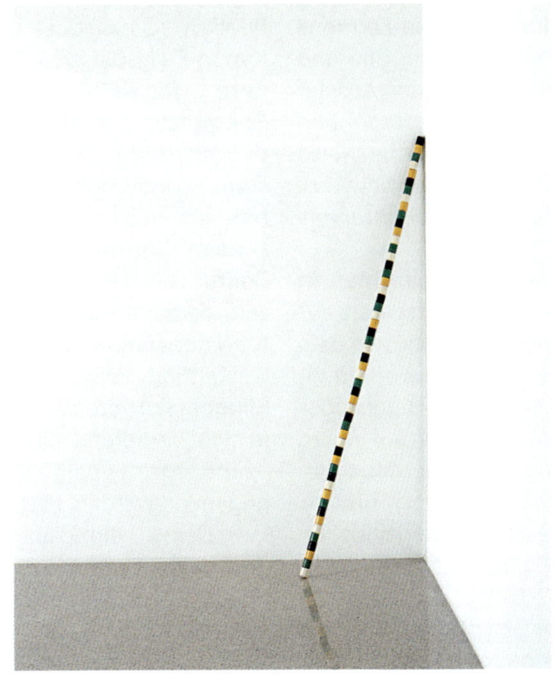

André Cadere
Barres de bois rond, 1971

83

Krauss): in addition to *non-sites,* the materiality of the neon tube is obviously reminiscent of Dan Flavin's exclusive use of these light tubes since the early 1960s, while its placement may make reference to the *Barres de bois rond,* colourfully painted wooden rods that André Cadere leaned against the walls of galleries and exhibition spaces in the 1970s as objects at the intersection of painting, sculpture and performance. ⟶ **83** These possible readings kindle the idea of an imitative, mimetic reference that *Taklit* explicitly contains in its title, which means *imitation, emulation,* or even *forgery.* Yet it remains intentionally unclear if the mimetic approach refers eclectically to the sculptural singularity of the above-mentioned artists or the situation encountered on the streets of Istanbul and its photographic documentation and material re-construction, or ultimately to the re-enactment of the first installation thirty years later in Leipzig in 2017. The imitation of nature, its mimesis, was, like *imitatio* (the pursuit of an artistic ideal), for many centuries the central point of reference in the Western understanding of art, especially in the three-dimensionality of sculpture, which is allegedly close to reality. Due to the renouncement of 'realistic' representation in modern abstraction, mimetic imitation seemingly disappeared from the arts; however, an expanded, action-oriented understanding of the concept of mimesis began to assert itself in recent aesthetic discourse, by which mimesis is conceived and consummated in its reference to reality and embraces the semantic areas of representation, expression and sensual perception.[13] Current mimesis research turns explicitly to the 'lesser' aesthetic phenomena that had been ignored culturally as not worthy of imitation or not imitable, and for which nevertheless mimetic techniques of representation have been established – for example, in cinematic re-enactment.[14] *Imitation / Taklit* emphatically challenges the hierarchy of values in the relationship of original or archetype to imitation. With its title semantically oscillating between imitation, emulation and forgery, the work problematises normative decisions in regards to what is culturally worth imitating or not. Moreover, it reflects upon the level of authenticity of a displaced work and also, in an art-historical perspective, upon the artist's own place within a genealogy of modern sculpture. It thus becomes clear that Ayşe Erkmen's references to places and spaces always contain a mimetic dimension by extension, since their appearance stresses a sensual presence, as the minimalistic, drawing-like space-structures of her early work *Imitating Lines* (*Uyumlu Çizgiler,* 1985) prove. ⟶ **42 + 84** A sensually stimulating spatial experience is the focus in two other rooms of the Leipzig Museum of Fine Arts: *Glassworks* (2015 / 2017)

13   See Koch / Vöhler / Voss 2010.

14   See the sub-project *Lesser Mimesis* in the DFG research group *Media and Mimesis* (FOR 1867), <http://www.fg-mimesis. de/teilprojekte/> (accessed 19 September, 2017).

Raum als begehbares Bild erfahrbar macht. Überdies lässt die Künstlerin die Fensterblenden des Raumes in fünfminütigem Intervall in Bewegung setzen (*Shutters*, 2017). ⟶ **90** Als »karnevalistische« Inszenierung knüpft die Arbeit an frühere Installationen Erkmens an, [15] die durch geringfügige farbliche Eingriffe und ihre Struktur die Atmosphäre des nüchternen Ausstellungsraumes neu definieren und die Betrachterinnen und Betrachter auf physische und psychische Weise in das Werk einbinden (vgl. etwa *Busy Colors*, New York, Long Island City, SculptureCenter, 2005; *Intervals*, London, Barbican, 2013).

Schafft *Glassworks* einen vereinheitlichten, in seiner malerischen Farbigkeit theatral-rätselhaft aufgeladenen Raum, so zielt die Toninstallation *Ewig Dein* (2011) im *Beethoven*-Saal des Museums auf einen gegenteiligen, fast dissoziativen Effekt. Max Klingers überlebensgroße Darstellung des Komponisten auf einem auskragenden Thron stellte das Leipziger Museum aufgrund ihrer eindrucksvollen Dimensionen und ungewöhnlich malerischen, expressiven Materialqualität schon zum Zeitpunkt der Erwerbung vor die Frage ihrer adäquaten Präsentation. ⟶ **87** War die 1902 nach langjähriger Arbeit vollendete Skulptur zunächst in einem eigens geschaffenen Anbau aufgestellt, so bezog sie nach Einrichtung des Museumsneubaus 2004 einen ihr gewidmeten, ansonsten nahezu leeren Raum

in der ersten Etage (einzig Klingers *Neue Salome* und *Kassandra* befinden sich noch im Saal). Diesem auf unabsehbare Zeit festgelegten, monumentalen Ort begegnet Ayşe Erkmen mit einer Toninstallation nach Beethovens 1863 posthum publiziertem dreistimmigen Kanon *Ewig Dein* (ca. 1811, WoO 161). In der verwendeten, gut einminütigen Einspielung singt dieselbe Sopranistin alle drei Stimmen, so dass sich die beiden Worte des Titels als einzige Textelemente in der steten Wiederholung immer dichter überlagern, während sich die Stimmlage immer höher zu schrauben scheint. Der physischen Schwere des ›leibhaftigen‹ Beethoven steht die körperlos-ephemere und doch zeitüberdauernde Wirkung seiner musikalischen Dichtung gegenüber, die in der polyphonisch reduzierten Gestaltung gleichwohl ähnlich hermetisch wirkt wie Klingers Porträtdarstellung. Zwar kann an dieser Stelle nicht vertiefend auf die wechselseitigen Raum- und Zeitbezüge der beiden Künste Skulptur und Musik eingegangen werden, die die räumliche Inszenierung von *Ewig Dein* in Leipzig anspricht, doch sei daran erinnert, dass der hier zum Tragen kommende Einsatz von Klang als gleichsam plastischem Material zu den konzeptuell-minimalistischen Raumerkundungen der 1960er und 1970er Jahre zurückverfolgt werden kann, etwa bei Max Neuhaus oder La Monte Young. Gegenüber deren faktizistischen und teils kakofonischen Klangereignis-

84

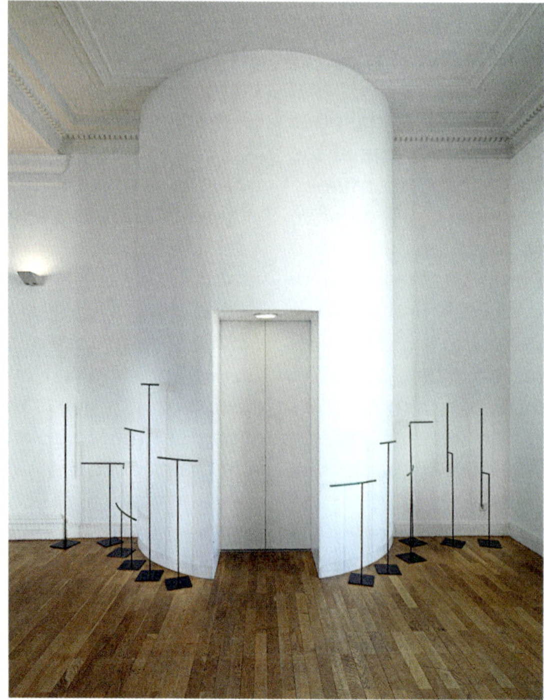

Ayşe Erkmen
Imitating Lines, 1985 / 2008
Ausstellungsansicht /
exhibition view, Hamburger
Bahnhof, Berlin

sen kann das dichte, lebendige Klanggewebe, das sich um die heroisch-isolierte skulpturale Inszenierung Beethovens herum entfaltet, auch als subtiler Kommentar zur kunsthistoriografischen Tradierung männlicher Künstlermythen gelesen werden, für die Klingers Denkmal ein visuell überwältigendes Beispiel abgibt.

Displacement als ästhetische Grenzverschiebung

Mit einer weiteren Intervention innerhalb des Museums der bildenden Künste Leipzig nimmt Ayşe Erkmen auf den Sammlungsbestand Bezug: August Gauls dunkel patinierte Bronzeplastiken von Pinguinen, die in einem Übergangsbereich des dritten Obergeschosses als gestaffelte Gruppe auf Wandkonsolen positioniert sind, nahm sie zum Anlass, eine eigene Sammlung tierischer Kleinstplastiken zu präsentieren (*By Nature*, 2015 / 2017). ⟶ **98** Gauls Tierplastiken, zur Entstehungszeit vor etwa hundert Jahren ebenso populär wie heute, sind von einer für die Jahrhundertwende ungewöhnlichen formalen Sachlichkeit gekennzeichnet; auch inhaltlich distanzierte sich der Bildhauer von exotistischen oder hierarchisierenden Darstellungskonventionen des Tieres. Mit seiner nahezu vollständigen Beschränkung auf das Tiermotiv hatte sich August Gaul, wie zuvor schon die französischen *animaliers* (Tierbildhauer), vom Menschenbild als wesentlichem Kunstinhalt verabschiedet. Die ästhetische Differenz, die zwischen den *animaliers* und den klassischen Bildhauern im späten 19. Jahrhundert geltend gemacht worden war – im Sinne eines Gegensatzes zwischen sklavischer Naturnachahmung einerseits und kreativem Ingenium andererseits –, war zu Gauls Schaffenszeit bereits überwunden. Eine neuerliche Differenzierung etablierte sich freilich in der Bronzebildnerei dort, wo die Limitation der realisierten Abgüsse Originalitäts- und Authentizitätsansprüche zu wahren suchte – ein Bestreben, das der Popularität eines ästhetischen Objekts, die sich in der Regel im Streben nach seinem physischen Besitz niederschlägt, gleichsam von Grund auf entgegensteht. Auf die aus diesem Streben resultierende Blüte kunstgewerblicher Plastik nimmt die Objektsammlung Ayşe Erkmens Bezug, eine Kollektion kleinstformatiger Porzellantiere vom Anfang des vergangenen Jahrhunderts – mithin Zeitgenossen von Gauls Pinguinen –, die die Künstlerin über Jahre hinweg auf Flohmärkten zusammengetragen hat. Diese Ansammlung bunter Tierfiguren aus Privathaushalten fällt gemeinhin in die Kategorie von Nippes und befindet sich damit unterhalb der ästhetischen Grenze, die sie vom Kunststatus der Kleinplastik trennt. Wie letztere wurden die Figuren jedoch in privaten Haushalten zur Zierde aufgestellt, wie jene spiegeln sie – mehr noch als die öffentlich-repräsentativen Aufgaben verpflichtete Großplastik – den Zeitgeschmack und die

85

casts the tinted light of a plethora of coloured glass panes that are mounted below the ceiling lights on the large corner space of the lower level. ⟶ **86 + 90** The variegated light that fills the space is reminiscent of the utopian architectural fantasies of colour glass at the beginning of the twentieth century: Bruno Taut's Crystal Pavilion for the 1914 exhibition of the Deutscher Werkbund (German Association of Craftsmen) in Cologne is the most prominent example. The installation has an immersive quality that allows the room to be experienced as a walk-in picture. In addition, the artist has the shutters of the room moved at five-minute intervals (*Shutters*, 2017). ⟶ **90** A 'carnivalesque' installation,[15] the work is linked to earlier installations by Erkmen due to its slight colour interventions and its structure that re-defines the matter-of-fact architecture and engages the viewer in ways both physical and psychological (see, for example, *Busy Colors,* New York, Long Island City, SculptureCenter, 2005; *Intervals,* London, The Curve, Barbican Centre, 2013).

While *Glassworks* creates a unified space that in its colourfulness is theatrically and mysteriously charged, the sound installation *Ewig Dein* (Forever Yours, 2011) in the *Beethoven* room of the museum has an almost dissociative effect. Due to its impressive dimensions and the unusual painterly, expressive quality of its materials, Max Klinger's monumental depiction of the composer on a spacious throne confronted the museum in Leipzig with the question of its adequate presentation at the time of its acquisition. ⟶ **87** Completed in 1902 after years of work, the sculpture was originally kept in a specially built extension. In 2004 it was moved into its own room on the first floor of the new museum building, a virtually empty room that only contains two other works by Klinger (*Neue Salome* [New Salome] and *Kassandra* [Cassandra]). Ayşe Erkmen responds to this monumental space, which is reserved for the work for an indeterminate period, with a sound installation. The work is based on Beethoven's three-part canon *Ewig Dein* (ca. 1811, WoO 161), which was published posthumously in 1863. In the recording, which lasts just over one minute, the same soprano sings all three voices, so that the two words in the title are the only text elements in the continuous repetition, overlapping evermore densely, while the register seems to get higher and higher. The physical heaviness of the corporeal Beethoven is contrasted with the bodiless, ephemeral and yet timeless effect of his musical creation, which in its reduced polyphony seems just as hermetic as the portrait by Klinger. Although the mutual spatial and temporal references in both sculpture and music that inform *Ewig Dein* in Leipzig can only be touched upon here, it is important to remember

15 Gregory Volk describes Erkmen's works as 'carnivalesque art' (Volk 2008, 157).

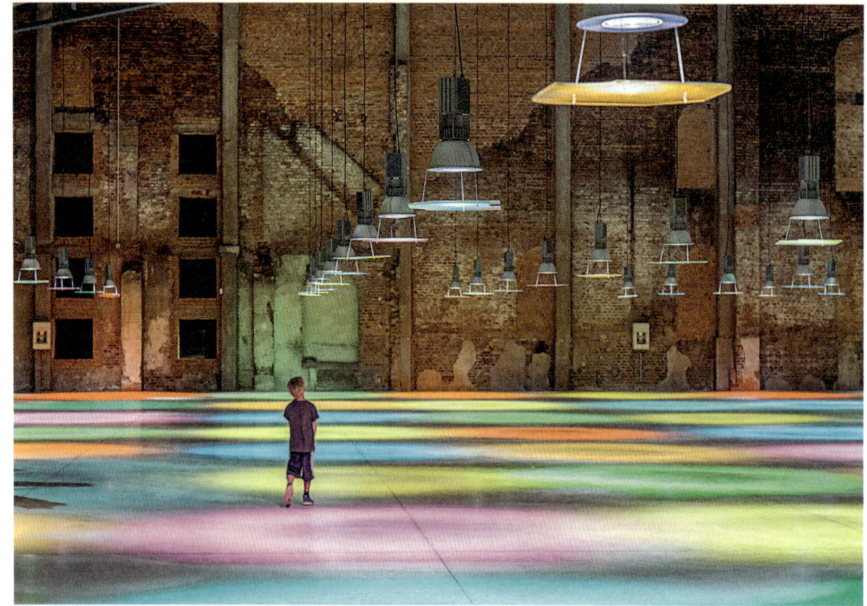

Ayşe Erkmen
Glassworks, 2015
Installationsansicht / installation
view, Cadhame Halle Verrière,
Meisenthal

86

that the use of sound as a quasi plastic material can be traced back to the spatial explorations of Minimal and Conceptual artists of the 1960s and 1970s such as Max Neuhaus and La Monte Young. Compared with their factitious and often cacophonic sound events, the thick fabric of lively sound that unfolds around Beethoven's heroically isolated sculptural staging can also be read as a subtle commentary on the art-historical tradition of male artist legends – of which Klinger's monument is a visually overwhelming example.

Displacement as an Aesthetic Shifting of Boundaries

Ayşe Erkmen makes reference to the museum's collection in a further intervention within the Leipzig Museum of Fine Arts: August Gaul's darkly patinated bronze sculptures of penguins, which are positioned in a transitional area of the third floor as a staggered group on wall consoles, provided the impulse for Erkmen to present her own collection of animal sculptures (*By Nature,* 2015 / 2017). ⟶ **98** Gaul's animal sculptures, which are just as popular today as they were one hundred years ago when they were created, are characterised by an unusual degree of formal objectivity for the turn of the century; the sculptor distanced himself from the exoticism and hierarchies of representing animals that were current at the time.

Like the French *animaliers* before him, August Gaul dismissed the human image as the key artistic subject by concentrating almost exclusively on animal motifs. The aesthetic difference between the *animaliers* and classic sculptors that had been debated in the nineteenth century – the contrast between the slavish imitation of nature on the one hand and creative genius on the other – had already been resolved by Gaul's time. It was replaced by a further differentiation that was established in the area of bronze sculpture, however: the limitations of casts intended to maintain standards of originality and authenticity conflicted with tendencies to popularise these aesthetic objects in larger numbers, since popularity typically manifests itself in the desire for physical possession. Popular sculptural objects, produced in large numbers in the applied arts, are the subject of Ayşe Erkmen's collection of miniature porcelain animals from the beginning of the twentieth century – thus contemporaries of Gaul's penguins – that the artist amassed at flea markets over the years. This collection of colourful animals from private homes usually falls into the category of knick-knacks, and is thus below the aesthetic border that separates them from the art status of the bronze sculptures. Similar to the latter, however, they were also displayed in private households as decoration, and they thus also reflect – even more than large-

persönlichen Vorlieben ihrer ehemaligen Besitzer wider (und offenbaren freilich ein vollends domestiziertes Bild vom Tier). Indem die Künstlerin dieses vielgestaltige Konvolut in stillen Dialog mit August Gauls genau beobachteten, differenzierten Pinguindarstellungen treten lässt, lädt Ayşe Erkmen zum Nachdenken über solche historisch wandelbaren ästhetischen Grenzziehungen ein.

Mit den *Gemütlichen Ecken* (2009) soll hier ein letztes Motiv der ästhetischen Grenzverschiebung angesprochen werden. Mit dieser Arbeit wird der Ausstellungsraum in den städtischen Raum erweitert. ⟶ 88+100 Zehn formal unterschiedliche, farbig lackierte Aluminiumtafeln finden in der Innenstadt Aufstellung, mal an Bäume oder Straßenschilder gelehnt, mal mitten auf dem Bürgersteig platziert. Die ungewöhnlichen Zuschnitte der Tafeln legen eine spezifische Funktionalität nahe, die sich den Passantinnen und Passanten jedoch ebenso wenig erschließt wie die Autorschaft und der Publikumsbezug der Objekte. Die konzeptuelle Paarung des städtischen Raums mit der Vorstellung von ›Gemütlichkeit‹ lässt unweigerlich an Karl Kraus' berühmten Ausspruch denken, mit dem er sich gegen die spätgründerzeitliche Dekoration seiner Wahlheimat Wien verwahrte: »Ich verlange von einer Stadt, in der ich leben soll: Asphalt, Straßenspülung, Haustorschlüssel, Luftheizung, Warmwasserleitung.

Gemütlich bin ich selbst.«[16] Womöglich bezog sich Ayşe Erkmen in ihrer ersten Realisierung der Arbeit, 2009 im Rahmen des *steirischen herbsts* in Graz, auf das beißende Diktum des österreichischen Kulturkritikers. In Leipzig artikuliert *Gemütliche Ecken* jedenfalls die unvermindert aktuelle Frage nach dem gesellschaftlichen Umgang mit dem städtischen Raum, der zunehmend wirtschaftlicher Nutzung unterworfen ist, und nach dem Ort der Kunst in dieser öffentlichen Sphäre. Wie überdimensionierte, weithin sichtbare visuelle Stolpersteine behaupten die Elemente der Gruppe ihre Buchstäblichkeit als gestaltete Objekte im Stadtbild. Jenseits einer vertrauten Design- und Verwertungslogik unterlaufen sie den an Kunst im öffentlichen Raum gemeinhin gestellten Anspruch eines kommunikativen oder identitätsstiftenden Angebots und verschieben so auch hier ästhetische Grenzziehungen zwischen Repräsentation und Funktionalität. In ihrer offensichtlich provisorischen Aufstellung widersprechen die *Gemütlichen Ecken* sowohl der Idee eines möglichst andauernden, positiven Gemütszustands wie auch der topologischen Besonderheit der Ecke. Als transportable Einheiten lassen sie sich vielmehr als weithin sichtbarer, bildhafter Ausdruck eines Displacement verstehen – als andauernde, das skulpturale Schaffen und die künstlerische Vita Ayşe Erkmens gleichermaßen kennzeichnende Entortung.

87

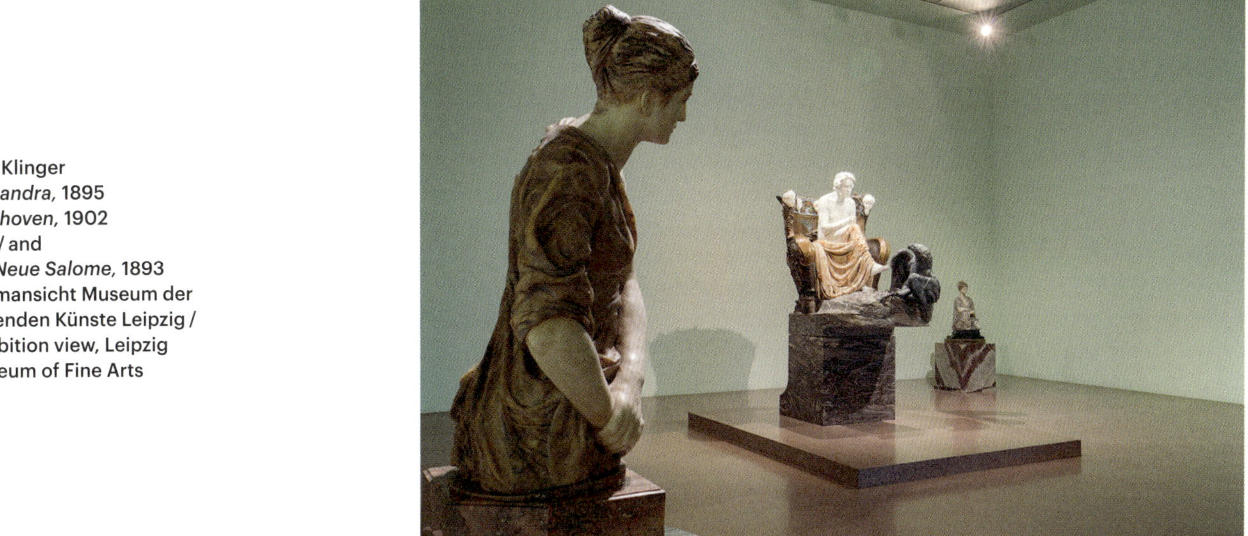

Max Klinger
Kassandra, 1895
Beethoven, 1902
und / and
Die Neue Salome, 1893
Raumansicht Museum der bildenden Künste Leipzig / exhibition view, Leipzig Museum of Fine Arts

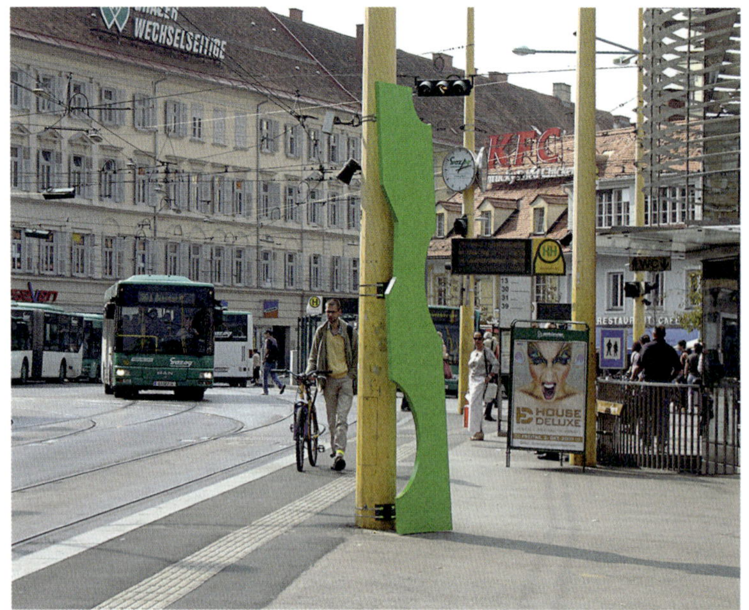

Ayşe Erkmen
Gemütliche Ecken, 2009
Installationsansicht /
installation view, Graz

88

format sculptures that had public duties of representation – the tastes of the times and the personal preferences of their former owners (and of course reveal a fully domesticated image of animals). By allowing this diverse flock to engage in silent dialogue with August Gaul's carefully observed and nuanced representations of penguins, Ayşe Erkmen encourages the viewer to contemplate such aesthetic demarcations that change over time.

The final motif of aesthetic shifting of borders to be mentioned here is *Gemütliche Ecken* (Cosy Corners, 2009). The work expands the exhibition sphere into urban space. ⟶ **88+100** Ten differently shaped and brightly enamelled aluminium panels are placed around the city centre of Leipzig, sometimes leaned against trees or street signs, and sometimes placed in the middle of the sidewalk. The unusual cuts of the panels suggest a specific function that remains just as enigmatic to passers-by as the authorship and the object's relationship to the audience. The conceptual pairing of urban space with the concept of *Gemütlichkeit,* or 'cosiness' inevitably recalls Karl Kraus' famous remark with which he protested against the turn-of-the-century decoration of his adopted home of Vienna: 'From a city in which I live I expect the following: asphalt, street cleaning, doors with locks, heating, hot running water – I am *gemütlich* on my own.'[16] Ayşe Erkmen was possibly referring to Kraus' caustic dictum when she created her first version of this work in 2009, in the context of *steirischer herbst* in Graz. In Leipzig *Gemütliche Ecken* also articulates the unabated current problem of society's interaction with urban space that is increasingly subjected to the interests of economic exploitation, and the issue of art's place in this public sphere. Like oversized visual 'stumbling blocks' that can be seen from a great distance, the elements of the group assert their literalness as designed objects in the urban landscape. Outside the familiar logic of design and economic use, they undermine the common expectation that art in public space should serve communicative purposes or endow identity, thus shifting the aesthetic demarcations between representation and functionality. The clearly provisional placement in urban space of *Gemütliche Ecken* contradicts both the idea of an enduring positive state of mind and the topological feature of the corner. As transportable units they can be understood as a vivid expression of displacement that can be seen from afar – a permanent displacement that equally characterises the sculpture and artistic biography of Ayşe Erkmen.

*Translated from
German by Tas Skorupa*

16   Kraus 1986, 109.

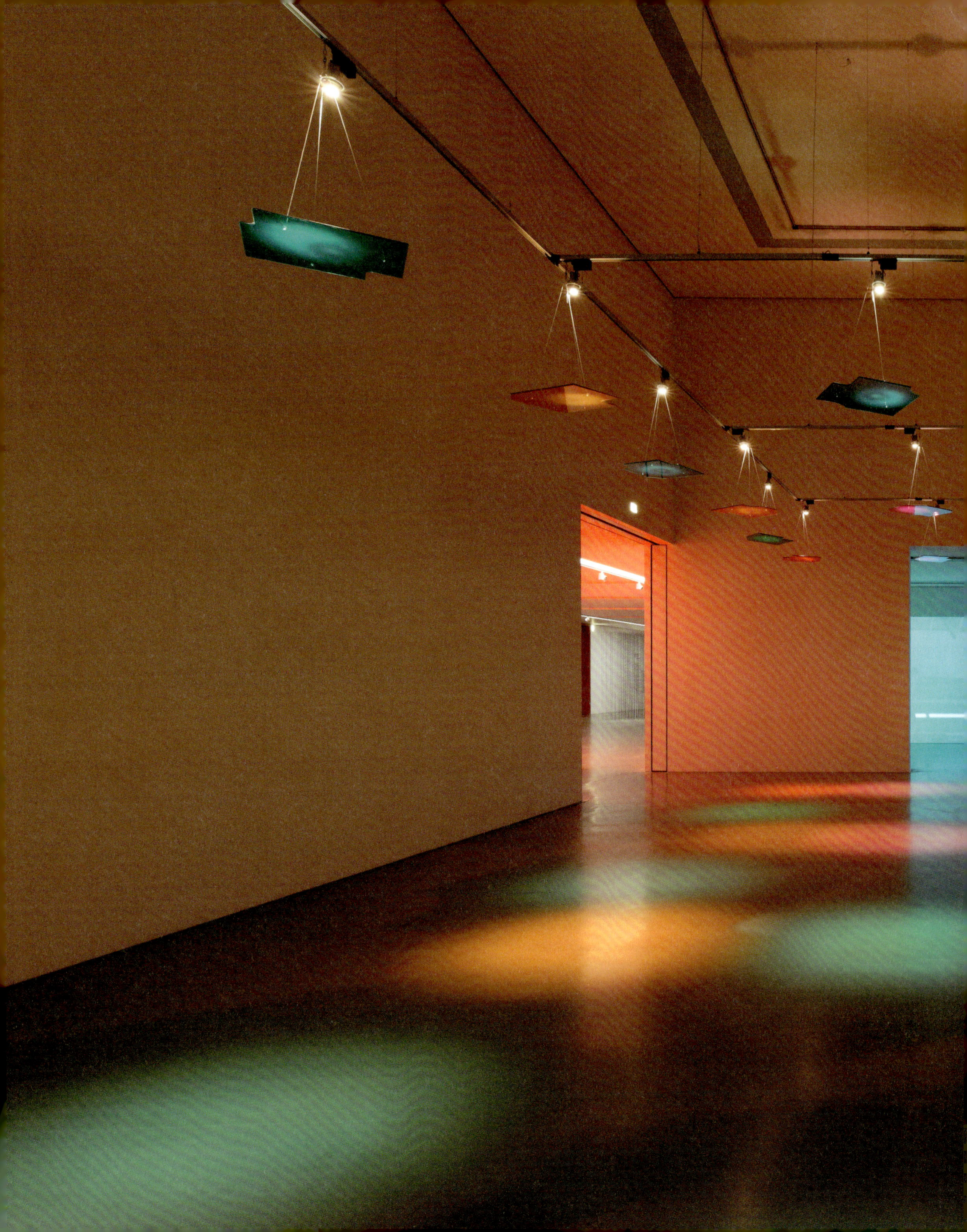

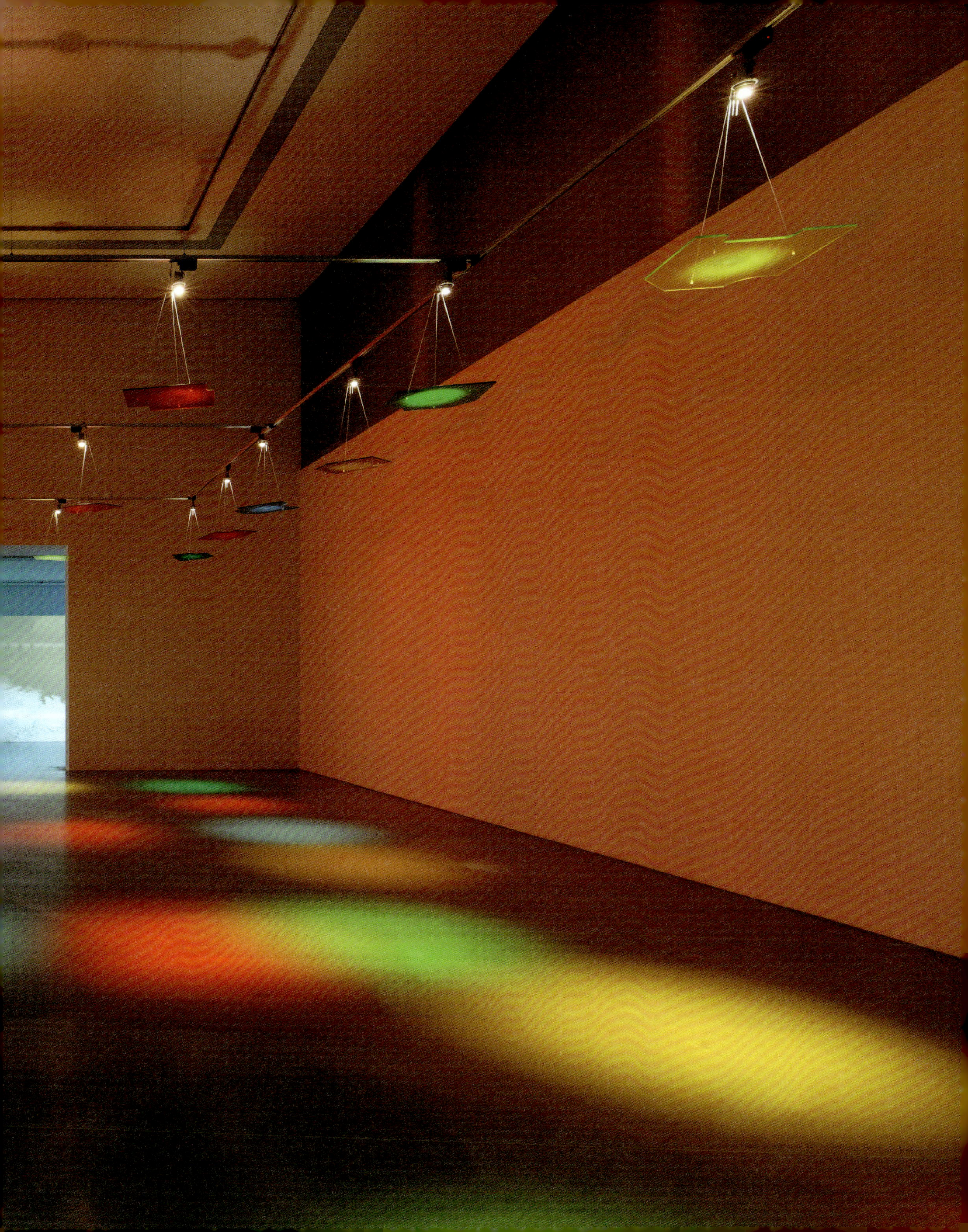

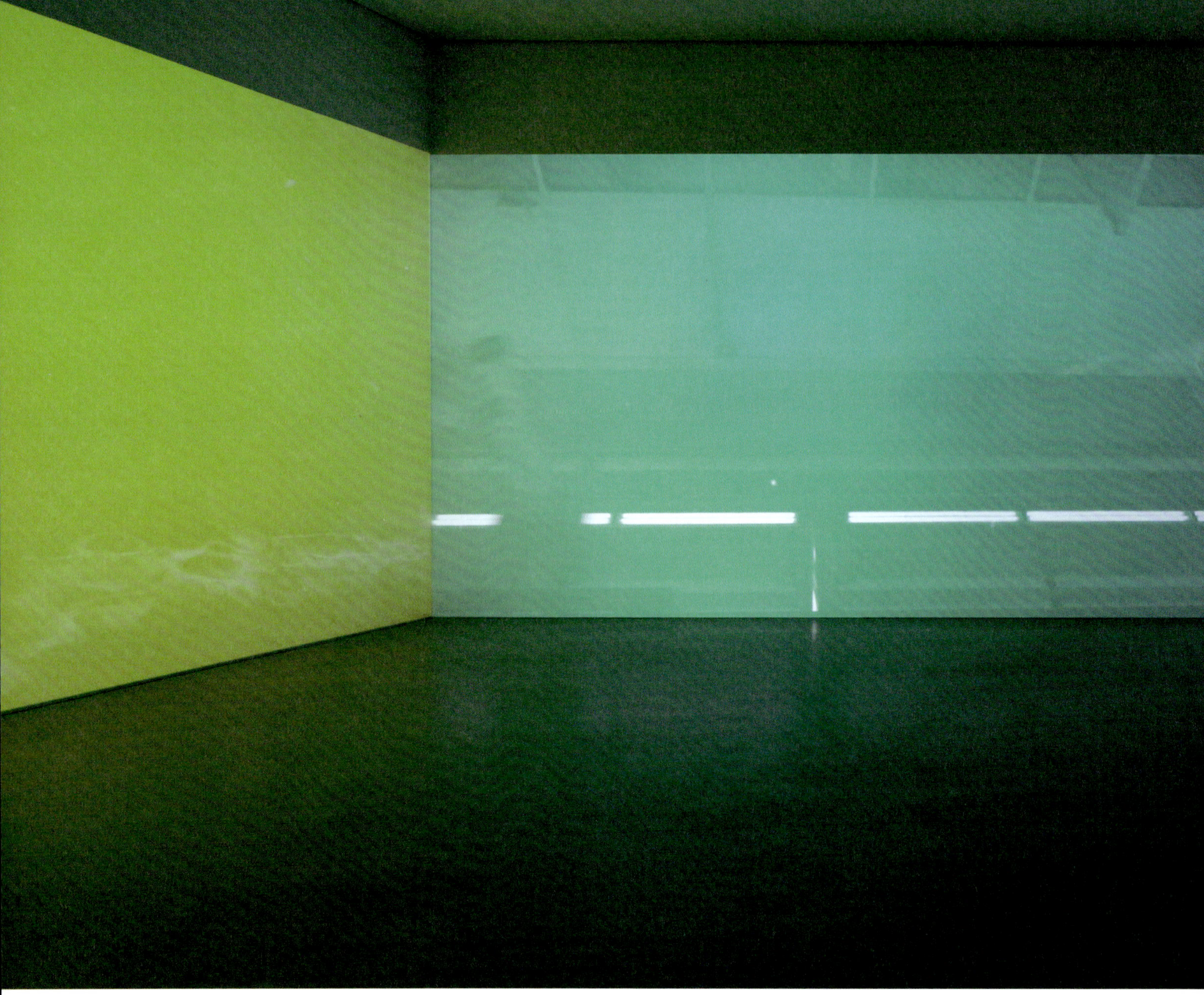

←— Ayşe Erkmen
Glassworks, 2015 / 2017
Shutters, 2017

Ayşe Erkmen
Bronze Acid Yellow, 2014
Bronze Acid Green, 2014

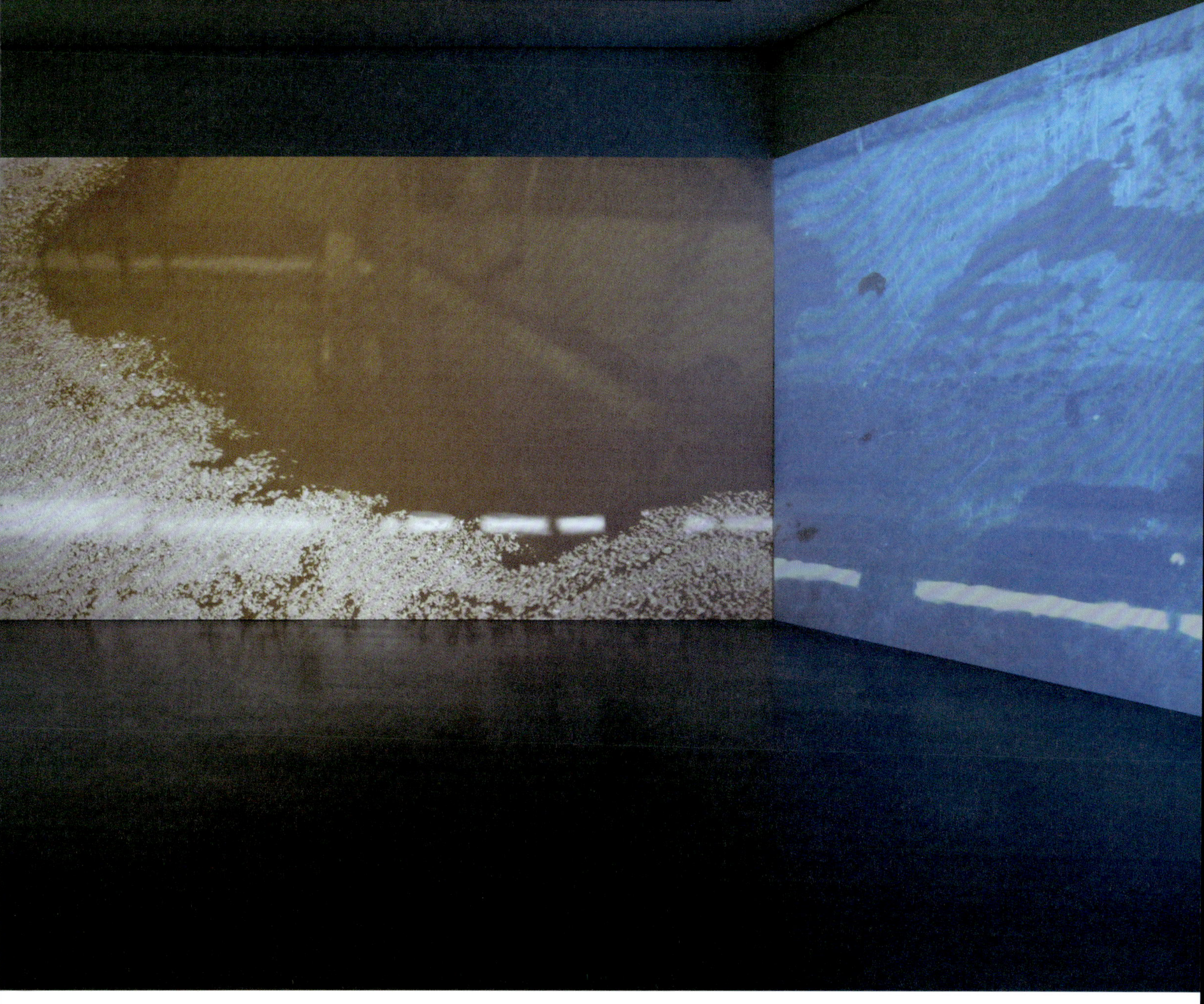

Ayşe Erkmen
Bronze Acid Ochre, 2014
Bronze Acid Blue, 2014

Ayşe Erkmen
Half of, 2017

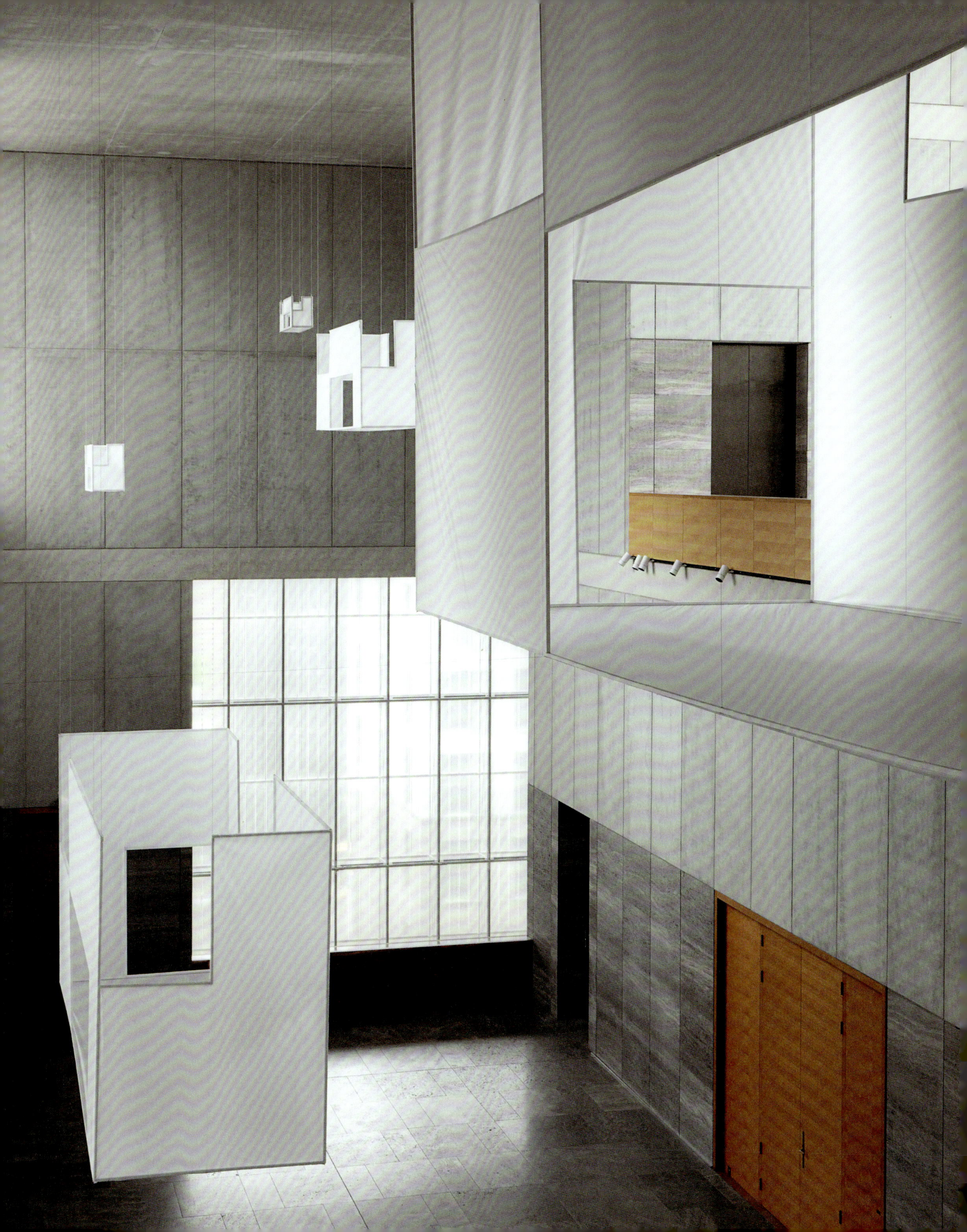

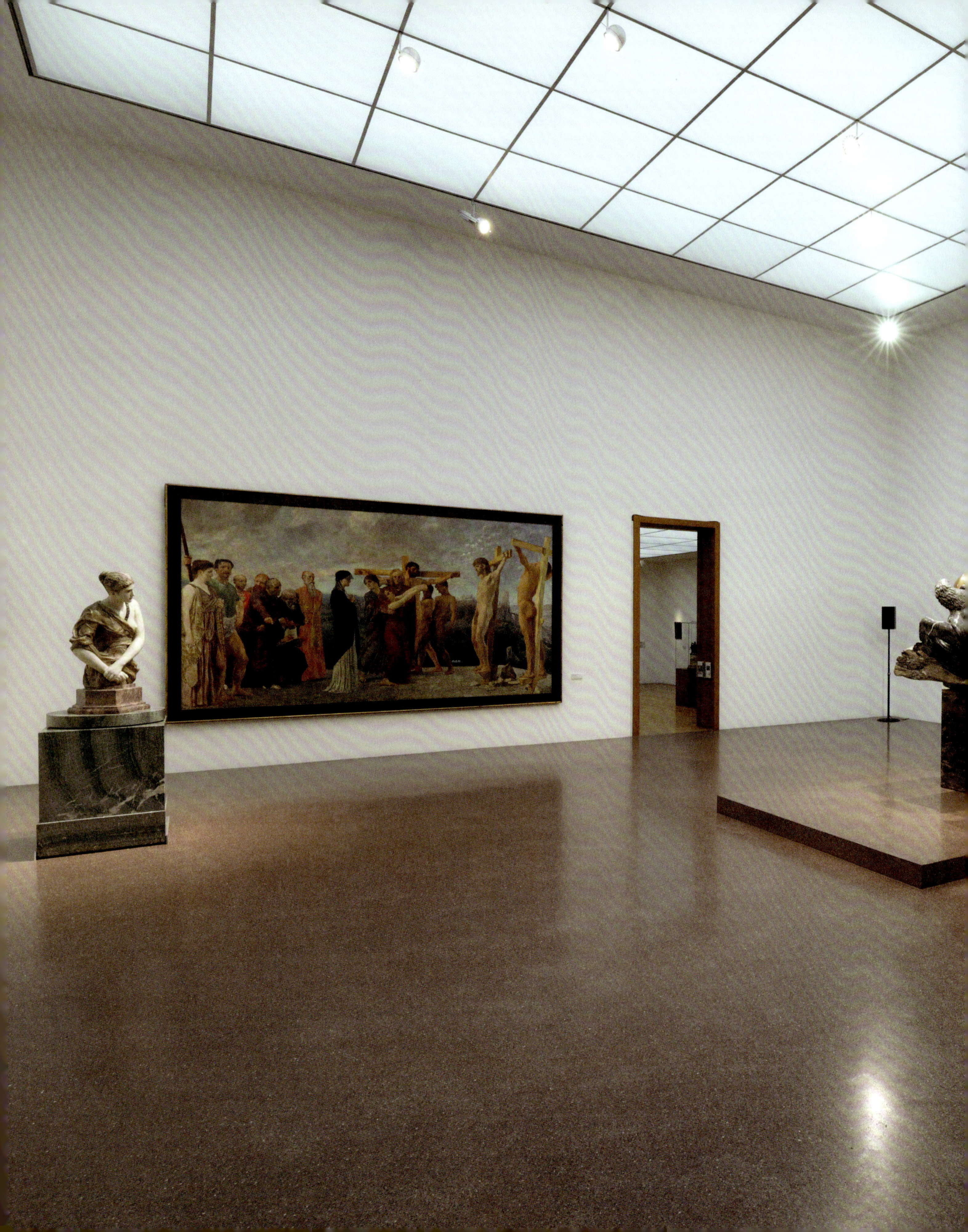

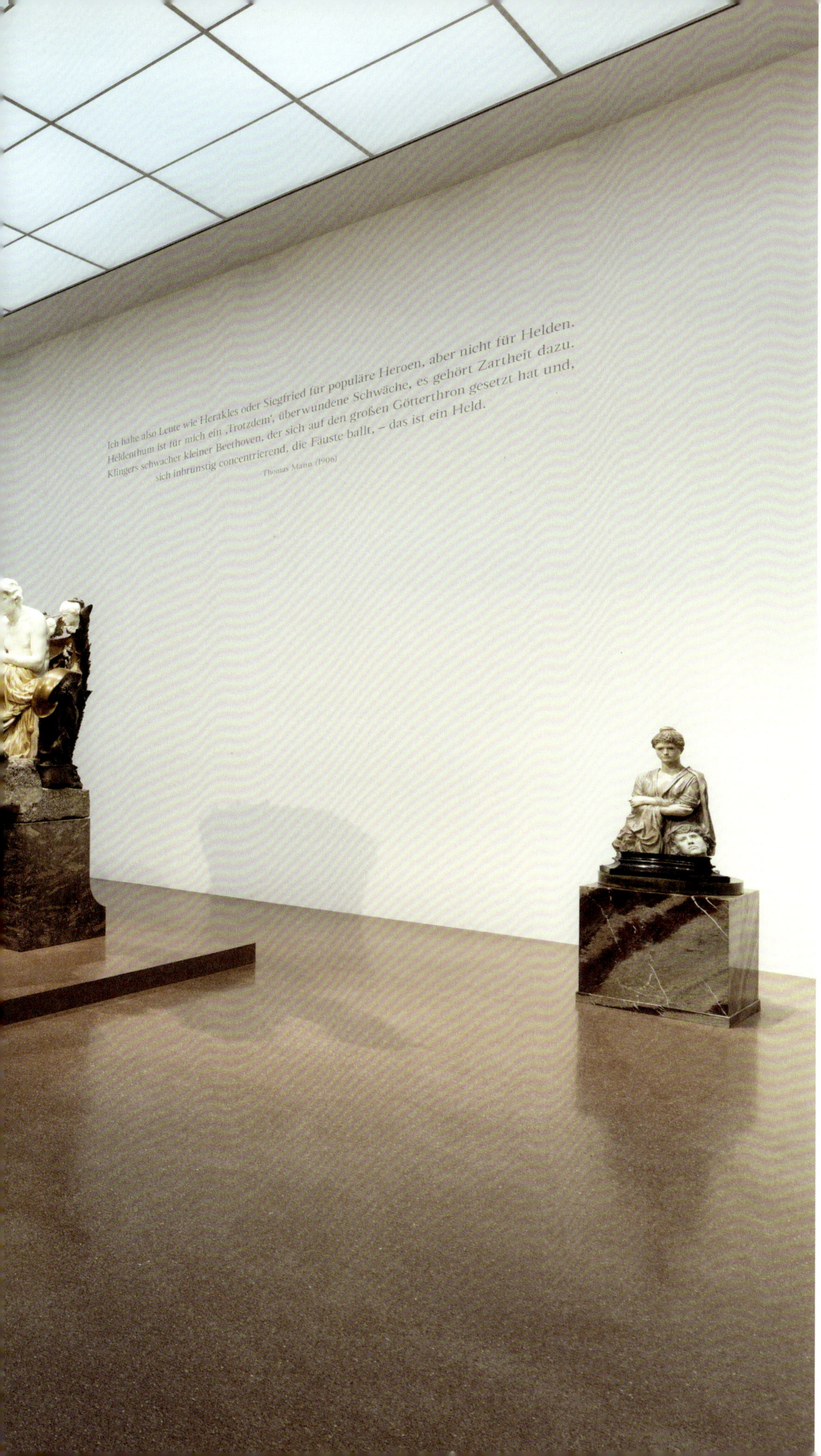

Ich halte also Leute wie Herakles oder Siegfried für populäre Heroen, aber nicht für Helden. Heldenthum ist für mich ein ‚Trotzdem', überwundene Schwäche, es gehört Zartheit dazu. Klingers schwacher kleiner Beethoven, der sich auf den großen Götterthron gesetzt hat und, sich inbrünstig concentrierend, die Fäuste ballt, – das ist ein Held.

Thomas Mann (1906)

Ayşe Erkmen
Ewig Dein, 2011

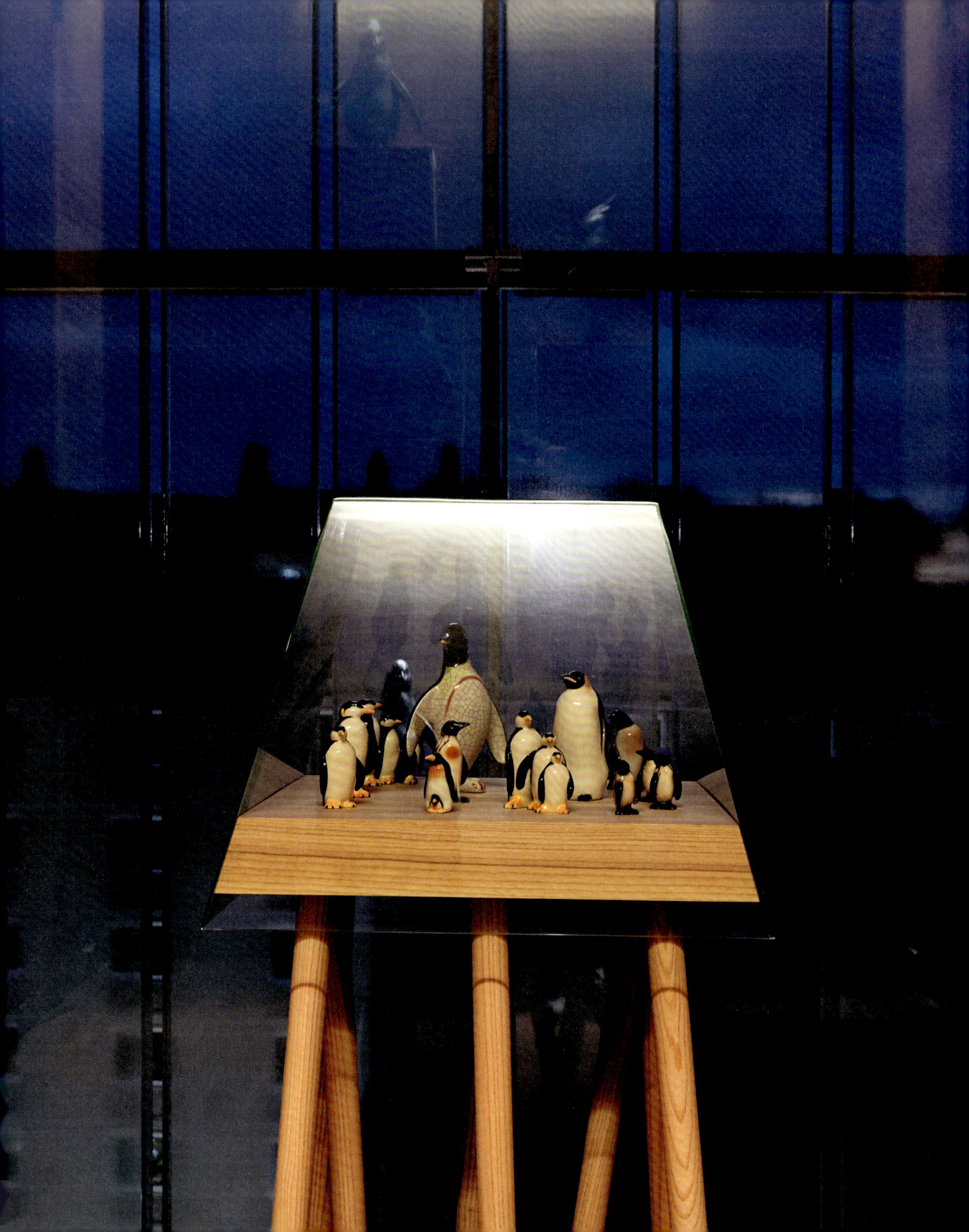

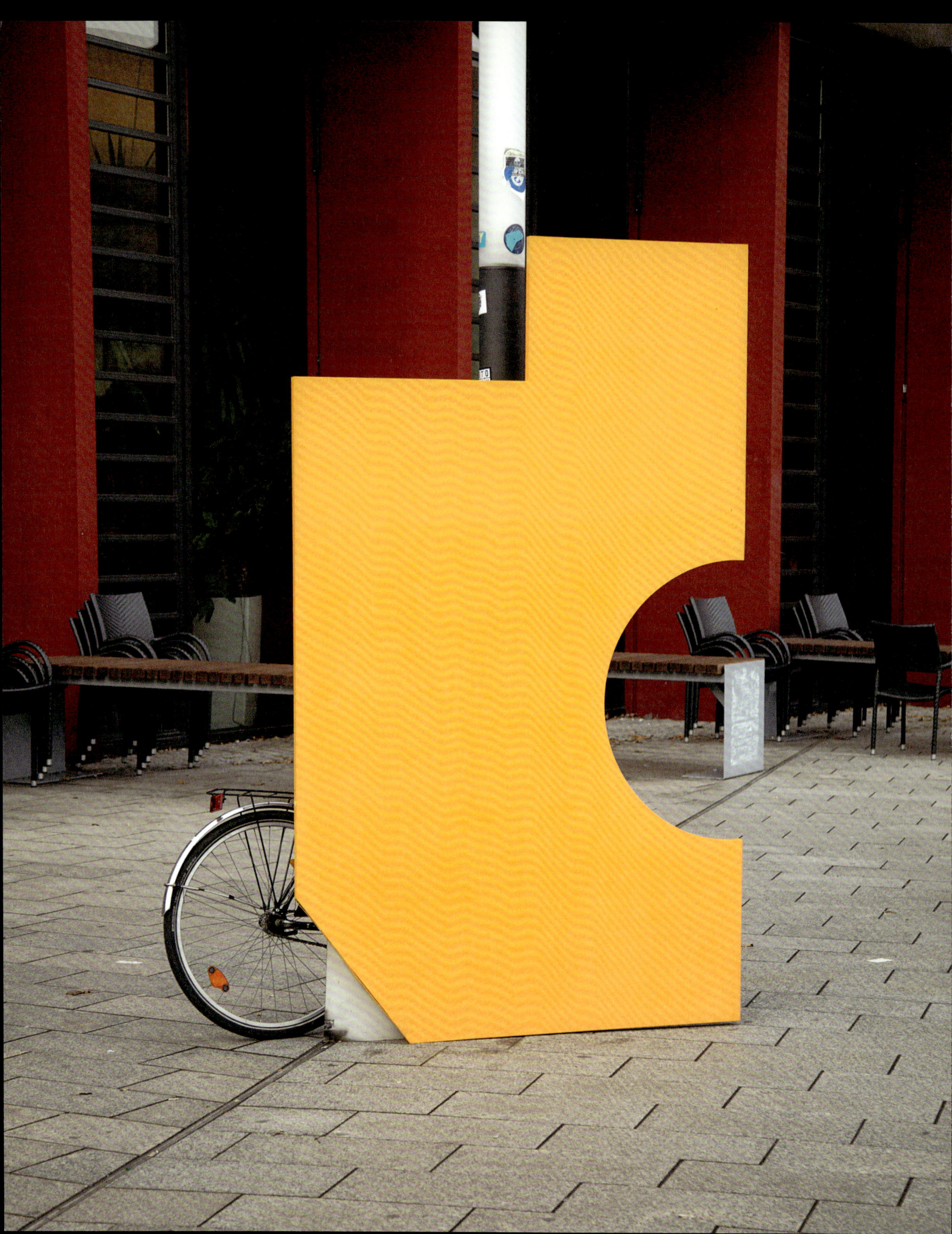

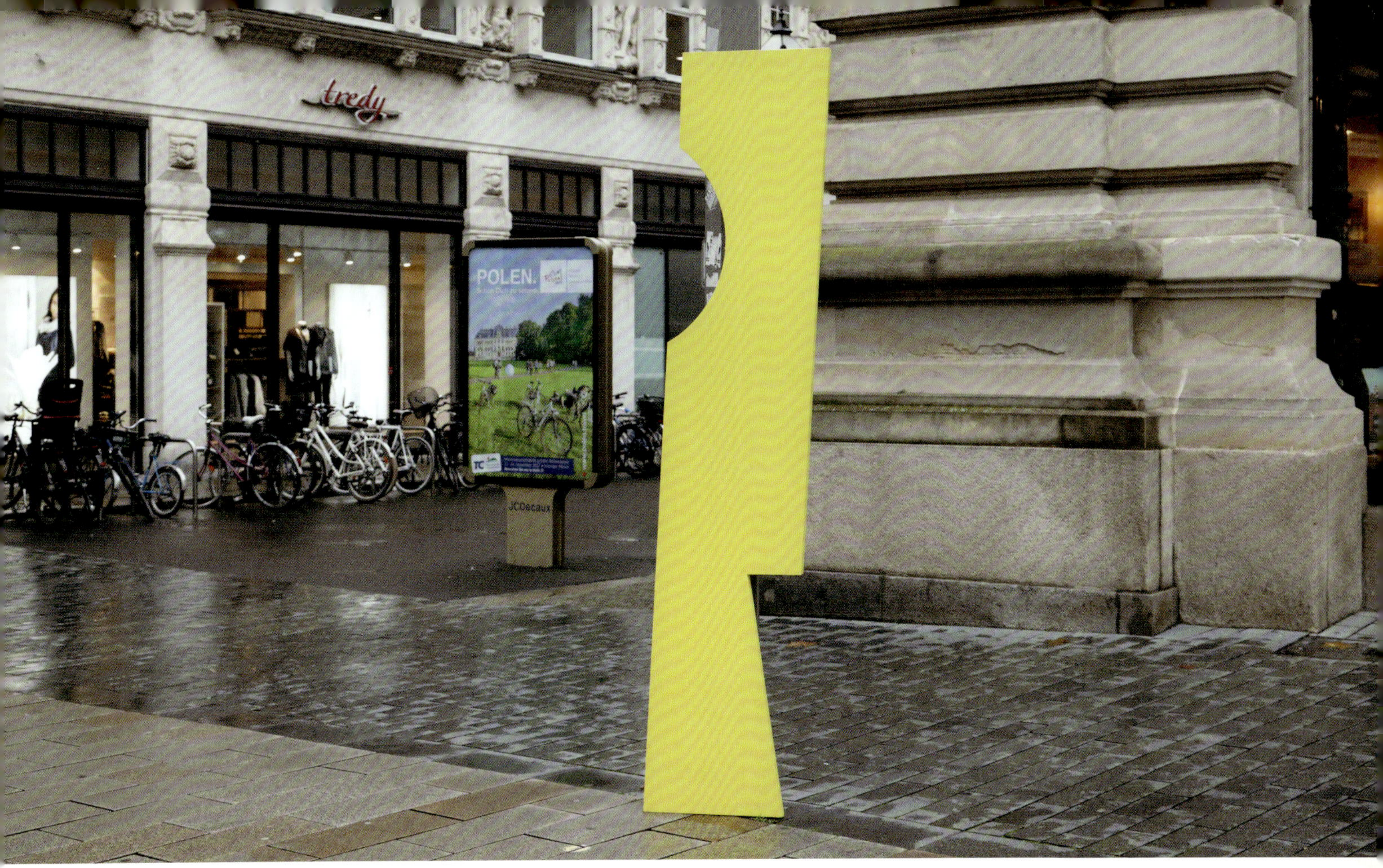
tredy
POLEN.
JCDecaux

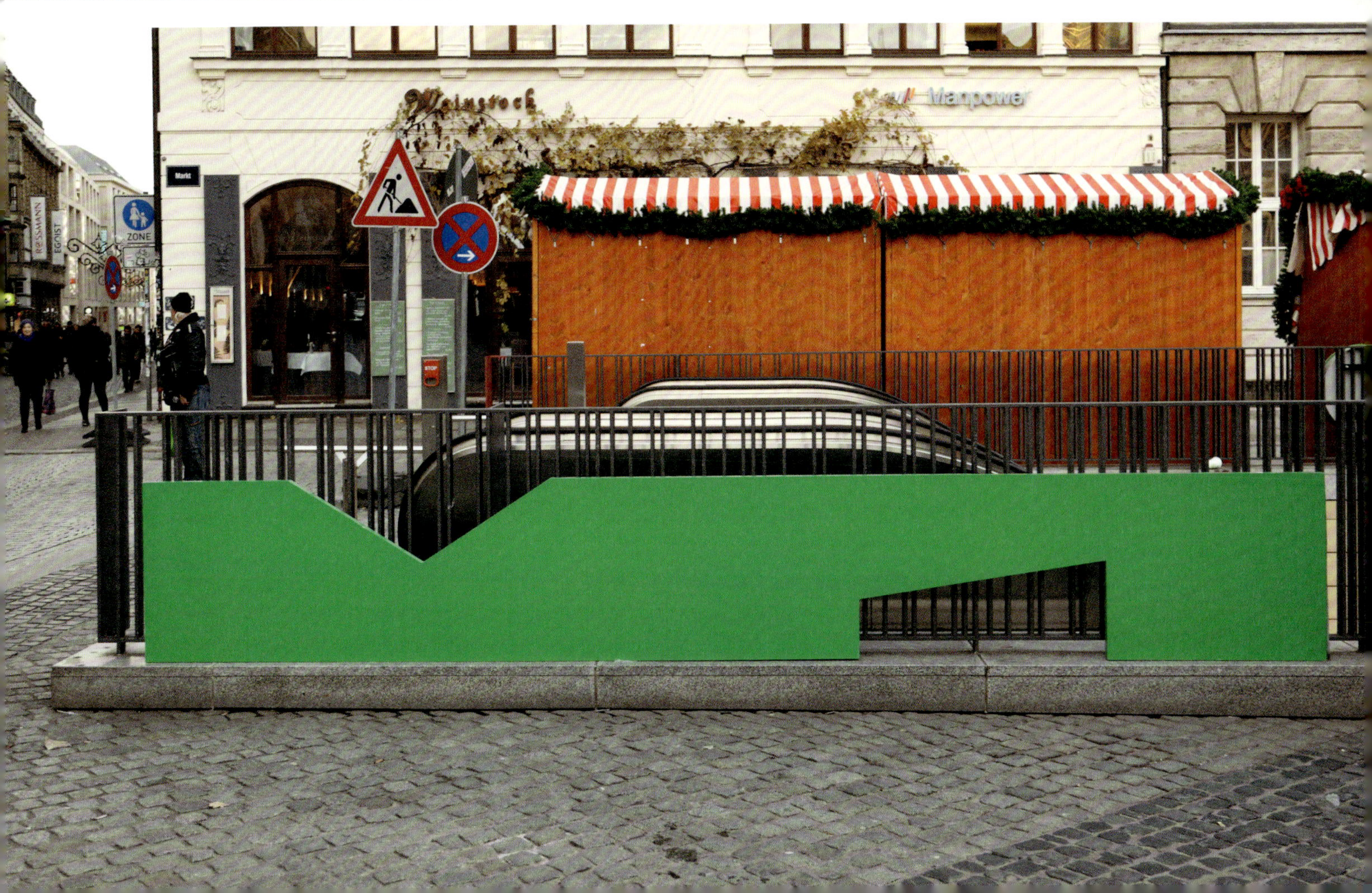
Manpower
ZONE

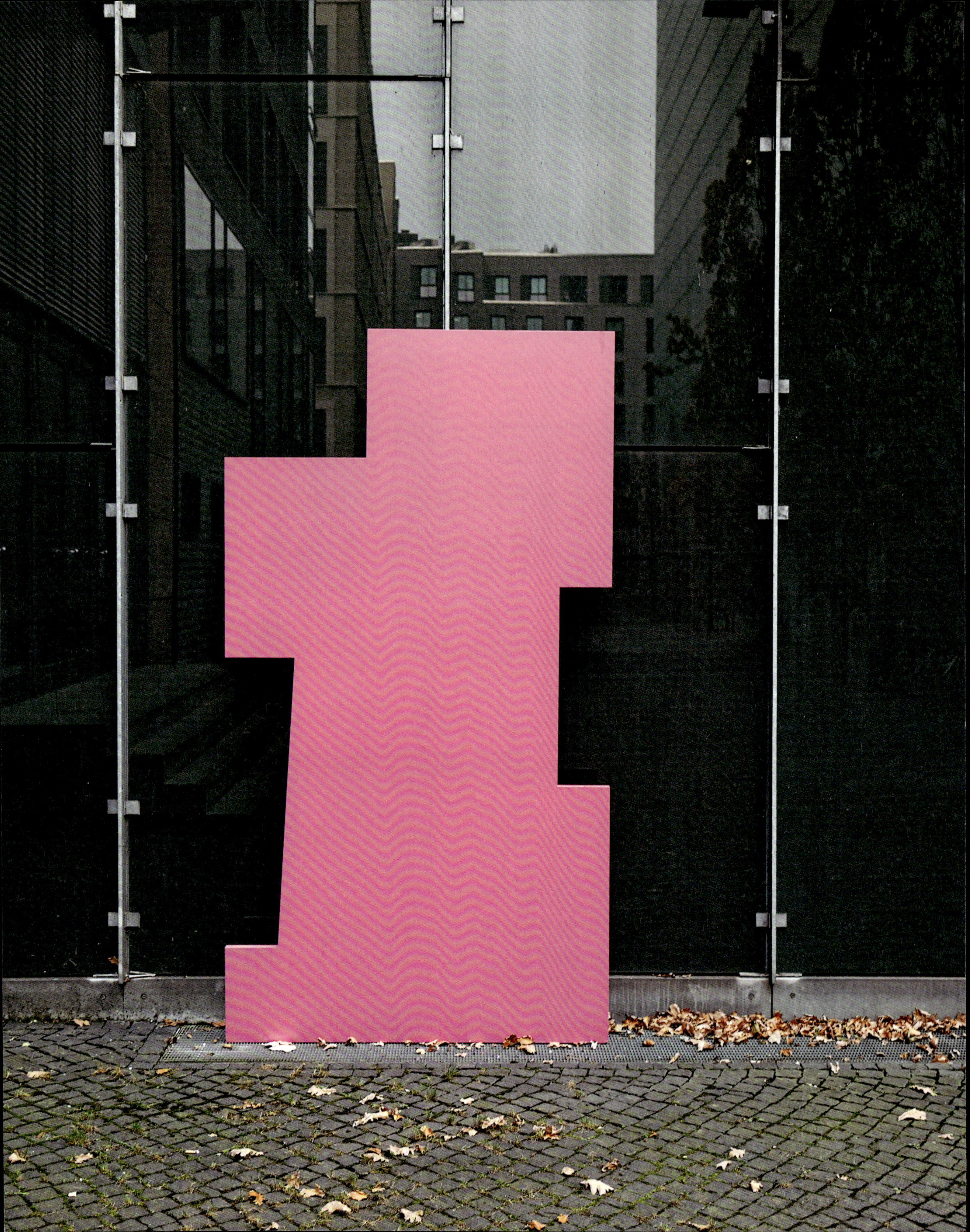

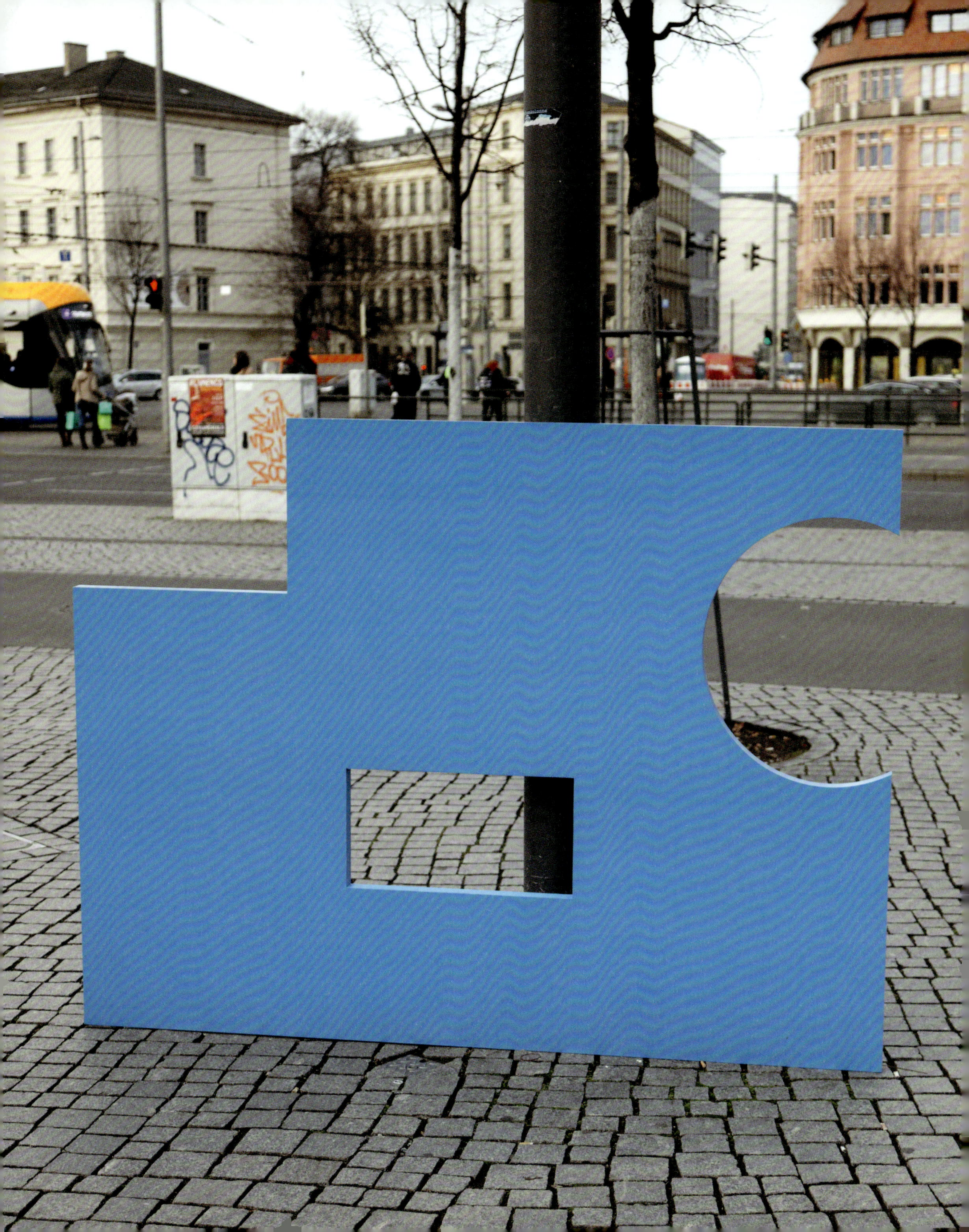

Mona Hatoum
Zustände
der Unsicherheit

Mona Hatoum
States
of Insecurity

Kelly Baum

1 Vgl. Butler 2004, 22; vgl. auch Butler 2005.

2 Vgl. Butler 2004, xii.

Es ist ein Gemeinplatz, dass Mona Hatoums Kunst von Politik handelt. Zu den politischen Themen, mit denen sie sich befasst, zählen Krieg, Exil, Verlust, Vorurteile und Überwachung. Doch schalten sich ihre Videos, Plastiken, Performances und Installationen nicht lediglich in kritische Debatten ein. Sie sprechen auch eine politische Sprache, sind politisch durch und durch. Dabei verdankt sich ein Großteil der politischen Wertigkeit ihrer Arbeit themenfremden Aspekten wie Form, Struktur, Materialität und Art der Ansprache. In ihrem entschiedenen Bestreben, politisch zu kommunizieren, verlässt sich die Künstlerin vor allem auf drei Arbeitsinstrumente: Affekt, Prekarität und Verkörperung. Für Hatoum haben diese sowohl funktionellen als auch strategischen Wert.

Prekarität, im Englischen ›precarity‹, gehört zu Hatoums ältesten Themen. Das Wort ›precarity‹ tritt seit der Jahrtausendwende dank der Arbeiten einiger maßgeblicher Autoren, vor allem dank Judith Butler, im Englischen immer häufiger auf. Ins *Oxford English Dictionary* allerdings wurde es noch nicht aufgenommen. Die nächstverwandte Form ist dort ›precarious‹ – ›prekär‹ –, abgeleitet von einem Terminus des klassischen Latein, der ›von fremder Gabe abhängig‹ bedeutet, insbesondere im Hinblick auf Pacht- und Eigentumsrechte. Erst im 17. und 18. Jahrhundert erhielt ›precarious‹ seinen zeitgemäßen Sinngehalt.

Heute ist damit ein Zustand der Unsicherheit, Instabilität und Verletzlichkeit konnotiert. Wer sich im Zustand der Prekarität befindet, ist einer andauernden Gefahr ausgesetzt und dem Willen anderer unterworfen. Judith Butler behandelt das Thema eloquent und prägnant in ihrem 2004 erschienenen Buch *Precarious Life: The Powers of Mourning and Violence*. Zwar sei Prekarität ungleich verteilt, seien Menschen bestimmter Abstammung, bestimmter Ethnien, Nationalitäten und Geschlechtsidentitäten stärker gefährdet als andere, doch sei die Erfahrung von Prekarität eine universelle. Zudem werde die Gewalt, für die wir anfällig sind, von anderen Menschen ausgeübt; jedem wohne das Potenzial inne, Grausamkeiten zu begehen und wiederum zu erdulden. Dieses Problem ist grundlegend für Butlers Verständnis von Subjektivität und bildet die Basis ihres Ethik- und Verantwortungsbegriffs. Nach Butler konstituieren wir uns *aus unseren* und *mittels unserer* Beziehungen zu unseren Mitmenschen, und insofern diese Beziehungen uns sowohl schützen als auch gefährden, stellen sie die Grundlage unserer Verantwortlichkeit gegenüber anderen dar.[1] Weil wir, mit anderen Worten, voneinander abhängig sind, sind wir einander auch verpflichtet.[2] Hatoum hat Butler nie zitiert, und ob sie mit ihren Schriften vertraut ist, ist nicht bekannt; aber auch, wenn das nicht der Fall sein sollte, deren allgemeine

106

It is an article of faith that Mona Hatoum's work speaks on politics. War, exile, deprivation, prejudice, surveillance: these are some of the political subjects that Hatoum addresses. Yet her videos, sculptures, performances, and installations do more than simply intervene in critical debates. They also speak politically. Everything about them is politically inflected. Indeed, much of the political valence of Hatoum's work derives from extra-thematic characteristics such as form, structure, material, and mode of address. In her determination to communicate politically, the artist relies on three tools above all: affect, precarity, and embodiment. For Hatoum, these have operative as well as strategic value.

Precarity is one of Hatoum's most long-standing subjects. Since the turn of the millennium, the word 'precarity' has appeared in the English language with increasing frequency, thanks to the writing of a few key authors, particularly Judith Butler. For all that, 'precarity' does not yet appear in the Oxford English Dictionary. The closest relation is 'precarious,' which derives from a classical Latin term meaning 'depending on the favor of another,' especially with regard to tenancy and property rights. It was not until the seventeenth and eighteenth centuries that 'precarious' acquired its modern meaning. Today it connotes a condition of insecurity, instability, or vulnerability. The

precarious person is chronically exposed to risk and subject to the will of others. In her 2004 book, *Precarious Life. The Powers of Mourning and Violence,* Butler speaks eloquently and incisively of precarity. Although it is unevenly distributed, with people of specific races, ethnicities, nationalities, and genders more imperiled by it than others, precarity is an experience we all share. Moreover, because the violence to which we are susceptible is inflicted by other human beings, every person has the potential to perpetrate and receive cruelty in turn. This conundrum is fundamental to Butler's conception of subjectivity, and it sets the stage for her account of ethics and responsibility. We are constituted, Butler argues, of and by our relations with other human beings, and insofar as these relations both protect and endanger us, they form the basis of our ethical accountability to others.[1] Because we are dependent on one another, in other words, so too are we beholden to one another.[2] Hatoum has never cited Butler, and it is unclear if she is familiar with her writing, but even if she is not, the artist still takes the general thrust of Butler's charge seriously. Throughout her work, Hatoum dramatizes the full spectrum of human relations, choreographing moments of intimacy and oppression, compassion and brutality, all in an effort to affirm our essential interdependence. In the process, she answers Butler's call to acknowledge – and even

1 Butler 2004, 22; see too Butler 2005.

2 Butler 2004, xii.

3   Die Unruhen von 1985
folgten auf die unrechtmäßige
Erschießung einer schwarzen
Frau, deren Sohn von der Poli-
zei gesucht wurde. Hatoum
schrieb über diese Arbeit: »The
body made vulnerable, walking barefoot with the boots of
the state following closely
behind.« (Hatoum 1987, 29.)

4   »Her own physical
involvement in these performances entailed an element of
endurance and risk. Exhaustion
was real not feigned, the struggle often a direct and physical
one.« (Ebd., 27.)

5   Vgl. den unbetitelten
Handzettel, den Hatoum
1983 in The Western Front in
Vancouver, Kanada, verteilt
hat; abgedruckt in Anastas /
Brenson 2006, 106.

Stoßrichtung nimmt die Künstlerin doch ernst. Hatoum bearbeitet in ihrem Œuvre das gesamte Spektrum menschlicher Beziehungen, choreografiert Augenblicke der Intimität und der Unterdrückung, des Mitleids und der Brutalität, immer bemüht, unsere unausweichliche wechselseitige Abhängigkeit zu demonstrieren. Dabei folgt sie Butlers Aufruf, das Leiden der Anderen anzuerkennen, und, wichtiger noch, Verantwortung dafür zu übernehmen, indem sie Prekarität repräsentiert, performativ umsetzt und sogar herbeiführt.

In den 1980er Jahren war es ihr eigener Körper, den Hatoum, oft im Bestreben, die prekären sozialen, politischen, wirtschaftlichen und physischen Lebensbedingungen anderer vor Augen zu führen, der Prekarität aussetzte. Das ist zum Beispiel in der Performance *Roadworks* (1985) der Fall, in der sie barfuß, mit einem Paar Dr. Martens um die Fußgelenke gebunden, durch die Straßen von Brixton ging. —→ **107** Sowohl der Schauplatz als auch der Zeitpunkt sind von Bedeutung: Hatoums Performance fand in einem überwiegend afrokaribischen Viertel im Londoner Süden statt, dessen Bewohner sich kurz zuvor gegen institutionalisierten Rassismus und polizeiliche Gewalt erhoben hatten. Das Publikum von *Roadworks* bezeugte also, wie Hatoum – ganz wörtlich, aber auch im politischen Sinne – von Symbolen verfolgt wurde, die sowohl auf britische Skinheads als auch auf die Metropolitan Police verwiesen.[3]

In weiteren, in England und Kanada durchgeführten Performances erhöhte Hatoum den Einsatz, indem sie ihr physisches und psychisches Wohl noch größerer Gefahr aussetzte. Diese Arbeiten »waren mit Belastung und Wagnis verbunden. Die Erschöpfung war real, nicht gespielt, der Kampf häufig unmittelbar und physisch«.[4] Das gilt etwa für die siebenstündige Performance *Under Siege*, die am 31. Mai 1982, eine Woche vor dem Einmarsch der israelischen Armee in den Libanon und der Belagerung Beiruts, in London aufgeführt und später in die Videoarbeit *Changing Parts* (1984) integriert wurde. —→ **108 + 126** Hatoum schloss sich in einer transparenten Plastikkonstruktion ein, wobei sie wieder und wieder versuchte, sich aus einer glitschigen Masse aus Schlamm zu erheben. Mehrere Lautsprecher erfüllten den Raum während der gesamten Performance mit den Klängen von Revolutionsliedern, Nachrichten und Deklarationen, die auf Arabisch, Englisch und Französisch vorgetragen wurden.[5] Die Performances und Videoarbeiten *The Negotiating Table* und *So much I want to say* (beide 1983), beide ein Jahr nach dem Massaker im Beiruter Flüchtlingslager von Schatila entstanden, fallen in dieselbe Kategorie. —→ **32** In der ersten Arbeit lag die Künstlerin mit blutüberströmtem, von Innereien

107

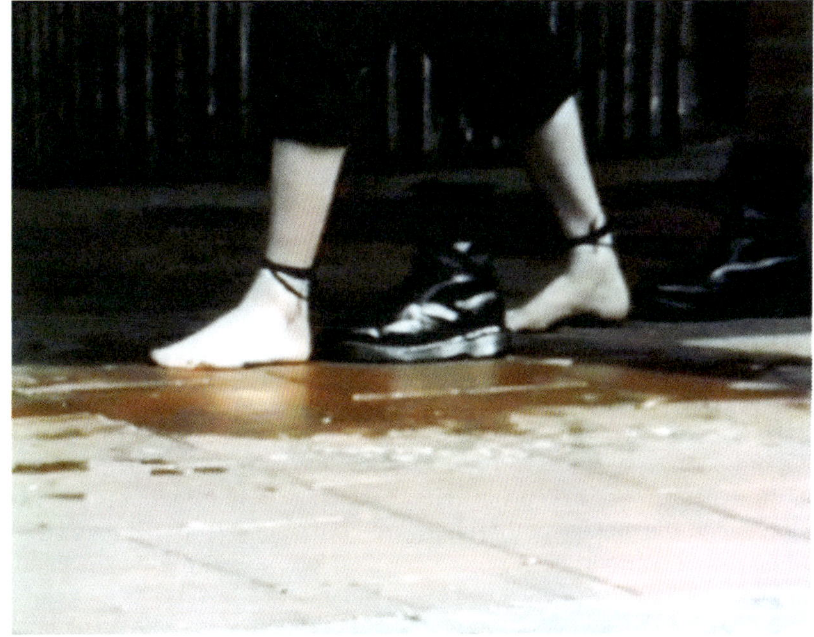

Mona Hatoum
Roadworks, 1985
Dokumentation der
Performance / documentation
of performance in Brixton,
London

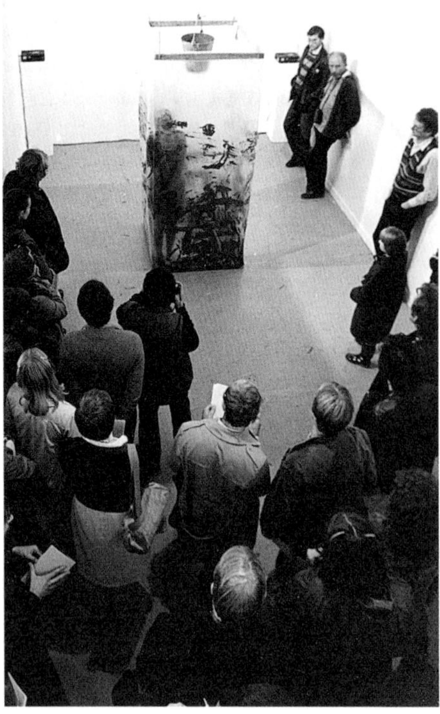

108

more importantly, to take responsibility for – the suffering of others. Hatoum does so by representing, performing, and even precipitating precarity.

In the 1980s, it was her own body that Hatoum placed in precarious circumstances, often in an effort to demonstrate the precarious social, political, economic, and physical circumstances in which others lived. Such is the case with *Roadworks* (1985), in which Hatoum walked barefoot through the streets of Brixton, England, with a pair of Dr. Martens tied to her ankles. ⟶ **107** The setting and the year are both important: Hatoum's performance took place in a predominantly Afro-Caribbean neighborhood in South London, whose residents had recently rebelled against institutionalized racism and police violence. Viewers of *Roadworks,* therefore, would have witnessed Hatoum being trailed, literally and politically, by symbols of both the British skinheads and the Metropolitan Police.[3]

In other performances staged in England and Canada, Hatoum increased the stakes, putting her physical and emotional well-being in even greater peril. As the artist stated, such works 'entailed an element of endurance and risk. Exhaustion was real not feigned, the struggle often a direct and physical one.'[4] Such is true of the seven-hour event *Under Siege*, realized in London on May 31, 1982, one week before the invasion of Lebanon and the siege of Beirut, and

later incorporated into *Changing Parts* (1984). ⟶ **108** + **126** In *Under Siege,* Hatoum confined herself inside a structure made of transparent plastic, trying repeatedly to raise herself up from a slippery mass of mud. Throughout the performance, multiple sets of speakers saturated the space with the sounds of revolutionary songs, news reports, and declarations read in Arabic, English, and French.[5] *The Negotiating Table* and *So much I want to say* (both 1983), both of which were made a year after the massacre in Beirut's Chatila refugee camp, also fall into this category. In the case of the former, the artist lay confined inside layers of cellophane, her body covered in blood and offal. In the latter, a video, she struggles to repeat the words of the title while a pair of hands tries to gag her mouth. Finally, in 1984, Hatoum performed *Them and Us … and Other Divisions* in Bracknell, England. ⟶ **109** As people sat smoking and drinking, the artist dragged herself along a 300-foot terrace wearing a hood and a pair of black overalls. Towards the end of her ordeal, which left her filthy and exhausted, Hatoum dipped a brush into a bucket of red paint and began scrubbing the stone steps with it. Her final gesture involved setting fire to a collection of newspapers. As they disintegrated, they revealed racist graffiti. Each of these works ultimately reduces the body to 'a human form denuded of status, property, rank or role.'[6]

3 The unrest in 1985 followed the wrongful shooting of a black woman whose son was sought by the police. Of this work Hatoum has written, 'The body made vulnerable, walking barefoot with the boots of the state following closely behind.' (Hatoum 1987, 29.)

4 Hatoum 1987, 27.

5 See the untitled leaflet from 1983 that Hatoum distributed at The Western Front in Vancouver, Canada; reproduced in Anastas / Brenson 2006, 106.

6 Hatoum 1987, 29.

6 »The body covered in clay, reducing the figure to a human form denuded of status, property, rank or role.« (Hatoum 1987, 29.)

7 In den späten 1980er Jahren gehörte Hatoum zum Beratungsausschuss von *Third Text*. Ebenso wie die feministische Theorie im Großbritannien der 1980er Jahre ist dieser Kontext von Bedeutung, will man Hatoums künstlerischen Werdegang verstehen. Vgl. D'Souza 2006, 109–111.

8 Hatoum 1987, 26.

9 »As a Palestinian woman this work was my first attempt at making a statement about a persistent struggle to survive in a continuous state of siege. Members of the audience, according to their own background, spoke of various powerful images of oppression: the Irish Hunger strikes, prisoners in solitary confinement, Bantustans […]« (Mona Hatoum, unbetitelter Handzettel in Anastas / Brenson 2006, 106; vgl. auch Archer 2016, 120.

bedecktem Körper da, eingewickelt in Schichten aus Polyäthylenfolie. In letzterer mühte sie sich damit ab, den Wortlaut des Werktitels zu wiederholen, während ein Händepaar versuchte, sie am Sprechen zu hindern. 1984 schließlich führte Hatoum im englischen Bracknell die Performance *Them and Us … and Other Divisions* auf. ⟶ **109** Vor trinkend und rauchend dasitzenden Leuten schleppte sie sich, bekleidet mit Kapuze und schwarzem Overall, über eine gut neunzig Meter lange Terrasse. Gegen Ende ihres Leidensweges tauchte Hatoum, schmutzig und erschöpft, eine Bürste in einen Eimer roter Farbe und machte sich daran, die Steinstufen zu schrubben. In der abschließenden Szene zündete sie eine Wand aus Zeitungspapier an. Als die Zeitungen zu Asche zerfielen, wurden darunter rassistische Graffiti sichtbar. All diese Arbeiten reduzieren den Körper letztlich auf »eine menschliche Form, die ihres Status, ihres Eigentums, ihres Rangs oder ihrer Rolle beraubt wurde«.[6]

Viele der besprochenen frühen Performances wurden fotografisch in einem Essay abgebildet, den Mona Hatoum 1987 in *Third Text*, einer bedeutenden Plattform für die Verbreitung globaler Kunst und postkolonialer Theorie, veröffentlicht hat.[7] Darin bezieht die Künstlerin »politisch Stellung« und bekundet auf der Grundlage einer »gemeinsamen Geschichte kolonialer Beherrschung« Solidarität mit Afrikanern und Mitgliedern der afrikanischen Diaspora.[8] Dadurch fühlt sie sich nicht nur in deren lange Geschichte der Diskriminierung und Entmündigung ein, sie verschmilzt auch ihren Status als 1952 im Beiruter Exil geborene und 1987 im Londoner Exil lebende Palästinenserin mit dem ganz ähnlichen Status jener Afrikaner. Und schließlich entwirft sie eine Identität, die beispielhaft für alle Entorteten und Marginalisierten steht und diese miteinschließt. Hatoums Stellungnahme in *Third Text* hat einen stark performativen Charakter. Der diskursive Akt findet seine logische Entsprechung in Arbeiten wie *Roadworks*, die Hatoums Identifikation mit afrokaribischen Einwanderern im wörtlichen Sinne verkörpern. Auch in *Under Siege*, der ersten Arbeit, in der Hatoum wirksam ihre weibliche palästinensische Identität einsetzte und den Überlebenskampf »im dauerhaften Belagerungszustand« thematisierte, spielt dies eine Rolle. Entscheidend ist, dass diese Arbeit bei Hatoums Publikum auch andere Fälle von Unterdrückung und Widerstand evozierte, darunter »die Irischen Hungerstreiks, Gefangene in Einzelhaft, die Bantustans«.[9] In diesem Sinne könnte man bei Hatoums Performances von Choreografien eines komplexes Tauschsystems sprechen, in dem zu gleichen Teilen Projektion, Identifikation und Mitgefühl zirkulieren. Ein solches System gewährleistet eine stellvertretende, einfühlende Übertragung des Selbst

109

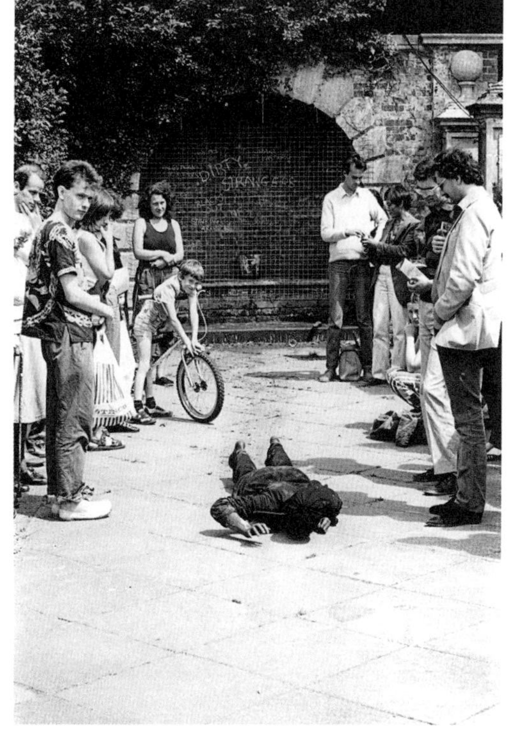

Mona Hatoum
Them and Us … and Other Divisions, 1984
Live-Performance aufgeführt im / live action performed at South Hill Park Arts Centre, Bracknell, Berkshire

auf den Anderen, eine Übertragung, die den Grund-
stein für eine Koalition mit breiter Basis legt, die sich
dem Recht und der Gerechtigkeit verpflichtet. Wie
Butler schreibt: In der Tatsache, dass wir allesamt »der
Gewalt ausgesetzt« sind, sowie in »unserer Verwund-
barkeit durch einen Verlust« finden wir eine »Grundlage für Gemeinschaft«.[10] Hatoums Werk scheint diese These zu bestätigen.

Im Verlauf ihrer Karriere in den 1990er Jahren
nahm Hatoum die eigene physische Präsenz in ihren
Arbeiten immer weiter zurück, bis ihr Körper schließlich ganz daraus verschwand. Doch sollte das Thema
Körper – bis in die Gegenwart – zentral bleiben. Anstatt explizit dargestellt zu werden oder eindeutig auf
die Künstlerin selbst zu verweisen, wird der Körper
jetzt aber lediglich impliziert. Hatoum beginnt nun,
aktiv um den Körper des Betrachters zu werben, sich
an diesen als verkörperten Stellvertreter zu wenden,
indem sie Plastiken und Installationen schafft, die einen kinästhetischen Aufmerksamkeitsmodus aktivieren, der alle Sinne anspricht, vor allem den Sehsinn,
den Tast- und den Hörsinn. In einem Interview mit
Janine Antoni erklärte sie 1998: »Mit den Installationen
wollte ich den Betrachter in eine phänomenologische
Situation verwickeln, in der Erfahrung physischer und
direkter wird. Ich wollte, dass der Betrachter über den
visuellen Aspekt der Arbeit physisch, sinnlich und

möglicherweise sogar emotional einbezogen wird.«[11]
Die Objekte und Räume, die Hatoum in der Folge schuf,
sind mithin vielleicht weniger didaktisch, nicht jedoch
weniger streitbar. Hatoum verlagert in diesen plasti-
schen Arbeiten die Bürde der Prekarität von sich selbst
auf den Betrachter. Anstatt ihre Verletzlichkeit vorzu-
führen oder auf die Verletzlichkeit anderer zu verweisen, setzt Hatoum das Publikum selbst einer poten-
ziellen Gefahr aus und betont damit dessen eigene
Anfälligkeit für Prekarität.

Als Beispiel kann Hatoums Installation *The
Light at the End* von 1989 dienen. ⟶ **110** Nachdem
sie einen abgedunkelten Raum betreten haben, werden die Besucher auf sechs orangefarbene Stäbe in
einem Metallrahmen aufmerksam. Sie nehmen das
Licht und die Wärme wahr, die davon ausgehen, und
merken bald, dass, was sie zunächst für einfache Ver-
strebungen hielten, eigentlich elektrische Heizstäbe
sind, deren Berührung ernsthafte Verletzungen ver-
ursachen würde. Die Skulpturen *Paravent* und *Daybed*
(beide 2008) operieren ähnlich. ⟶ **112 + 170** Es handelt sich um vergrößerte Versionen zweier unterschiedlicher Küchenreiben. Hatoum verwandelt diese
Haushaltsgegenstände im einen Fall in einen Wand-
schirm, im anderen in ein Bett. Während die ursprünglichen Geräte für den Handgebrauch vorgesehen waren, wenden sich die Skulpturen an unsere Körper. Sie

110

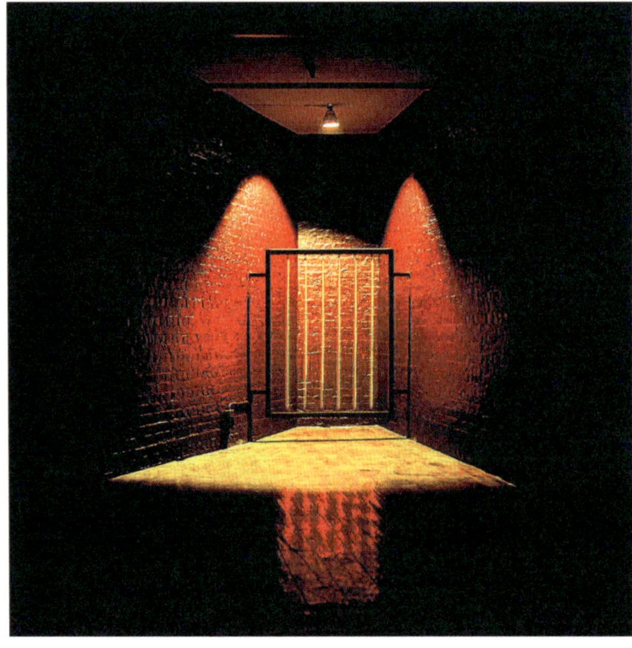

Mona Hatoum
The Light at the End, 1989
Installationsansicht /
installation view,
The Showroom, London

12 Edward Saids prägnante Ausführungen zu diesen Arbeiten und zur Rolle des ›Häuslichen‹ in Hatoums Werk im Allgemeinen finden sich in Said 2000.

laden uns ein, uns zu nähern, hinter ihnen zu stehen, uns auf sie zu legen. Doch ginge dies auf Kosten unserer körperlichen Unversehrtheit, eignet Hatoums anziehenden Objekten doch zugleich eine recht unheilvolle Seite. Beide Konstruktionen bestehen aus unerbittlichem Stahl und sind von Löchern durchstoßen, deren scharfe Kanten exponierte Körperpartien zu verletzen drohen. In *Impenetrable* (2009), einem von der Decke hängenden, aus Stacheldraht bestehenden Kubus, wird auf ganz ähnliche Weise der Schein gegen das Sein ausgespielt. ⟶ **113**+**164**

Im Spannungsfeld zwischen Einladen und Einschüchtern bewegen sich auch die Arbeiten *Doormat* (1996) ⟶ **114** und *Home* (1999). Bei *Doormat* handelt es sich um einen kleinen Vorleger, der aus Edelstahl und vernickelten Nadelstiften besteht, die das Wort ›Welcome‹ formen, bei *Home* um die drahtumzäunte Installation einer Ansammlung von Küchenutensilien und Wohnmöbeln, die allesamt unter Strom stehen. Der Strom, der durch diese Gegenstände fließt, ist hör- und spürbar.[12] Man denke auch an Hatoums irritierende Plastik *Incommunicado* (1993), im Falle deren die Künstlerin ein Kinderbett – eine Katalogbestellung – aus Stahlteilen montiert hat, wobei sie den stabilen Lattenrost, der eigentlich dafür vorgesehen ist, eine weiche Matratze und darauf einen verletzlichen Säugling zu tragen, durch messerscharfen dünnen Draht ersetzte. Ihrer ursprünglichen Bestimmungen, Assoziationspotenziale und Funktionen entledigt, bereiten die von Hatoum zweckentfremdeten Alltagsgegenstände allesamt Schmerzen statt Behagen.

Entscheidend ist, dass Hatoum sich unsere Vertrautheit mit den zitierten Formen und deren Assoziationskontexte – Trost, Privatsphäre, Häuslichkeit – zunutze macht, um uns in einem trügerischen Zustand der Sicherheit zu wiegen. Denn es sind gerade unsere Gewissheiten, seien es körperliche, kognitive, subjektive oder politische, auf deren Erschütterung die Künstlerin abzielt. *Light Sentence* (1992) entzieht den Betrachtern auf weniger unmittelbare, aber nicht weniger eindringliche Art und Weise den Boden. ⟶ **114** Hatoum schuf hier eine dreiseitige Einfriedung, indem sie verschließbare Gitterboxen übereinanderstapelte. An einem langen Kabel baumelt eine Glühbirne; während sie sich hin und her bewegt, manchmal in sanften Schwüngen, erzeugt sie Schatten an der Wand und dramatisiert diese zugleich, wodurch die Sinnestäuschung einer Gleichgewichtsstörung hervorgerufen wird. Der Werktitel, der sich auf das Licht (›light‹) der Glühbirne beziehen lässt und gleichzeitig wortspielerisch eine lebenslange Haftstrafe (›life sentence‹) heraufbeschwört, verortet dieses Schwindelgefühl eindeutig im Bereich des Eingesperrtseins; wie die verwandte Arbeit *Quarters* (2017) evoziert er Gefängnisse,

111

Many of the early performances discussed above were reproduced in a 1987 essay that Hatoum published in *Third Text*, an important venue for the dissemination of global art and postcolonial theory.[7] Here the artist takes a 'political stance' and, based on a 'shared history of colonial domination,' declares her solidarity with Africans and members of the African diaspora.[8] In so doing, Hatoum not only empathizes with their long history of discrimination and disenfranchisement, she also elides her position as a Palestinian woman who was born in exile in Beirut in 1952 and who was living, in 1987, in exile in London with their own, very similar position. Ultimately, she forges an identity that is inclusive of – and exemplary of – all dislocated, marginalized subjects. Hatoum's assertion in *Third Text* is highly performative. This discursive operation has its corollary in pieces such as *Roadworks*, where the artist literally embodies her identification with Afro-Caribbean immigrants. It is also a factor in *Under Siege*, the first work to leverage Hatoum's identity as a Palestinian woman and to comment on the struggle for survival 'in a continuous state of siege.' Importantly, the work evoked for Hatoum's viewers other instances of oppression and resistance, including 'the Irish Hunger strikes, prisoners in solitary confinement, Bantustans.'[9] With this in mind, we might say that Hatoum choreographs in her performances a complex system of exchange involving equal parts projection, identification, and compassion. Such a system generates a vicarious, empathetic relay between self and other, one that lays the foundations for a broad-based coalition dedicated to justice and equity. As Butler writes: in 'our [common] exposure to violence' and our mutual 'vulnerability to loss,' we find 'a basis for community.'[10] Hatoum's work seems to give truth to this claim.

As her career progressed over the course of the 1990s, Hatoum began to withdraw physically from her work, absenting her body in the process. Yet the body remained – and still remains – one of her most important subjects. Instead of being represented outright or identified explicitly with the artist, however, the body is now implied. It is at this moment that Hatoum starts to actively solicit the viewer's body, petitioning the viewer as an embodied agent. She does so by creating sculptures and installations that enable a kinesthetic mode of attention engaging all the senses, especially sight, touch, and hearing. As the artist explained to Janine Antoni in a 1998 interview: 'With the installation work, I wanted to implicate the viewer in a phenomenological situation in which the experience is more physical and direct. I wanted the visual aspect of the work to engage the viewer in a physical, sensual, maybe even emotional way.'[11] The objects and spaces Hatoum would go on to create

7 In the late 1980s, Hatoum was a member of the Advisory Committee of *Third Text*. This is an important context for understanding Hatoum's formation as an artist, as is British feminist theory of the 1980s. See D'Souza 2006, 109–11.

8 Hatoum 1987, 26.

9 Hatoum, untitled leaflet, in Anastas / Brenson 2006, 106; see too Archer 2016, 120.

10 Butler 2004, 17; see too ibid., 22.

11 Antoni 1998 / 2016, 141.

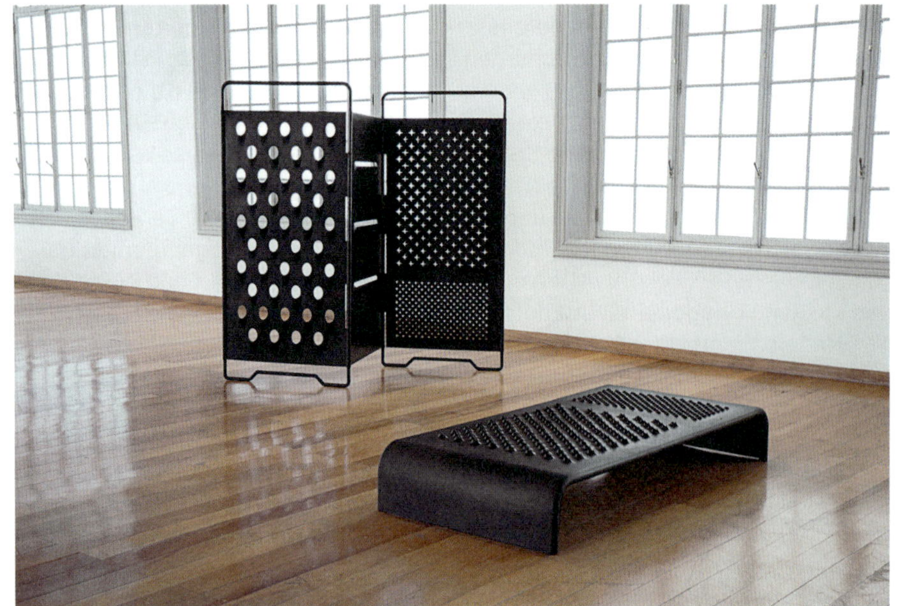

112

might be less didactic, as a result, but they are no less polemical. Indeed, it is in this three-dimensional work that Hatoum shifts the burden of precarity from herself to viewers. Instead of enacting vulnerability or referencing the vulnerability of others, Hatoum exposes the audience itself to potential harm, underscoring their own susceptibility to precarity.

Take, for instance, Hatoum's 1989 installation *The Light at the End*. ⟶ **110** Upon entering a darkened room, viewers are drawn toward six orange rods set within a metal frame. Sensing the light and heat emanating from the beams, they soon realize that what at first look like ordinary struts are in fact electric heating elements. Touching them would bring great harm to their person. The sculptures *Paravent* and *Daybed* (both 2008) operate in a similar manner. ⟶ **112**+**170** Both are inflated versions of two different types of graters. Hatoum transforms these domestic implements into a folding screen, on the one hand, and a bed, on the other. While the original tools addressed themselves to our hands, the sculptures address themselves to our bodies. They invite us to approach them, to stand behind them, to lie down on them. We do so, however, at great cost to our bodily integrity, for Hatoum's appealing objects are also quite sinister. Both structures are made of unforgiving steel and punctured with holes whose sharp edges threaten to

cut exposed patches of skin. *Impenetrable* (2009), a cube suspended from the ceiling and made with lengths of barbed wire, similarly pits appearance against reality. ⟶ **113**+**164**

The tension between hospitality and intimidation is also at play in *Doormat* (1996) ⟶ **114**, a small carpet comprised of stainless steel and nickel-plated pins that spell the word 'Welcome,' and *Home* (1999), an installation enclosed behind a wire fence that includes an assemblage of kitchen utensils and household furniture, all of them electrified. The current that courses through these implements is audible and palpable. [12] Consider also Hatoum's disconcerting sculpture *Incommunicado* (1993). In this case, the artist adapted a crib acquired ready-made through a catalogue, substituting the sturdy slats that would have supported a soft mattress and, by extension, a vulnerable infant, with razor-thin pieces of wire. Stripped of their original identities, associations, and functions, the everyday items that Hatoum repurposes are all made hurtful instead of comforting.

Importantly, the familiarity of the forms cited by Hatoum, and likewise their association with solace, privacy, and domesticity, serves to lure viewers into a false state of security, and it is precisely our state of security, whether bodily, cognitive, subjective, or political, that the artist seeks to repudiate. *Light*

12 For Edward Said's incisive statements on these pieces and on the role of 'home' in Hatoum's work overall, see Said 2000.

Lager und Ghettos. ⟶ **134** Indem sie die Betrachter in einen Zustand physischer und kognitiver Prekarität versetzt und den erschütternden, entortenden Bedingungen ausliefert, unter denen Flüchtlinge und Häftlinge leben, zwingt Hatoum sie, sich mit der Situation eines bedrängten Anderen auseinanderzusetzen – und diese einzunehmen.[13]

In ihrem nach 1990 entstandenen Œuvre stellt dieser Ansatz für Hatoum nur eine der Möglichkeiten dar, Prekarität zu aktivieren. Bloßstellung, Fehlbarkeit und Verletzlichkeit sind in Hatoums künstlerischer Praxis der letzten beiden Jahrzehnte auf vielen Ebenen am Werk. Sie erzeugt diese Zustände nicht nur beim Betrachter, etwa in *Paravent* und *Light Sentence*, sie kleidet Prekarität auch in Symbole, indem sie die Idee und das Gefühl von Verletzlichkeit über den Gebrauch von Stellvertretern von Körpern wie Kinderbetten oder architektonische Strukturen konkretisiert – so bei *Marrow* (1996), einem Krankenhausbett für Kinder, das aus weichem, nachgiebigem, orangerotem Gummi besteht. ⟶ **116** Zu einem unförmigen Haufen auf dem Boden zusammengefallen und seiner inneren Stabilität beraubt, thematisiert *Marrow* »die Zerbrechlichkeit des Körpers«, wie Antoni 1998 im Interview mit Hatoum bemerkte.[14] Ähnliches könnte von der Skulptur *Bourj* (2010) behauptet werden. ⟶ **117 + 166** Die für eine Ausstellung in Beirut geschaffene

Arbeit – in die Stadt war Hatoums Familie nach der Vertreibung aus Palästina 1948 geflohen – besteht aus gestapelten Stahlrohren, deren verbrannte, vernarbte Oberflächen an Kriegsschäden denken lassen, besonders an die des Libanesischen Bürgerkriegs, der einen großen Teil der Stadtbebauung unbewohnbar zurückließ. Als Beispiel kann auch die Installation *Remains of the Day (s version)* (2016) dienen, die aus Stühlen (für Erwachsene und Kinder), einem Tisch, einem Spielzeuglastwagen und einem Nudelholz besteht, die allesamt aus stark beschädigtem Drahtgitter gefertigt sind. ⟶ **162** Diese Gegenstände sind nicht nur instabil, sie bedrohen durch diese Instabilität überdies die Sicherheit ebenjener Körper, deren Schutz sie eigentlich gewährleisten sollten. Sogar die Arbeit *Cellules* (2012–2013**) ⟶ 174,** bestehend aus Metallstrukturen, die an Gefängnisse oder Käfige erinnern, in welche die Künstlerin blutrote Glasobjekte eingeschlossen hat, suggeriert Gewalt und Verletzlichkeit, ebenso *Hot Spot III* (2009) ⟶ **158**, eine Edelstahlplastik des Erdballs, in der mit rotem Neonlicht die sieben Kontinente konturiert werden – allesamt, so legt Hatoum nahe, Schauplätze für sozialen, wirtschaftlichen und politischen Aufruhr, der die Bewohner der Gefahr aussetzt.

Damit verwandt sind Arbeiten Hatoums, die mit unbeständigen Materialien operieren, um allge-

113

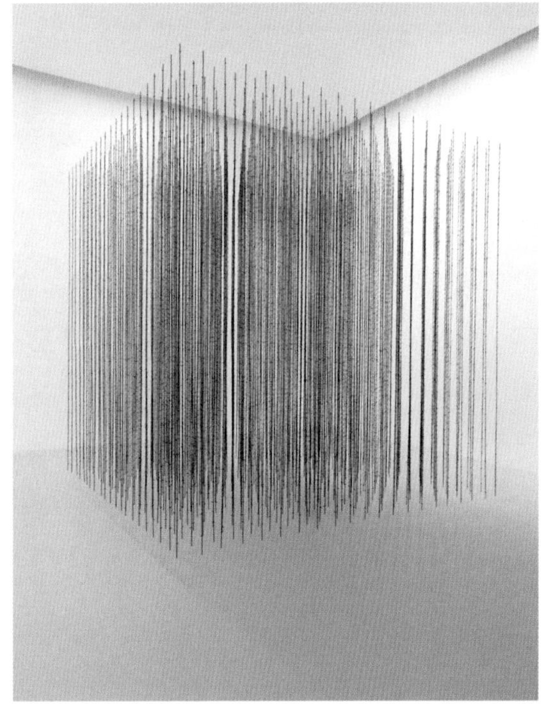

Mona Hatoum
Impenetrable, 2009
Installationsansicht /
installation view,
Mathaf: Arab Museum
of Modern Art, Doha

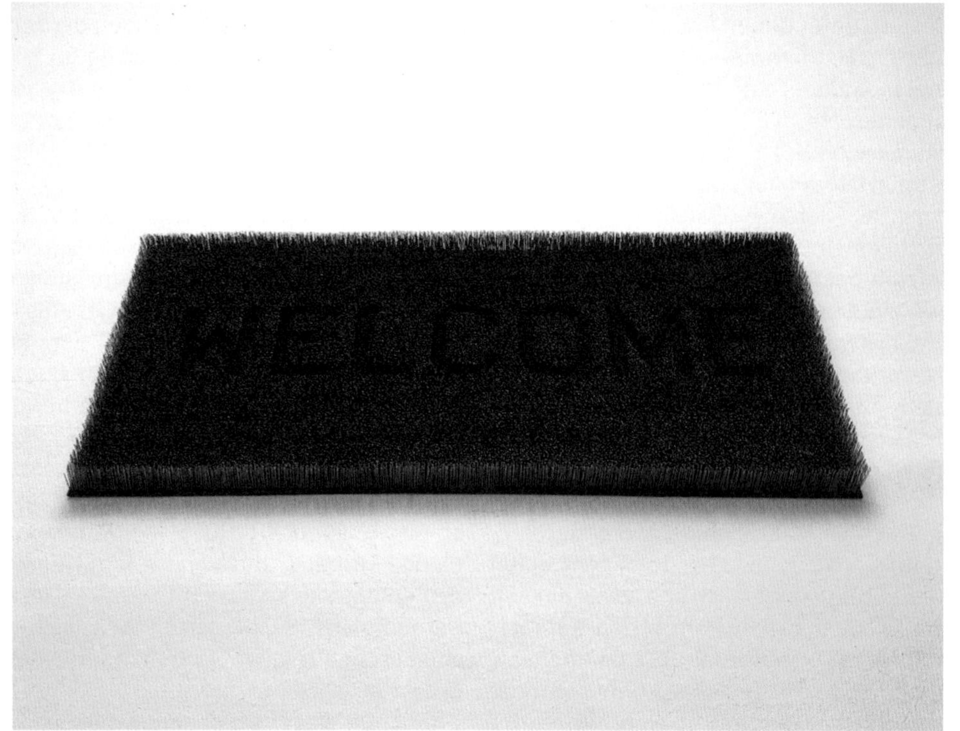

Mona Hatoum
Doormat, 1996

114

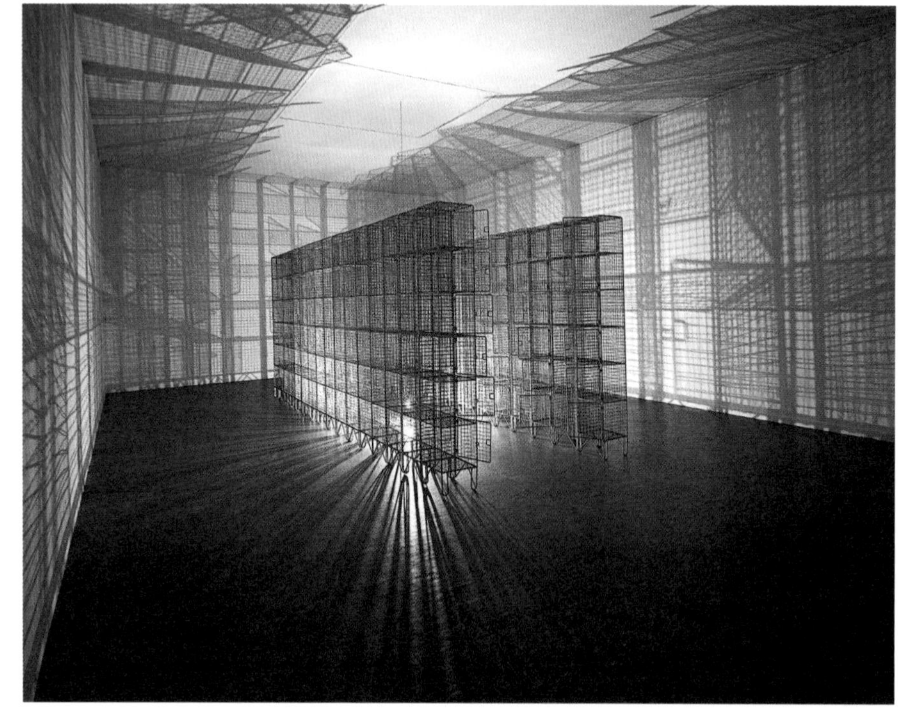

Mona Hatoum
Light Sentence, 1992
Installationsansicht /
installation view,
Centre Pompidou, Paris

meinere Zustände von Prekarität – von emotionalen bis hin zu physischen und geopolitischen – zu symbolisieren und im gleichen Zug zu konkretisieren. Von besonderer Bedeutung sind hierbei die vielen Objekte, die die Künstlerin aus menschlichem Haar gefertigt hat, darunter die Arbeit *Interior Landscape* (2008), in der sie in ein Kissen eine historische Landkarte Palästinas eingestickt hat – eine Karte, die nach 1948 hinfällig wurde. Die hier abgebildete politische Geografie, und im weiteren Sinne die durch diese verkörperte menschliche Gemeinschaft, ist infolge der israelischen Besatzung nicht stabiler oder haltgebender als eine menschliche Haarsträhne, so scheint Hatoum anzudeuten. *Recollection* (1995) besteht aus Haaren, die die Künstlerin über Jahre hinweg verloren und anschließend zu Kugeln gerollt hat. Die lose im Ausstellungsraum liegenden Haarkugeln werden von Luftströmungen umhergetragen.

Schließlich könnte man an dieser Stelle noch auf die Arbeit *Keffieh* (1993–1999) verweisen, die aus Frauenhaar gewoben wurde und ein arabisches Tuch darstellt, das traditionell von Männern getragen wird und palästinensische Selbstbestimmung symbolisiert. ⟶ **118** Lose Strähnen durchbrechen die Begrenzungen des Flechtmusters, wodurch der Eindruck von lebendigem, wachsendem Gewebe entsteht. Haar, im Grunde körperlicher Abfall, lässt viele Assoziationen

zu, darunter Abjektion und Ekel, evoziert aber auch Verfall und Degenerierung.[15]

Hatoum ist für den Gebrauch von Materialien bekannt, die ihren Werken Vergänglichkeit oder strukturelle Instabilität verleihen. Ein Beispiel hierfür ist die während eines Aufenthalts in Jerusalem geschaffene Arbeit *Present Tense* (1996). ⟶ **119** Die Installation besteht aus 2 200 Stück Nablus-Seife – ein traditionelles palästinensisches Produkt –, in welche die Künstlerin farbige Glasperlen eingedrückt hat. Zusammen bilden diese Perlen die Konturen einer Landkarte von 1993, welche die unzusammenhängenden Landparzellen dokumentiert, die entsprechend der Bedingungen der Oslo-Abkommen unter palästinensische Kontrolle gestellt werden und so die Grundlage eines künftigen palästinensischen Staates bilden sollten. Wie bei der Landkarte, die der Arbeit zugrunde liegt, so handelt es sich auch bei *Present Tense* um ein kartografisches Wunschbild, das vollständig aus Grenzen, Ghettos und Mauern besteht. Doch im Gegensatz zur harten Realität der Kontrollpunkte, die Palästinenser täglich zu bewältigen haben, ist Hatoums Grenzlinien Zeitlichkeit eingeschrieben. Kämen die Seifenstücke in Kontakt mit Wasser, löste sich das Grundmaterial der Arbeit mitsamt den dargestellten Grenzlinien auf. Mit der Erosion der Grenzen ginge die metaphorische, wenn nicht gar buchstäbliche Aufhebung

115

Sentence (1992) unsettles the ground on which viewers stand in less direct, but no less emphatic ways. ⟶ **114** Here Hatoum has constructed a three-sided enclosure by stacking mesh lockers one on top of the other. A light bulb dangles from a long cord, and as it moves up and down, swaying gently at times, it simultaneously activates and dramatizes the shadows cast on the wall, creating a sense of hallucinatory disequilibrium. The title of the work clearly frames this vertigo in terms of incarceration, evoking prisons, camps, and ghettos, as does the related work *Quarters* (2017). ⟶ **134** In precipitating physical and cognitive precarity in viewers, in putting them in the same kind of upsetting, dislocating circumstances as refugees and prisoners, Hatoum forces viewers to consider – and to inhabit – the position of a besieged other.[13]

This is only one way that Hatoum mobilizes precarity in her work after 1990. Indeed, exposure, fallibility, and vulnerability operate on many levels in her practice from the last two decades. Besides instigating it in viewers, as she does in *Paravent* and *Light Sentence*, she also symbolizes precarity, concretizing the concept and sensation of vulnerability through the use of bodily substitutes like cribs and architectural structures. This is the case in *Marrow* (1996), a children's hospital cot comprised of soft, pliable red-orange rubber. ⟶ **116** Collapsed into a disheveled

heap on the floor, bereft of its internal support, *Marrow* speaks to the 'fragility of the body,' as Antoni commented in her 1998 interview with Hatoum.[14] Something similar might be said of the sculpture *Bourj* (2010). ⟶ **117**+**166** Created for an exhibition in Beirut, the city to which Hatoum's family fled after being forced out of Palestine in 1948, *Bourj* consists of vertical stacks of steel tubing whose burnt, scarred surfaces evoke the ravages of war, especially the Lebanese Civil War, which left much of the city's buildings unfit for habitation. Another instance is *Remains of the Day (s version)* (2016), with its chairs (for both adults and children), table, toy truck and rolling pin, all of them made of ravaged wire mesh. Insofar as these items are rendered unstable, they moreover threaten the safety of the very bodies that they were originally intended to engage. ⟶ **162** Even *Cellules* (2012–13) ⟶ **174**, a set of metal structures reminiscent of prisons or cages into which the artist has inserted objects made of blood-red glass, suggests violence and vulnerability, as does *Hot Spot III* (2009) ⟶ **158**, a stainless steel sculpture of the globe that uses red neon to delineate its seven continents. All of them, Hatoum suggests, are sites of social, economic, and political upheaval that expose their inhabitants to risk.

Related are works by Hatoum that use fragile materials to simultaneously symbolize and concretize

13 See Hatoum's comments on this work in Antoni 1998 / 2016, 136.

14 Ibid., 142.

16 Butler / Spivak 2007b, 39; vgl. Butler / Spivak 2007a, 55, 66, 68.

17 Vgl. ausführlicher zu diesem Werk Mikdadi 2008, 67; zu Hatoums Bemerkungen bezüglich dieser Arbeit vgl. Archer / Brett / de Zegher 1997, 26–27.

18 Vgl. ausführlicher hierzu Baykal 2012, 62–63.

der Einschränkungen palästinensischer Freiheit und Mobilität sowie des palästinensischen Austauschs einher. In dieser Hinsicht stellt *Present Tense* einen subversiven Akt der Wunscherfüllung dar – Judith Butler nannte das »performativen Widerspruch«. Nach Butler beinhaltet ein performativer Widerspruch das Ergreifen eines Rechts, das noch nicht gewährt wurde, und die Herstellung von Gerechtigkeit, die noch nicht existiert. Er ist eine Art politischer Rede, die einen »Ansporn, ein Anstacheln, ein Einfordern« darstellt.[16] Gleichzeitig bezeugt *Present Tense* eine maßlos unterdrückerische geopolitische Realität. Schließlich sollte die Landkarte von 1993 ursprünglich die Zuteilung von Eigentum und Souveränität an Palästinenser veranlassen, erreichte letztlich aber kaum etwas, stellte sich als ebenso fehlbar und mangelhaft heraus wie Hatoums unbeständige Skulptur.[17] *Map* (1999), die Darstellung einer Weltkarte, deren Konturen von auf dem Boden liegenden Glasmurmeln gebildet werden, ist ebenso instabil. ⟶ **121** Jeder Schritt erzeugt Erschütterungen, die die Murmeln aus ihrer ursprünglichen Position lösen. Während sie sich verteilen, verzerrt sich die Karte bis zur Unkenntlichkeit. Eine ungenaue Karte ist eine dysfunktionale Karte, geeignet weder zur Darstellung noch zur Durchsetzung territorialer Integrität.[18] Hatoum verfolgt mit *Present Tense* und *Map* gleich mehrere Ziele. Einerseits thematisiert sie durch den Gebrauch instabiler, unberechenbarer Materialien die geopolitische Prekarität, von der Flüchtlinge betroffen sind, deren Status per se schon Entortung impliziert, von den Gefahren der Grenzüberquerung ganz zu schweigen. Gleichzeitig untergräbt sie die Autorität der Karten. Ihre politische Intervention legt es, mit anderen Worten, darauf an, den politischen Einfluss der Kartografie anzufechten, die, besonders in Zusammenhang mit dem israelisch-palästinensischen Konflikt, eine so entscheidende Rolle bei der Stabilisierung ungleicher Machtverhältnisse spielt. Und zuletzt demonstriert Hatoum durch die Verfremdung von Karten, die wir so häufig als naturgegeben ansehen, die Künstlichkeit aller kartografischen und geopolitischen Definitionen.

In all den genannten Skulpturen und Installationen verunsichert Hatoum Wahrnehmung und Erfahrung: Wir sehen nie, was wir zu sehen erwartet, und wir erfahren nur selten, was wir zu erfahren erwartet haben. Ein ums andere Mal werden wir aus unseren Gewohnheiten gerissen und unserer Überzeugungen beraubt, ganz unmittelbar im Falle von *Projection* (2006) ⟶ **121** + **160**, einer Arbeit, in der mit Baumwolle und Zellstoff aus Abacá eine Weltkarte ohne Grenzen dargestellt wird, die auf der kaum bekannten, aber genaueren und gerechteren Peters-Projektion beruht, oder *Natura morta (medical cabinet)*

116

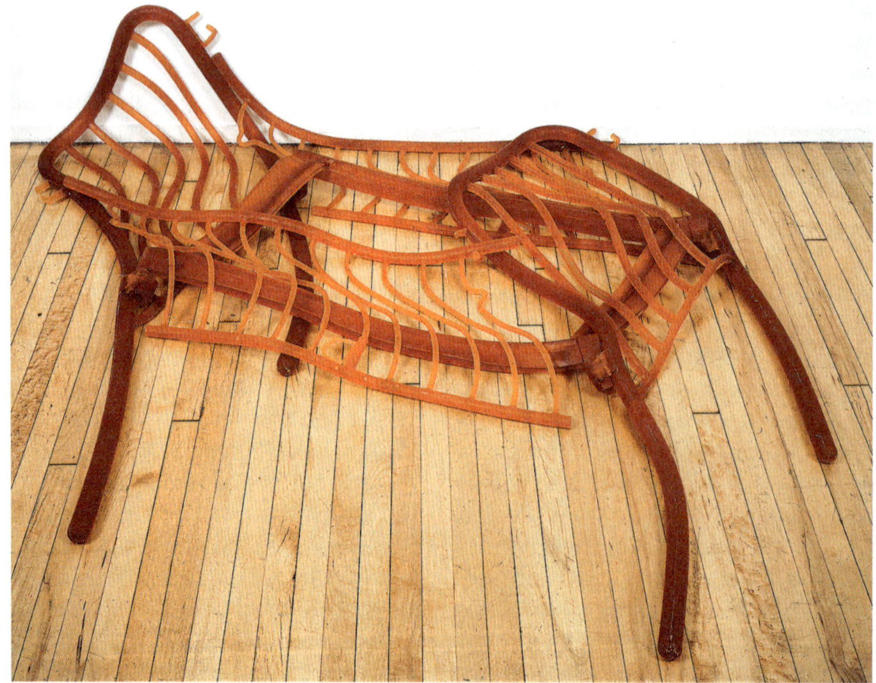

Mona Hatoum
Marrow, 1996

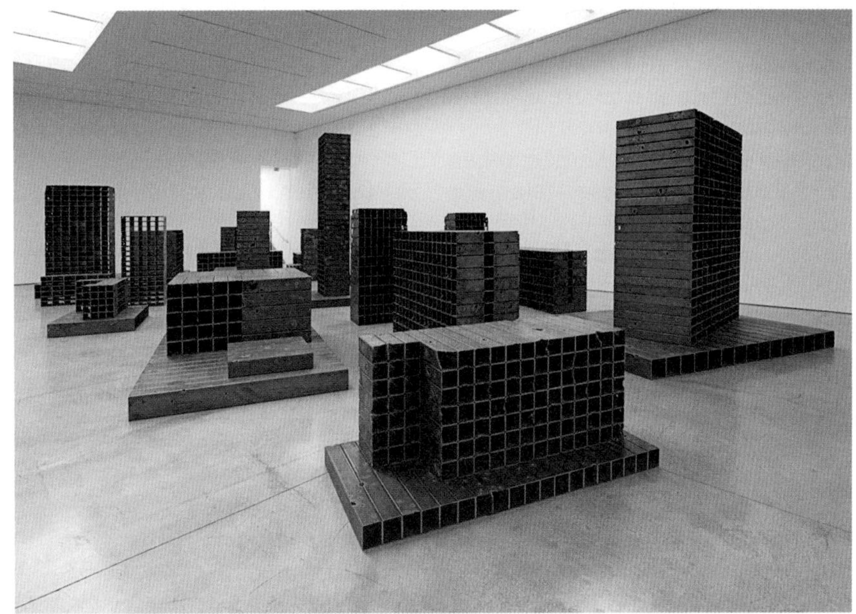

Mona Hatoum
Bunker, 2011
Installationsansicht /
installation view,
White Cube, London

117

more general states of precarity, from the emotional to the physical to the geopolitical. Especially relevant here are the many objects the artist has made out of human hair, including *Interior Landscape* (2008), in which she created a historical map of Palestine on a pillow, a map made obsolete after 1948. The political geography represented by this map, and by extension the human community it embodies, is, Hatoum seems to suggest, thanks to the Israeli occupation, no more sturdy or binding than a strand of human hair. *Recollection* (1995) consists of hair the artist shed over the course of many years and subsequently rolled into balls. Left unsecured on the floor of the space where they are installed, the hair balls drift along with the air currents. Finally, we might consider *Keffieh* (1993–99), an Arab scarf traditionally worn by men and a symbol of Palestinian self-determination woven out of pieces of women's hair. ⟶ **118** Stray wisps exceed the boundaries of the plaited grid, creating the impression of living, growing tissue. Hair, which is essentially the body's waste, has many associations, including abjection and repulsion, but it also evokes decay and degeneration.[15]

Hatoum is known for using materials that render her works either ephemeral or structurally unstable as well. Take *Present Tense* (1996), for instance, created while Hatoum was in residence in Jerusalem. ⟶ **119**

The installation consists of 2,200 bars of Nablus soap, a traditional Palestinian product, into which the artist pressed beads of red glass. Together these beads trace the outlines of a 1993 map documenting the discontinuous parcels of land to be transferred to Palestinian control under the terms of the Oslo Accords, thereby forming the basis of a future Palestinian state. Like the map that serves as its referent, *Present Tense* is a cartographic fantasy comprised entirely of limits, ghettos, and walls. Unlike the very real checkpoints that Palestinians are forced to navigate every day, however, Hatoum's boundaries are inherently temporary. Were the soap to come into contact with water, the work's very ground would dissolve and along with it the demarcations it illustrates. With the erosion of borders comes the metaphorical, if not literal, lifting of restrictions on Palestinian freedom, mobility, and exchange. In this respect, *Present Tense* constitutes a subversive act of wish fulfilment, what Judith Butler has called 'performative contradiction.' According to Butler, performative contradiction involves taking a right that has not yet been granted and engendering justice even though it does not yet exist. It is a form of political speech that leverages 'inducement, incitation, solicitation.'[16] At the same time, *Present Tense* acknowledges an all-too-oppressive geopolitical reality. After all, the 1993 map was supposed to prompt the allocation of

15   For Hatoum's comments on *Keffieh,* see her conversation with Mark Francis, published in an unpaginated pamphlet that accompanied the artist's 2000 exhibition at fig-1 in London. For a detailed discussion of this work, see Mansoor 2010, 49–52, 61–64.

16   Butler / Spivak 2007a, 55, 66, 68.

19 »The same action which presents the body with often bloody directness as an object of brutality and oppression, also contains its energy and resistance.« (Hatoum 1987, 27.)

20 »With a gathering sense of alarm, I realise that I am in the direct line of fire.« (Elwes 1981/2006, 118.)

(2012), einem dreidimensionalen Stillleben, das aus geblasenen Glasrepliken von Handgranaten besteht. ⟶ **136** Diese Werke verdeutlichen: Hatoum hat sich darauf spezialisiert, den psychischen Apparat, mithilfe dessen wir die Welt verstehen, und die Kategorien, mit denen wir die Objekte unseres Alltags fassen, zu destabilisieren und außer Kraft zu setzen. Dadurch erzeugt sie nicht nur kognitive Dissonanz, sondern auch tiefgreifende ontologische Prekarität.

Doch Hatoum bringt nicht nur Körper, Gegenstände, Gruppen und Klassifizierungssysteme aus dem Gleichgewicht. Von Beginn ihres Schaffens an hat sie stets auch den Status des Subjekts stark in Zweifel gezogen. In der Regel geschieht das, indem sie die Differenzierbarkeit zweier scheinbar unvereinbarer Subjektpositionen unterminiert. ›Opfer‹ und ›Täter‹ etwa geraten in Hatoums Œuvre ständig durcheinander. 1987 schrieb die Künstlerin in diesem Sinne: »Der Akt, den Körper in oft blutiger Direktheit als Objekt von Brutalität und Unterdrückung darzustellen, enthält gleichzeitig auch dessen Energie- und Widerstandspotenzial.«[19] Das gilt etwa für die Arbeit *Video Performance* (1980), in der Hatoum unter Verwendung einer Speziallinse eine Kamera auf das Publikum richtet, um es in Nahaufnahme zu examinieren. Diese Bilder werden auf einen Monitor im selben Raum übertragen. (Die Zuschauerin Catherine Elwes schreibt über

den Moment, kurz bevor die Kamera sie erfasste: »Die Unruhe steigt und mir wird klar, dass ich mich genau in der Schusslinie befinde.«)[20] Nach Abschluss der Publikumsmusterung dreht Hatoum den Spieß um. Die Kamera richtet sie nun auf sich selbst, untersucht in extremer Nahsicht aufs Genaueste ihr Haar, ihren Kopf und ihr Gesicht. Nicht der Betrachter, sondern die Künstlerin wird nun Zielscheibe eines besitzergreifenden, voyeuristischen, entmenschlichenden Blicks. Die Macht dieses Blicks – und sein Verletzungspotenzial – werden noch verstärkt von den auf dem Monitor übertragenen Bildern. Das Bildmaterial deckt sich zunächst mit den Aufnahmen, die Hatoum von sich selbst macht, dann aber kommt es zur Aufspaltung, und anstatt der erwarteten Detailaufnahmen bekommt das Publikum ein im Vorfeld aufgenommenes Video des nackten Körpers der Künstlerin zu sehen, welches das Vermögen der Kamera aufzeigt, ihre Motive nach Belieben zu entblößen. Indem Hatoum ihre Kleidung verliert, verliert sie auch ihre Identität, Privatsphäre und Autonomie.

Ähnliches könnte man im Falle von *Variation on Discord and Divisions* (1984) behaupten, einer Performance, in der Hatoum mit einer Kopfbedeckung aus schwarzem Stoff, die zugleich als Schleier, Maske, Kapuze oder Sturmhaube interpretiert werden kann, vor das Publikum tritt. ⟶ **122** Insofern dieses Stück

118

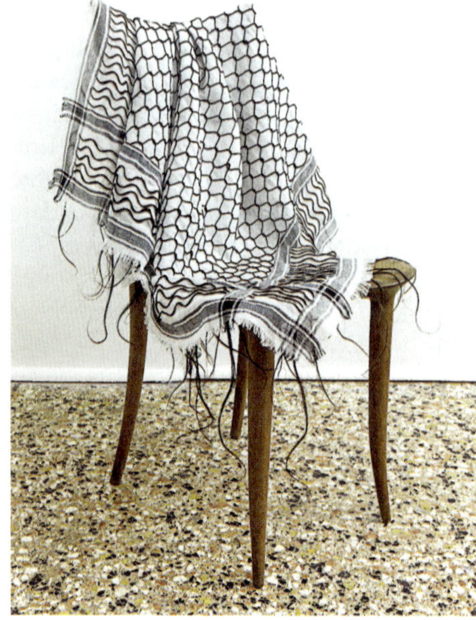

Mona Hatoum
Keffieh, 1993–1999

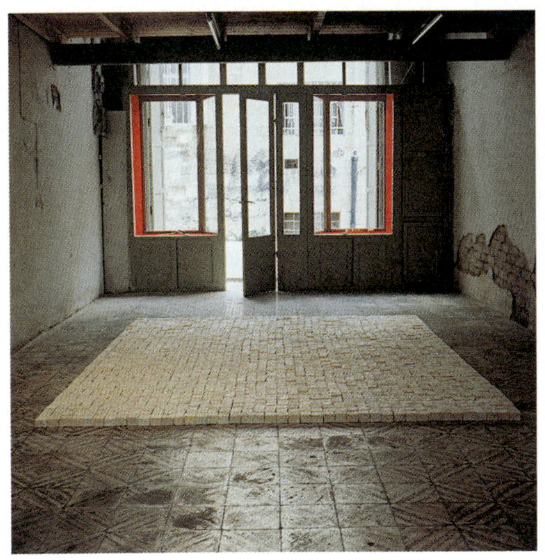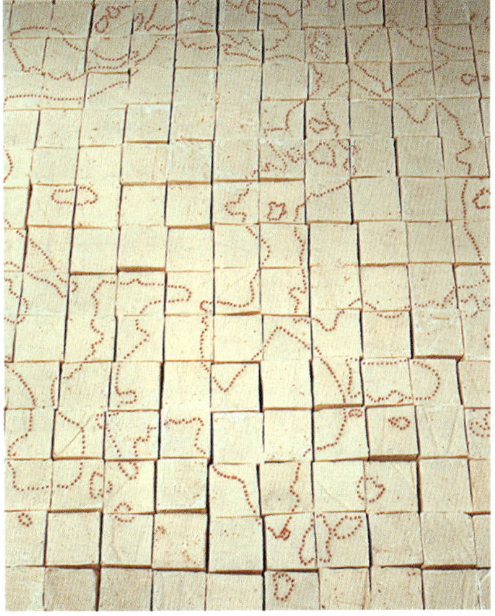

Mona Hatoum
Present Tense, 1996
Installationsansicht /
installation view, Gallery
Anadiel, Jerusalem 1996

Present Tense
(Detail / detail), 1996

119

property and sovereignty to Palestinians, but in the end it achieved very little, proving as fallible and as flawed as Hatoum's fragile sculpture.[17] *Map* (1999), a picture of a world map made with glass marbles placed directly on the floor, is also subject to instability. ⟶ **121** Every footfall produces a vibration that dislodges the marbles from their original locations. As they disperse, the map becomes distorted and unrecognizable. An inaccurate map is also a dysfunctional map: it can neither represent nor enforce territorial integrity.[18] Hatoum's goals in the case of both *Present Tense* and *Map* are several-fold. On the one hand, the artist dramatizes through her use of fragile, unpredictable materials the geopolitical precarity of refugees, whose very status as refugees involves displacement, not to mention the dangerous traversal of borders. At the same time, she undermines the authority of maps themselves. Hers is, in other words, a political intervention, designed to contest the political clout of cartography, which plays such a crucial role in reinforcing unequal relations of power, especially in the context of the Israeli-Palestinian conflict. Finally, Hatoum demonstrates the inherent artificiality of all cartographic and geopolitical definitions, denaturalizing the maps we so often take for granted.

In each of the sculptures and installations above, Hatoum stimulates perceptual and experiential uncertainty: we never see what we expect to see, and we rarely experience what we expect to experience. We are repeatedly exiled from our habits and dispossessed of our convictions, directly so in the case of *Projection* (2006) ⟶ **121+160**, a work that uses cotton and abaca pulp to picture a borderless world map according to the less familiar, but more accurate and equitable Peters projection, and *Natura morta (medical cabinet)* (2012), a three-dimensional still life comprised of blown-glass replicas of hand grenades. ⟶ **136** As these works suggest, Hatoum specializes in disabling – in rendering uncertain – the mental apparatus we use to make sense of the world as well as the categories into which we place the objects of our everyday lives. In so doing, she generates not only cognitive dissonance, but profound ontological precarity as well.

Yet it is not only bodies, things, groups, and classification systems that Hatoum destabilizes. From the beginning of her career, the artist has also cast the status of the subject into grave doubt. Generally speaking, she does so by undermining the distinction between two seemingly irreconcilable subject positions. 'Victims' and 'assailants' are constantly confused in Hatoum's work, for instance. As the artist wrote in 1987, 'The same action which presents the body with often bloody directness as an object of brutality and oppression, also contains its energy and resistance.'[19]

17 For more on this work, see Mikdadi 2008, 67. For Hatoum's words on this work, see Archer 1997, 26–27.

18 For more see Baykal 2012, 62–63.

19 Hatoum 1987, 27.

21 »She has to transform the mask of anonymity and prejudice into an image of a living, fighting person.« (Hatoum 1987, 32; vgl. auch D'Souza 2006, 111.)

Stoff die Künstlerin entpersonalisiert und einsperrt, bedeutet es Unterwerfung. Doch setzt sich Hatoum schon bald zur Wehr. Nachdem sie eine Zeitlang zwischen Besucherreihen herumgekrochen ist und Schlieren roten Wassers auf dem Boden zurückgelassen hat, ergreift sie ein Messer und fängt an, Löcher in den Stoff zu schneiden. So befreit sie sowohl ihren Blick als auch ihre Stimme und »verwandelt die Maske der Anonymität und des Vorurteils in das Bild eines lebendigen, kämpfenden Menschen«.[21] Die dialektische Beziehung von Opfer und Täter ist auch in der Plakatarbeit *Over my dead body* (1988/2002) im Spiel, Hatoums bisher vielleicht publikumswirksamster Arbeit, die eine Nahaufnahme des Gesichts der Künstlerin im Profil zeigt. ⟶ **132** Auf Hatoums Nase thront ein Spielzeugsoldat, der sein Gewehr zwischen ihre Augenbrauen richtet. Es ist vollkommen unklar, auf welchen Gegner es Hatoum in dieser Inszenierung genau abgesehen hat. Zwar ist der Soldat bewaffnet, doch handelt es sich lediglich um eine Spielzeugfigur, deren Gewehr so machtlos ist wie sie selbst. Indem sie den Soldaten der Lächerlichkeit preisgibt, nimmt Hatoum ihm auf wirkungsvolle Weise Macht und Maskulinität. Ihr vernichtender Blick und ihr herrisches Auftreten weisen ihm einen klaren Ort zu. Andererseits dienen Spielzeugsoldaten auch der Romantisierung und Rechtfertigung äußerst realer Gewalthandlungen.

Hatoums Spielfigur mag zwar nur das Surrogat eines tatsächlichen Soldaten sein, doch verkörpert sie die Autorität und das Brutalitätspotenzial des Militärs oder einer Polizeibehörde. Auch die Arbeit *Corps étranger* (1994), deren französischer Titel Ausländer, Fremde und invasive Arten assoziieren lässt, stellt das Schema von Opfer und Täter infrage. Aufnahmen des Körperinneren der Künstlerin, die mit einer Endoskopkamera gemacht wurden, werden auf den Boden projiziert. Um diese Aufnahmen sehen zu können, müssen die Betrachter eine hohe, enge Zylinderkonstruktion betreten und den Blick nach unten richten. Daraufhin werden sie von zumindest zwei widerstreitenden Erfahrungen erwartet. Zwar thronen sie über den entblößten Organen, über dem erniedrigten Körper der Künstlerin, doch ist ihre Herrschaftsposition dabei keineswegs gefestigt. Die Blickperspektive verursacht bei den Betrachtern ein Soggefühl, ein Gefühl, als wären sie mit Haut und Haar von einer Bestie verschlungen worden. Weder der abstoßenden Szene vor ihren Augen noch dem begrenzten, beengenden Raum können sie entkommen. Auch wenn die Künstlerin gleich zweifach belagert wird, zunächst von der Kamera und dann vom Betrachter, gibt sie ihre Machtposition und Autorität zu keiner Zeit preis. Wie in anderen Fällen zwingt Hatoum das Publikum nicht nur, sich das eigene Gewaltpotenzial einzugestehen, sie

120

Such is the case with *Video Performance* (1980), in which Hatoum turns a camera on spectators, using a special lens to examine them in close-up. The resulting images are transmitted to a monitor in the same room. (As audience member Catherine Elwes writes of the moment just before the camera reached her: 'With a gathering sense of alarm, I realise that I am in the direct line of fire.'[20]) The tables turn after Hatoum finishes scanning the audience. At this point, she points the camera at her own head, scrutinizing her hair, head, and face in extreme detail. Now the artist, not the viewer, is the target of a possessive, voyeuristic, dehumanizing gaze. The power of this gaze – and its ability to violate – are made even more manifest by the images broadcast on the monitor. At first, the footage corresponds to the film Hatoum is making of herself, but eventually the two diverge, and instead of the expected close-ups, viewers are treated to a pre-recorded tape of her naked body that suggests the camera's ability to disrobe its subjects at will. Stripped of her clothes, Hatoum is also stripped of her identity, privacy, and sovereignty.

Much the same could be said of *Variation on Discord and Divisions* (1984), a performance in which Hatoum appears to the audience with her head covered by a piece of black fabric that reads simultaneously as a veil, mask, hood, and balaclava. ⟶ **122**

Insofar as it depersonalizes and imprisons the artist, the cloth signifies subjection. Yet Hatoum soon fights back. After a period spent crawling through rows of spectators and smearing red water across the floor, the artist picks up a knife and begins carving holes through the cloth. In so doing, she liberates both her sight and her speech, 'transform[ing] the mask of anonymity and prejudice into an image of a living, fighting person.'[21] The dialectical relationship between victims and bullies is also at play in the billboard *Over my dead body* (1988/2002), perhaps Hatoum's most declamatory work to date, which represents a close-up of the artist's face in profile. ⟶ **132** Perched on the bridge of her nose is a toy soldier, who points a rifle at her eyebrow. It is entirely unclear who Hatoum means to position as the antagonist in this mise-en-scène. The soldier wields a weapon, but he is only a plaything, and his gun is as impotent as he is. Indeed, by picturing the solider as nothing more than a trifle, Hatoum effectively deflates both his power and his masculinity. Her withering stare and commanding demeanor also keep him firmly in his place. Then again, toy soldiers serve to romanticize and legitimize very real acts of violence. Hatoum's doll might only be a surrogate for an actual soldier, but he still embodies all the authority and all the potential for brutality of the military or a police department. *Corps étranger*

20 Elwes 1981/2006, 118.

21 Hatoum 1987, 32; see too D'Souza 2006, 111.

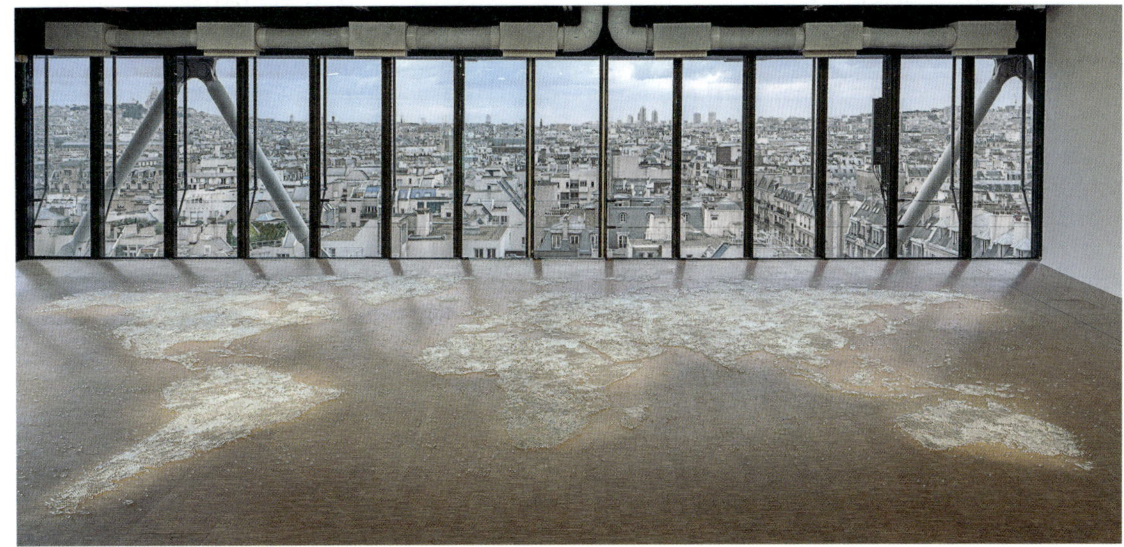

Mona Hatoum
Map (clear), 2015
Installationsansicht /
installation view,
Centre Pompidou, Paris

121

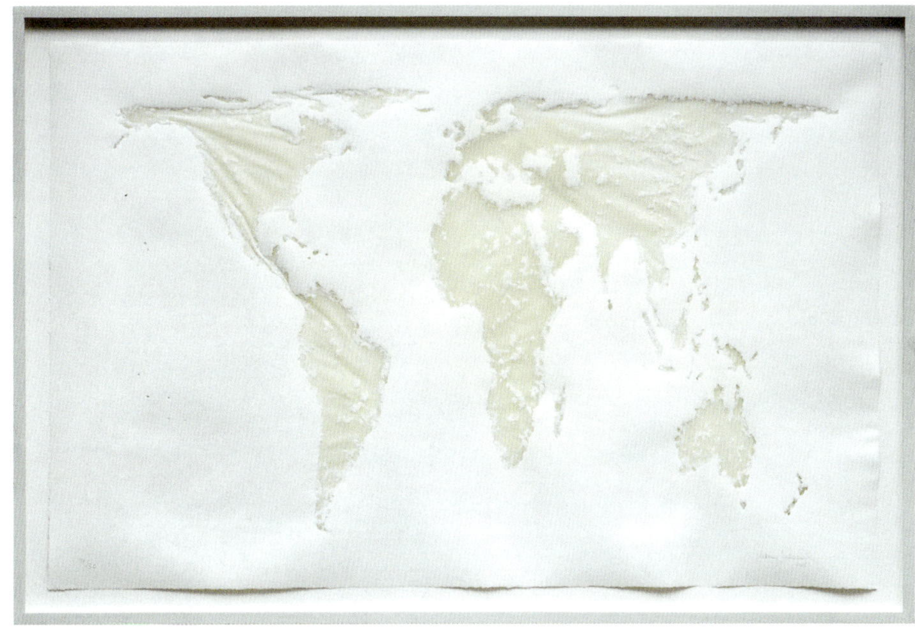

Mona Hatoum
Projection, 2006

22 »Hatoum's critique of hegemonic culture problematizes accepted notions of victimization, displacement and oppression.« (Hatoum 1987, 27.) Hatoums Bemühungen decken sich mit jüngeren Versuchen, Verletzlichkeit als konstitutiv für – als Möglichkeitsbedingung von – Handlungsfähigkeit, Kontrolle und Widerstand neu zu denken. Vgl. Butler / Gambetti / Sabsay 2016b. Zu einer anders gelagerten Erörterung des Themas Hatoum und Prekarität mit spezifischem Fokus auf den Körper vgl. Tzelepis 2016.

23 »[…] is the presentation of identity as unable to identify with itself, but nevertheless grappling with the notion (perhaps only the ghost) of identity to itself.« (Said 2000, 15.)

befähigt auch die Entrechteten, sich zu behaupten, wodurch sie »etablierte Vorstellungen von Diskriminierung, Displacement und Unterdrückung hinterfragt«.[22]

Wichtig ist, dass durch die Infragestellung der Unterscheidung von Selbst und Anderem sowie durch die Konfrontation von Identität mit Differenz und Unbestimmtheit der traditionelle Subjektbegriff in seinen Grundfesten erschüttert wird. Tatsächlich hat Hatoum ihre gesamte Laufbahn hindurch das Ziel verfolgt, Subjektivität aufzulösen, oder, genauer gesagt, zu demonstrieren, inwiefern Subjektivität immer schon dezentriert ist. Die Arbeit *Roadworks*, in der sich Hatoum mit afrokaribischen Bewohnern Südlondons identifiziert, stellt nach wie vor eines der stärksten Beispiele für diesen Vorgang dar, ebenso wie *Light Sentence*, wo der vorgeblich mündige Betrachter die Rolle des Gefangenen verkörpert. Auch die paradoxale Arbeit *You Are Still Here* (1994), die aus einem Spiegel besteht, in den die Künstlerin im Sandstrahlverfahren den titelgebenden Schriftzug eingraviert hat, behandelt die Widersprüchlichkeiten von Identität. Mit seiner reflektierenden Oberfläche scheint der Spiegel den Anspruch des Werktitels zu erfüllen, das Subjekt ein für alle Mal festzulegen. Letztlich erreicht er jedoch das genaue Gegenteil. Denn schließlich befindet sich der Spiegel, in dem wir uns sehen, ge-

nau dort, wo wir nicht sind. Insofern die Arbeit *You Are Still Here* das Abbild vom Körper trennt, entortet sie das Subjekt unwiderruflich. ⟶ **123** Letzten Endes treibt Hatoum uns alle ins Exil. Der Exilierte stellt von Natur aus das prekäre Subjekt par excellence dar. Wie Edward Said einmal geschrieben hat, ist Hatoums Werk »die Demonstration, dass Identität sich nicht mit sich selbst identifizieren kann, sich aber dennoch mit der Vorstellung (oder nur mit der Illusion) von Identität mit sich selbst auseinandersetzt«.[23] Sowohl für Said als auch für Hatoum handelt es sich beim Exilierten nicht nur um eine Person, er verkörpert nicht nur eine Kategorie oder einen Zustand, sondern auch ein Erklärungsmodell, eine Denkfigur, durch die Erfahrung gefiltert und Objekte geschaffen werden. Mona Hatoums vom Status des Exilierten angeregte Perspektive neigt dazu, jedwede Gewissheit zu unterminieren, von der physischen und der perzeptiven bis hin zur kognitiven, ontologischen und geopolitischen.

Wenn es Hatoums Objekten gelingt, nicht nur Subjekte, sondern im Allgemeinen auch Überzeugungen, Kategorien und Dualismen in den Zustand der Prekarität zu versetzen, dann liegt das an deren hohem Affektpotenzial. Zu affizieren bedeutet, eine Wirkung zu erzielen oder einen Eindruck zu machen – für gewöhnlich den Eindruck von Bedrängtsein und Unbehagen. Affiziert werden heißt heimgesucht werden.

122

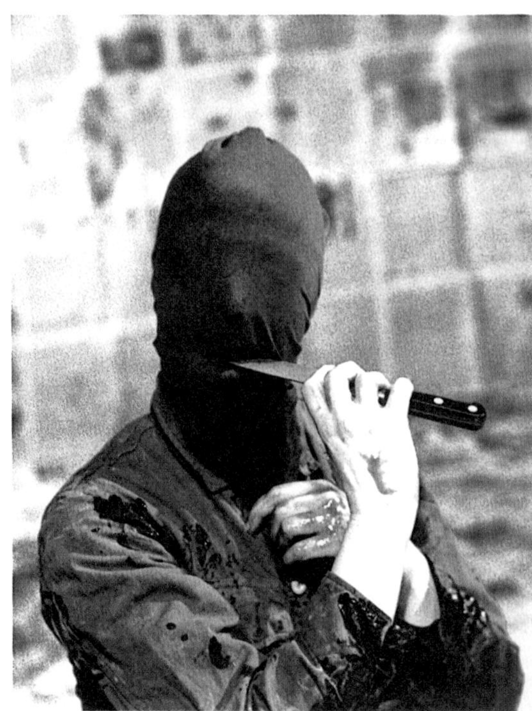

Mona Hatoum
Variation on Discord and Divisions, 1984
Live-Performance aufgeführt in / live action performed at The Western Front, Vancouver

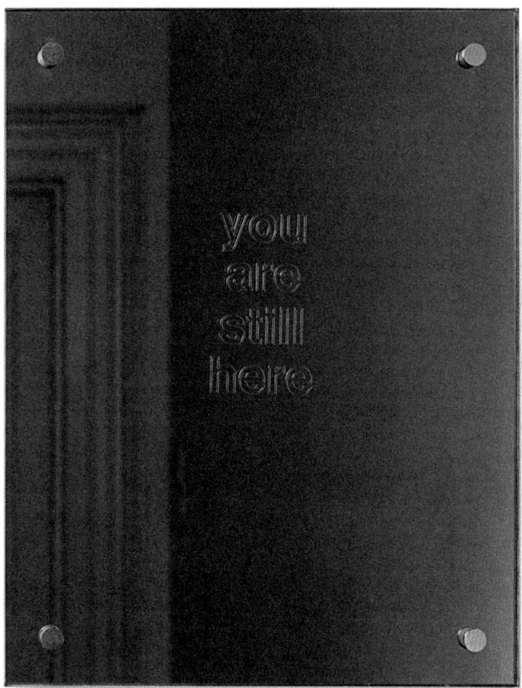

Mona Hatoum
You Are Still Here, 1994

123

(1994), a French phrase that evokes aliens, strangers, and invasive species, also unsettles the relative positions of predator and prey. Here footage of the inside of the artist's body, shot with an endoscopic camera, is projected onto the floor. In order to see the footage, viewers must step inside a tall, narrow cylinder and look down. Once they do, at least two contradictory experiences await them. On the one hand, they find themselves towering over the artist's exposed organs, her debased body. Their place of dominance is by no means secure, however. By virtue of this same perspective, they also feel themselves engulfed, as if they had been swallowed whole by a devouring beast. There is no escaping the abject scene before them, nor the confined, suffocating space of the structure. Although the artist is occupied twice over, once by the camera and again by the viewer, she never cedes her power or authority. Here and elsewhere, Hatoum not only forces viewers to acknowledge their own potential for violence, she also enables the disenfranchised to assert themselves, thereby 'problematiz[ing] accepted notions of victimization, displacement and oppression.'[22]

Importantly, challenging the distinction between self and other and exposing identity to difference and uncertainty both represent a profound assault on the traditional notion of the subject. Indeed, Hatoum has sought throughout her career to defix subjectivity – or, rather, to demonstrate how subjectivity is always already decentered. *Roadworks,* in which she identifies with an Afro-Caribbean inhabitant of South London, remains one of the most powerful examples of this operation, as is *Light Sentence,* in which ostensibly enfranchised viewers embody the role of prisoner or detainee. The oxymoronic *You Are Still Here* (1994), which consists of a mirror onto which the artist sandblasted an eponymous phrase, also dramatizes the contradictions of identity. ⟶ **123** By virtue of its reflective surface, the mirror would seem to achieve exactly what the title claims: to situate the subject once and for all. In the end, however, it accomplishes the very opposite. After all, the mirror in which we see ourselves is precisely where we are not. Insofar as it splits her image from her body, *You Are Still Here* irrevocably dislocates the subject. Ultimately, Hatoum makes exiles of us all. The exile, of course, is the precarious subject par excellence. As Edward Said once noted, Hatoum's work 'is the presentation of identity as unable to identify with itself, but nevertheless grappling with the notion (perhaps only the ghost) of identity to itself.'[23] For Said as for Hatoum, exile is not only a person, a category, or a condition, it is also an explanatory structure – a mode of thinking – through which experience is filtered and objects

22   Hatoum 1987, 27. Hatoum's efforts dovetail with recent attempts to rethink vulnerability as constitutive of – as a condition of possibility of – agency, mastery, and resistance. See Butler / Gambetti / Sabsay 2016b, 1–11. For a different discussion of Hatoum and precarity, one that focuses specifically on the body, see Tzelepis 2016, 147–66.

23   Said 2000, 15.

24 »Affect arises in the midst of in-between-ness: in the capacities to act and be acted upon. [...] Affect [...] is the name we give to those [...] visceral forces [...] that can serve to drive us toward movement, toward thought.« (Seigworth / Gregg 2010, 1–2.)

Ein affektives Objekt ist im Wesentlichen ein Katalysator, und insofern es sowohl eine emotionale als auch eine körperliche Reaktion einfordert, bringt es Konsequenzen und Verantwortlichkeiten für den Rezipienten mit sich. In einer solchen Konstellation ist weder die Position des Objekts noch die des Subjekts eine neutrale. Wie die Herausgeber eines kürzlich erschienenen Bandes zur Affekttheorie formulieren: »Affekt entsteht inmitten des Dazwischen-Seins: im Vermögen, zu handeln und Objekt von Handlungen zu werden. [...] Affekt [...] ist der Begriff, mit dem wir jene [...] inneren Kräfte bezeichnen [...], die uns in Bewegung versetzen und unser Denken anstoßen können.«[24] In Hatoums Werk werden ebenjene kraftvollen Begegnungen von Objekt und Subjekt inszeniert, und diese Begegnungen lassen uns keine andere Wahl, als auf sie zu reagieren.

Aus dem amerikanischen Englisch von Peter Sondermeyer

124

created. Taking its cue from the status of the exile, Hatoum's exilic perspective tends to destabilize any and all certainties, from the physical and the perceptual to the cognitive, ontological, and geopolitical.

If Hatoum's objects succeed at rendering not only subjects but convictions, categories, and dualisms in general precarious, it is because they have such strong affective powers. To affect means to have an effect or make an impression on, usually one of distress and discomfort. To be affected is to be afflicted. An affective object is essentially a catalyst, and insofar as it demands an emotional as well as a physical response, it comes with consequences and responsibilities for the receiver. In such a scenario, the position of neither the object nor the subject is neutral. As the editors of a recent volume on affect theory write: 'Affect arises in the midst of in-between-ness: in the capacities to act and be acted upon. [...] Affect [...] is the name we give to those [...] visceral forces [...] that can serve to drive us toward movement, toward thought.'[24] Hatoum's work stages precisely this kind of forceful encounter between object and subject, and, after such an encounter, we have no choice but to respond.

24 Seigworth / Gregg 2010, 1–2.

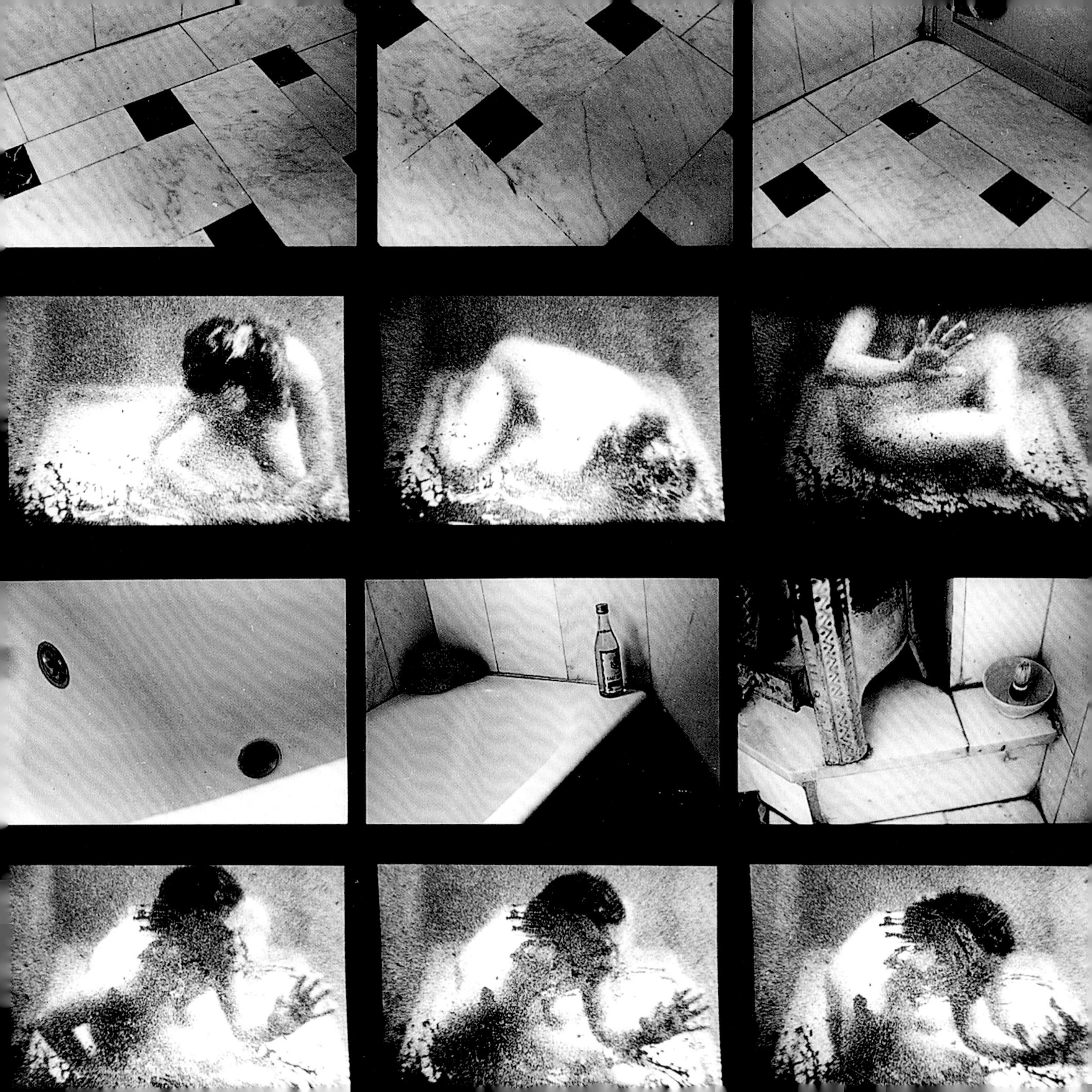

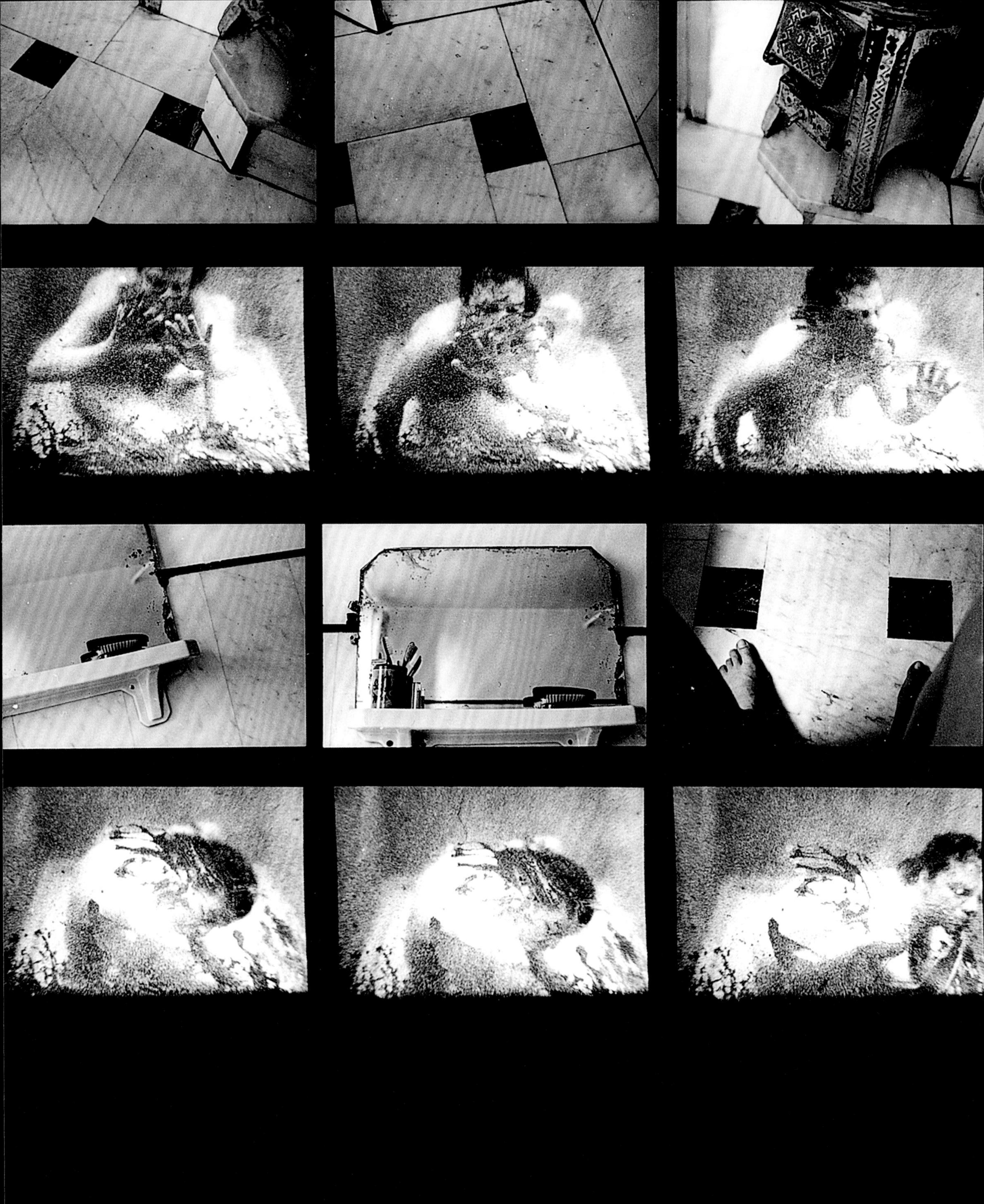

←— Mona Hatoum
Changing Parts, 1984

Mona Hatoum
Roadworks, 1985

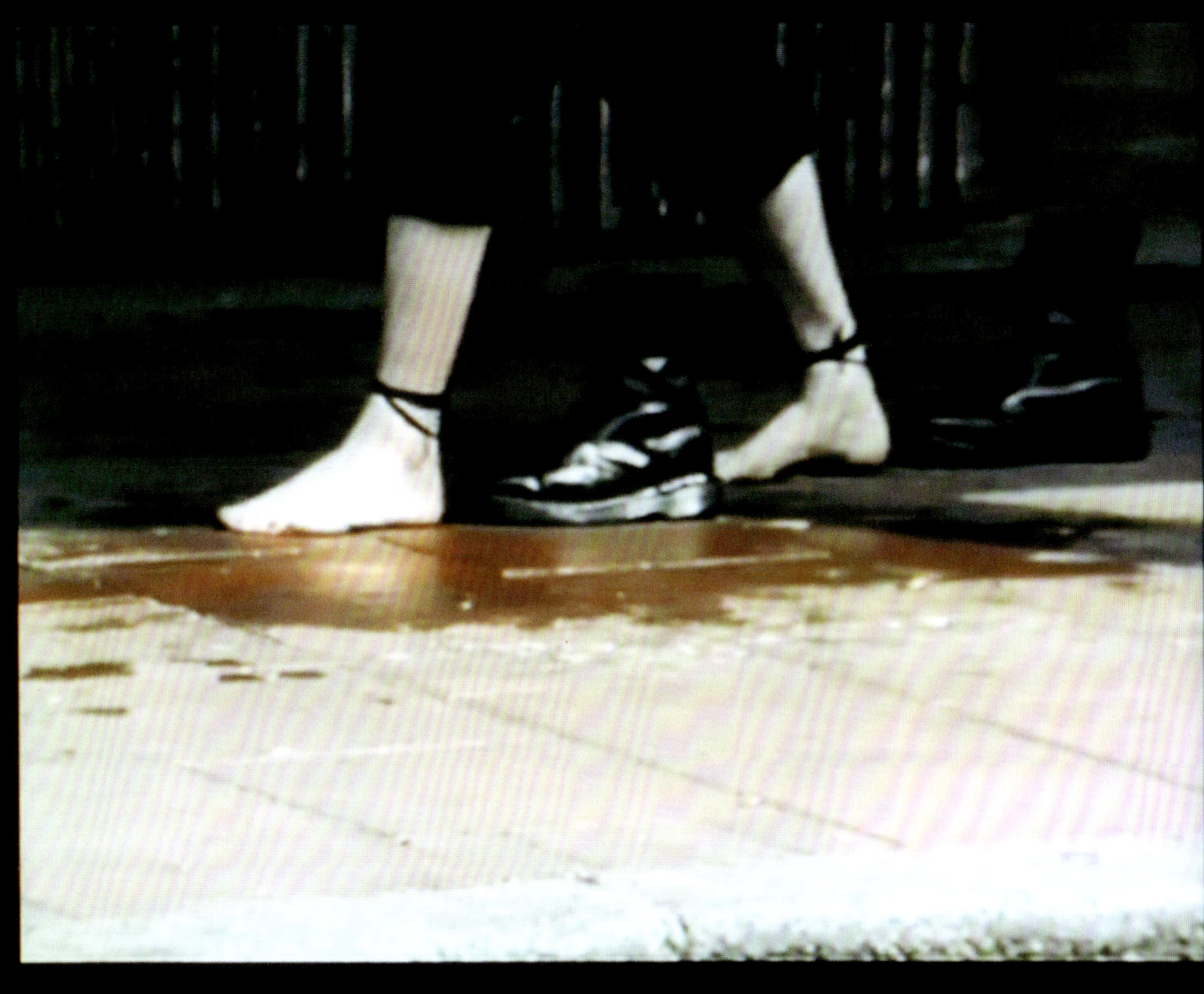

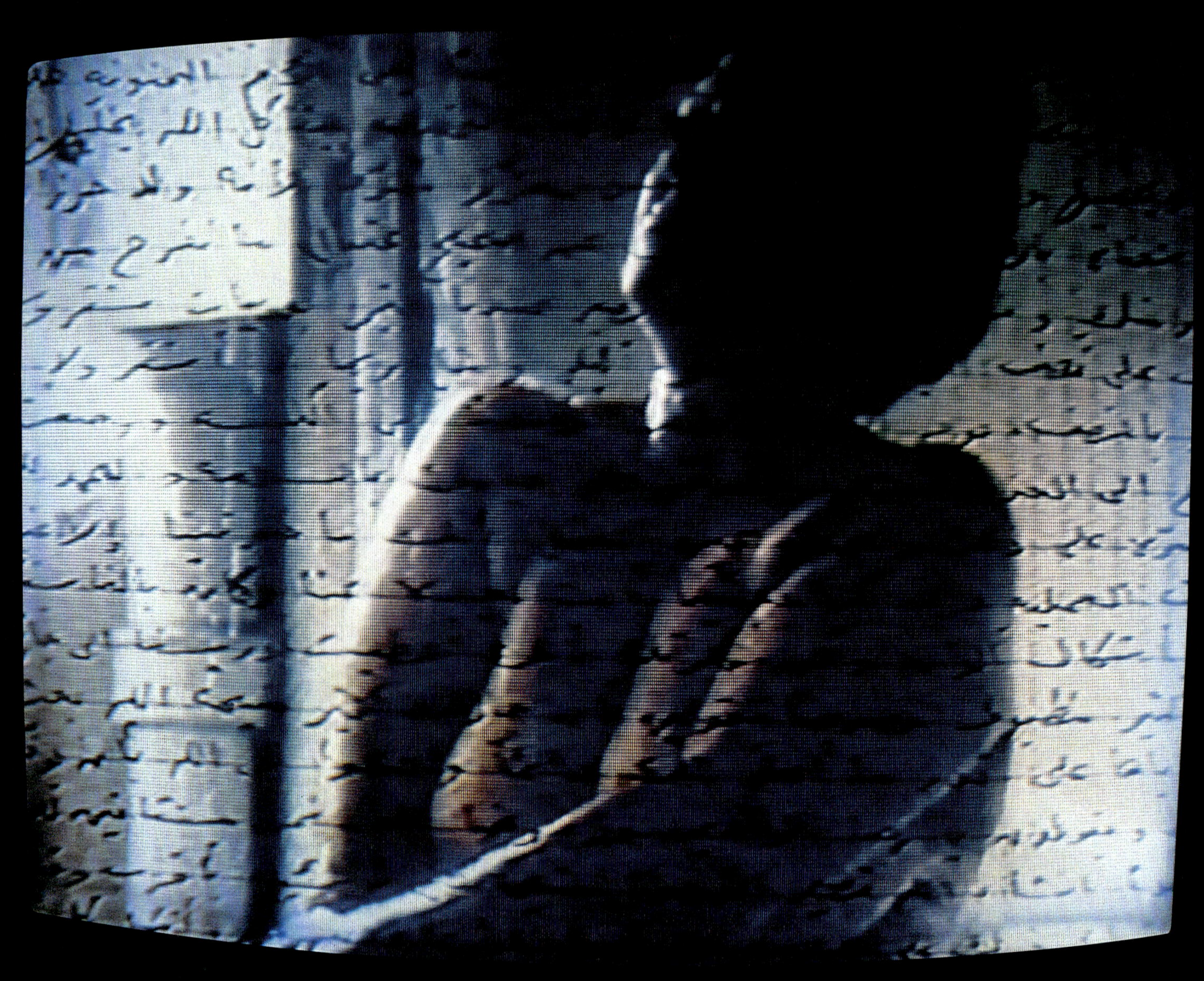

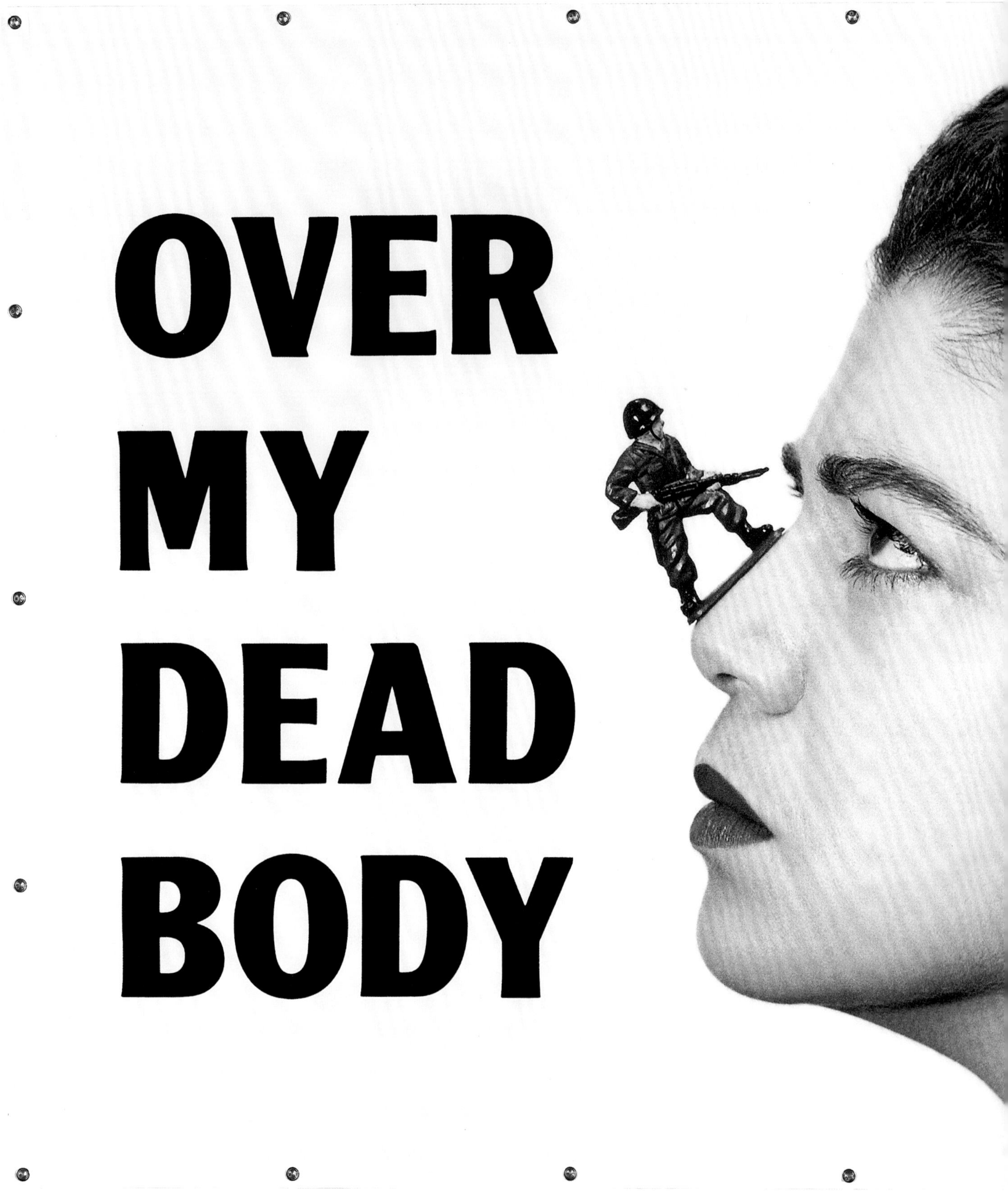

OVER
MY
DEAD
BODY

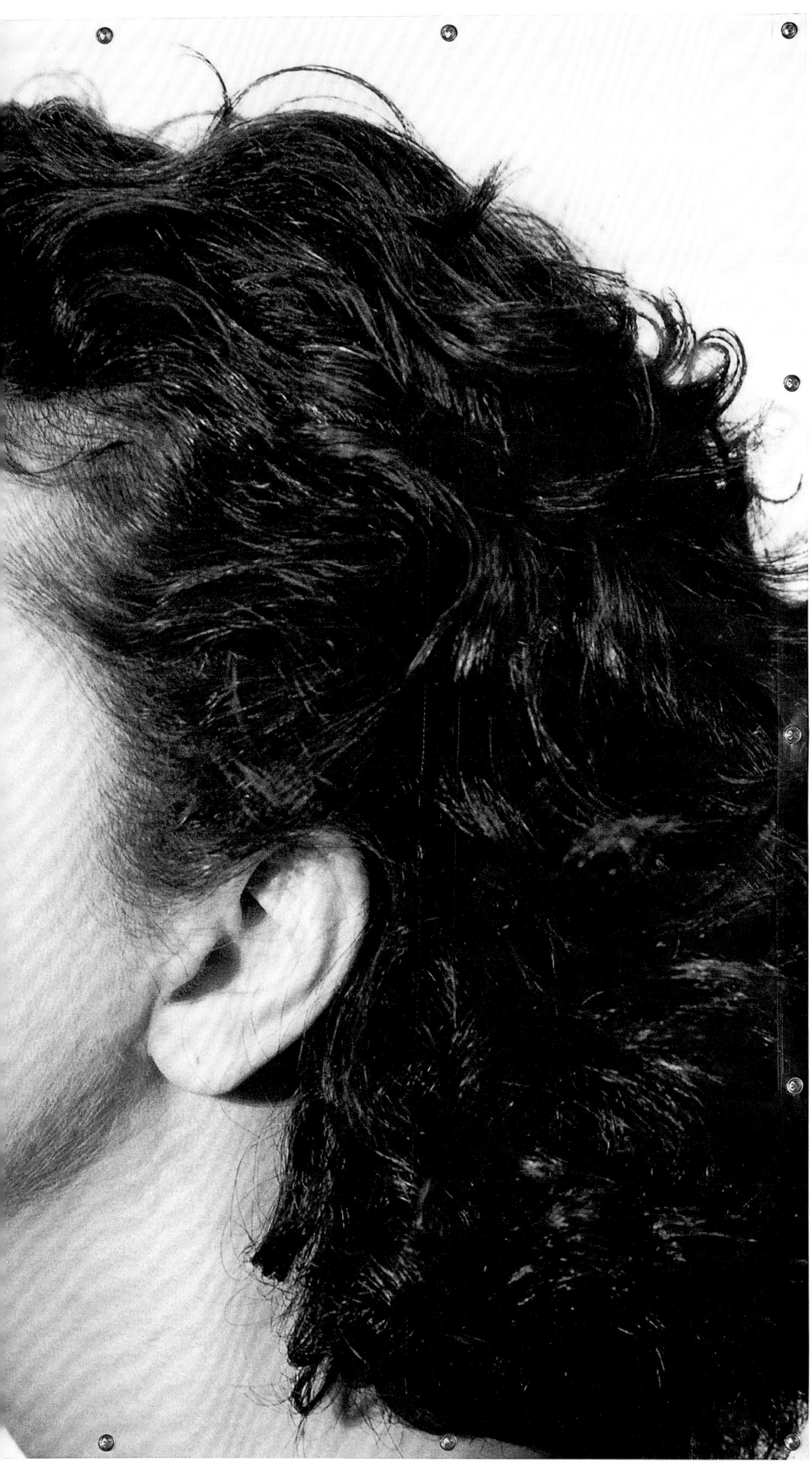

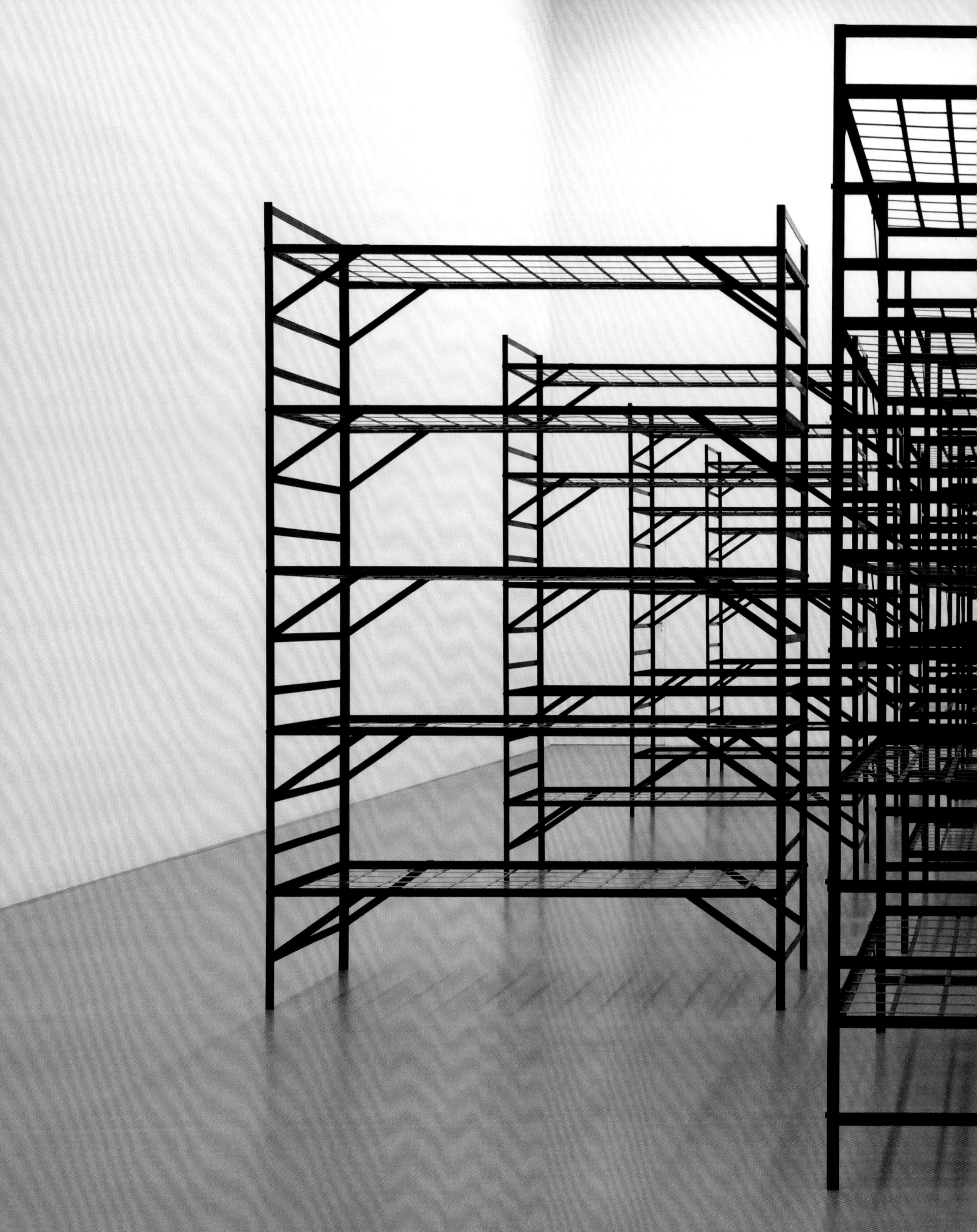

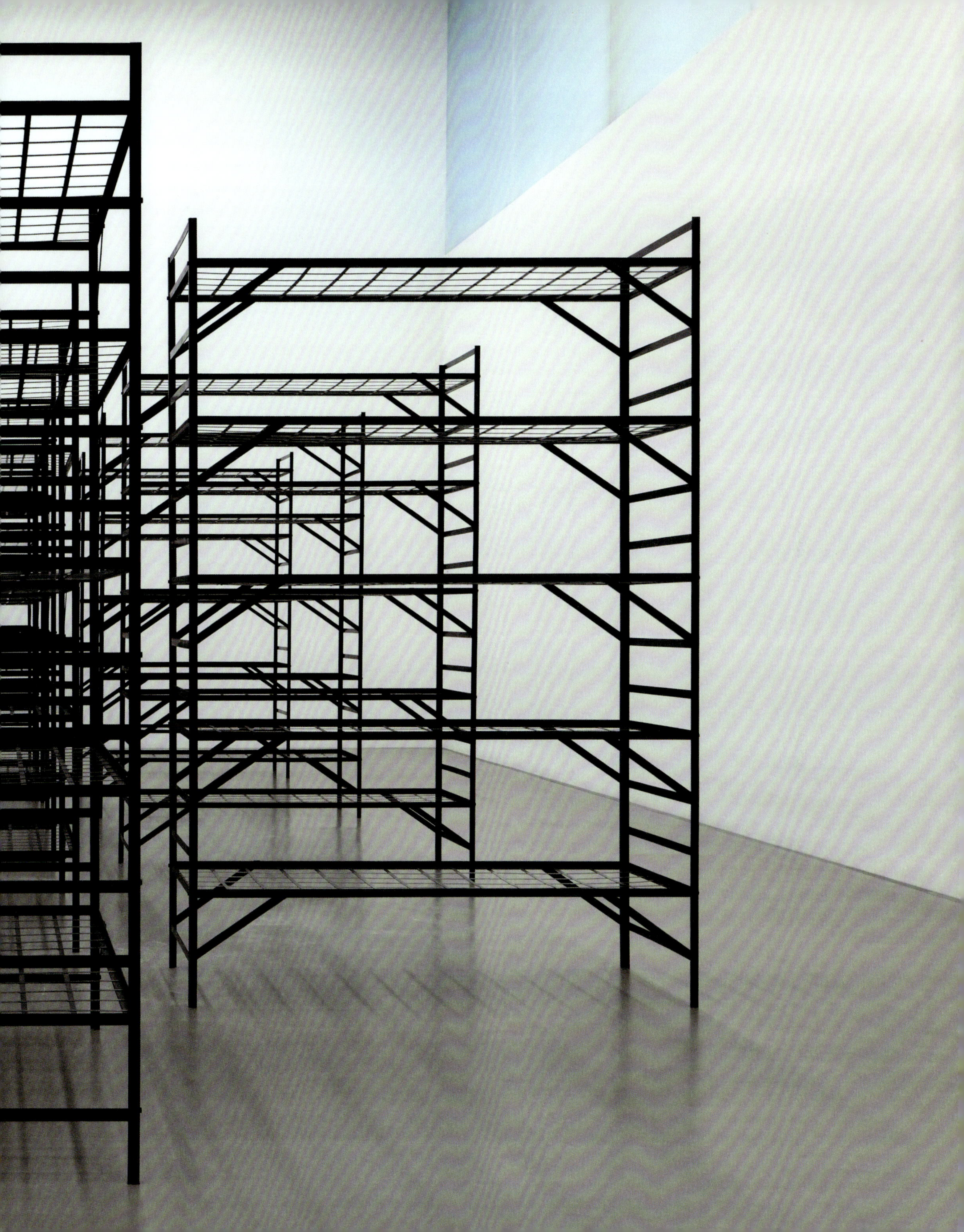

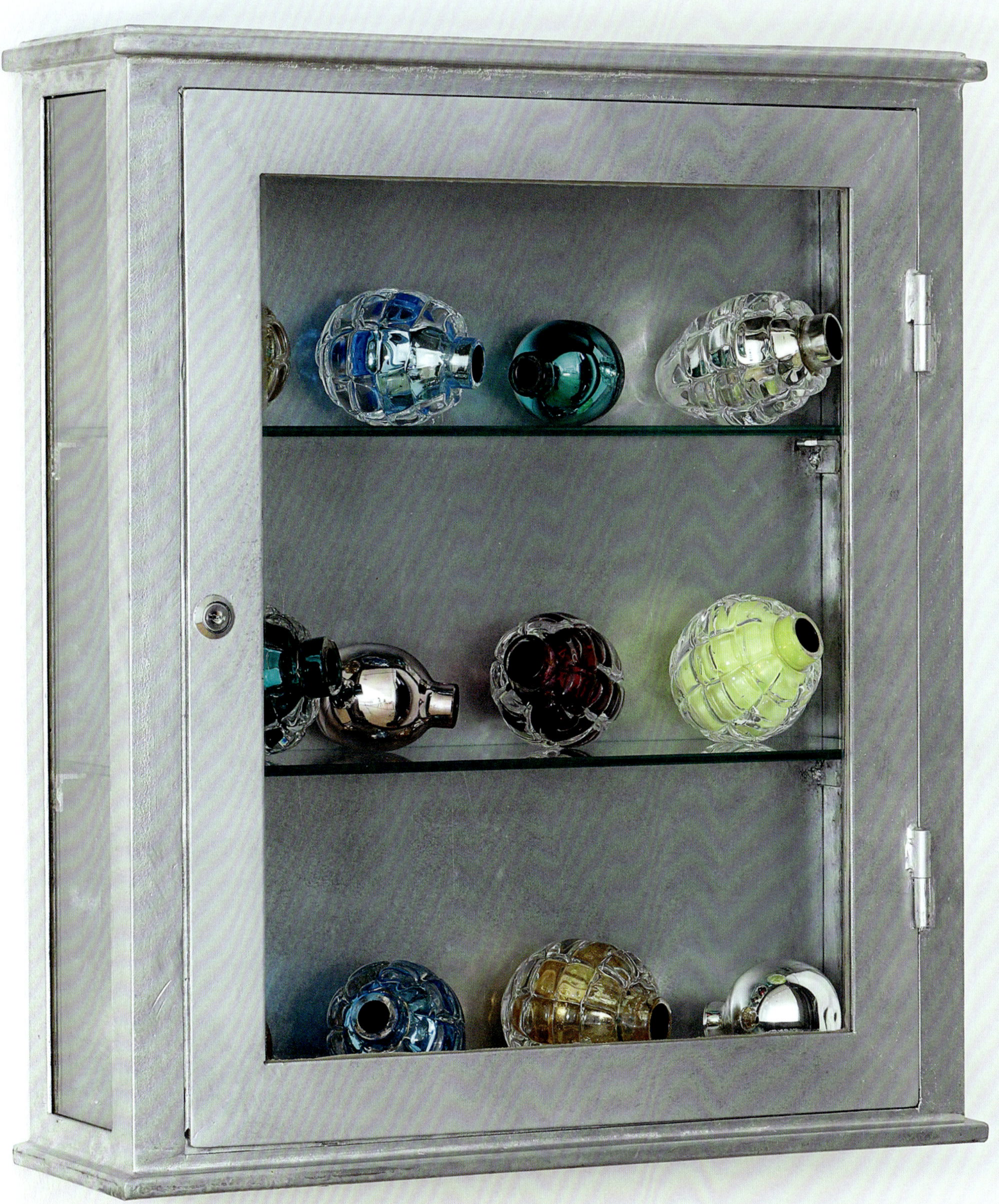

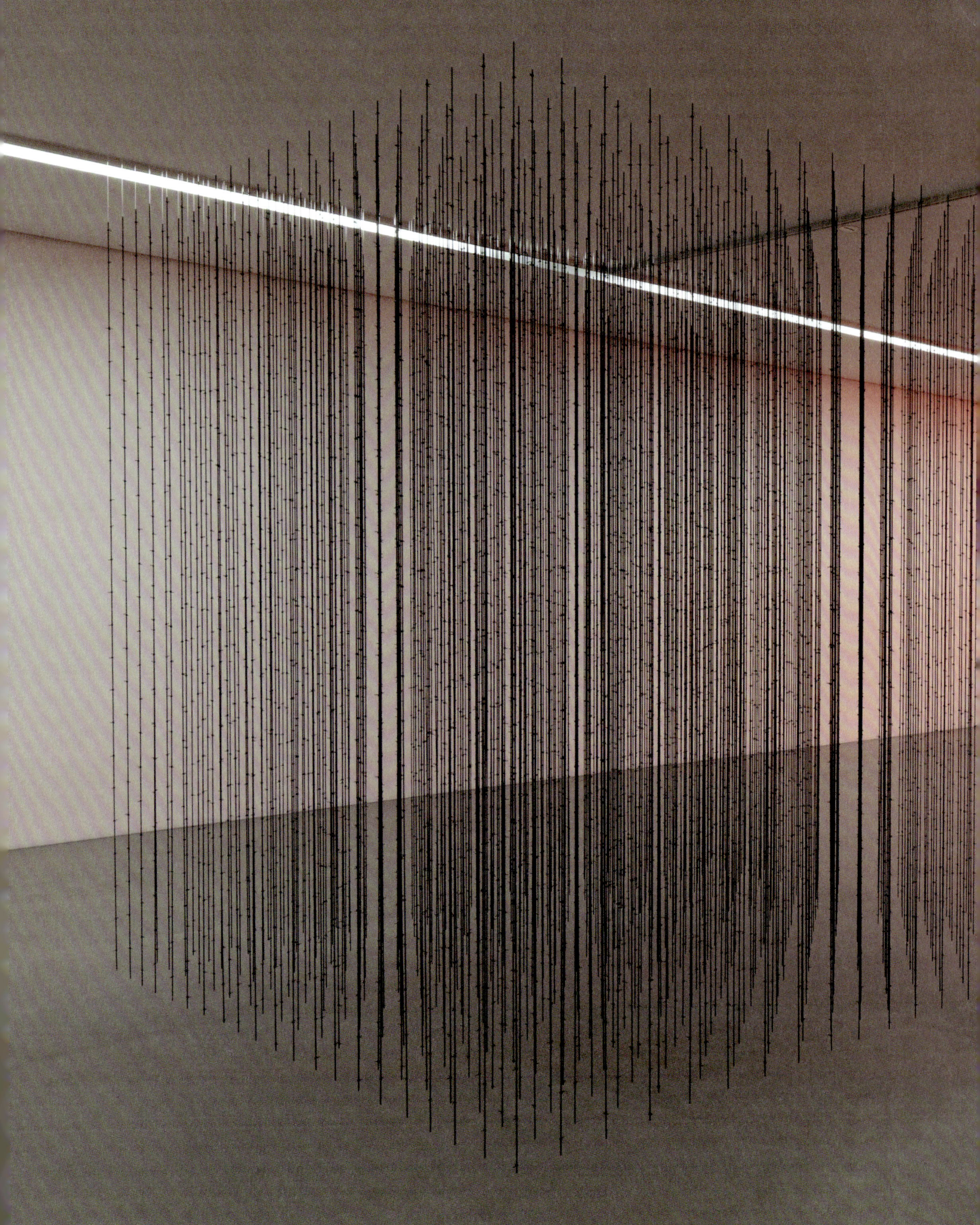

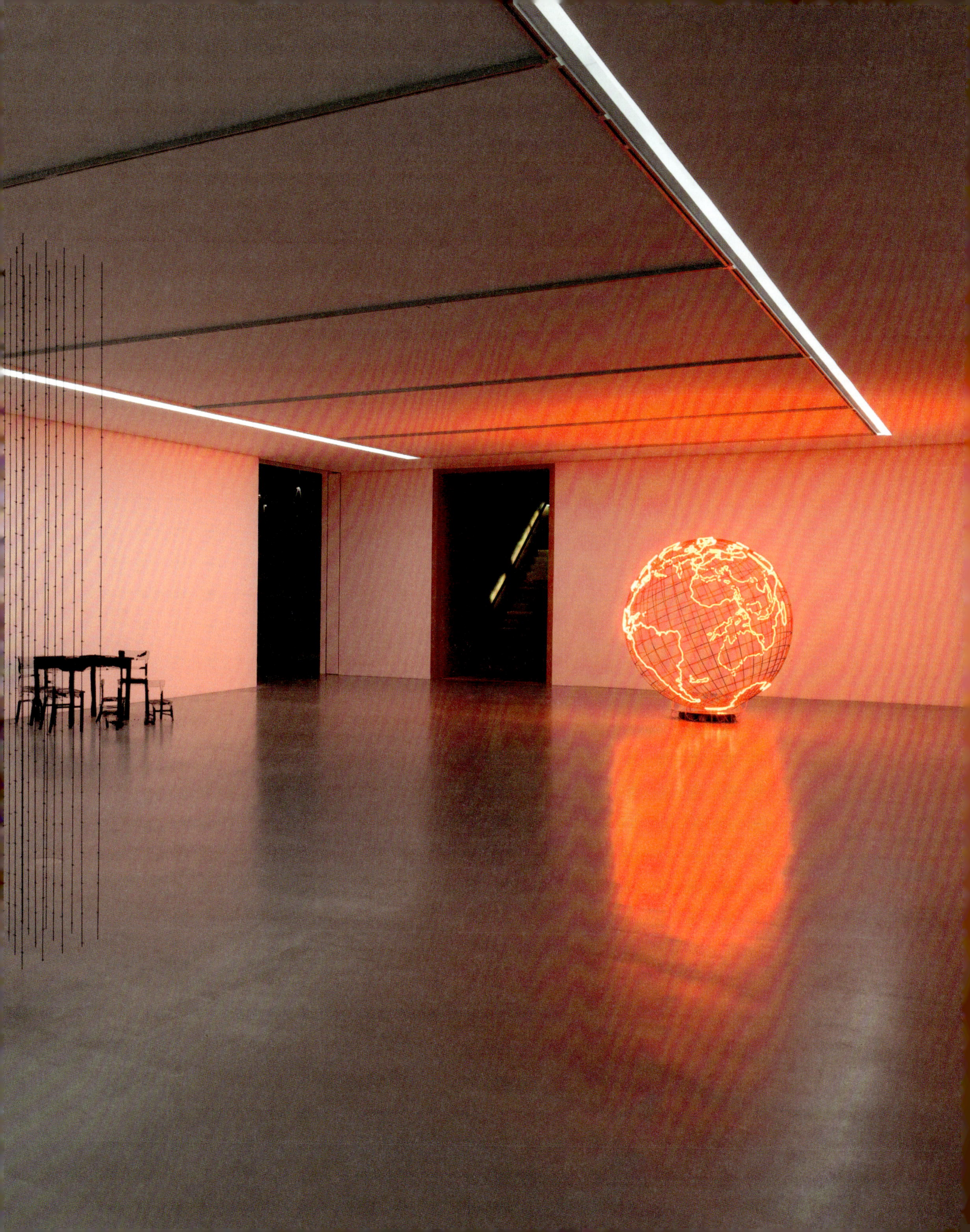

⟵ Mona Hatoum
Impenetrable, 2009
Remains of the Day (s version), 2016
Hot Spot III, 2009

Feminismus, Postkolonialismus und zeitgenössische Kunst

Feminism, Postcolonialism and Contemporary Art

Kea Wienand

1 Vgl. Schmidt-Linsenhoff 2005, 19; Karentzos 2012, 250–251.

2 Ich verwende im Folgenden immer dann den Unterstrich bzw. den sogenannten Gender-Gap, wenn alle Geschlechter gemeint sind; der Unterstrich hat sich jüngst als Schreibweise durchgesetzt, mit der angezeigt wird, dass mehr als nur zwei Geschlechter existieren.

3 Diskussionen darüber, von wo aus antirassistische und antisexistische Kritik geübt werden könne, sind bis heute virulent, vgl. dazu z. B. Micossé-Aikins 2015.

4 Vgl. Pejic 2008.

5 Zu der der Situation von Künstlerinnen in der Bundesrepublik Deutschland vgl. die Kommentierung der Studie des deutschen Kulturrats von 2014 durch Larissa Kikol (Kikol 2016); zur Situation von Künstlerinnen in den Vereinigten Staaten vgl. die Ausführungen von Maura Reilly (Reilly 2007).

Ausstellungen zeitgenössischer Kunst stellen schon seit längerem Orte bereit, an denen feministische und postkoloniale Standpunkte artikuliert und diskutiert werden.[1] Nicht mehr nur in eher alternativ organisierten Ausstellungsräumen, sondern auch bei prominenten Kunstveranstaltungen und in großen Museen werden künstlerische Arbeiten ausgestellt, die das Verhältnis der Geschlechter sowie Bilder von Männlichkeit und Weiblichkeit kritisch hinterfragen. Thematisierungen von kolonialen Machtstrukturen und rassistischen Stereotypen sind im Kunstfeld ebenfalls keine Seltenheit mehr. So haben seit Catherine Davids *documenta X* (1997) beispielsweise auch alle folgenden *documenta*-Ausstellungen die Aktualität und Notwendigkeit der politischen und theoretischen Positionen Feminismus und Postkolonialismus (nicht nur in der Kunst) konstatiert und damit die Etablierung von künstlerischen Reflexionen über Sexismen und Rassismen als Thema des Kunstfeldes befördert. Nach wie vor sind sich die Akteur_innen[2] feministischer und postkolonialer Kritik uneinig, ob die bekannten und zum ›Mainstream‹ gehörenden Kunstinstitutionen geeignete Räume für die eigentlich ›von unten‹ kommenden Proteste gegen hegemoniale Strukturen sein können, oder ob diese Proteste durch die institutionellen ›Umarmungen‹ von dominierenden Diskursen affirmiert werden und an politischer Aussagefähigkeit und Schlagkraft verlieren.[3] Denn auch wenn sich nicht in Abrede stellen lässt, dass künstlerische Einsprüche gegen Geschlechterhierarchien und koloniale Dominanz- und Ausbeutungsstrukturen im Ausstellungsbetrieb der zeitgenössischen Kunst präsent sind (etwa jüngst in der Ausstellung *Uncertain States*, Berlin, Akademie der Künste, oder in *Postwar*, München, Haus der Kunst, beide 2016–2017), lässt sich gleichzeitig eine erhebliche Zurückhaltung von Kurator_innen und Künstler_innen ausmachen, wenn es darum geht, Kunstwerke als feministisch, postkolonial oder gar antirassistisch zu bezeichnen und sich damit offensiv politisch zu verorten.[4] Gewiss birgt das Labeln von künstlerischen Arbeiten immer gewisse Probleme (was macht nun eine feministische oder postkoloniale Kunst aus und wer darf darüber entscheiden?), insofern jede Bezeichnungspraxis immer auch zu vereinheitlichen droht und Grenzen zieht, aber gerade angesichts einer aktuell global auszumachenden erneuten Konsolidierung weißer männlicher Vorherrschaft und imperialistischer Tendenzen ist eine eindeutige politische Stellungnahme zu gegenwärtigen Machtstrukturen und Dominanzverhältnissen notwendig.

Die bereits genannten positiven neueren Entwicklungen sollten nicht darüber hinwegtäuschen, dass die *Art World* weiterhin überwiegend den weißen – meist aus Westeuropa oder Nordamerika stam-

142

For quite some time exhibitions of contemporary art have provided platforms for articulating and discussing feminist and postcolonial perspectives.[1] The days when artworks that critically question gender relationships and images of masculinity and femininity were exhibited only in alternative exhibition spaces are past; these works are now included in prominent art events and shown at major museums. Likewise, colonial power structures and racist stereotypes as subject matter are no longer rare in the art world. Since Catherine David's *documenta X* (1997) all subsequent *documenta* exhibitions have attested to the topicality of and necessity for political and theoretical positions on feminism and postcolonialism (not only in art), thus promoting the establishment of artistic reflections on sexism and racism as subjects in the field of art. Participants[2] in feminist and postcolonial criticism are at odds about whether well-known, mainstream art institutions are suitable spaces for protests against hegemonial structures that really need to come 'from below', or if these protests are affirmed by institutional 'embracing' of the dominant discourses, thus robbing them of their meaningfulness and punch.[3] For even if it cannot be denied that artistic objections to gender hierarchies and colonial structures of dominance and exploitation are present in exhibitions of contemporary art (for example, recently in the exhibitions *Uncertain States* at the Akademie der Künste in Berlin or *Postwar* at the Haus der Kunst in Munich, both in 2016–17), at the same time curators and artists are cautious about designating artworks as feminist, postcolonial or even anti-racist, which could put them in an aggressively political position.[4] It is certainly problematic to label artistic works (what constitutes feminist or postcolonial art, and who is authorised to decide about it?), since every labelling practice always threatens to generalise and draw borders. However, especially now – in light of the current global developments that again consolidate white male domination and imperialistic tendencies – an unambiguous political position on current power structures and relationships of dominance is much needed.

The above-mentioned positive new developments should not obscure the fact that *Art World* continues to favour mainly white, male and heterosexual artists – mostly from western Europe or North America – and remains predominantly elitist, that is, characterised by exclusion. Although there have been considerable changes in the participation of female artists, who are considerably more present in exhibitions, collections and galleries today than they were thirty years ago, they are still underrepresented in comparison to their male counterparts.[5] Since 1998

1 See Schmidt-Linsenhoff 2005, 19; Karentzos 2012, 250–51.

2 In the German original, the author uses the term 'Gender_Gap' to indicate all genders; the use of a space with the underline symbol is common in German to acknowledge that more than two genders exist.

3 There is much debate today about how anti-racial and anti-sexual critique can be practiced; see, for example, Micossé-Aikins 2015.

4 See Pejic 2008.

5 On the situation of artists in Germany see the commentary on the German Cultural Council's study of 2014 by Larissa Kikol (Kikol 2016); on the situation of artists in the United States see Maura Reilly's study (Reilly 2007).

6   Zu ihren vielfältigen Aktionen vgl. unter anderem ihre Homepage, online: <http://www.guerrillagirls.com>, letzter Zugriff: April 2017.

7   Vgl. Schade / Wenk 2011, 8 ff.

8   Die Bezeichnung ›Women of Color‹ wird als Solidaritätsbekundung verwendet und bezeichnet alle Frauen, die die Erfahrung teilen, als Andere der weißen Mehrheitsgesellschaft zu gelten.

9   Der Begriff ›Rassisierung‹ und das Adjektiv ›rassisiert‹ sind kritisch-analytische Bezeichnungen einer sozialen Praxis des Konstruierens von hierarchisierten Differenzen, die auf der Annahme von biologisch fundierten ›Rassen‹ gründen.

menden – männlichen und heterosexuellen Künstler bevorzugt und zu großen Teilen elitär, das heißt von Ausschließungen geprägt bleibt. Auch wenn sich erhebliche Veränderungen beispielsweise hinsichtlich der Teilhabe von weiblichen Kunstproduzentinnen bemerken lassen und diese heute wesentlich stärker in Ausstellungen, Sammlungen und Galerien präsent sind als noch vor 30 Jahren, sind sie im Vergleich zu ihren männlichen Kollegen nach wie vor unterrepräsentiert. [5] Die Guerrilla Girls, eine feministisch-aktivistische Künstlerinnengruppe aus New York, machen seit 1998 mit Postern und verschiedenen Aktionen immer wieder darauf aufmerksam, [6] dass die Forderung nach einer paritätischen Teilhabe der Geschlechter im Feld der Kunst weiter notwendig ist. 2016 wurden sie vom Kölner Museum Ludwig eingeladen, dessen Sammlung in den Blick zu nehmen, woraufhin sie ihre schon verschiedentlich gestellte Frage erneut artikulierten: »Do women have to be naked to get into the Museum?« (»Müssen Frauen nackt sein, um ins Museum zu kommen?«) Nur 5 % der ausgestellten Künstler_innen – so das Ergebnis ihrer Recherche – seien Frauen, dafür aber 85 % der Akte weiblich. Thematisiert wird damit ein Paradox, auf das die feministische Kritik seit den 1970er Jahren immer wieder hingewiesen hat: Die bloße Sichtbarkeit von Weiblichkeit in Kunstgeschichte und visueller Kultur führt *nicht* per

se zu einer größeren Anerkennung von Frauen – zum Beispiel als kreative Subjekte –, vielmehr geht der Objektstatus, der Frauen in der europäischen Kulturgeschichte zugewiesen wurde und weiter zugewiesen wird, sowie ihre visuelle Präsenz in verschiedenen Medien mit ihrem Ausschluss aus der politischen Öffentlichkeit einher. [7]

Dass die Erfahrungen von Ausschluss und Marginalisierung nicht für alle Frauen gleich sind, wurde von weißen Feministinnen jedoch übersehen, von ›Women of Color‹ [8] aber immer wieder in die Diskussion eingebracht. Auf verschiedene Weise machten diese auf ihre doppelte Diskriminierung als Frauen *und* als rassisierte [9] Andere aufmerksam. So begab sich die Künstlerin Adrian Piper 1975 im Rahmen ihrer Performance *The Mythic Being* mit Bart, ›Afroperücke‹, Sonnenbrille und Zigarre in die Öffentlichkeit. —→ 143 Durch diese überzeichneten Attribute des ›schwarzen Machos‹ blieb die Künstlichkeit ihrer Figur offensichtlich, und die absichtsvoll unperfekte Inszenierung ließ Geschlechtergrenzen ebenso wie rassisierte Einteilungen eher verschwimmen als sie zu bestätigen. Zugleich kann man in Videoaufnahmen der Aktion erkennen, wie sich Piper in ›männlichem Habitus‹ in der Öffentlichkeit bewegte. Sie berichtet, dass sie zwar nie Gefallen an der von ihr performten Figur habe finden können, dass ihr die Auftritte aber eine gewisse

143

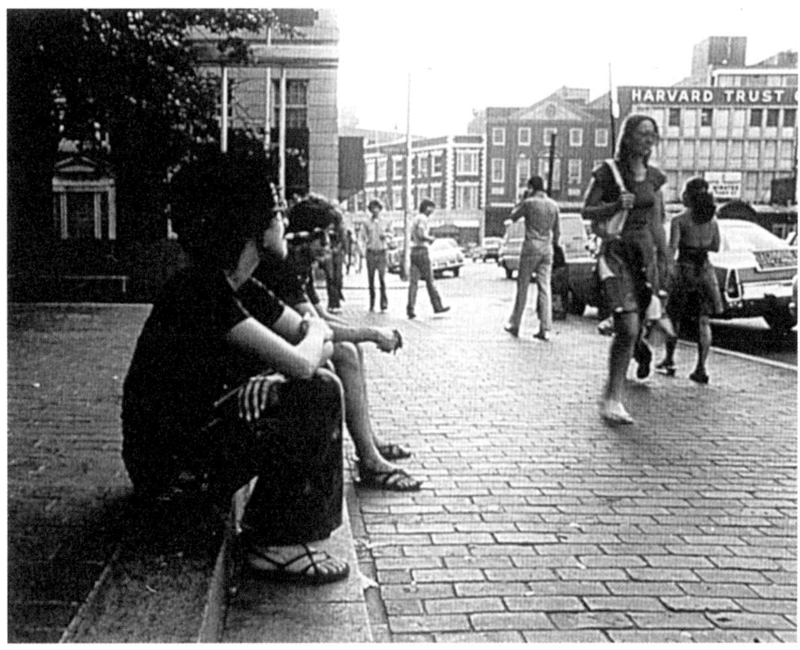

Adrian Piper
The Mythic Being: Cruising White Women, 1975

10 Vgl. Bowles 2007,
621–622.

11 Vgl. Marchart 2008.

12 Die Ausstellung war Teil eines größeren Projektes von cross links e. V.; sie wurde kuratiert von Bettina Knaup und Beatrice E. Stammer und in Partnerschaft mit der Akademie der Künste, Berlin, realisiert.

13 Die Ausstellung bestand aus Werken der Sammlung Verbund, Wien, und wurde kuratiert von Gabriele Schor und Merle Radtke.

14 Auf eine solche Ambivalenz verweist auch die Rezension der genannten Hamburger Ausstellung von Bettina Uppenkamp (Uppenkamp 2015).

Freiheit im Verhalten ermöglicht und Spaß bereitet haben.[10] Die Arbeit lässt sich als Hinweis darauf lesen, dass schwarze Frauen nicht nur in der Öffentlichkeit, sondern auch im Feminismus sowie innerhalb der schwarzen Bewegung darum kämpfen mussten, überhaupt als Akteurinnen wahrgenommen und anerkannt zu werden. Indem Piper während ihrer Aktion die Betrachter_innen (aber auch sich selbst) mit einer hinsichtlich Geschlecht und rassisierter Kategorisierung uneindeutigen Figur konfrontierte, setzte sie sie der Erfahrung aus, sich zu dieser verhalten zu müssen. Dabei entkoppelt *The Mythic Being* geschlechtliche und rassisierte Kategorien von jeglichem Essentialismus und eröffnet eine Möglichkeit, deren soziale Bedingtheiten und Auswirkungen – auch in Bezug auf die eigene Person – zu reflektieren.

Der Wandel des etablierten Kanons ist insofern nicht der einzige Effekt, den feministische und antirassistische Strömungen bewirkt haben. Dadurch, dass der exklusive Charakter der Kunst – zumindest teilweise – aufgebrochen wurde und Akteur_innen verschiedener Geschlechter, Hautfarben und Herkünfte sich eine Präsenz im Kunstfeld erkämpften, finden auch andere Themen und unterschiedliche Perspektiven auf gesellschaftliche und kulturelle Phänomene Eingang in Museen und Ausstellungen. Die Institutionen der Kunst und Kunstgeschichtsschreibung mit ihren Regeln, Ordnungen und Methoden geraten dabei selbst in einen kritisch-analytischen Blick. Oliver Marchart konstatiert, dass die westlichen Institutionen des Kunstfeldes gegenwärtig von einer gegenhegemonialen Verschiebung erfasst würden.[11] Wenn heute Künstler_innen in der Kunstwelt etabliert sind, die mit ihren Arbeiten eurozentrische Blicke irritieren sowie als gesichert geltende Annahmen stören und hinterfragen, dann folgen sie immer auch den Traditionslinien der Kämpfe sowie der Debatten von Feminismus und Postkolonialismus und agieren auf einem Feld (einem Kunstfeld), das durch diese Auseinandersetzungen maßgeblich (vor)bereitet wurde.

Zahlreiche Ausstellungen haben in den letzten Jahren die ›feministischen Avantgarden‹ der 1960er und 1970er Jahre zu präsentieren versucht (in Deutschland etwa *re.act.feminism – performancekunst der 1960er und 70er jahre heute,* Berlin, Akademie der Künste, 2008–2009[12], oder *Feministische Avantgarde der 1970er Jahre,* Hamburger Kunsthalle, 2015[13]). Auch wenn die Arbeiten in den White Cubes dieser historisierenden Ausstellungen eine gewisse Nobilitierung erfuhren, drohten sie doch von ihrer ursprünglich linksaktivistischen Herkunft abgeschnitten und die Schärfe ihrer Tabubrüche und Regelverletzungen normalisiert zu werden.[14] Diesem Eindruck standen die Erzählungen und Reflexionen der Künstlerinnen entge-

144

with their posters and other activities, the Guerrilla Girls, a feminist group of activist artists from New York, have been calling attention to the fact that equal participation of the genders is still needed in the field of art.[6] In 2016 they were invited by the Museum Ludwig in Cologne to examine the museum's collection; they re-articulated their questions that had already been similarly phrased: 'Do women have to be naked to get into the museum?' Their research revealed that while only five percent of the exhibited art was by women artists, eighty-five percent of the nude images were of women. This casts light on the paradox that feminist criticism has highlighted again and again since the 1970s: the mere visibility of femininity in art history and in the visual arts does not per se lead to greater respect for women – as creative subjects, for example. Instead, the status as objects that has been and continues to be allocated to women in European art history along with their visual presence in different media has resulted in their exclusion from the political public.[7]

That the experiences of exclusion and marginalisation are not the same for all women was overlooked by white feminists, but women of colour have brought this into discussions repeatedly.[8] In different ways they called attention to their double discrimination as women and as racially classified Others.[9]

In 1975, as part of her performance *The Mythic Being,* the artist Adrian Piper went out in public wearing a moustache, afro wig, sunglasses and cigar. → 143 These exaggerated attributes of a 'black macho' made the artificiality of her figure perfectly clear, and the consciously imperfect staging blurred the borders of gender and racially classified categorisation even more than confirming them. Yet the video of the performance shows how Piper moved in public as her 'male alter ego'. She discloses that she never liked the figure in her performance, but that it gave her a certain sense of freedom and fun.[10] The work can be read as an indication of how black women had to fight to be noticed and recognised as participants not only in public but also in the feminist and black movements. By confronting the viewers (but also herself) with a figure that was ambiguous in terms of gender and racial classification, she exposed them to the experience of having to react. *The Mythic Being* separates gender and racial categories from any essentialism and gives the opportunity to reflect on social conditionality and its consequences – also in terms of one's self.

In this respect the transformation of the established cannon was not the only result of feminist and anti-racist movements. Due to the breakdown of art's exclusive character – at least partially – and the

6 On their diverse activities see their website: <http://www.guerrillagirls.com> (accessed 20 August, 2017).

7 See Schade / Wenk 2011, 8ff.

8 The term 'woman of colour' is used to show solidarity and refers to all women who share the experience of being an Other in white majority society.

9 The term 'Rassisierung' and the adjective 'rassisiert' are terms of critical analysis in German that refer to a social practice of constructing hierarchic differences that are based on biological 'races'.

10 See Bowles 2007, 621–22.

15 Feminismus ist keine Erfindung des globalen Nordens, sondern wird auch in den verschiedenen Regionen des globalen Südens praktiziert. Ich konzentriere mich hier allerdings auf die mir – teilweise aus eigener Erfahrung und Beteiligung – bekannten Diskussionsprozesse westlicher Feminismen und die Einsprüche von ›Women of Color‹ und von postkolonialen Positionen.

16 Sigrid Adorf geht in ihrer Studie zu Videoarbeiten der 1970er Jahre der Frage nach, welche repräsentationskritischen Bedeutungen diesen künstlerischen Auseinandersetzungen zugesprochen werden können (vgl. Adorf 2008).

gen, die die zweite Welle des Feminismus prägten. So machten zum Beispiel Erläuterungen von Suzanne Lacy zu ihren frühen Arbeiten auf dem Symposium zu *re.act.feminism* im Januar 2009 deutlich, wie stark die Künstlerinnen der sozialen Bewegung und den Aktionen ›auf der Straße‹ verbunden waren beziehungsweise an diesen teilhatten. Unter dem Titel *In Mourning and in Rage* hatten Suzanne Lacy und Leslie Labowitz 1977 zusammen mit verschiedenen Frauenprojekten in Los Angeles einen Protest organisiert, der sich gegen die sensationslüsterne Berichterstattung der lokalen Presse über eine Serie von Vergewaltigungen und Morden an Frauen wandte. ⟶ **146** Mit einem Autokorso und einem Auftritt in schwarzen Gewändern und roten Umhängen waren die Künstlerinnen und Aktivistinnen vor das örtliche Rathaus gezogen, wo sie ihre Analyse der Ereignisse vortrugen, betroffenen Frauen Unterstützung anboten und ihre Trauer um die Verstorbenen zum Ausdruck brachten.

Mit Blick auf solche Aktionen lässt sich der Feminismus in erster Linie als eine Bewegung charakterisieren, die sich sowohl aus Anteilen sozialen Engagements als auch aus akademischen und künstlerischen Elementen konstituiert. Keinesfalls aber ist damit eine einheitliche politische Position benannt, vielmehr umfasst der Feminismus verschiedene Auslegungen und Vorstellungen davon, was eine femi-

nistische Politik sein könnte und wie sie auszuführen sei. Gemeinsam ist den verschiedenen Ansätzen zwar der Widerstand gegen patriarchale Strukturen und Gewalt sowie die Forderung nach einer gleichberechtigten Teilhabe aller Geschlechter; welche Themen akut sind und wie Emanzipation erreicht werden könnte, bleibt allerdings umstritten. In den feministischen Kunstszenen Westeuropas und Nordamerikas waren es in den 1960er und 1970er Jahren neben den spezifisch weiblichen Lebensrealitäten und Alltagserfahrungen vor allem patriarchale Bilder von Weiblichkeit, die in den kritischen Blick gerieten. **15** Die als männlich verstandenen Repräsentationen wurden auf verschiedene Art und Weise kritisiert und artikulieren sich bis heute in unterschiedlichen künstlerischen Strategien. Während einige Künstlerinnen alternative und ›eigene‹ Bilder von Weiblichkeit entwerfen, befragen andere die tradierten Visualisierungen und ihre medialen Repräsentationen auf deren Bedeutungsproduktionen und Effekte im Kontext einer von Machtstrukturen durchzogenen Gesellschaft. **16** Eine Kontroverse, die einen wesentlichen Dissens in den Auffassungen von feministisch-künstlerischer Praxis deutlich macht, entzündete sich an der mittlerweile berühmten Installation *The Dinner Party* (1974–1979) von Judy Chicago. ⟶ **149** Die Arbeit besteht aus einem zum Dreieck arrangierten großen Tisch mit 39 Gedecken, die

---

rise in visibility of participants of different genders, skin colours and origins in the field of art, new topics and different perspectives on social and cultural phenomena have entered museums and exhibitions. This has the effect that art institutions and art writing rules, regulations and methods are beginning to scrutinise themselves critically and analytically. Oliver Marchart notes that Western art institutions are presently in the grips of anti-hegemonial displacement. [11] When nowadays established artists disturb Eurocentric views, disturbing and questioning established assumptions, they always follow the traditional lines of battle as well as the debates of feminism and postcolonialism and act on a field (a field of art) that was decisively prepared by these discussions.

Numerous exhibitions in recent years have tried to present the 'feminist avant-gardes' of the 1960s and 1970s (in Germany such exhibitions as *re.act.feminism – performancekunst der 1960er und 70er jahre heute,* 2008–09, in the Akademie der Künste in Berlin [12] or *Feministische Avantgarde der 1970er Jahre,* 2015, in the Hamburger Kunsthalle [13]). Although the works were ennobled in the White Cubes of these historicising exhibitions, their originally leftist and activist origins were weakened and normalised as was the sharpness of their breaches of taboo and violation of rules. [14] The stories and reflections of the artists who

formed the second wave of feminism are opposed to this impression. Suzanne Lacy's explanations of her early works at the symposium *re.act.feminism* in January 2009, for example, makes it clear how strong the artists' links to and participation in the social movement and the activities 'on the street' were. In 1977 Suzanne Lacy and Leslie Labowitz organised a protest with different women's projects in Los Angeles, entitled *In Mourning and in Rage,* that appealed to the sensationalising reporting of the local press on a series of rapes and murders of women. ⟶ **146** Dressed in black robes and red capes the artists and activists made a procession with a motorcade to the local city hall, where they analysed the events, offered support to women and expressed their grief about the deceased.

Keeping such actions in mind, feminism can be characterised first and foremost as a movement that constitutes an interest in social engagement as well as academic and artistic elements. However, there is hardly a unified political position; instead feminism embraces different interpretations and ideas about what feminist politics could be and how it could be implemented. One common element in the different approaches is opposition to patriarchal structures and violence as well as the demand for equal participation of all genders; which subjects are acute and

11 See Marchart 2008.

12 The exhibition was part of a larger project by cross links e. V.; it was curated by Bettina Knaup and Beatrice E. Stammer and implemented by the Akademie der Künste, Berlin.

13 The exhibition consisted of works from the Verbund Collection, Vienna, and was curated by Gabriele Schor and Merle Radtke.

14 The review of the abovementioned exhibition in Hamburg by Bettina Uppenkamp shows this short of ambivalence (Uppenkamp 2015).

17 *The Dinner Party* wurde 1987 in der Schirn Kunsthalle in Frankfurt am Main ausgestellt. Für eine deutschsprachige Kritik an der Arbeit vgl. die Beiträge der 1. Ausgabe der Zeitschrift *FrauenKunstWissenschaft* von 1987.

18 Vgl. Walker 1989, 193 ff.

jeweils einer bedeutenden historischen Frauenfigur gewidmet sind, weitere 999 Namen sind in goldener Schrift auf die weißen Porzellankacheln geschrieben, mit denen der Boden ausgelegt ist. Kunstvoll bestickte Tischläufer und Porzellanteller, die mit blumenähnlichen Vaginamotiven bemalt sind, sollen nicht nur die nahezu vergessenen weiblichen Persönlichkeiten, sondern auch die als weiblich geltenden Tätigkeiten Porzellanmalerei und Nadelarbeit aufwerten. Chicagos Installation wurde jedoch in den Jahren nach ihren ersten Präsentationen der Vorwurf des Essentialismus gemacht – Frauen würden hier auf ihre Körperlichkeit beziehungsweise ihr Geschlecht reduziert und als natürliche Referenz entworfen.[17] Bemängelt wurde weiterhin, dass nur wenige Plätze für lesbische oder schwarze Frauen bereitgehalten würden. Signifikant ist, dass fast alle Teller florale Vulvamotive zeigen, ausgerechnet aber auf demjenigen der schwarzen Frauenrechtlerin Sojourner Truth drei Gesichter abgebildet sind, die nicht nur klischeehaft ausgestaltet sind, sondern auch schwarzer Weiblichkeit eine eigene Sexualität verwehren, wie die Schriftstellerin Alice Walker hervorhob.[18]

Ein Versuch, Bilder schwarzer Weiblichkeit aufzuwerten und umzucodieren, ist Betye Saars Assemblage *The Liberation of Aunt Jemima* von 1972. Zu sehen ist zentral die ursprünglich aus Minstrel Shows und aus der US-amerikanischen Werbung stammende stereotype Figur der Aunt Jemima, die in der rechten Hand einen Besen, in der linken aber – abweichend vom Stereotyp – ein Gewehr hält. Vor ihr befindet sich ein Bild einer schwarzen ›Mammy‹ mit einem weißen Baby auf dem Arm, davor wiederum eine schwarze Faust als Symbol der Black-Power-Bewegung. Im Hintergrund ist in Form einer aus der Werbung stammenden Darstellung Aunt Jemimas eine Anspielung auf Andy Warhols Siebdrucke von Marilyn Monroe ins Bild gesetzt. Die schwarzer Weiblichkeit zugeschriebenen Rollen der Hausfrau, des Hausmädchens und letztlich der Sklavin für Weiße werden konterkariert, der tradierte weibliche Charakter mit den Insignien der schwarzen Bürgerrechtsbewegung versehen und zu einer militanten Kämpferin umgestaltet. Anders als Chicago rekurriert Saar nicht auf Bilder vermeintlich natürlicher weiblicher Eigenheiten, sondern arbeitet ein bekanntes Stereotyp um, indem sie dieses mit Zeichen schwarzen Widerstands ausstattet.

Künstlerinnen wie Cindy Sherman versuchen dagegen nicht, die Frau aufzuwerten oder umzucodieren. In ihren *Untitled Film Stills* (1977–1980) fotografiert Sherman sich selbst in unterschiedlichen Posen, die an bekannte filmische Stereotype weißer weiblicher Filmstars erinnern, aber keine natürliche Weiblichkeit behaupten. ⟶ **150** ›Die Frau‹ wird

146

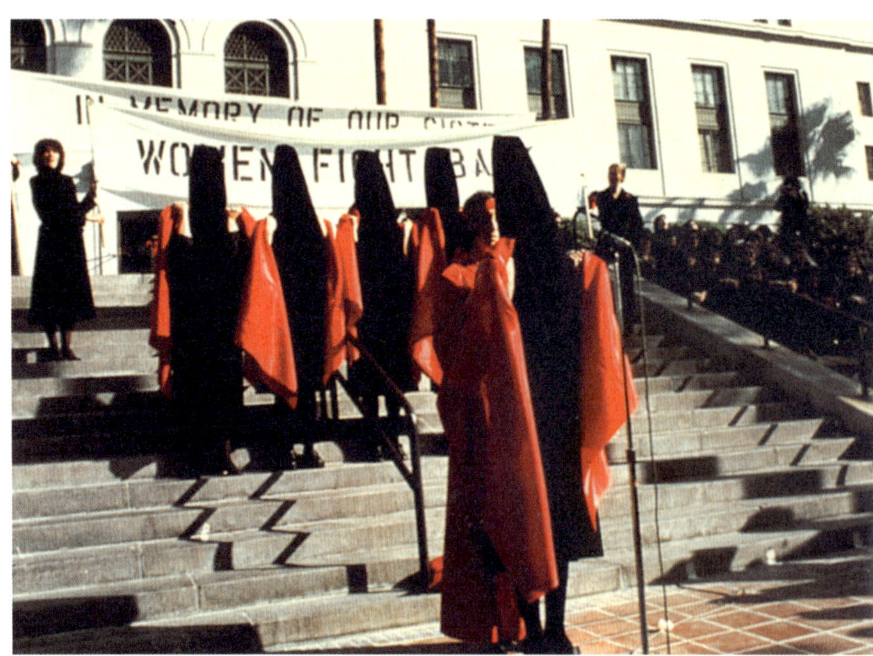

Suzanne Lacy & Leslie Labowitz
In Mourning and in Rage, 1977

19   Für eine ausführliche Analyse dieser Arbeit vgl. Brandes 2010, 59 ff. und 168 ff.

hier in ihrem Bildstatus dargestellt, Weiblichkeit in diesen inszenierten Fotografien als Maskerade vorgeführt, hinter der sich kein unveränderlicher Kern verbirgt. In die von der Lacanschen Psychoanalyse inspirierten feministischen Debatten darüber, ob Weiblichkeit lediglich ein patriarchales Bild sei und ob es jenseits patriarchaler Weiblichkeitskonstruktionen überhaupt eine weibliche Essenz gebe, lassen sich die Fotografien von Carrie Mae Weems einbringen: Ihre Arbeit *Mirror, Mirror* (aus der *Ain't Jokin'*-Serie, 1987–1988) zeigt eine schwarze Frau, die in einen Spiegel schaut, der aber nicht ihr Gesicht reflektiert, sondern das einer Weißen. Laut Bildunterschrift fragt die Frau: »Mirror, Mirror on the wall, who's the finest of them all?« (»Spieglein, Spieglein an der Wand, wer ist die Schönste im ganzen Land?«), der Spiegel antwortet: »Snow White, you black bitch! And don't you forget it!!!« (»Schneewittchen, du schwarze Schlampe! Und merk' dir das mal!!!«). ⟶ **151** Deutlich wird, dass das Bild von Weiblichkeit in der westlichen Dominanzkultur ein (schnee)weißes ist, dem das Bild schwarzer Weiblichkeit lediglich als kontrastive Folie dient. In weiteren Serien, zum Beispiel in *From Here I Saw What Happened and I Cried* (1995–1996), macht Weems in Bild-Text-Kombinationen deutlich, wie Schwarze in der Geschichte der Vereinigten Staaten mithilfe der Fotografie in stereotypen Bildern fixiert wurden, die

bis heute ihre Wahrnehmung als ›Andere‹ prägen. Anthropologisch-ethnografische fotografische Praktiken geraten dabei ebenso in den Blick wie solche aus dem Kontext von Kunst, Pornografie oder privater fotografischer Erinnerungskultur.[19] Auch ›Rasse‹ wird somit als soziale Konstruktion erkennbar, die in der Moderne durch verschiedene visuelle Repräsentationstechniken mitkonstituiert wurde.

Im Kontext künstlerischer Dekonstruktion geschlechtlicher und rassisierter Kategorien werden auch dominierende Vorstellungen von Künstlerschaft, Genie und Originalität – nicht ohne Humor – als beteiligt an der Herstellung von Differenzen entlarvt. Wenn die Künstlerin Elaine Sturtevant sich mit Hut, Fliegerweste und Jeans als Joseph Beuys verkleidet, legt sie damit nicht nur die Inszenierung des selbsternannten Kunstrevolutionärs offen, sondern evoziert ebenso die Frage, ob sich eine solche Position auch von einer Frau einnehmen ließe (*Beuys La Rivoluzione Siamo Noi,* 1988). Mit Rosemarie Trockels Malmaschine (*Ohne Titel, Malmaschine,* 1990) kann die Signatur eines Gemäldes maschinell hergestellt werden, wodurch die in der westlichen Kunstgeschichte als originär geltende Handschrift ersetzt wird. In ähnlicher Manier konterkariert Shigeko Kubota Mythen männlicher Künstlerschaft, wenn sie das in den 1960er Jahren von vielen männlichen Künstlern praktizierte

147

how emancipation could be achieved is debated. In the feminist art scene of western Europe and North America in the 1960s and 1970s it was – in addition to the specifically female life realities and everyday experiences – particularly patriarchal images of femininity that came under the critical gaze.[15] The type of representation that was considered masculine was criticised in different ways and continues to be articulated to this day using different artistic strategies. While some artists create their own alternative images of femininity, others question the established representations and their presentation in the media in terms of the production of meaning and effects in the context of a society that is infused with structures of power.[16] The now famous installation *The Dinner Party* (1974–79) by Judy Chicago sparked a controversy that makes apparent one fundamental point of dissent in the concepts of feminist artistic practice. ⟶ **149** The work consists of a triangular table with thirty-nine place settings, each of which are dedicated to an important woman figure from history; an additional 999 names are inscribed in golden lettering on the porcelain tiles that cover the floor. Artfully embroidered table runners and porcelain plates painted with flower-like vagina motifs are not only meant to raise appreciation for these largely forgotten female figures, but also for activities such as porcelain painting and

needlework that are associated with women. However, Chicago's installation was criticised for its essentialism in the years after its first presentations – for reducing women to their bodies or sex and understanding them as a natural reference.[17] It was also criticised for reserving so few places for lesbian or black women. It is significant that almost all of the plates have floral vulva motifs, but ironically there are three faces on the plate of Sojourner Truth, the black activist for women's rights; not only are these based on clichés, they also deny black women their own sexuality, as the writer Alice Walker criticised.[18]

Betye Saar's 1972 assemblage *The Liberation of Aunt Jemima* is an attempt to upgrade and re-encode the image of black femininity. At the centre of the work is the stereotype figure of Aunt Jemima, originally from a minstrel show and widely known through American advertising, who holds a broom in her right hand and – diverging from the stereotype – a rifle in her left hand. In front of her there is a picture of a black 'mammy' with a white baby in her arm and, in front of that, a black fist, the symbol of the Black Power movement. The background is plastered with the image of Aunt Jemima known from advertising in reference to Andy Warhol's silk screens of Marilyn Monroe. The roles attributed to black femininity – housewife, housemaid and ultimately slave for white

15   Feminism is not an invention of the Global North but is also practiced in the different regions of the Global South. However, my focus here is the discussion process – that I am aware of due to my own experience and participation – in Western feminisms and the protests of women of colour and of postcolonial positions.

16   In her study on video works of the 1970s, Sigrid Adorf examined the question of which means of critical representation can be ascribed to this artistic debate (see Adorf 2008).

17   *The Dinner Party* was exhibited at the Schirn Kunsthalle in Frankfurt am Main in 1987. See the contributions of the first edition of the magazine *FrauenKunstWissenschaft* of 1987 for critiques of the work in German.

18   See Walker 1989, 193ff.

20 Vgl. dazu auch die ein-
führende Darstellung von postkolonialer Theorie von Ina
Kerner (Kerner 2012).

21 Für eine ausführliche Darstellung dieser Perspektive
und ihrer verschiedenen Referenzen vgl. Kravagna 1999.

Action Painting kommentiert, indem sie mit einem Pinsel, den sie zwischen ihren Beinen an ihrer Unterwäsche befestigt hat, rote Striche auf ein am Boden liegendes Blatt Papier malt (*Vagina Painting*, 1965). Künstlerisches Schaffen, das von der westlichen Kunstgeschichte seit der Moderne immer wieder mit dem männlichen Zeugungsakt gleichgesetzt und sexuell aufgeladen wurde, wird dadurch ins Lächerliche gezogen. Es wird gleichzeitig als etwas dargestellt, das Frauen auf diesem Weg nicht erreichbar ist. Dass auch Materialität geschlechtlich kodiert ist, wird in Objekten im Stil von Pop und Minimal Art verhandelt, die in Materialien und Techniken umgesetzt werden, die als weiblich gelten, wie es unter anderem Rosemarie Trockel in ihren Strickbildern gelungen ist. ⟶ **152**

Seit den 1980er Jahren werden im Kunstfeld zunehmend Arbeiten präsentiert, die sich mit der kolonialen Vergangenheit und deren bis heute andauernden vielfältigen Fortwirkungen und Kontinuitäten auseinandersetzen. Unter dem Begriff des Postkolonialismus, der eine Perspektive beschreibt, die auf antikolonialistische und antirassistische Kämpfe und Proteste politischer Bewegungen zurückzuführen ist,[20] werden dabei nicht nur ökonomische und politische Verhältnisse thematisiert, sondern vor allem auch historische und aktualisierte Formen der Wahrheits- und Wissensproduktion, mit denen koloniale

Ausgrenzungs- und Diskriminierungsverhältnisse legitimiert werden. Analysiert werden die oft zwischen Faszination und Abwehr changierenden Bilder, die sich die Kolonisatoren von ›den Anderen‹ machten und die bis heute auch teilweise die Selbstbilder der ehemals Kolonisierten prägen.[21] Insofern ist die Auseinandersetzung mit Repräsentationen aus der Gegenwart immer auch eine Auseinandersetzung mit der Vergangenheit. Koloniale Verhältnisse und interkulturelle ›Kontakte‹ rücken dabei in den Blick und werden auf ihre Verwobenheit mit gegenwärtigen Realitäten befragt. Geschlechterverhältnisse spielen auch hier auf verschiedenen Ebenen eine Rolle. Der Film *Not So Nice Coloured Girls* (1987) der Künstlerin Tracey Moffatt zeigt das zeitgenössische Nachtleben von Sydney und folgt drei jungen schwarzen Frauen, die sich von einem betrunkenen Weißen ihr Abendvergnügen bezahlen lassen. Über Schriftinserts erfahren die Betrachter_innen, dass sie mit diesem von ihnen selbst als ›picking up Captain‹ bezeichneten Verhalten letztlich eine Überlebensstrategie ihrer Mütter und Großmütter fortführen (auch wenn diese das nicht gutheißen). Während die Betrachter_innen die ungelenken Annäherungsversuche beobachten können, trägt eine Stimme aus dem Off Aufzeichnungen der ersten Kolonisatoren Australiens vor, die vom neu entdeckten Kontinent und vor allem von dessen

148

people – are foiled, while the established female character is equipped with the insignias of the black civil rights movement and transformed into a militant fighter. Unlike Chicago, Saar does not refer to imagery of supposed *natural* feminine characteristics, but instead transforms a famous stereotype by fitting it with symbols of black opposition.

Artists such as Cindy Sherman, on the other hand, did not try to upgrade or re-encode the image of women. In her *Untitled Film Stills* (1977–80) Sherman photographed herself in different poses that are reminiscent of known film stereotypes of white female stars, but do not portray natural femininity. ⟶ **150** In these staged photographs, 'woman' is represented as an image, and femininity is presented as a masquerade, behind which there is no consistent core. The feminist debate that was inspired by Lacanian psychoanalysis about whether femininity is just a patriarchal image or if there is a female essence at all beyond patriarchal constructions of femininity, can be related to the photographs of Carrie Mae Weems. Her work *Mirror, Mirror* (from the *Ain't Jokin'* series, 1987–88) shows a black woman looking into a mirror that does not reflect her own face but the one of a white woman. According to the captions the woman asks, 'Mirror, mirror on the wall, who's the finest of them all?' The mirror says, 'Snow White, you black

bitch, and don't you forget it!!!'. ⟶ **151** It becomes clear that the image of femininity in the Western dominant culture is as white as snow, of which the image of black femininity is just a contrasting foil. Using combinations of text and images in other series such as *From Here I Saw What Happened and I Cried* (1995–96), Weems shows how in American history photography cast black people in stereotype images that continue to mark their perception of themselves as 'Others' to this day. Photographs from anthropological and ethnographic practices are in focus as well as those from the context of art, pornography and photographic cultures of private remembrance.[19] Race also becomes noticeable as a social construction that was created in the modern era through various visual techniques of representation.

The dominant concepts of authorship, genius and originality are revealed in the context of artistic deconstruction of gender and racial categories – not without humour – to be involved in the production of differences. When the artist Elaine Sturtevant dressed up as Joseph Beuys in a hat, fishing vest and jeans, she was not only disclosing the pose of the self-proclaimed art revolutionary, she was also evoking the question of whether such a position can be held by a woman (*Beuys La Rivoluzione Siamo Noi*, 1988). The signature of a painting can be made by a machine,

19 For a comprehensive analysis of this work see Brandes 2010, 59ff and 168ff.

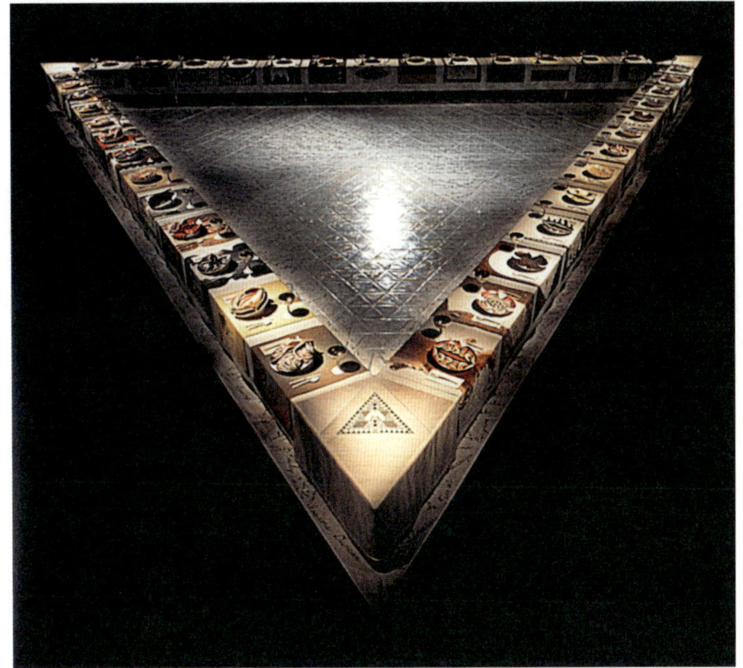

149

as Rosemarie Trockel's painting machine (*Ohne Titel, Malmaschine* [Untitled, Painting Machine], 1990) proves, thus replacing the 'handwriting' or style that is considered original in Western art history. In a similar manner, Shigeko Kubota foiled myths of male artistry when in the 1960s she commented on male-dominated Action painting by using a brush attached to her underwear between her legs to paint red lines on a sheet of paper on the ground (*Vagina Painting*, 1965). Artistic production, which since the modern period has repeatedly been equated with the male act of procreation and sexually loaded, is thus made ridiculous and simultaneously shown as something that cannot be achieved by women. The notion that materials are also sexually coded is explored in objects in the style of Pop art and Minimalism that are executed using materials and techniques that are considered feminine, for example in Rosemarie Trockel's knitted works. ⟶ **152**

Since the 1980s there has been an increase in artworks that deal with colonial past and its various consequences and continuity that continue to this day. Under the rubric of postcolonialism, which describes a perspective that is based on anticolonial and antiracist struggles and protests of political movements,[20] not only economic and political circumstances are addressed, but predominantly historical and current forms of producing truth and knowledge, with which the colonial relationships of exclusion and discrimination are legitimised. The images that fluctuate between fascination and hostility are analysed, which the colonisers made of the 'Others' and which to this day to a great extent characterise the self-images of those who were formerly colonised.[21] In this respect dealing with representations from the present is also dealing with the past. Colonial conditions and intercultural 'contacts' are noticeable and questioned in terms of their entanglement with present realities. Gender relations also play a role on different levels. The film *Not So Nice Coloured Girls* (1987) by Tracey Moffatt shows contemporary Australian nightlife in Sydney and follows three young black women who let a white man pay for their evening of fun. Intertitles inform the viewers that this type of behaviour, which they called 'picking up Captain', is actually a continuation of the strategy of survival practiced by their mothers and grandmothers (although they do not condone it). While the viewers can observe the awkward advances, the voice-over recites notes written by the first colonists of Australia who tell of the newly discovered continent and especially of their inhabitants, using known stereotypes. The filmed images do not always correspond to visual expectations; the camera seldom focuses on the women themselves,

20 See also the introductory overview of postcolonial theory by Ina Kerner (Kerner 2012).

21 See Kravagna 1999 for a comprehensive look at this perspective and its different references.

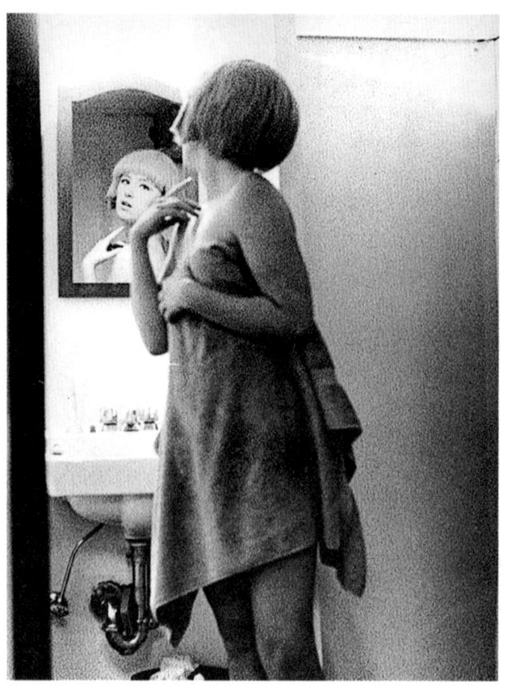

Cindy Sherman
Untitled Film Still #2, 1977

150

and the film narration is repeatedly interrupted by images of framed drawings by European 'conquerors' and staged scenes that concisely show the relationship between the 'Captain' and the women. [22] Simple polarisation of abuser / perpetrator and victim is made impossible – at the latest when the women steal the wallet of the man they have picked up. Moffatt's film does not create new heroines, but instead of simply repeating colonial images and relationships of gazes, it addresses the space between the colonisers and the colonised as one of lust and economy as well as a continuity in which stereotypes stubbornly persist. In a similar way the works of Kara Walker cite established parameters of depiction, exposing them as still influential but also putting them in motion. In her large-format paper-cuts Walker makes panoramas of racist and sexist stereotypes, such as in *Slavery, Slavery!* (1997). ⟶ **153** Although viewers initially believe that they are seeing images of a southern family idyll with slaves in the nineteenth century, on second glance they recognise that they are disturbing pornographic scenes full of violence, in which the roles of perpetrators and victims – similar to the work of Moffatt – are ambiguous in a disturbing way. What some read as parodying alienation, which works on both the level of content and representation, has been criticised massively and rejected by others as unbroken repetition of clichés and ingratiation to a dominant white art world. [23] The strategy of parodistic repetition and simultaneous thwarting of image traditions from the colonial period remains controversial in its readability and critical effectiveness.

The experiences of migration, flight and displacement as well as life in the diaspora and generally in a globalised world form another thematic area of postcolonial art discourse. While it was initially understood as an appeal against the dominant discourse of memory, in which migration stories for a long time only came up occasionally, many artists have since created alternative imagery that contrasts with the current overpowering presence of stereotypical images of migration in the media. In this context few claim to be able to just represent the specific experiences and living realities. While some try to represent the memories of travelling and being on the road or also the living situations of migrants, as for example Anny and Sibel Öztürk did in their recent installations with travelling routes or packed cars, others more selectively examine experiences of exclusion, displacement and painful violence. ⟶ **155** Ayşe Erkmen, Mona Hatoum and Gülsün Karamustafa are some of the artists who addressed these subjects early on and saw mobility and migration not only as a geographic and economic, but also the cultural and ideological

22   Christian Kravagna also cites Moffatt's film as an example. See Kravagna 1999, 50; for a comprehensive reading of the film see Vercoe 1997.

23   Anja Zimmermann (Zimmermann 2007), Birgit Haehnel (Haehnel 2007) and Alexandra Karentzos (Karentzos 2012) read Walker's works as parodies; for additional commentary of the critiques, which were predominantly expressed by Afro-American artists of an older generation, see Wall 2010.

22 Auch Christian Kravagna nennt Moffatts Film als Beispiel. Vgl. ebd., 50; für eine ausführliche Lektüre der Arbeit vgl. Vercoe 1997.

23 Eine Lektüre von Walkers Arbeiten als Parodie nehmen Anja Zimmermann (Zimmermann 2007), Birgit Haehnel (Haehnel 2007) und Alexandra Karentzos (Karentzos 2012) vor; für eine zusätzliche Kommentierung der Kritiken, die überwiegend von afroamerikanischen Künstlerinnen älterer Generationen artikuliert wurden, vgl. Wall 2010.

Bewohnerinnen erzählen, wobei bekannte Stereotype reproduziert werden. Die Filmaufnahmen entsprechen dabei jedoch nicht den Sehgewohnheiten; selten fokussiert die Kamera die Frauen direkt, immer wieder wird die filmische Narration unterbrochen von Aufnahmen gerahmter Zeichnungen der europäischen ›Eroberer‹ und gestellten Szenen, die das Verhältnis zwischen dem ›Captain‹ und den Frauen pointiert vor Augen führen. [22] Einfache Polarisierungen von Täter und Opfer werden dabei verunmöglicht – spätestens wenn die Frauen dem umworbenen weißen Mann die Brieftasche klauen. Moffatts Film schafft keine neuen Heroinen, wiederholt aber auch nicht einfach koloniale Bilder und Blickverhältnisse, vielmehr thematisiert er den Zwischenraum zwischen Kolonisator und Kolonisierter als einen des Begehrens und der Ökonomie sowie als Kontinuum, in dem Stereotype sich hartnäckig halten. In ähnlicher Weise zitieren auch die Arbeiten von Kara Walker tradierte Darstellungsparameter, um sie als bis heute wirkmächtige zu entlarven, aber auch, um sie in Bewegung zu bringen. In großformatigen Scherenschnittbildern entwirft Walker Panoramen rassistischer und sexistischer Bildstereotype, zum Beispiel in *Slavery, Slavery!* (1997). ⟶ **153** Meint man zunächst noch Bilder einer Familienidylle samt Sklaven in den Südstaaten des 19. Jahrhunderts zu sehen, erkennt man auf den zweiten Blick verstörende pornografische Szenen voller Gewalt, in denen die Rollen von Tätern und Opfern – ähnlich wie bei Moffatt – auf irritierende Weise uneindeutig werden. Was die einen als parodistische Verfremdung lesen, die sowohl auf inhaltlicher als auch auf Ebene der Repräsentation funktioniert, haben andere als ungebrochene Wiederholung von Klischeebildern und Anbiederung an eine dominante weiße Kunstwelt massiv kritisiert und abgelehnt. [23] Die Strategie des parodierenden Wiederholens und gleichzeitigen Durchkreuzens von tradierten Bildern der Kolonialzeit bleibt hinsichtlich ihrer Lesbarkeit und kritischen Effektivität umstritten.

Erfahrungen von Migration, Flucht und Vertreibung sowie vom Leben in der Diaspora und generell in einer globalisierten Welt bilden ein weiteres Themenfeld des postkolonialen Kunstdiskurses. Während dieser zunächst als Einspruch gegen dominierende Erinnerungsdiskurse zu verstehen war, in denen Migrationsgeschichten lange Zeit nur selten vorkamen, entwerfen viele Künstler_innen mittlerweile eher Gegenbilder zu einer aktuell zu verzeichnenden medialen Überpräsenz stereotyper Bilder von Migration. Auch in diesem Kontext behaupten die wenigsten, die spezifischen Erfahrungen und Lebensrealitäten einfach abbilden zu können. Während einige die Erinnerungen an Reisen und Unterwegssein oder auch

151

Carrie Mae Weems
Mirror, Mirror, 1987–1988

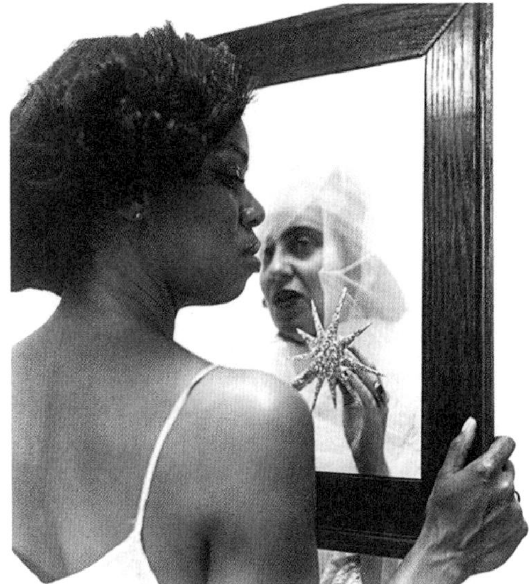

24 Darauf hat mit Bezug auf Ayşe Erkmen, Romuald Hazoumé und Yinka Shonibare unter anderem auch Melanie Ulz verwiesen (Ulz 2011).

25 Für eine feministische Lektüre von Arbeiten der Minimal-Art-Künstler, denen – entgegen ihrer Intention – aufgrund von Material und Größe Bedeutungen und geschlechtliche Konnotationen anhaften, vgl. Chave 1990 / 1998.

26 Gattungshierarchien, die auf geschlechtsspezifischen Zuordnungen, aber auch auf der Vorstellung von ›außereuropäischer Kunst‹ als einer bloß reproduktiven basieren, sind ein wiederkehrendes Thema feministischer Künstlerinnen (z. B. Joyce Kozloff und Miriam Schapiro), das Aladağ um den Aspekt der Raumerfahrung und das Thema Migration ergänzt.

migrantische Wohnsituationen zu visualisieren suchen wie jüngst etwa Anny und Sibel Öztürk in ihren Installationen mit Reiserouten oder bepackten Autos, nehmen andere gezielter Erfahrungen der Ausgrenzung, des Vertriebenseins und schmerzhafter Gewalt in den Blick. ⟶ **155** Ayşe Erkmen, Mona Hatoum und Gülsün Karamustafa gehören zu den Künstlerinnen, die sich schon früh mit diesen Sujets befasst und Mobilität und Migration nicht nur als geografische und ökonomische, sondern auch als kulturelle und ideologische Grenzverschiebung thematisiert haben.[24] Bei ihnen wie auch bei anderen Künstlerinnen spielt die Auseinandersetzung mit Räumen und Orten eine zentrale Rolle. Häufig geht es dabei nicht um ein bloßes Besetzen und Für-sich-Reklamieren des Ausstellungs- oder des öffentlichen Raumes, wie es beispielsweise Arbeiten von Minimal-Art-Künstlern wie Richard Serras riesigen Stahlkonstruktionen unterstellt werden könnte.[25] Vielmehr bestehen die Arbeiten eher aus fast schon alltäglich wirkenden Interventionen und im Eröffnen von spezifischen ästhetischen Erfahrungen. So hat Nevin Aladağ mit *Paravent / Social Fabric #3* (2013) Paravents konzipiert, die aus zusammengenähten Teppichen verschiedener Länder und Traditionen bestehen und die im Raum aufgestellt als Schutz, aber auch als Barrieren wahrgenommen werden können. Was ursprünglich den Boden bedeckt, ist nun in die

Vertikale gebracht, was als textiles Material eher dem privaten Raum zugeordnet wird, steht nun in einem öffentlichen Raum. Weitere Ambivalenzen finden sich in den verwendeten Teppichen, deren unterschiedliche Muster, Formen und Farben zwar einerseits auf kulturelle Differenzen verweisen, andererseits aber auch kulturübergreifende Gemeinsamkeiten in der Gestaltung privater Wohnräume erkennen lassen. Textile Materialien und kunsthandwerkliche Teppiche wiederum sind weiblich konnotiert, werden aber auch außereuropäischen Kulturen zugeordnet.[26] In der europäischen Kulturgeschichte gelten sie als lediglich dekorative sowie reproduktive Objekte und sind seit der Moderne von der als ›rein‹ verstandenen Abstraktion der ›hohen Kunst‹ abgegrenzt. Aladağs Paravents geben sich jedoch als Skulpturen aus, wodurch sie tradierte Hierarchien negieren und Gattungsgrenzen überschreiten und diese humorvoll in Frage stellen. Zu Recht ist verschiedentlich darauf hingewiesen worden, dass die Ästhetik von Aladağs Objekten an Bauhaus und De Stijl erinnert, die Kunst und Leben zu einer neuen Synthese verhelfen wollten. Aladağ bringt über die verschiedenen Teppiche die Lebensrealität von Migrationserfahrungen, aber auch Ästhetiken privaten Wohnens in ihre Arbeit ein und stellt somit auf mehreren Ebenen Grenzziehungen in sozialen Gefügen zur Disposition.

152

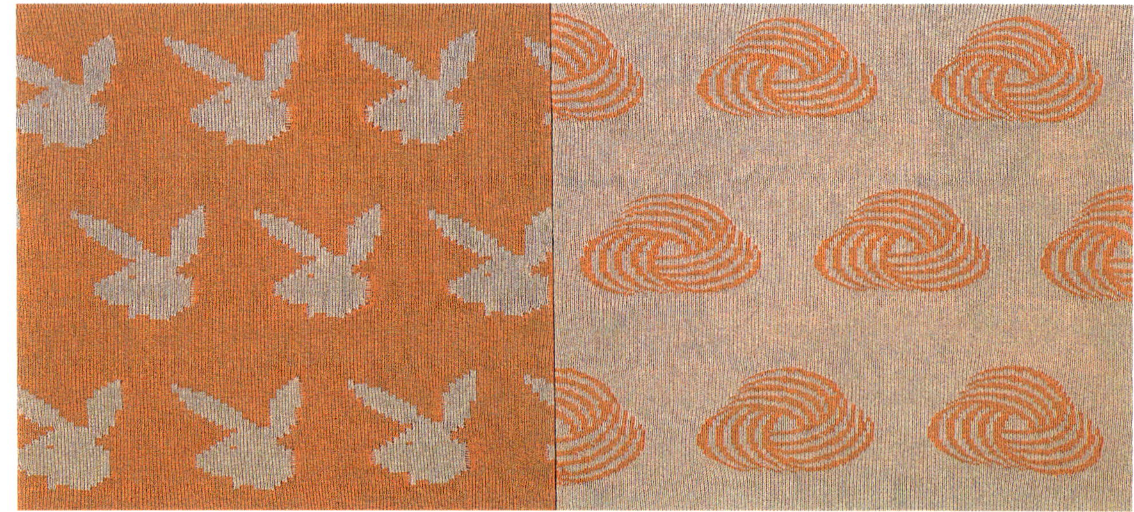

Rosemarie Trockel
Ohne Titel, 1985

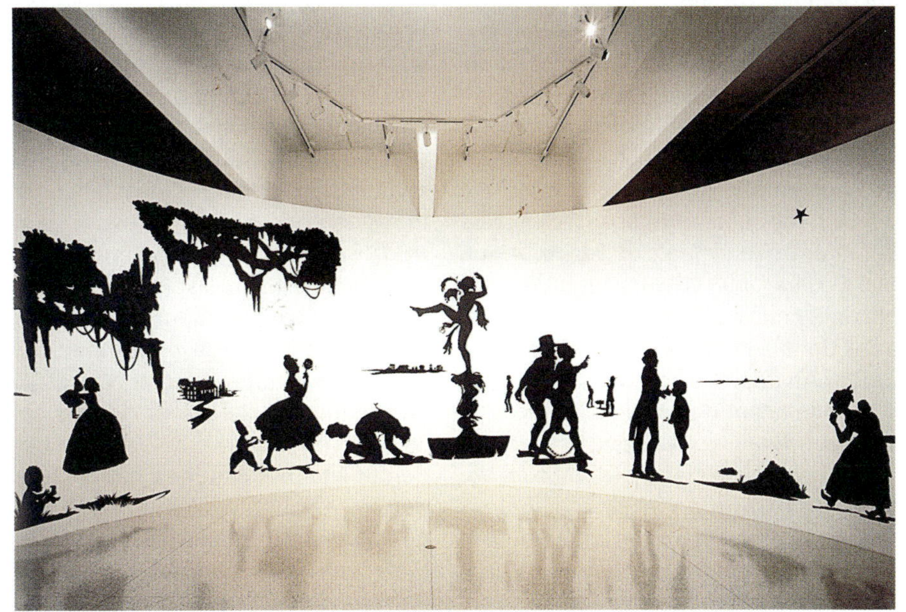

Kara Walker
Slavery, Slavery!, 1997

153

shifting of borders.[24] Dealing with spaces and places is central to the work of these artists. Frequently it is not about merely occupying and re-claiming the exhibition space or public space, as Minimal artists have been accused of doing, such as Richard Serra with his enormous steel constructions.[25] Instead, the works consist of interventions that seem almost inconsequential and are aimed at opening up specific aesthetic experiences. For example, Nevin Aladağ created screens (*Paravent / Social Fabric #3*, 2013) that consist of carpets from different countries and traditions that are sewn together and placed in the space as protection but can also be perceived as barriers. What once covered the floor is now displayed vertically; textiles that were associated with the private space are now in a public space. Other ambivalences are to be found in the carpets, whose different patterns, forms and colours all refer to cultural differences on the one hand, but on the other hand they also reveal similarities in the design of private living spaces that are transcultural. Textiles and hand-crafted carpets have female connotations, but are also associated with non-European cultures.[26] In European art history they are considered merely decorative and reproductive objects that have been excluded from the 'pure' abstraction of 'high art' since the modern period. Aladağ's screens masquerade as sculptures, thus ne-

gating established hierarchies and overstepping genre borders and questioning these with humour. Many have rightly commented that the aesthetics of Aladağ's objects are reminiscent of Bauhaus and De Stijl, which set out to create a new synthesis of art and life. By means of the different carpets Aladağ brings the real-life experience of migration as well as the aesthetics of private living into her work and thus places demarcations in social structures on several levels.

Making the experiences, realities and knowledge of migrants and in current world politics also of marginalised people – especially women – visible and perceptible has been repeatedly addressed in recent times in artistic works. Sanja Iveković demanded, for example, in 2007 in the context of her work at *documenta 12*: 'Now it's time for women's voices to be heard.'[27] The artist Gülsün Karamustafa has long focused on the real-life experience of migrants and women in general in the context of constantly changing processes of globalisation. The starting point for her work *Objects of Desire / A Suitcase Trade (100 Dollars Limit)* (1989) was the change triggered by the end of the Soviet Union and the Fall of the Berlin Wall that began to be perceived even in Turkey: in towns along the coast of the Black Sea, but also in Istanbul, informal markets were formed in which mostly women from former Soviet republics offered goods from bank-

24 See for example Melanie Ulz (Ulz 2011) who has examined this with reference to Ayşe Erkmen, Romuald Hazoumé and Yinka Shonibare.

25 For a feminist reading of works by Minimal artists, whose works – contrary to their intentions – adhere to meanings and sexual connotations due to the materials used and size, see Chave 1990 / 1998.

26 The topic of hierarchies of genre that are based on sex-specific categories but also on the idea of 'non-European art' as a merely reproductive art, is a recurring theme of feminist artists (for example, Joyce Kozloff and Miriam Schapiro), which is expanded by Aladağ to include the aspects of spatial experience and the topic of migration.

27 Press release, *documenta 12*, 11 July, 2007, <http://www.documenta12.de/fileadmin/Ivekovic_11.7/070711_PMAIvekovic_form_en.pdf> (accessed 22 September, 2017).

27 Pressemitteilung der *documenta 12*, 10.7.2007, online: <http://documenta12.de/fileadmin/pdf/PM/NEU070711_PMAIvekovic_form_de.pdf>, letzter Zugriff: 1.5.2017.

28 Vgl. Karamustafa 2001, 171.

Die Erfahrungen, die Realitäten und das Wissen von Migrant_innen und in der aktuellen Weltpolitik Marginalisierten – hier insbesondere von Frauen – sichtbar und hörbar zu machen, ist ein in jüngster Zeit wieder mehrfach aufgegriffenes künstlerisches Anliegen. So forderte etwa Sanja Iveković 2007 im Zusammenhang mit ihrer Arbeit auf der *documenta 12*: »Es ist an der Zeit, dass die Stimmen der Frauen gehört werden.«[27] Die Künstlerin Gülsün Karamustafa fokussiert schon seit längerem die Lebensrealitäten von Migrantinnen und Frauen im Allgemeinen im Kontext sich ständig transformierender Globalisierungsprozesse. Ausgangspunkt für ihre Arbeit *Objects of Desire / A Suitcase Trade (100 Dollars Limit)* (1989) waren Veränderungen, die mit dem Ende der Sowjetunion und dem sogenannten Fall der Mauer auch in der Türkei wahrnehmbar wurden: An Küstenorten des Schwarzen Meeres, aber auch in Istanbul, entwickelten sich informelle Märkte, auf denen vorwiegend Frauen aus ehemaligen Sowjetrepubliken Waren günstig zum Verkauf anboten, die aus bankrotten Textil- und Keramikfabriken sowie aus eigenen Haushalten stammten. Von den Einheimischen wurden diese Märkte gern angenommen, und für die Händlerinnen, die auf dem Rückweg Waren aus der Türkei mitnahmen, war das Geschäft so attraktiv, dass sich einige durch Prostitution das nötige Startkapital verschafften. Der Begriff ›Kofferhandel‹, der sich für diese Form des Warenaustauschs etabliert hat, spielt darauf an, dass die gehandelten Güter als persönliches Reisegepäck über die Grenzen geschmuggelt und so weder registriert noch besteuert wurden. Für die Volkswirtschaften der beteiligten Länder wurden diese Geschäfte enorm wichtig, was wiederum die Bedeutung von Westeuropa als Wirtschaftsmacht dezentralisierte.[28] Karamustafa studierte das wechselnde Warenangebot und die Verkaufsstrategien der überwiegend weiblichen Akteur_innen. Für Ausstellungen, zu denen sie in Westeuropa eingeladen wurde, kaufte sie für 100 US-Dollar (diesen Betrag konnten die Händlerinnen als Prostituierte pro Nacht verlangen) auf diesen Märkten verschiedene Produkte ein, um sie in den Kunstinstitutionen den Besucher_innen zum Kauf anzubieten. Unterwäsche, diverser Nippes, Kinderspielzeug und Schminkartikel in allen denkbaren Farben wurden so präsentiert, wie Karamustafa es auf den Marktständen in Istanbul gesehen hatte. Jeden Gegenstand, den sie verkaufte, dokumentierte sie im eher flüchtigen Medium des Polaroidfotos. Mittlerweile hat die Künstlerin ihre Recherchen auf ähnliche Märkte, zum Beispiel in Berlin, ausgeweitet beziehungsweise aktualisiert. Ihre daraus entstehenden Installationen entsprechen zwar nicht dem bürgerlichen Kunstgeschmack westlicher Provenienz, entbehren dabei aber

154

rupt textile and ceramic factories as well as from their own households for sale at cheap prices. These markets were very popular among locals, and for the women dealers – who took back products from Turkey when they returned to their own countries – the business was so attractive that some of them collected the necessary seed capital through prostitution. The term 'suitcase trade', which was established for this type of exchange of goods, alludes to the fact that the goods were smuggled over the border as personal baggage and could thus not be registered or taxed. For the economies of the countries involved, this business was extremely important, and it also decentralised the importance of western Europe as an economic power.[28] Karamustafa studied the changing range of goods and the sales strategies of the mostly female participants. For exhibitions that she was invited to in western Europe, she bought various products at these markets for one hundred American dollars (the amount that the dealers charged as prostitutes for the night), which she offered for sale to the exhibition visitors at the art institutions. Underwear, knickknacks, children's toys and makeup in all possible colours were presented in the way that Karamustafa had seen them in the markets of Istanbul. Each item that she sold was first quickly documented in Polaroids. In the meantime the artist had expanded and updated her concept by doing research at similar markets, for example, in Berlin. Although the installations that she composed as a result no longer conform to Western bourgeois tastes, they do not lack a certain fascination. More importantly, however, is the attention brought to how marginalised women seek possibilities of survival in the changed economic and social conditions. The circumstances of these business forms are neither euphemistically romanticised nor are the women represented as mere victims. The artist does not claim to speak for them, to be able to understand their experiences adequately or to be able to make their voices heard unaltered. Instead she presents the women as active business women, without producing a fixed image of them. She thus displaces the tendency to view (or ignore) women from southeastern Europe – if at all – as victims.

In conclusion it can be said that the relationship between feminism and postcolonialism is not only determined by similarities and connections; it is still one of mutual criticism and struggle for solidarities and alliances.[29] Particularly the objections raised by Chandra Talpade Mohanty and Gayatri Chakravorty Spivak, two theoreticians from India, against white feminism are famous and still current.[30] Mohanty and Spivak have spoken out vehemently about the fact that women from the Global South are not only exposed

28 See Karamustafa 2001, 171.

29 The history of transnational feminism has been described by Elisabeth Fink and Uta Ruppert as 'the history of struggling for solidarity' (Fink / Ruppert 2009, 64).

30 See Mohanty 1984; Spivak 1988.

29 Als »Geschichte des Ringens um Solidarität« haben Elisabeth Fink und Uta Ruppert die Geschichte des transnationalen Feminismus beschrieben (Fink / Ruppert 2009, 64).

30 Vgl. Mohanty 1984; Spivak 1988.

31 Castro Varela / Dhawan 2005, 60.

auch nicht einer gewissen Faszination. Wesentlicher ist jedoch, dass darauf aufmerksam gemacht wird, wie marginalisierte Frauen sich unter sich verändernden ökonomischen und gesellschaftlichen Bedingungen (Über-)Lebensmöglichkeiten suchen. Weder sind die Bedingungen dieser Handelsformen dabei beschönigend verklärt, noch werden die Frauen als bloße Opfer dargestellt. Auch behauptet die Künstlerin nicht, für sie zu sprechen, ihre Erfahrungen adäquat nachvollziehen zu können oder ihre Stimmen ungebrochen hörbar zu machen. Vielmehr stellt sie die Frauen als aktive und handelnde vor, ohne ein feststehendes Bild von ihnen zu produzieren. Damit verschiebt sie den Blick, der es gewohnt ist, südosteuropäische Frauen – wenn überhaupt – nur als Opfer zu (über)sehen.

Zusammenfassend lässt sich sagen, dass das Verhältnis von Feminismus und Postkolonialismus nicht nur von Ähnlichkeiten und Verknüpfungen bestimmt, sondern nach wie vor eines der wechselseitigen Kritik und des Ringens um Solidaritäten und Allianzen ist.[29] Bekannt geworden und nach wie vor aktuell sind insbesondere die Einsprüche, die von Chandra Talpade Mohanty und Gayatri Chakravorty Spivak,[30] zwei aus Indien stammenden Theoretikerinnen, gegen den weißen Feminismus erhoben wurden. Vehement haben Mohanty und Spivak darauf hingewiesen, dass Frauen des globalen Südens nicht nur der Gewalt patriarchaler Systeme ausgesetzt seien, sondern auch den ökonomischen Ausbeutungen eines weltweiten kapitalistischen Systems. Mohanty hat 2003 erneut gefordert, die Restrukturierungen eines flexibilisierten globalen Kapitalismus in den Blick zu nehmen und diesen analytisch mit den Mikropolitiken des Alltagslebens, der Kultur und geschlechtsspezifischen Kontexten zu verbinden. Spivak betont, dass im globalen Norden das durch koloniale und neokoloniale Interessen korrumpierte Wissen zunächst verlernt werden müsse, bevor »der Prozess der Globalisierung und seine Effekte auf den Lebensalltag der subalternen Frauen im Süden verstanden werden« könnten.[31] Mit ›verlernen‹ ist eine Dekolonialisierung des Denkens gemeint, zu verlernen sind dabei Annahmen, die als universell und allgemein gültig angesehen werden und die Beschränktheit der eigenen Perspektive sowie die eigene Positioniertheit in globalen Machtstrukturen unreflektiert lassen. Im Kunstfeld scheinen genau solche Prozesse des Verlernens und der Dekolonialisierung möglich zu sein. Künstler_innen wie Gülsün Karamustafa oder Ayşe Erkmen (etwa mit *Shipped Ships*, 2001 —→ **28**, oder *Plan B*, 2011) lenken unseren Blick auf weltweite Machtsysteme und die Positionen (nicht nur) von Frauen innerhalb dieser Systeme. Erprobt werden Möglichkeiten, vielfältige Differenzen anzuerkennen beziehungsweise überhaupt

155

Anny & Sibel Öztürk
Behind the Wheel, 2004

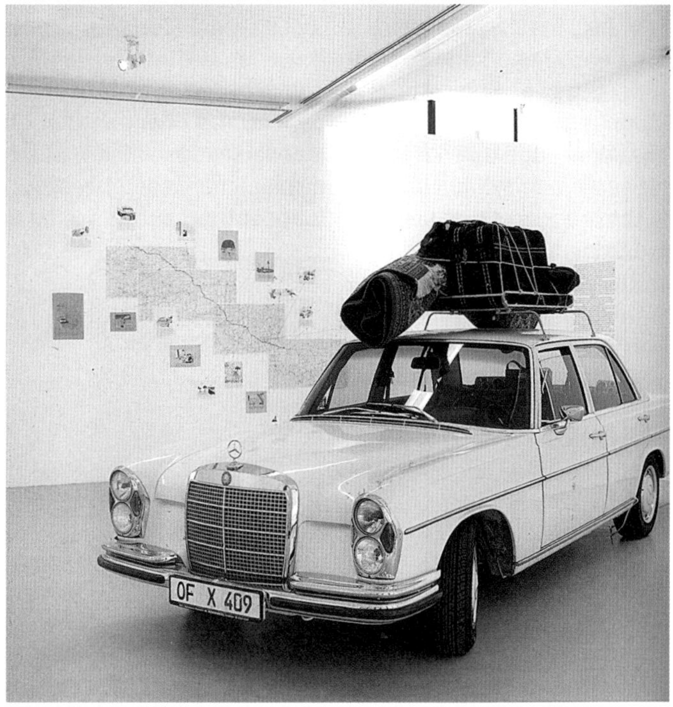

zu erkennen sowie vermeintlich feststehendes und medial vermitteltes Wissen zu irritieren sowie die Wahrnehmung für andere Realitäten zu sensibilisieren (etwa von Mona Hatoum in *Projection,* 2006 ⟶ **160**). Weiterhin arbeiten sie sich dabei an der Dominanz des globalen Nordens und seiner Traditionen ab, womit auch deutlich wird, dass dessen große Erzählungen immer noch wirkmächtig sind. Diesen Erzählungen wird jedoch nicht mit ebenso gewaltigen Gegenerzählungen oder Gesten geantwortet, sondern vielmehr mit Störungen und Veränderungen, die zwar zunächst oft eher leise und unscheinbar erscheinen, aber zu wesentlichen Verschiebungen und möglicherweise auch zu einem Verlernen eurozentrischer Blick- und Denkweisen führen können.

156

to the violence of patriarchal systems, but also the economic exploitation of a worldwide capitalist system. In 2003 Mohanty reiterated that flexible restructuring of global capitalism be examined and analytically linked with the micropolitics of everyday life, culture and gender-specific contexts. Spivak highlights that in the Global North the knowledge that has been corrupted by colonial and neo-colonial interests has to first be unlearnt, before 'the process of globalisation and its effects on the everyday life of subordinate women in the south can be understood'.[31] By 'unlearning' they mean a de-colonialisation of thinking; including unlearning assumptions seen as universal and generally valid that allow the narrow-mindedness of one's own perspective as well as one's own position in the global systems of power to be unlearnt. In the area of art such processes of unlearning and decolonisation seem to be possible. Artists such as Gülsün Karamustafa or Ayşe Erkmen (for example, with *Shipped Ships,* 2001 ⟶ **28**, or *Plan B,* 2011) direct our gaze at worldwide systems of power and the positions (not only) of women within these systems. The acknowledgement and mere recognition of manifold differences, the disturbance of established knowledge that is mediated by the media and a creation of awareness of other realities are all being tested by artists (in Mona Hatoum's *Projection,* 2006 ⟶ **160**, for example).

They continue to work on dismantling the dominance of the Global North and its traditions, making it clear that its great stories are still influential. These stories, however, are not answered with equally powerful counter-stories or gestures, but instead with disturbances and changes that often seem rather soft or inconspicuous initially, but can lead to fundamental displacements and possibly also to the unlearning of Eurocentric ways of seeing and thinking.

Translated from German
by Tas Skorupa

31 Castro Varela / Dhawan 2005, 60.

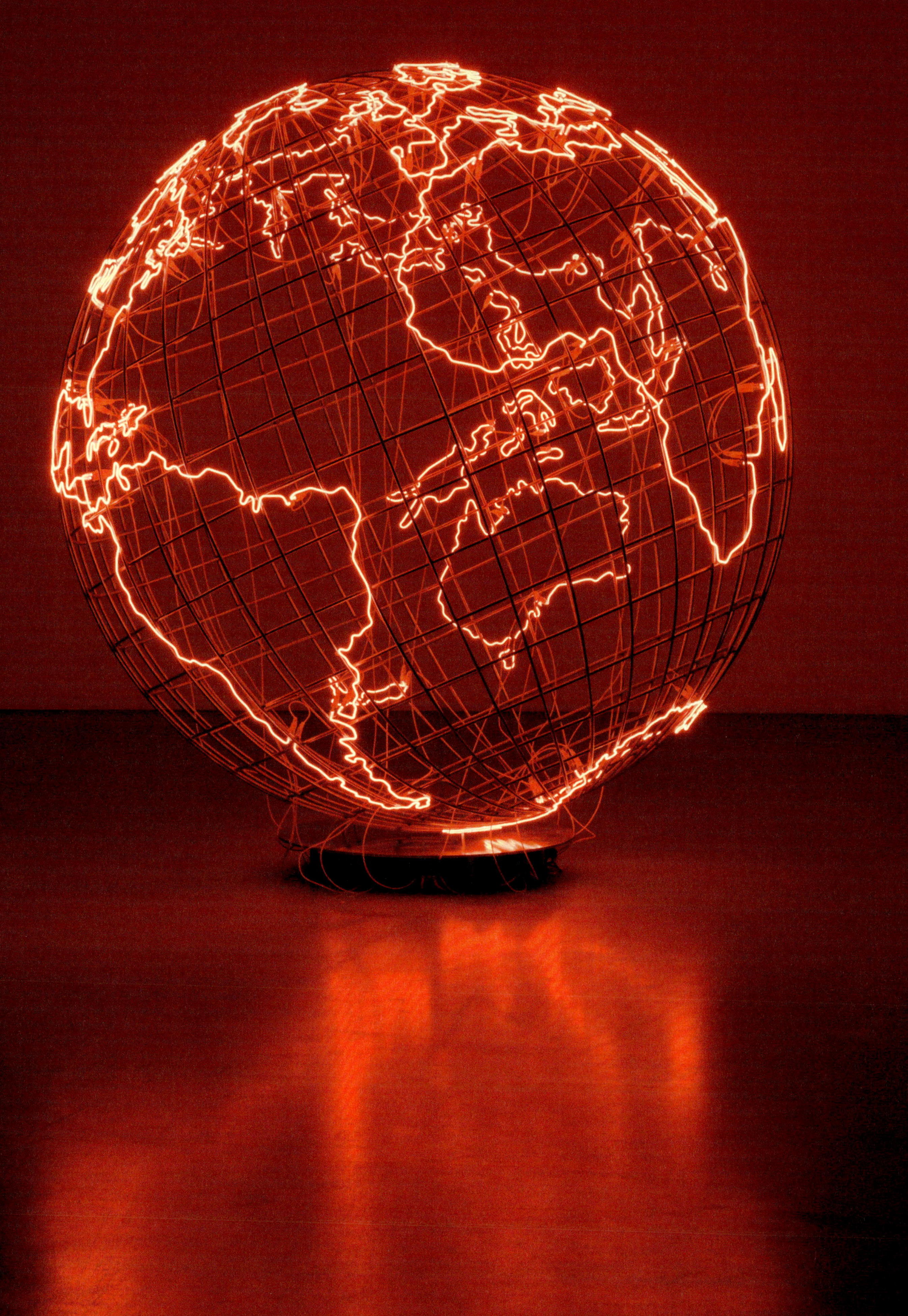

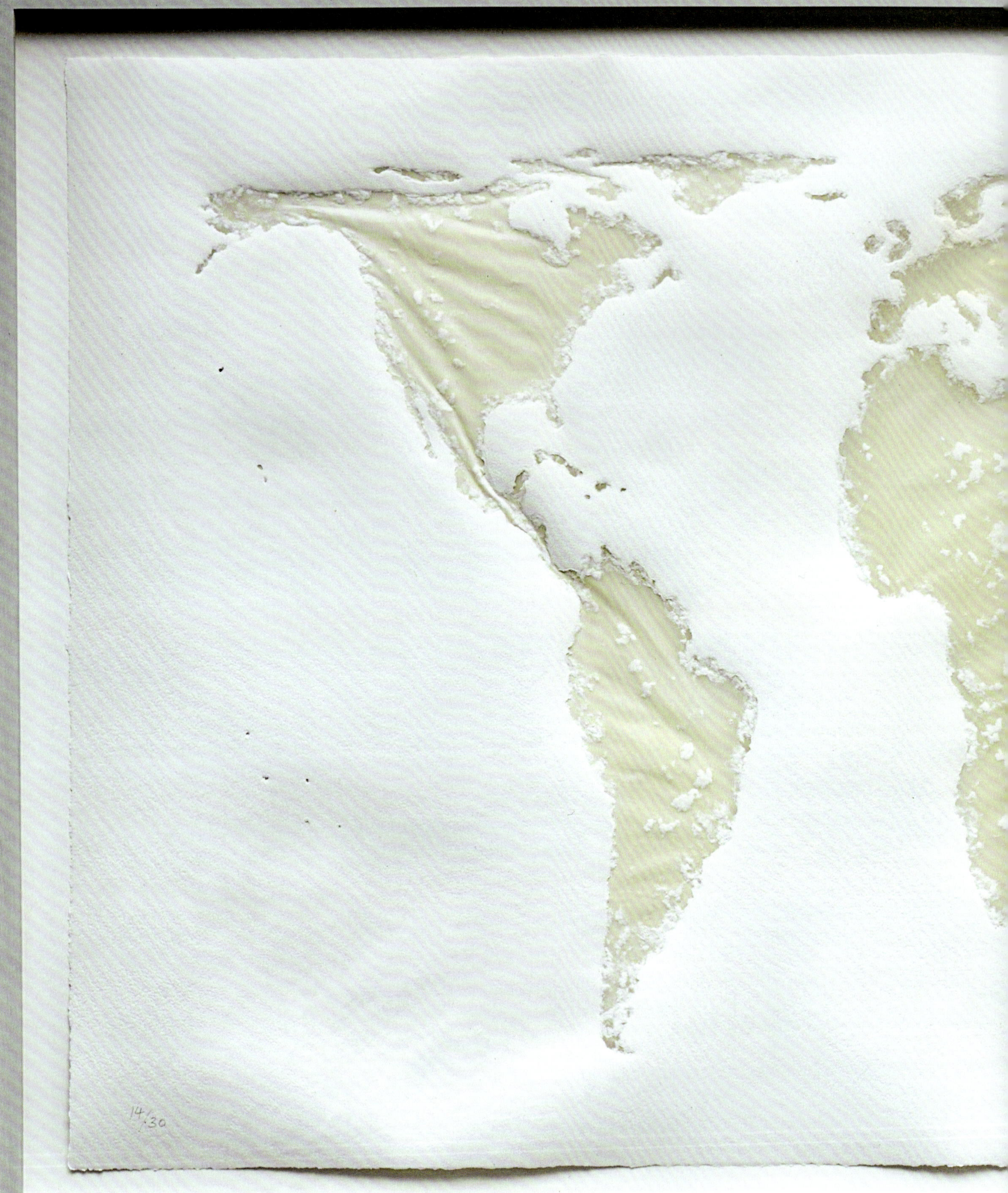

14/30

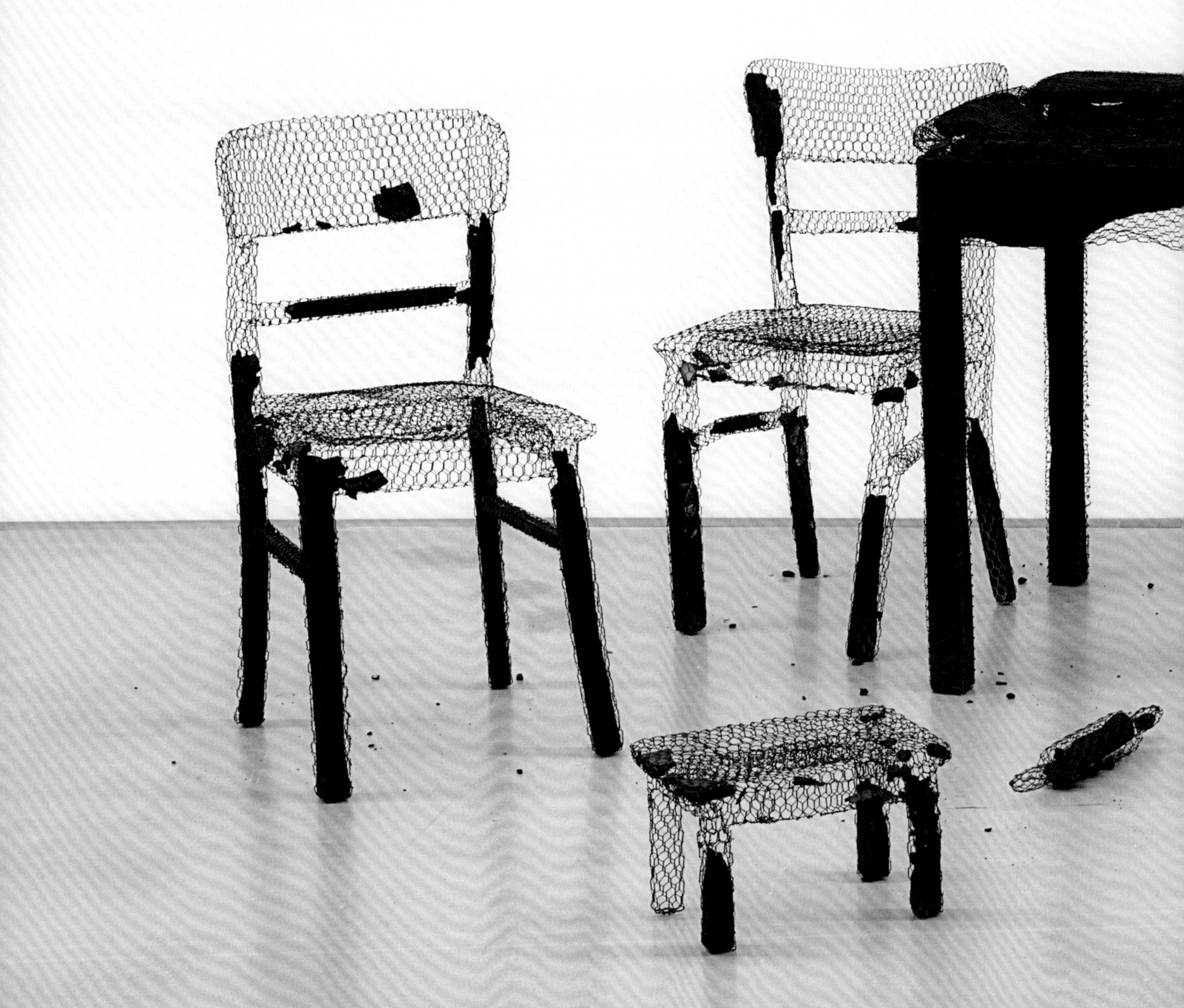

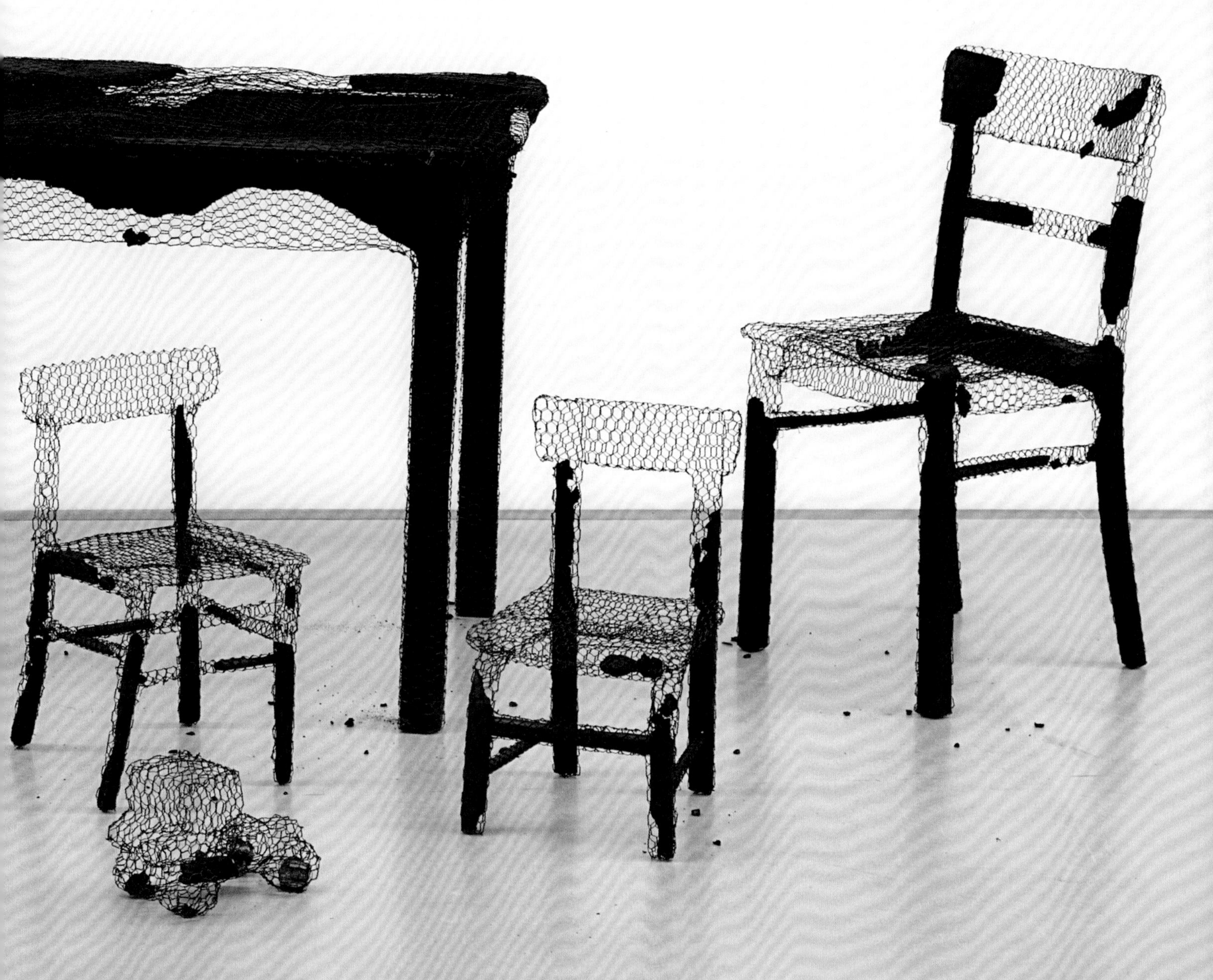

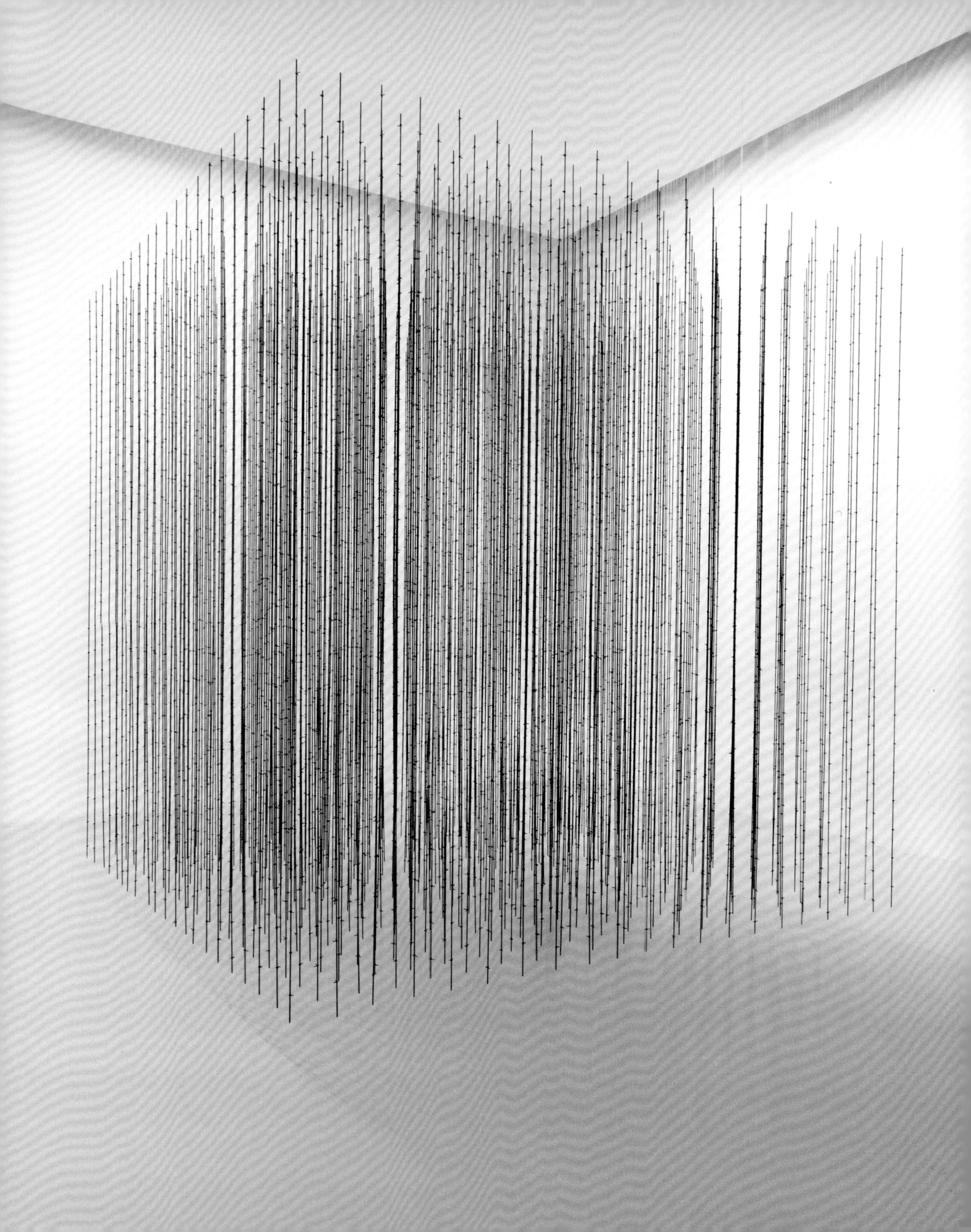

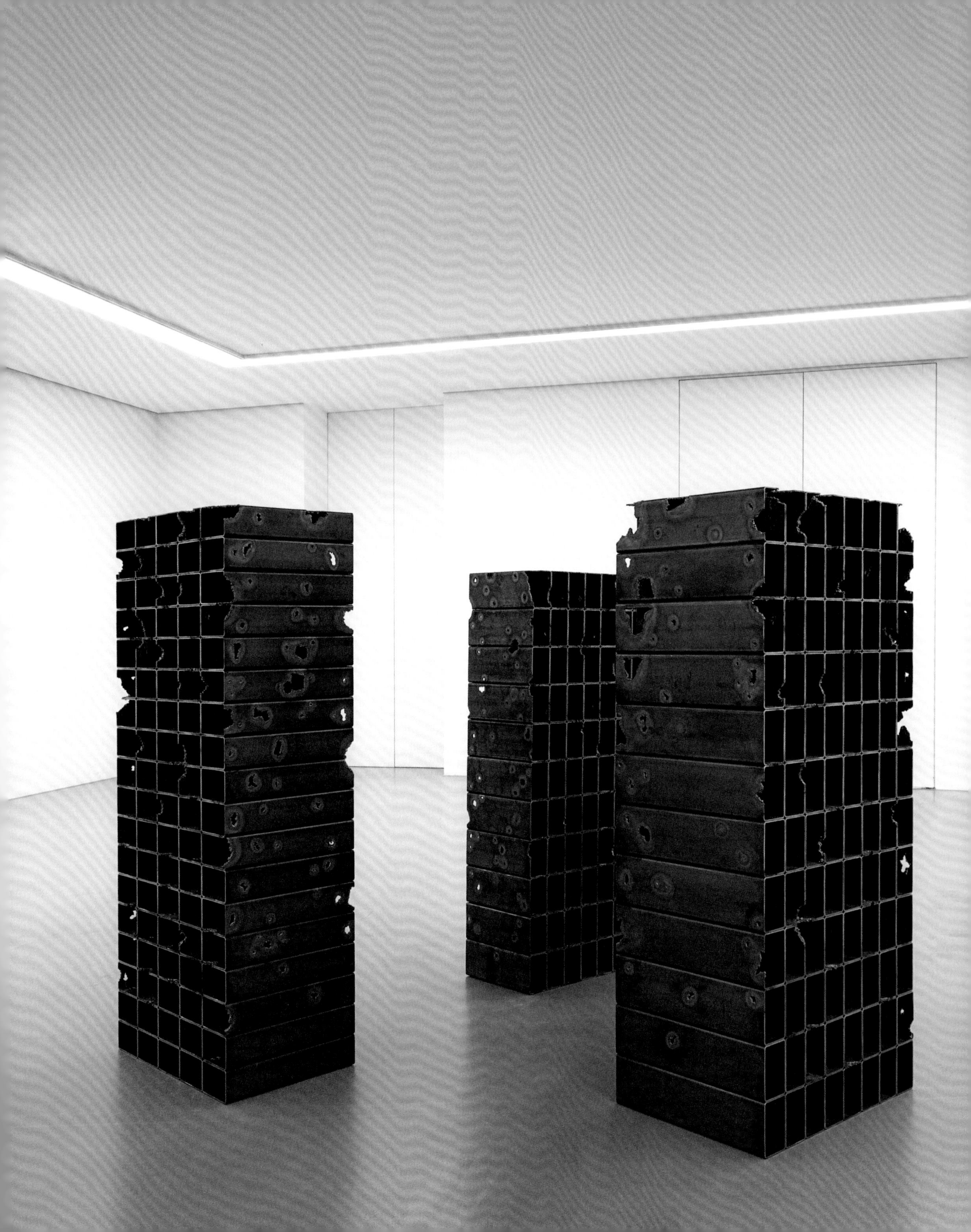

Mona Hatoum
Bourj A, Bourj II und / and *Bourj III,* 2011

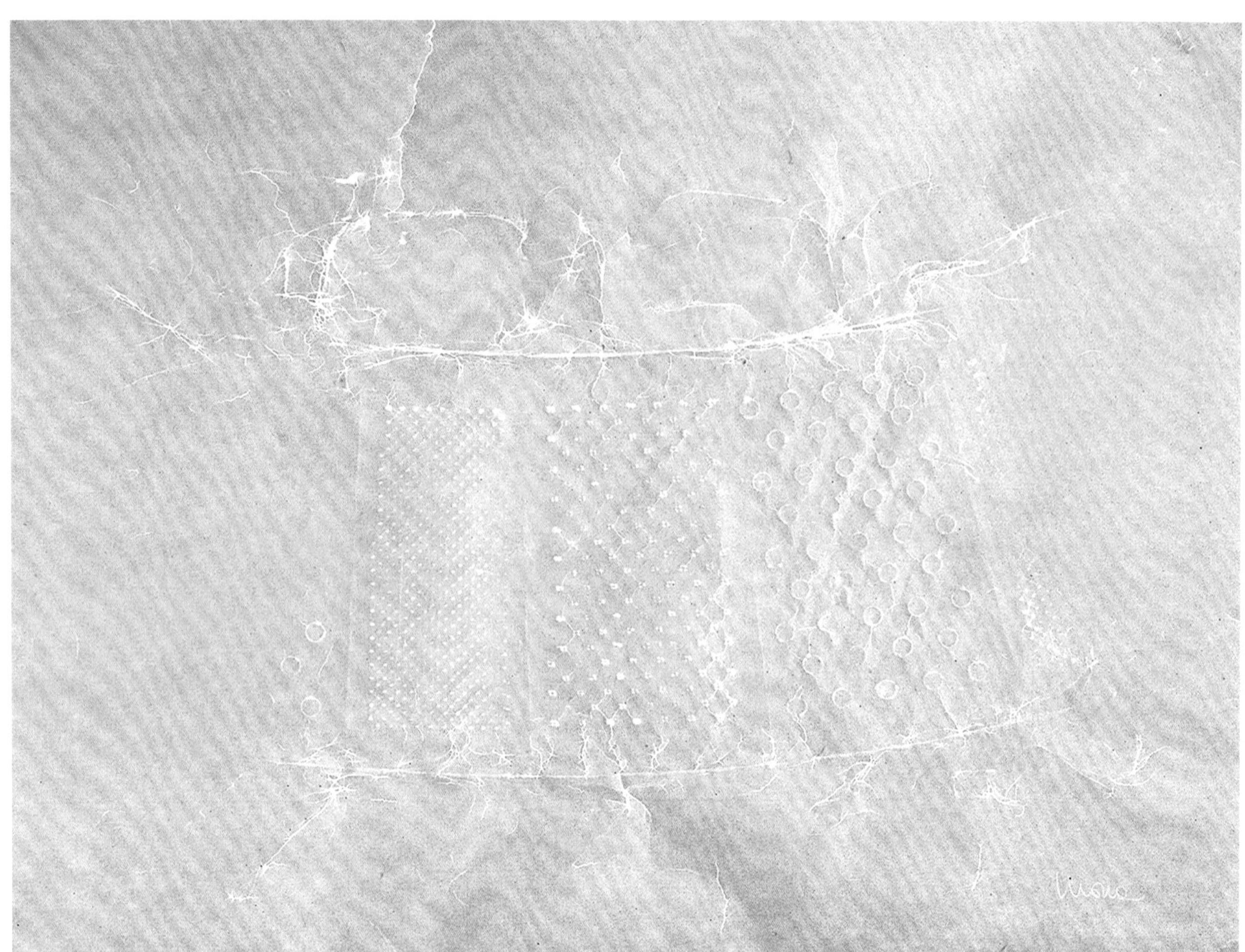

Mona Hatoum
Untitled (râpe cylindrique), 1999

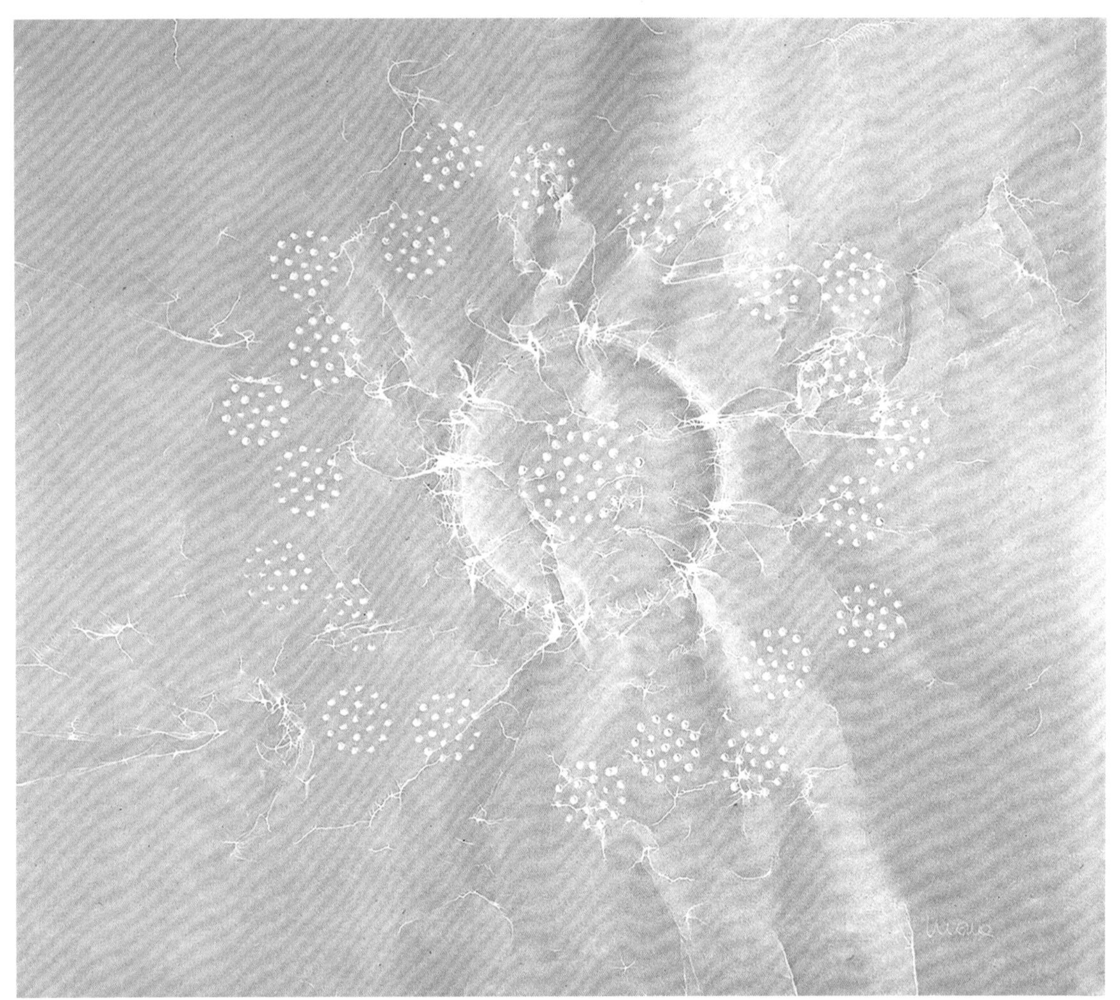

Mona Hatoum
Untitled (passoire de J-L), 1999

Mona Hatoum
Paravent, 2008
Daybed, 2008

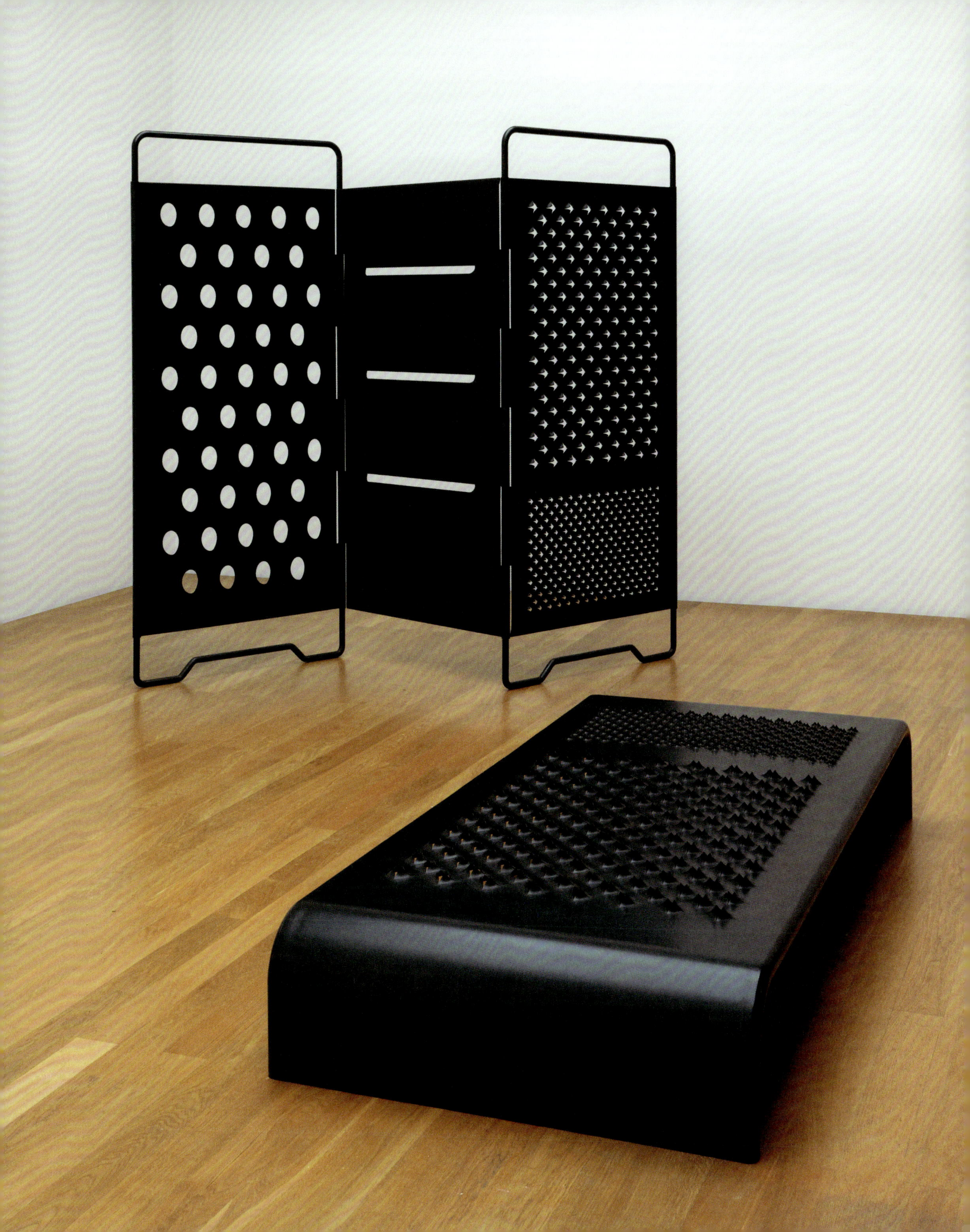

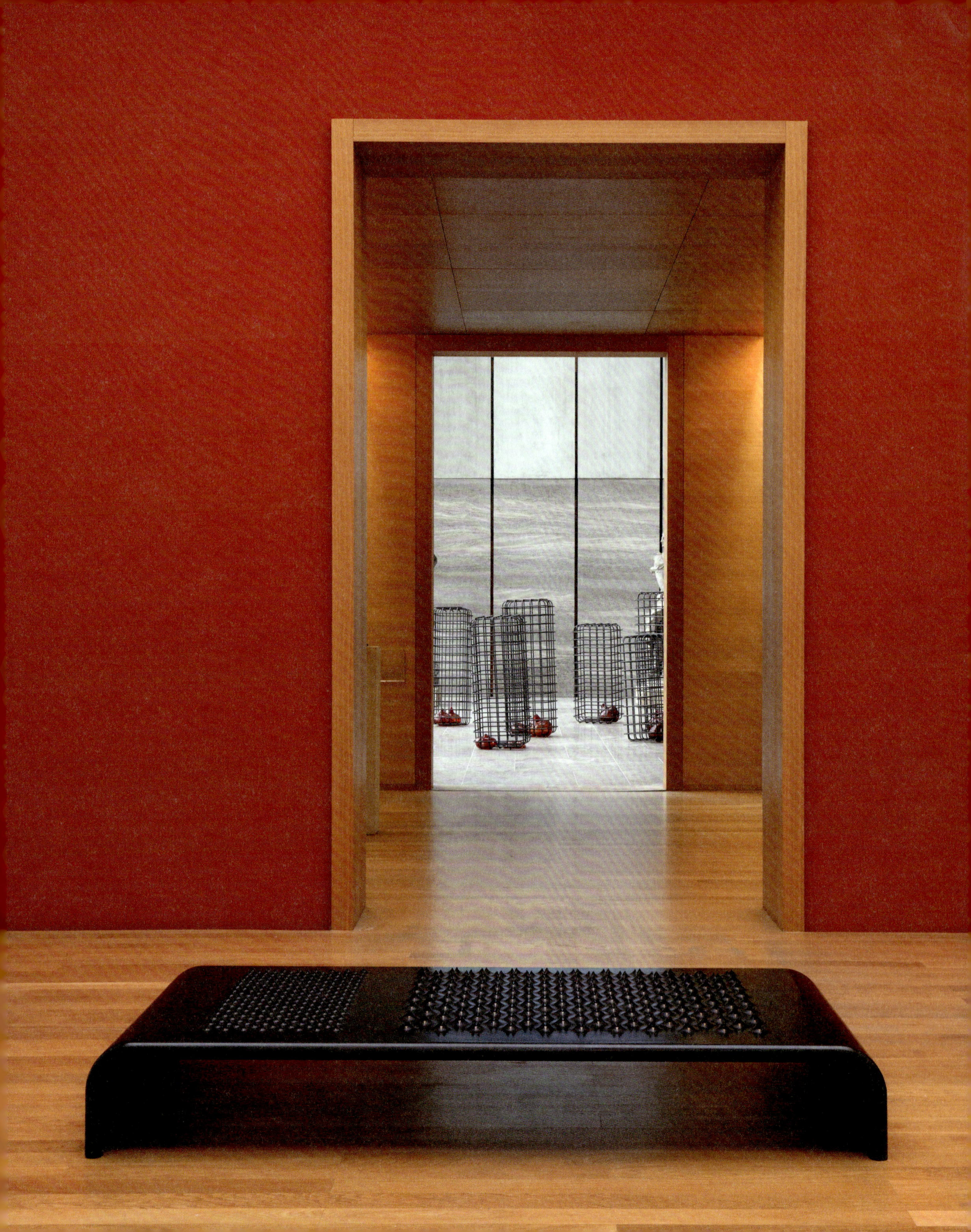

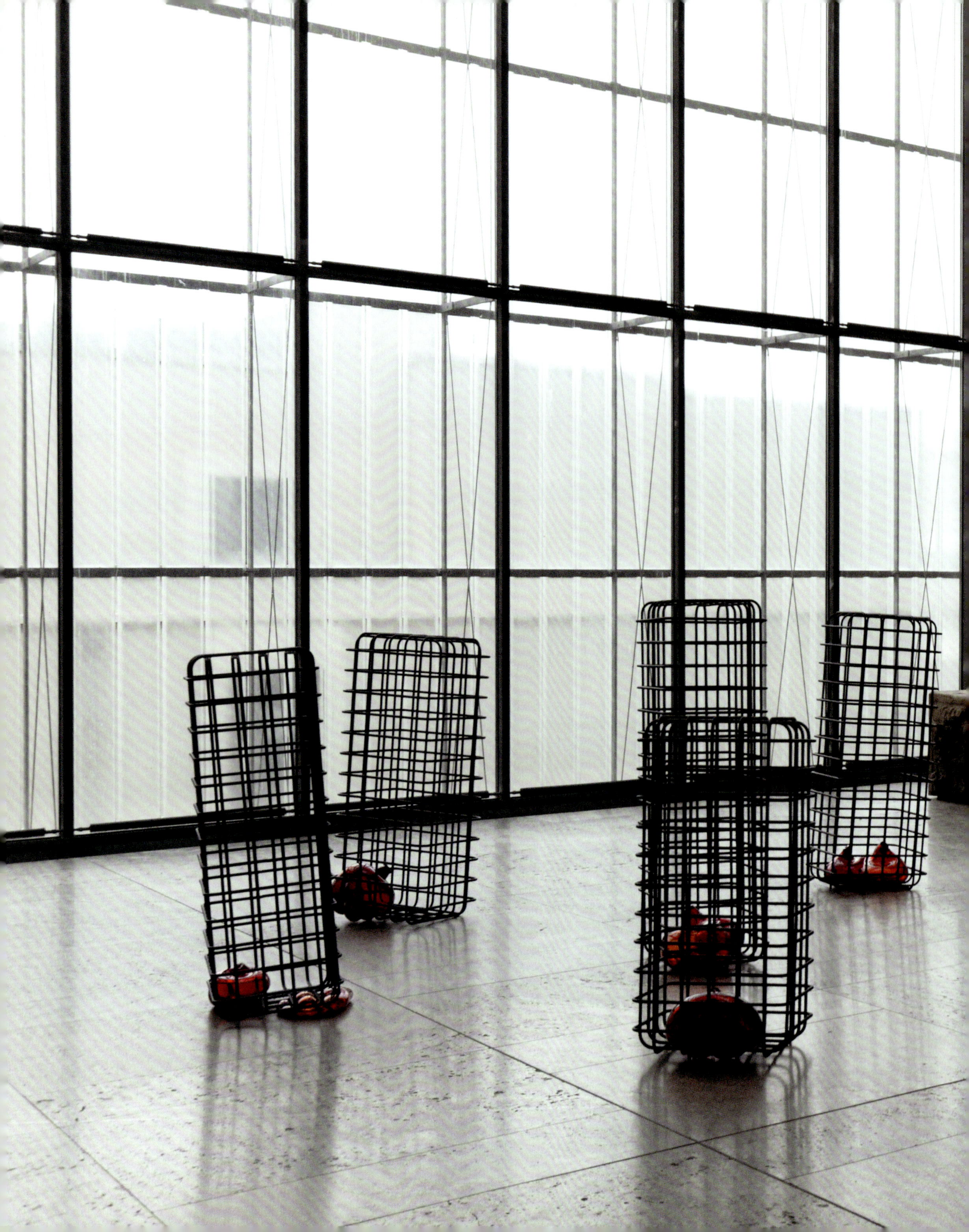

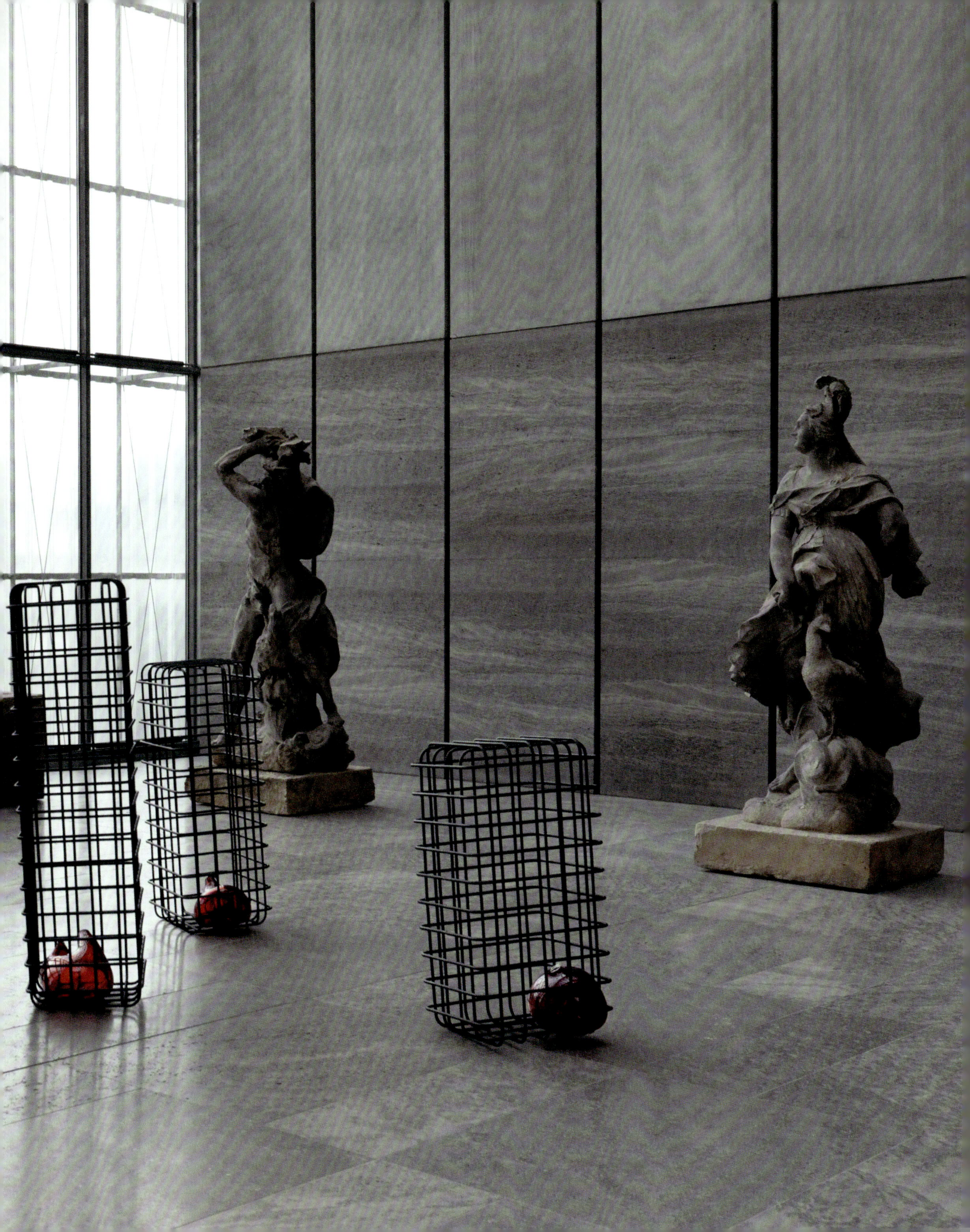

Anhang / Appendix

Ayşe Erkmen

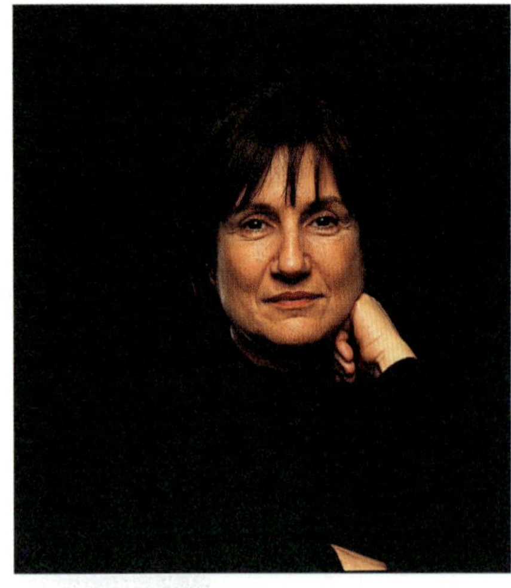

1949
geboren in Istanbul, lebt und arbeitet in Istanbul und Berlin (seit 1993) / born in Istanbul, lives and works in Istanbul and Berlin (since 1993)

Auszeichnungen und Lehrtätigkeiten / Awards, posts and prizes

Seit / Since 2012
Mitglied der / Member of the Akademie der Künste, Berlin – Sektion Bildende Kunst / Visual Arts section

2010–2015
Gastprofessur (2010) und Professur (ab 2011) / Visiting professor (2010) and professor (since 2011), Kunstakademie Münster

2002
Maria Sibylla Merian-Preis des Hessischen Ministeriums für Wissenschaft und Kunst, Wiesbaden

2000
Gastprofessur / Visiting professor, Staatliche Hochschule für Bildende Künste, Städelschule, Frankfurt am Main

1998
Gastdozentur / Visiting lecturer, Universität Gesamthochschule Kassel

Preis der 7. Triennale Kleinplastik Fellbach

1993
Stipendium des DAAD / DAAD scholarship in Berlin

Ausbildung / Education

1969–1977
İstanbul Devlet Güzel Sanatlar Akademisi

Einzelausstellungen (Auswahl) / Solo exhibitions (selection)

2016
Unlikely, Barbara Gross Galerie, München / Munich

2015
Fingerspitzengefühl, Galerie Barbara Weiss, Berlin

.A|Ayşe Erkmen & Ann Veronica Janssens, S.M.A.K. Stedelijk Museum voor Actuele Kunst, Gent

By Nature, Kunsthal 44 Møen, Askeby

2013
Vanille, chocolat et roue de bicyclette, Fondation Speerstra, Apples

Intervals, The Curve, Barbican Centre, London

Wesenszug, Galerie Barbara Weiss, Berlin

2011
itself, Magazin4, Bregenzer Kunstverein

Plan B, La Biennale di Venezia, Esposizione Internationale d'Arte, Türkischer Pavillon / Turkish pavilion, Venedig / Venice

2010
15-5519, Between You and I – Intervention 4, Witte de With Center for Contemporary Art, Rotterdam

Doppelhaushälfte, Galerie Barbara Weiss, Berlin

2009
Bluish, Kunstverein Freiburg

2008
Hausgenossen, K21 Kunstsammlung Nordrhein-Westfalen, Düsseldorf

Chrystal Rock, NRW.BANK, Düsseldorf

Weggefährten, Nationalgalerie im Hamburger Bahnhof – Museum für Gegenwart – Berlin, Staatliche Museen zu Berlin – Preußischer Kulturbesitz

Aşağı Yukarı / Ups and Downs, Yapı Kredi Kâzım Taşkent Sanat Galerisi, Istanbul

2007
Special Project – Ayşe Erkmen: Coffee, Extra City, Centrum voor hedendaagse kunst, Antwerpen / Antwerp

Habenichts, Galerie Barbara Weiss, Berlin

2006
Awesome, The Physics Room, Christchurch

2005
Busy Colors, SculptureCenter, Long Island City, New York

Habseligkeiten, Galerie Barbara Weiss, Berlin

2004
durchnässt, Schirn Kunsthalle Frankfurt, Frankfurt am Main

bound to / gebunden an, Städtisches Museum Abteiberg, Mönchengladbach

Bis August, GAK Gesellschaft für Aktuelle Kunst, Bremen

2003
Tidvatten, Magasin III Stockholm Konsthall

Kuckuck, Kunstmuseum St. Gallen

2002
Müßiggang, Galerie Barbara Weiss, Berlin

Ketty und Assam, Kokerei Zollverein, Essen

Kein gutes Zeichen, Vereinigung bildender KünstlerInnen Wiener Secession, Wien / Vienna

2001
Kuaförde İki Kadın, Chambal, Eudora, Emre ve Dario / Two Women at the Coiffeur, Chambal, Eudora, Emre & Dario, Maçka Sanat Galerisi, Istanbul

Shipped Ships, Projekt für die Kunstreihe *Moment* der Deutschen Bank / project for the series *Moment* by the Deutsche Bank, Frankfurt am Main

1999
Half of, Galerie Deux, Tokio / Tokyo

choo-choo, Städtische Galerie Göppingen

1997
PFM-1 ve diğerleri / PFM-1 and others, Maçka Sanat Galerisi, Istanbul

I-MA-GES, Kunstausstellung der Ruhrfestspiele Recklinghausen, Kunsthalle Recklinghausen

1996
Images, Kunstverein Arnsberg

1995
Bu Galeri / This Gallery, Maçka Sanat Galerisi, Istanbul

1994
Am Haus, Dauerhafte Installation / permanent installation, Oranienstraße 18, Berlin

1993
Zum Haus, Galerie von der Tann, Berlin

Das Haus, daadgalerie, Berlin

Gruppenausstellungen (Auswahl) / Group exhibitions (Selection)

2017
Art and Alphabet, Hamburger Kunsthalle

Skulptur Projekte Münster 2017

Luther und die Avantgarde, Altes Gefängnis, Wittenberg

2016
Uncertain States – Künstlerisches Handeln in Ausnahmezuständen, Akademie der Künste, Berlin

Projects at 8 Shrines and Temples / Travelling over 1300 Years of Time and Space, Saidaiji Temple, Nara

2015
Strange Pilgrims, The Contemporary Austin

2014
Une Histoire – Art, architecture, design des années 1980 à nos jours, Musée national d'Art moderne, Centre national d'art et de culture Georges-Pompidou, Paris

2013
Anne ben barbar mıyım? / Mom, Am I Barbarian?, 13. İstanbul Bienali

2011
Hayal ve Hakikat – Türkiye'den Modern ve Çağdaş Kadın Sanatçılar / Dream and Reality – Modern and Contemporary Women Artists from Turkey, Istanbul Modern Sanat Müzesi

2010
Tactics of Invisibility, Thyssen-Bornemisza Art Contemporary, Wien / Vienna; TANAS, Berlin, 2010, ARTER – space for art, Istanbul, 2011

2009
For the blind man in the dark room looking for the black cat that isn't there, Contemporary Art Museum St. Louis

2008
SCAPE 2008 Christchurch Biennial of Art in Public Space

Translocalmotion, 7th Shanghai Biennale

Above The Fold. Ayşe Erkmen, Ceal Floyer, David Lamelas, Kunstmuseum Basel, Museum für Gegenwartskunst

2007
57. Internationale Filmfestspiele Berlin

2006
3rd Echigo-Tsumari Art Triennial, Nigata

2005
Raum.Prolog, Akademie der Künste, Berlin

2004
OPEN / INVITED e v+ a 2004 Imagine Limerick, Limerick

2003
Performative Installation #1, Gegeben sind … Konstruktion und Situation, Galerie im Taxispalais, Innsbruck

2001
2. Berlin Biennale für zeitgenössische Kunst, Postfuhramt und / and KW Institute for Contemporary Art, Berlin

2000
Man and Space, III. Gwangju Biennale

1999
Zeitenwenden – Rückblick und Ausblick, Kunstmuseum Bonn; Museum Moderner Kunst Stiftung Ludwig Wien, Wien / Vienna

Under the Same Sky, Nykytaiteen museo Kiasma, Helsinki

1998
7. Triennale Kleinplastik Fellbach

Arte all'Arte, Associazione Arte Continua: Casola D'Elsa, San Gimignano

1997
Skulptur. Projekte in Münster

1996
Manifesta 1, Rotterdam

Zuspiel – Ayşe Erkmen, Andreas Slominski, Portikus, Frankfurt am Main

1995
4. Uluslararası İstanbul Bienali

Für eine detailliertere Biografie und Ausstellungsliste von Ayşe Erkmen verweisen wir auf die Ausstellungskataloge Gent 2015 und Berlin 2008a sowie ihre Website http://ayseerkmen.com.

For a more detailed biography and exhibition list please see the exhibition catalogues Gent 2015 and Berlin 2008a and Ayşe Erkmen's website http://ayseerkmen.com.

Mona Hatoum

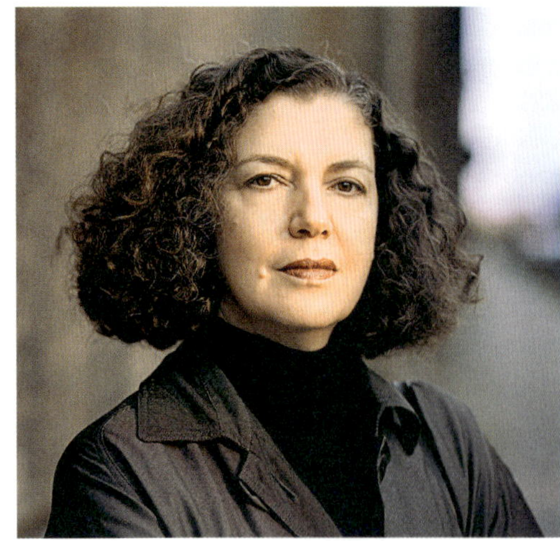

1952
geboren in Beirut, lebt und arbeitet in London (seit 1975) / born in Beirut, lives and works in London (since 1975)

Auszeichnungen und Lehrtätigkeiten / Awards, posts and prizes

2017
10th Hiroshima Art Prize, Hiroshima City Museum of Contemporary Art

2016
School of the Museum of Fine Arts Medal Award, Tufts University, Boston

2011
Premio Joan Miró, Fundació Joan Miró, Barcelona

2010
Käthe-Kollwitz-Preis, Akademie der Künste, Berlin

Ehrendoktor / Honorary Doctorate, University of Southampton

2009
Creative Arts Fellowship, Bellagio Center – The Rockefeller Foundation, Bellagio

2008
Ehrendoktor / Honorary Doctorate, American University of Beirut

Rolf Schockprisen, Kungliga Vetenskapsakademien, Stockholm

2007
Ehrenmitglied / Honorary Fellowship, University of the Arts London

2004
Sonning-Preis, Københavns Universitet, Kopenhagen / Copenhagen

Roswitha Haftmann-Preis, Roswitha Haftmann-Stiftung, Zürich / Zurich

2003
Stipendium des DAAD / DAAD scholarship in Berlin

2000
George-Maciunas-Preis der Stadt Wiesbaden

1995
Nominierung für den / Nominated for the Turner Prize, London

1994–1995
Gastprofessur / Visiting scholar, École nationale supérieure des beaux-arts de Paris

1992–1997
Lehrtätigkeit / Part time teaching post, Jan van Eyck Academie, Maastricht

1989–1992
Senior Fellow, Cardiff Institute of Higher Education

Ausbildung / Education

1979–1981
Slade School of Fine Art, London

1975–1979
Byam Shaw School of Art, London

1970–1972
Beirut University College, Beirut

Einzelausstellungen (Auswahl) / Solo exhibitions (selection)

2017
Terra Infirma, The Menil Collection, Houston

10th Hiroshima Art Prize, Hiroshima City Museum of Contemporary Art

2015
The Institute of Contemporary Art, Boston

Musée national d'Art moderne, Centre national d'art et de culture Georges-Pompidou, Paris; Tate Modern, London, 2016; Nykytaiteen museo Kiasma, Helsinki, 2016

Twelve Windows, The Museum of Fine Arts, Houston

2014
Pinacoteca do Estado de São Paulo; Fundación PROA, Buenos Aires, 2015

Turbulence, Mathaf: Arab Museum of Modern Art, Doha

2013
Kunstmuseum St. Gallen

Mappings, Centre d'art Les Pénitents Noirs, Aubagne

2012
Projection, Fundació Joan Miró, Barcelona

You Are Still Here, ARTER – space for art, Istanbul

2011
Sammlung Goetz, München / Munich

2010
Le Grand Monde, Fundación Marcelino Botín, Santander

Electrified, Kunsthal 44 Møen, Askeby

Käthe-Kollwitz-Preis 2010, Akademie der Künste, Berlin

Witness, Beirut Art Center

Suspendu, MAC/VAL Musée d'art contemporain du Val-de-Marne, Vitry-sur-Seine

2009
Collected Works, Rennie Museum, Vancouver

Natura Morta, Fondazione Merz, Turin

Interior Landscape, Fondazione Querini Stampalia ONLUS, Venedig / Venice

Hanging Garden, Kunsthalle Wien, Wien / Vienna

Measures of Entanglement, Ullens Center for Contemporary Art, Peking / Beijing

2008
Darat al Funun – The Khalid Shoman Foundation, Amman

Present Tense, Parasol Unit Foundation for Contemporary Art, London

Hanging Garden, daadgalerie, Berlin

Undercurrents, XIII Biennale Donna, Palazzo Massari PAC, Ferrara

2005
Douglas F. Cooley Memorial Art Gallery, Reed College, Portland

Over My Dead Body, Museum of Contemporary Art Australia, Sydney

2004
Hamburger Kunsthalle; Kunstmuseum Bonn; Magasin III Stockholm Konsthall

2003
Photo and video works, Uppsala Konstmuseum

Museo de Arte Contemporáneo de Oaxaca; Exconvento de Conkal, Yucatán

2002
Centro de Arte de Salamanca; Centro Galego de Arte Contemporánea, Santiago de Compostela

Laboratorio Arte Alameda, Mexiko Stadt / Mexico City

2001
Sala Mendoza, Caracas

2000
SITE Santa Fe; als / as *Domestic Disturbance,* Massachusetts Museum of Contemporary Art, North Adams, 2001

The Entire World as a Foreign Land, Tate Britain, London

1999
Le Creux de l'enfer – Centre d'art contemporain, Thiers; Le Collège, FRAC Fonds régional d'art contemporain Champagne-Ardenne, Reims, 2000; Museum van Hedendaagse Kunst Antwerpen / Antwerp, 2000

ArtPace Foundation for Contemporary Art, San Antonio

Castello di Rivoli, Museo d'Arte Contemporanea, Turin

1998
Scottish National Gallery of Modern Art, Edinburgh

Measures of Distance, Contemporary Arts Center, Cincinnati

Kunsthalle Basel

1997
Museum of Contemporary Art, Chicago; New Museum of Contemporary Art, New York; Museum of Modern Art, Oxford, 1998

1996
De Appel, Amsterdam

Quarters, Viafarini DOCVA, Mailand / Milan

Current Disturbance, Capp Street Project, San Francisco

Anadiel Gallery, Jerusalem

The Fabric Workshop and Museum, Philadelphia

1995
The British School at Rome, Rom / Rome

1994
Centre national d'art et de culture Georges-Pompidou, Paris

1993
Positionings / Transpositions (with Barbara Steinman), Art Gallery of Ontario, Toronto

South London Gallery (with Andrea Fisher), London

Recent Work, Arnolfini, Bristol

1992
Dissected Space, Chapter, Cardiff

1989
Forest City Gallery, London, Ontario

Obscure, Quebec

The Light at the End, The Showroom, London; Oboro, Montreal

Mind the Gap, A Space, Toronto (performance)

1986
Nine One One Contemporary Arts Center, Seattle

1985
Between the Lines, The Orchard Gallery, Derry (performance)

1984
Variation on Discord and Divisions, ABC No Rio, New York; AKA Gallery, Saskatoon; The Western Front, Vancouver; Articule, Montreal, 1985 (performance)

The Negotiating Table, Franklin Furnace, New York (performance)

1983
The Negotiating Table, SAW Gallery, Ottawa; Niagara Artists Centre, St Catharines; The Western Front, Vancouver (performance)

Für eine detailliertere Biografie und Ausstellungsliste von Mona Hatoum verweisen wir auf die Monografie Archer 2016 und den Ausstellungskatalog Paris / London / Helsinki 2015.

For a more detailed biography and exhibition list please see the publication Archer 2016 and the exhibition catalogue Paris / London / Helsinki 2015.

Ayşe Erkmen

Imitating Lines, 1985 / 2008
26 Stahlrohre mit Standplatten, angeschweißte Rohre, grün lackiert, Maße variabel / 26 steel pipes with base plates and additional welded-on pipes, varnished in green, dimensions variable
Courtesy of the artist and Galerie Barbara Weiss, Berlin, Barbara Gross Galerie, München / Munich, Dirimart, Istanbul

Imitation / Taklit, 1987 / 2017
Installation, Ziegelsteine, Leuchtstoffröhre, Maße varia-bel / installation, bricks, neon tube, dimensions variable
Courtesy of the artist and Galerie Barbara Weiss, Berlin, Barbara Gross Galerie, München / Munich, Dirimart, Istanbul

PFM-1 and others, 1997
Computeranimation in Farbe mit Ton, auf DVD übertragen, 6 Monitore, 4 Min., Loop / computer animation in colour with sound, transferred to DVD, 6 screens, 4 min, loop
Courtesy of the artist and Galerie Barbara Weiss, Berlin, Barbara Gross Galerie, München / Munich, Dirimart, Istanbul

PFM-1 and others, 1997 / 2013
90 Keramikobjekte, Maße variabel / 90 ceramic objects, dimensions variable
Privatsammlung / private collection

Alkoven, 1997 / 2017
Keramikfliesen, Tisch (von UNA / Giulia Foscari) / ceramic tiles, table (by UNA / Giulia Foscari), 101×450×200 cm
Courtesy of the artist and

Galerie Barbara Weiss, Berlin, Barbara Gross Galerie, München / Munich, Dirimart, Istanbul

Die Farben der Buchstaben (M), 2006
ausgestanztes, farbiges Plexiglas / die-cut, coloured Plexiglas, ca. / ca 45×47 cm
Courtesy of the artist and Galerie Barbara Weiss, Berlin, Barbara Gross Galerie, München / Munich, Dirimart, Istanbul

Die Farben der Buchstaben (5), 2006
ausgestanztes, farbiges Plexiglas / die-cut, coloured Plexiglas, 40,5×24 cm
Courtesy of the artist and Galerie Barbara Weiss, Berlin, Barbara Gross Galerie, München / Munich, Dirimart, Istanbul

Netz, 2006 / 2008
Polyester-Textilband, ca. 10 000 Meter in unterschied-lichen Längen / ribbon, poly-ester, ca 10,000 m in variable dimensions
Courtesy of the artist and Galerie Barbara Weiss, Berlin, Barbara Gross Galerie, München / Munich, Dirimart, Istanbul

Jalousie, 2007
7 Jalousien, Kunststoff, Baum-wolle, Maße variabel / 7 blinds, plastic, cotton, dimensions variable
Courtesy of the artist and Galerie Barbara Weiss, Berlin, Barbara Gross Galerie, München / Munich, Dirimart, Istanbul

Gemütliche Ecken, 2009
10 Aluminiumverbundplatten, lackiert, Maße variabel / 10 alu-

minium composite boards, varnished, dimensions variable
Courtesy of the artist and Galerie Barbara Weiss, Berlin, Barbara Gross Galerie, München / Munich, Dirimart, Istanbul

Ewig Dein, 2011
Klanginstallation, 1 Min. 11 Sek., Loop / sound installation, 1 min 11 s, loop
Courtesy of the artist and Galerie Barbara Weiss, Berlin, Barbara Gross Galerie, München / Munich, Dirimart, Istanbul

Row-row, 2012
Metall, Farbe / metal, colour, 93×266 cm
Privatsammlung / private collection

Großes grünes Pompon, 2012
Kleidungsetiketten aus Baumwolle, gebeizter Chrom-ständer / clothing labels made out of cotton, stained chrome stand, 120×31 cm, Ø 41 cm
Courtesy of the artist and Galerie Barbara Weiss, Berlin, Barbara Gross Galerie, München / Munich, Dirimart, Istanbul

Kleines grünes Pompon, 2012
Kleidungsetiketten aus Baumwolle, gebeizter Chrom-ständer / clothing labels made out of cotton, stained chrome stand, 100×31 cm, Ø 36 cm
Courtesy of the artist and Galerie Barbara Weiss, Berlin, Barbara Gross Galerie, München / Munich, Dirimart, Istanbul

Bronze Acid Blue, 2014
Video in Farbe mit Ton, 4 Min. 1 Sek., Loop / colour video with sound, 4 min 1 s, loop
Courtesy of the artist and

Galerie Barbara Weiss, Berlin, Barbara Gross Galerie, München / Munich, Dirimart, Istanbul

Bronze Acid Ochre, 2014
Video in Farbe mit Ton, 4 Min. 1 Sek., Loop / colour video with sound, 4 min 1 s, loop
Courtesy of the artist and Galerie Barbara Weiss, Berlin, Barbara Gross Galerie, München / Munich, Dirimart, Istanbul

Bronze Acid Green, 2014
Video in Farbe mit Ton, 3 Min., Loop / colour video with sound, 3 min, loop
Courtesy of the artist and Galerie Barbara Weiss, Berlin, Barbara Gross Galerie, München / Munich, Dirimart, Istanbul

Bronze Acid Yellow, 2014
Video in Farbe mit Ton, 5 Min., Loop / colour video with sound, 5 min, loop
Courtesy of the artist and Galerie Barbara Weiss, Berlin, Barbara Gross Galerie, München / Munich, Dirimart, Istanbul

green / not the color it is, 2014
Bronze, Patina / bronze, patina, 30×20×10 cm
Courtesy of the artist and Galerie Barbara Weiss, Berlin, Barbara Gross Galerie, München / Munich, Dirimart, Istanbul

grass green / not the color it is, 2014
Bronze, Patina / bronze, patina, 30×20×10 cm
Courtesy of the artist and Galerie Barbara Weiss, Berlin, Barbara Gross Galerie, München / Munich, Dirimart, Istanbul

*light green / not the color
it is,* 2014
Bronze, Patina / bronze, patina,
30 × 20 × 10 cm
Courtesy of the artist and
Galerie Barbara Weiss, Berlin,
Barbara Gross Galerie,
München / Munich, Dirimart,
Istanbul

Glassworks, 2015 / 2017
Installation, 22 farbige Glas-
platten, Strahler / installation,
22 coloured glass plates,
spotlights
Courtesy of the artist and
Galerie Barbara Weiss, Berlin,
Barbara Gross Galerie,
München / Munich, Dirimart,
Istanbul

By Nature, 2015 / 2017
Installation, Porzellantier-
figuren, Plexiglasvitrine, Maße
variabel / installation, porcelain
figurines, showcase in Plexi-
glass, dimensions variable
Courtesy of the artist and
Galerie Barbara Weiss, Berlin,
Barbara Gross Galerie,
München / Munich, Dirimart,
Istanbul

Shutters, 2017
Installation, Fensterblenden
in Bewegung / installation,
moving shutters
Courtesy of the artist and
Galerie Barbara Weiss, Berlin,
Barbara Gross Galerie,
München / Munich, Dirimart,Is-
tanbul

Half of, 2017
Installation, 5-teilig, Stoff,
Aluminium, Maße variabel /
installation, 5 pieces, fabric,
aluminium, dimensions variable
Courtesy of the artist and
Galerie Barbara Weiss, Berlin,
Barbara Gross Galerie,
München / Munich, Dirimart,
Istanbul

Mona Hatoum

Changing Parts, 1984
Video in Schwarz-Weiß mit Ton,
24 Min. / black and white video
with sound, 24 min
Eine / A Western Front Video
Production, Vancouver
Courtesy of the artist

Roadworks, 1985
Dokumentation der Aufführung
von / documentation of
performance for *Roadworks,*
Brixton, London
Video in Farbe mit Ton, 6 Min.
45 Sek. / colour video with
sound, 6 min 45 s
Courtesy of the artist

Measures of Distance, 1988
Video in Farbe mit Ton,
15 Min. 35 Sek. / colour video
with sound, 15 min 35 s
Eine / A Western Front Video
Production, Vancouver
Courtesy of the artist

Over my dead body,
1988 / 2002
Tintenstrahldruck auf PVC
mit Ösen / ink jet on PVC with
eyelets, 204,5 × 305 cm
Courtesy of the artist

*Untitled (couteaux étalons
thiernois II)*, 1999
Japanisches Wachspapier /
Japanese wax paper,
32,5 × 54,5 cm
Courtesy of the artist

*Untitled
(passoire à queue),* 1999
Japanisches Wachspapier /
Japanese wax paper,
43,5 × 54,5 cm
Courtesy of the artist

Untitled (passoire de J-L), 1999
Japanisches Wachspapier /
Japanese wax paper,
43,5 × 50 cm
Courtesy of the artist

*Untitled
(petite passoire à queue)*, 1999
Japanisches Wachspapier /
Japanese wax paper,
30 × 46,5 cm
Courtesy of the artist

*Untitled
(râpe cylindrique),* 1999
Japanisches Wachspapier /
Japanese wax paper,
40 × 54,5 cm
Courtesy of the artist

Projection, 2006
Baumwolle, Abacá / cotton,
abaca, 89 × 140 cm
Courtesy of the artist

Paravent, 2008
Geschwärzter Stahl / black
finished steel, 215 × 302 × 5 cm
Sammlung Sander / The Sander
Collection, Darmstadt

Daybed, 2008
Geschwärzter Stahl / black
finished steel, 31,5 × 219 × 98 cm
Courtesy of the artist

Impenetrable, 2009
Geschwärzter Stacheldraht,
Angelschnur / black finished
steel, fishing wire,
300 × 300 × 300 cm
Courtesy of the artist

Hot Spot III, 2009
Edelstahl, Neonröhren /
stainless steel, neon tube,
234 × 223 × 223 cm
Sammlung Goetz, München /
Munich

Bourj A, 2011
Baustahlrohre / mild steel
tubing, 165 × 70 × 40 cm
Courtesy of the artist

Bourj II, 2011
Baustahlrohre / mild steel
tubing, 180 × 75 × 50 cm
Courtesy of the artist

Bourj III, 2011
Baustahlrohre / mild steel
tubing, 180 × 80 × 55 cm
Courtesy of the artist

*Natura morta
(medical cabinet),* 2012
Muranospiegelglas, Stahl,
Glas / Murano mirrored glass,
steel, glass, 61,5 × 54 × 17,5 cm
Courtesy of the artist

Cellules, 2012–2013
Baustahl, mundgeblasenes
Glas in 8 Teilen, 170 cm × Maße
variabel / mild steel, hand-
blown glass in eight parts,
170 cm × variable dimensions
Courtesy of the artist and
Galerie Chantal Crousel, Paris

*Remains of the Day
(s version),* 2016
Drahtgeflecht, Holz, Maße
variabel / wire mesh, wood,
dimensions variable
Courtesy of the artist

Quarters, 2017
Baustahl / mild steel,
275 × 516 × 1515 cm
Courtesy of the artist and
White Cube

Aufgeführt wird hier nur die im Zusammenhang mit der Ausstellung und den gezeigten Werken verwendete Literatur. Für einen Überblick über die Literatur zu Ayşe Erkmen verweisen wir auf die Austellungskataloge Berlin 2008a und Gent 2015 sowie ihre Website http://ayseerkmen.com, für einen Überblick über die Literatur zu Mona Hatoum auf den Ausstellungskatalog Paris / London / Helsinki 2015.

Only the literature used in connection with the exhibition and the works on display is listed in the following. For an overview of the literature on Ayşe Erkmen see the exhibition catalogues Berlin 2008a and Gent 2015 as well as her website http://ayseerkmen.com; for an overview of the literature on Mona Hatoum see exhibition catalogue Paris / London / Helsinki 2015.

Adorf 2008
Sigrid Adorf, *Operation Video. Eine Technik des Nahsehens und ihr spezifisches Subjekt: die Videokünstlerin der 1970er Jahre,* Bielefeld: transcript 2008.

Adorno 1951 / 2005
Theodor W. Adorno, *Minima Moralia* (1951), 2005 ins Englische übersetzt von / translated to English by Dennis Redmond, online: <http://www.efn.org/~dredmond/MinimaMoralia.html>, letzter Zugriff / last access: 1.7.2017.

Adorno 1951 / 2014
Theodor W. Adorno, *Minima Moralia. Reflexionen aus dem beschädigten Leben,* Frankfurt am Main: Suhrkamp ⁹2014 (Erstauflage / first edition 1951).

Amman 2008
Mona Hatoum, Ausst.-Kat. / exh. cat. Amman, Darat al Funun – The Khalid Shoman Foundation 11.10.2008–22.1.2009, Amman: Darat al Funun 2008.

Anastas / Brenson 2006
Witness to Her Art. Art and Writings by Adrian Piper, Mona Hatoum, Cady Noland, Jenny Holzer, Kara Walker, Daniela Rossell and Eau de Cologne, hrsg. von / ed. by Rhea Anastas, Michael Brenson, Annandale-on-Hudson: Bard College. Center for Curatorial Studies 2006.

Antoni 1998 / 2016
Janine Antoni, »Interview with Mona Hatoum«, in *BOMB* 63 (Frühling / Spring 1998), online: <http://bombmagazine.org/article/2130/monahatoum>, letzter Zugriff / last access: 29.1.2015 (zuletzt Wiederabdruck / reprinted in Archer 2016, 136–144)

Antwerpen 2000
Mona Hatoum, Ausst.-Kat. / exh. cat. Antwerpen, Museum van Hedendaagse Kunst 18.6.–17.9.2000, hrsg. von / ed. by Jo Glencross, Antwerpen: MUHKA 2000.

Archer 1996
Michael Archer, »Mona Hatoum«, in *Dimensions. Fünf Künstler aus Großbritannien: Hannah Collins, Alan Currall, Mona Hatoum, Tanya Leighton, Marcus Taylor,* Ausst.-Kat. / exh. cat. Städtische Kunsthalle Mannheim 11.5.–30.6.1996, Mannheim: Städtische Kunsthalle 1996, 40–41.

Archer 1997 / 2016
Michael Archer, »Michael Archer in conversation with Mona Hatoum«, in Archer 2016, 8–30 (Erstabdruck / first published in Archer / Brett / de Zegher 1997, 8–30).

Archer / Brett / de Zegher 1997
Michael Archer, Guy Brett, Catherine de Zegher, *Mona Hatoum,* London, New York: Phaidon Press 1997.

Archer 2016
Michael Archer u. a. / et al., *Mona Hatoum,* London, New York: Phaidon Press 2016 (erweiterte Neuauflage von / revised and extended edition of Archer / Brett / de Zegher 1997).

Arendt 1943
Hannah Arendt, »We Refugees«, in *Menorah Journal* 31 / 1 (1943), 69–77 (Deutsch / German: »Wir Flüchtlinge«, in Hannah Arendt, *Zur Zeit. Politische Essays,* hrsg. von / ed. by Marie Luise Knott, Berlin: Rotbuch 1986, 7–21).

Arnsberg 1996
Ayşe Erkmen. Images, Ausst.-Kat. / exh. cat. Arnsberg, Kunstverein 30.5.–15.6.1996, hrsg. von / ed. by Johannes Teiser, Arnsberg: Kunstverein 1996.

Barcelona 2012
Mona Hatoum. Projecció, Ausst.-Kat. / exh. cat. Barcelona, Fundació Joan Miró 22.6.–24.9.2012, Barcelona: Fundació Joan Miró 2012.

Basel 1996
Fremdkörper. Videoinstallationen von Matthew Barney, Mona Hatoum, Gary Hill, Bruce Nauman, Marcel Odenbach, Bill Viola und speziell zusammengestellte Programme von Videobändern, Ausst.-Kat. / exh. cat. Kunstmuseum Basel, Museum für Gegenwartskunst 1.6.–29.9.1996, hrsg. von / ed. by Theodora Vischer, Basel: Museum für Gegenwartskunst 1996.

Basel 2008
Above the Fold. Ayşe Erkmen, Ceal Floyer, David Lamelas, Ausst.-Kat. / exh. cat. Kunstmuseum Basel, Museum für Gegenwartskunst 1.7.–12.10.2008, hrsg. von / ed. by Nikola Dietrich, Ostfildern-Ruit: Hatje Cantz Verlag 2008.

Batty 2013
David Batty, »Istanbul Biennial under fire for tactical withdrawal from contested sites«, in *The Observer,* 14.9.2013, online: <https://www.theguardian.com/world/2013/sep/14/istanbul-biennial-art-protest-under-fire>, letzter Zugriff / last access: 22.5.2017.

Baykal 2012
Emre Baykal, »For Your Own Safety, at Your Own Risk«, in Istanbul 2012, 60–68.

Bell 2008
Kirsty Bell, »A Mapping of Mona Hatoum«, in *Mona Hatoum. Unhomely,* Ausst.-Kat. / exh. cat. Berlin, Galerie Max Hetzler 2.5.–28.6.2008, hrsg. von / ed. by Max Hetzler Galerie, Berlin: Holzwarth Publications 2008, 61–73 (Deutsch / German: »Mona Hatoum – eine Kartographie ihres Werkes«, in ebd. / ibid., 75–89).

Belting 2005
Hans Belting, *Szenarien der Moderne: Kunst und ihre offenen Grenzen,* hrsg. von / ed. by Peter Weibel, Hamburg: Philo and Philo Fine Arts 2005 (Fundus-Bücher; 164).

Belting / Buddensieg 2016
Hans Belting, Andrea Buddensieg, »Kunst im Zeitalter der Globalisierung: Zeitgenossenschaft als neues Axiom«, in *Grenzenlos Kunst?*, Dokumentation der Vortragsreihe in / documentation of the lectures at Berlin, Akademie der Künste, 2010–2012, hrsg. im Auftrag der / ed. on behalf of the Akademie der Künste, Berlin, von / by Robert Kudielka, Angela Lammert, Dortmund: Kettler Verlag 2016, 15–22.

Berlin 1994
Erzählen, Ausst.-Kat. / exh. cat. Berlin, Akademie der Künste 9.10.–27.11.1994, hrsg. von / ed. by Michael Glasmeier, Ostfildern-Ruit: Hatje Cantz Verlag 1994.

Berlin 1995
Ayşe Erkmen. In Berlin, Ausst.-Kat. / exh. cat. Berlin, DAAD-Galerie, Galerie von der Tann 1995, für das / for the DAAD-Künstlerprogramm und die / and the Galerie von der Tann, hrsg. von / ed. by Friedrich Meschede, Iris von der Tann, Berlin 1995.

Berlin 2004 / 2006
Topos Raum. Die Aktualität des Raumes in den Künsten der Gegenwart, Tagungsband / proceedings Berlin, Akademie der Künste 17.–20.11.2004, hrsg. von / ed. by Angela Lammert u. a. / et al., Nürnberg: Verlag für moderne Kunst 2006.9

Berlin 2005
Raum. Prolog, Ausst.-Kat. / exh. cat. Berlin, Akademie der Künste 3.4.–4.6.2005, hrsg. von / ed. by Julia Bernhard, Berlin: Akademie der Künste 2005.

Berlin 2006
U2 Alexanderplatz 2006. Kunst im U-Bahnhof Alexanderplatz, Ausst.-Kat. / exh. cat. Berlin, U-Bahnhof Alexanderplatz 27.9.–29.10.2006, hrsg. von / ed. by Uwe Jonas u. a. / et al., Berlin: Neue Gesellschaft für Bildende Kunst 2006.

Berlin 2008a
Ayşe Erkmen. Weggefährten, Ausst.-Kat. / exh. cat. Berlin, Nationalgalerie im Hamburger Bahnhof 13.9.2008–11.1.2009, hrsg. von / ed. by Britta Schmitz, Bettina Schaschke, Köln: Verlag der Buchhandlung Walther König 2008.

Berlin 2008b
Political, Minimal, Ausst.-Kat. / exh. cat. Berlin, KW Institute for Contemporary Art 30.11.2008–25.1.2009, hrsg. von / ed. by Klaus Biesenbach, Nürnberg: Verlag für moderne Kunst 2008.

Berlin 2010
Mona Hatoum. Käthe-Kollwitz-Preis 2010, Ausst.-Kat. / exh. cat. Berlin, Akademie der Künste 31.7.–5.9.2010, hrsg. von / ed. by Akademie der Künste, Berlin: Akademie der Künste 2010.

Berlin 2012
Mona Hatoum. Shift, Ausst.-Kat. / exh. cat. Berlin, Galerie Max Hetzler 8.9.–13.10.2012, hrsg. von / ed. by Max Hetzler Galerie, Berlin: Holzwarth Publications 2012.

Bertola 2009
Chiara Bertola, »Mona Hatoum. Forme instabili, vive, organiche e in movimento / Mona Hatoum. Unstable, Living, Organic and Moving Forms«, in Venedig 2009, 18–33.

Bertola 2016
Chiara Bertola, »Interview with Mona Hatoum (2014)«, in Archer 2016, 152–159.

Bessling 2010
Rainer Bessling, »Ayşe Erkmen – Migration der Formen«, in *Künstler. Kritisches Lexikon der Gegenwartskunst* 91 / 15 (3. Quartal / 3rd Quarter 2010).

Birmingham 2005
Ayşe Erkmen. Under the Roof, Ausst.-Kat. / exh. cat. Birmingham, Ikon Gallery 9.4.–30.5.2005, hrsg. von / ed. by Nigel Prince, Anna Pike, Birmingham: Ikon Gallery 2005.

Bitterli / Veronese 2014
Konrad Bitterli, Nadia Veronese, »Parcours. Anmerkungen zur Ausstellung«, in St. Gallen 2014, 9–23.

Block 2008
Ayşe Erkmen.)>ucucu</ =simdi=(.)>temporary</ =contemporary=(, hrsg. von / ed. by René Block, Istanbul: YKY 2008 (Contemporary Art in Turkey; 5).

Boltanski / Chiapello 1999 / 2003
Luc Boltanski, Ève Chiapello, *Der neue Geist des Kapitalismus,* aus dem Französischen übersetzt von / translated from French by Michael Tillmann, Konstanz: UVK 2003 (Original: *Le nouvel esprit du capitalisme,* Paris: Éditions Gallimard 1999).

Bourriaud 2009
Nicolas Bourriaud, *Radikant,* aus dem Französischen übersetzt von / translated from French by Katharina Grän, Berlin: Merve 2009 (Original: *Radicant. Pour une esthétique de la globalisation,* Paris: Denoël 2009).

Bowles 2007
John P. Bowles, »›Acting like a Man‹: Adrian Piper's Mythic Being and Black Feminism in the 1970s«, in *Signs* 32 / 3 (2007), 621–647.

Brandes 2010
Kerstin Brandes, *Fotografie und »Identität«. Visuelle Repräsentationspolitiken in künstlerischen Arbeiten der 1980er und 1990er Jahre,* Bielefeld: transcript 2010.

Brett 1997
Guy Brett, »Itinerary«, in Archer / Brett / de Zegher 1997, 34–87.

Brohl 2003
Christiane Brohl, *Displacement als kunstpädagogische Strategie,* Norderstedt: Books on Demand 2003, zugleich Diss. Universität Lüneburg 2001.

Buchhart 2004
Dieter Buchhart, »Ayşe Erkmen. Wahrnehmungsbrüche« (Interview), in *Kunstforum. International* 168 (2004), 248–261.

Butler 1990 / 1991
Judith Butler, *Das Unbehagen der Geschlechter,* aus dem Englischen übersetzt von / translated from English by Kathrina Menke, Frankfurt am Main: Suhrkamp 1991 (Original: *Gender Trouble. Feminism and the Subversion of Identity,* New York u. a. O. / et al.: Routledge 1990).

Butler 2004
Judith Butler, *Precarious Life. The Powers of Mourning and Violence,* London, New York: Verso 2004.

Butler 2004 / 2005
Judith Butler, *Gefährdetes Leben. Politische Essays,* aus dem Englischen übersetzt von / translated from English by Karin Wördemann, Frankfurt am Main: Suhrkamp 2005 (Übersetzung von / translation of Butler 2004).

Butler 2005
Judith Butler, *Giving an Account of Oneself,* New York: Fordham University Press 2005.

Butler / Spivak 2007a
Judith Butler, Gayatri Chakravorty Spivak, *Who Sings the Nation-State? Language, Politics, Belonging,* New York: Seagull Books 2007.

Butler / Spivak 2007b
Judith Butler, Gayatri Chakravorty Spivak, *Sprache, Politik, Zugehörigkeit,* aus dem Englischen übersetzt von / translated from English by Michael Heitz, Sabine Schulz, Zürich, Berlin: Diaphanes 2007 (Übersetzung von / translation of Butler / Spivak 2007a).

Butler / Gambetti / Sabsay 2016a
Judith Butler, Zeynep Gambetti, Leticia Sabsay (Hrsg. / ed.), *Vulnerability in Resistance,* Durham, NC: Duke University Press 2016.

Butler / Gambetti / Sabsay 2016b
Judith Butler, Zeynep Gambetti, Leticia Sabsay, »Introduction«, in Butler / Gambetti / Sabsay 2016a, 1–11.

Casid / D'Souza 2014
Jill H. Casid, Aruna D'Souza (Hrsg. / ed.), *Art History in the Wake of the Global Turn,* Williamstown, MA: Sterling and Francine Clark Art Institute 2014.

Castro Varela / Dhawan 2005
María do Mar Castro Varela, Nikita Dhawan, *Postkoloniale Theorie. Eine kritische Einführung,* Bielefeld: transcript 2005.

Chadwick 2008
Whitney Chadwick, »Situated and Unsettled: An Introduction to the Work of Mona Hatoum«, in Ferrara 2008, 19–35.

Chave 1990 / 1992
Anna C. Chave, »Minimalism and the Rhetoric of Power«, in *Art in Modern Culture: An Anthology of Critical Texts,* hrsg. von / ed. by Francis Frascina, Jonathan Harris, New York: Icon Editions 1992, 264–281 (Erstabdruck / first published in *Arts Magazine* 64 (5.1.1990), 44–63).

Chave 1990 / 1998
Anna C. Chave, »Minimalismus und die Rhetorik der Macht«, in *Minimal Art. Eine kritische Retrospektive,* hrsg. von / ed. by Gregor Stemmrich, Dresden, Basel: Verlag der Kunst ²1998, 647–677 (gekürzte deutsche Fassung von / shortened German version of Chave 1990 / 1992).

Christchurch 2006
Ayşe Erkmen. Awesome, Ausst.-Kat. / exh. cat. Christchurch, The Physics Room 1.4.–29.4.2006, Christchurch: The Physics Room 2006.

Deleuze 1988 / 2000
Gilles Deleuze, *Die Falte. Leibniz und der Barock,* aus dem Französischen übersetzt von / translated from French by Ulrich Johannes Schneider, Frankfurt am Main: Suhrkamp 2000 (Original: *Le pli. Leibniz et le baroque,* Paris: Les Éditions de Minuit 1988).

Deleuze 1990 / 1993
Gilles Deleuze, »Postskriptum über die Kontrollgesellschaften«, in ders. / id., *Unterhandlungen 1972–1990,* aus dem Französischen übersetzt von / translated from French by Gustav Roßler, Frankfurt am Main: Suhrkamp 1993, 254–262 (Original: »Post-scriptum sur les sociétés de contrôle«, in *L'autre Journal* 1 (Mai / May 1990), 229–247).

Deleuze / Guattari 1980 / 2005
Gilles Deleuze, Félix Guattari, *Tausend Plateaus. Kapitalismus und Schizophrenie,* aus dem Französischen übersetzt von / translated from French by Gabriele Ricke, Ronald Vouillé, Berlin: Merve 2005 (Original: *Mille plateaux,* Paris: Les Éditions de Minuit 1980).

Demos 2013
T. J. Demos, *The Migrant Image. The Art and Politics of Documentary during Global Crisis,* Durham, NC: Duke University Press 2013.

Diamond 1987 / 1997
Sara Diamond, »Interview with Mona Hatoum«, in Archer / Brett / de Zegher 1997, 124–133 (Erstabdruck / first published in *Fuse* (April 1987), 46–52).

Didi-Huberman 1992 / 1999
Georges Didi-Huberman, *Was wir sehen blickt uns an. Zur Metapsychologie des Bildes,* aus dem Französischen übersetzt von / translated from French by Markus Sedlaczek, München: Fink 1999 (Original: *Ce que nous voyons, ce qui nous regarde,* Paris: Les Éditions de Minuit 1992).

Dogramaci 2013a
Burcu Dogramaci, *Fotografieren und Forschen. Wissenschaftliche Expeditionen mit der Kamera im türkischen Exil nach 1933,* Marburg: Jonas Verlag 2013.

Dogramaci 2013b
Burcu Dogramaci (Hrsg. / ed.), *Migration und künstlerische Produktion. Aktuelle Perspektiven,* Bielefeld: transcript 2013.

Dogramaci 2016
Burcu Dogramaci, *Heimat. Eine künstlerische Spurensuche,* Köln, Weimar, Wien: Böhlau Verlag 2016.

Doha 2014
Mona Hatoum. Turbulence, Ausst.-Kat. / exh. cat. Doha, Mathaf: Arab Museum of Modern Art 7.2.–18.5.2014, Mailand: Silvana Editoriale 2014.

D'Souza 2006
Aruna D'Souza, »Measures of Difference«, in Anastas / Brenson 2006, 107–115.

Düsseldorf 2009
Ayşe Erkmen. Hausgenossen. Crystal Rock, Ausst.-Kat. / exh. cat. Düsseldorf, K21 Kunstsammlung Nordrhein-Westfalen 8.11.2008–17.1.2010, hrsg. von / ed. by Julian Heynen, Köln: Verlag der Buchhandlung Walther König 2009.

Eiblmayr 2011
Silvia Eiblmayr, »Gemütliche Grazer Ecken – ein Widerspruch«, in Graz 2011, 66–69.

Elwes 1981 / 2006
Catherine Elwes, »Notes from a Video Performance by Mona Hatoum (1980)«, in Anastas / Brenson 2006, 118–119 (Erstabdruck / first published in *Undercut* 1 (März / March–April 1981), 28–29).

Erkmen 2001
Ayşe Erkmen, »Kunst im Raum / Art in Space«, in *Public Art. Kunst im öffentlichen Raum,* hrsg. von / ed. by Florian Matzner, Ostfildern-Ruit: Hatje Cantz Verlag 2001, 71–81.

Ferrara 2008
Mona Hatoum. Undercurrents (XIII Biennale Donna), Ausst.-Kat. / exh. cat. Ferrara, Ferrara Palazzo Massari PAC 6.4.–1.8.2008, hrsg. von / ed. by Lola G. Bonora u. a. / et al., Ferrara: Gallerie d'Arte Moderna e Contemporanea 2008.

Fink / Ruppert 2009
Elisabeth Fink, Uta Ruppert, »Postkoloniale Differenzen über transnationale Feminismen. Eine Debatte zu den transnationalen Perspektiven von Chandra T. Mohanty und Gayatri C. Spivak«, in *Femina Politica. Zeitschrift für feministische Politikwissenschaft* 2 / 2009, 64–73.

Flusser 1994
Vilém Flusser, *Von der Freiheit des Migranten. Einsprüche gegen den Nationalismus,* Bensheim: Bollmann Verlag 1994.

Flusser 1994 / 2003
Vilém Flusser, *The Freedom of the Migrant: Objections to Nationalism,* hrsg. von / ed. by Anke K. Finger, aus dem Deutschen übersetzt von / translated from German by Kenneth Kronenberg, Urbana: University of Illinois Press 2003 (Übersetzung von / translation of Flusser 1994).

Foucault 1967 / 1986
Michel Foucault, »Of Other Spaces«, aus dem Französischen übersetzt von / translated from French by Jay Miskowiec, in *Diacritics* 16 / 1 (Herbst / autumn 1986), 22–27.

Foucault 1967 / 1992
Michel Foucault, »Andere Räume«, in *Aisthesis. Wahrnehmung heute oder Perspektiven einer anderen Ästhetik,* hrsg. von / ed. by Karlheinz Barck u. a. / et al., Leipzig 1992, 34–46 (Original: »Des espaces autres«, Vortrag auf der Konferenz / lecture at the conference Cercle d'études architecturales, Tunis 14.3.1967, publ. in *Architecture, Mouvement, Continuité* 5 (Oktober / October 1984), 46–49).

Frankfurt am Main 1996
Zuspiel. Ayşe Erkmen, Andreas Slominski, Ausst.-Kat. / exh. cat. Frankfurt am Main, Portikus 3.2.–24.3.1996, hrsg. von / ed. by Matthias Winzen für das / for the Siemens Kulturprogramm, Ostfildern-Ruit: Hatje Cantz Verlag 1996.

Freud 1900 / 2000
Sigmund Freud, *Die Traumdeutung* (1900), in ders. / id., *Studienausgabe,* Bd. / vol. II, Frankfurt am Main: Fischer Taschenbuchverlag 2000.

Freud 1900 / 2015
Sigmund Freud, *The Interpretation of Dreams* (1900 / 1913), aus dem Deutschen übersetzt von / translated from German by Abraham Arden Brill, Mineola, New York: Dover 2015 (Übersetzung von / translation of Freud 1900 / 2000).

Garb 2006
Tamar Garb, »Hairlines«, in *Women Artists at the Millennium,* hrsg. von / ed. by Carol Armstrong, Catherine de Zegher, Cambridge, London: MIT Press 2006.

Gent 2015
Ayşe Erkmen, Ausst.-Kat. / exh. cat. Gent, S.M.A.K. 31.10.2015–14.2.2016, hrsg. von / ed. by Jan Verwoert, Philippe Van Cauteren, Gent: MER. Paper Kunsthalle 2015.

Graz 1996
Inklusion: Exklusion. Versuch einer neuen Kartographie der Kunst im Zeitalter von Postkolonialismus und globaler Migration, Ausst.-Kat. / exh. cat. Graz, *steirischer herbst* im Reininghaus 22.9.–26.10.1996, hrsg. von / ed. by Peter Weibel, Köln: Dumont 1997.

Graz 2011
Utopie und Monument: Ausstellung für den öffentlichen Raum, Publikation zum *steirischen herbst,* Graz 2009 und 2010, hrsg. von / ed. by Sabine Breitwieser, Wien u. a. O. / et al.: Springer 2011.

Haehnel 2007
Birgit Haehnel, »›[...] so bitter wie der Geschmack von heißen gerösteten Kaffeebohnen [...]‹. Trauma, Medialität und Hautfarbe in Kara Walkers *Safety Curtain* der Staatsoper Wien«, in *FrauenKunstWissenschaft* 43 (Juni / June 2007), 22–36.

Hatoum 1987
Mona Hatoum, »Body & Text«, in *Third Text* 1 / 1 (Herbst / autumn 1987), 26–33.

Hatoum 2015a
»Mona Hatoum. Parole aux artistes«, Vortrag von / lecture by Mona Hatoum in Paris, Musée national d'Art moderne, Centre national d'art et de culture Georges-Pompidou, 25.9.2015, online: <https://www.centrepompidou.fr/id/cBgjb4G/rEBApM6/de>, letzter Zugriff / last access 1.11.2015.

Hatoum 2015b
Mona Hatoum im Gespräch mit / in conversation with Christine van Assche anlässlich ihrer Ausstellung / on the occasion of her exhibition in Paris, Musée national d'Art moderne, Centre national d'art et de culture Georges-Pompidou, online: <https://www.centrepompidou.fr/cpv/resource/cMbapqd/rLbapLy>, letzter Zugriff / last access: 1.11.2015.

Hamburg / Bonn / Stockholm 2004
Mona Hatoum, Ausst-Kat. / exh. cat. Hamburger Kunsthalle 26.3.–31.5.2004, Kunstmuseum Bonn 17.6.–29.8.2004, Magasin III Stockholm Konsthall 9.10.–19.12.2004, hrsg. von / ed. by Christoph Heinrich, Ostfildern-Ruit: Hatje Cantz Verlag 2004.

Herbstreuth 1997
Peter Herbstreuth, »Ayşe Erkmen. Mißverständnisse sind Teil des Werks« (Interview), in *Kunstforum. International* 139 (1997), 276–287.

Huber 2013
Thomas R. Huber, *Ästhetik der Begegnung. Kunst als Erfahrungsraum der Anderen,* Bielefeld: transcript 2013.

Ianniciello 2014
Celeste Ianniciello, »Postcolonial Art: A Living Archive of Border-Crossing and Migrant Matters«, in *Critical Cartography of Art and Visuality in the Global Age,* hrsg. von / ed. by Anna Maria Guasch Ferrer, Nasheli Jiménez del Val, Cambridge: Cambridge Scholars Publishing 2014, 19–33.

Istanbul 2012
Mona Hatoum. You are still here. Hâlâ Buradasın, Ausst.-Kat. / exh. cat. Istanbul, ARTER – space for art 17.3.–17.5.2012, hrsg. von / ed. by İlkay Baliç, Istanbul: ARTER – space for art 2012.

Karamustafa 2001
Gülsün Karamustafa, »Objects of Desire – A Suitcase Trade (100 Dollars Limit). Eine Kunst-Performance«, in Sabine Hess, Ramona Lenz (Hrsg. / ed.), *Ein kulturwissenschaftlicher Streifzug durch transnationale Räume,* Königstein: Ulrike Helmer 2001, 166–180.

Karentzos 2012
Alexandra Karentzos, »Postkoloniale Kunstgeschichte. Revisionen von Musealisierungen, Kanonisierungen, Repräsentationen«, in Julia Reuter, Alexandra Karentzos (Hrsg. / ed.), *Schlüsselwerke der Postcolonial Studies,* Wiesbaden: Springer 2012, 249–266.

Kassel 1997
Politics:poetics. Das Buch zur documenta X, Ausst.-Kat. / exh. cat. Kassel, *documenta X* 21.6.–28.9.1997, im Auftrag der documenta und der Museum Fridericianum Veranstaltungs-GmbH, hrsg. von / ed. by Catherine David, Jean-François Chevrier, Ostfildern-Ruit: Hatje Cantz Verlag 1997.

Kassel 1998
Echolot oder 9 Fragen an die Peripherie, Ausst.-Kat. / exh. cat. Kassel, Museum Fridericianum 22.3.–21.6.1998, hrsg. von / ed. by René Block, Kassel: Museum Fridericianum 1998.

Keidel 2006
Matthias Keidel, *Die Wiederkehr der Flaneure. Literarische Flanerie und flanierendes Denken zwischen Wahrnehmung und Reflexion,* Würzburg: Königshausen und Neumann 2006.

Kerner 2012
Ina Kerner, *Postkoloniale Theorien – zur Einführung,* Hamburg: Junius Verlag 2012.

Kikol 2016
Larissa Kikol, »Frauen, wagt mehr Größenwahn!«, in *Die Zeit* 37 (1.9.2016).

Koch / Vöhler / Voss 2010
Gertrud Koch, Martin Vöhler, Christiane Voss (Hrsg. / ed.), *Die Mimesis und ihre Künste,* München: Fink 2010.

Kölle 2008
Brigitte Kölle, »Grenzen und Schwellen – Gedanken zum künstlerischen Werk von Ayşe Erkmen«, in Berlin 2008a, 159–167.

Kowalewski 2016
Laura Kowalewski, *Über Körper und Konflikte: Mona Hatoums The Negotiating Table (1983),* Master-Arbeit, Leuphana Universität Lüneburg 2016, online: <http://opus.uni-lueneburg.de/opus/volltexte/2016/14404/>, letzter Zugriff / last access: 1.10.2016.

Kraus 1986
Karl Kraus, *Aphorismen. Sprüche und Widersprüche. Pro domo. Nachts,* Frankfurt am Main: Suhrkamp 1986.

Krauss 1977 / 1998
Rosalind E. Krauss, *Passages in Modern Sculpture,* Cambridge: MIT Press [12]1998 (Erstauflage / first edition 1977).

Kravagna 1999
Christian Kravagna, »Die Moderne im Rückspiegel. Über postkoloniale Kunst und Formen der Aneignung«, in *Springerin. Hefte für Gegenwartskunst* 5 / 2 (1999), 48–53.

Kravagna 2013
Christian Kravagna, »Reinheit der Kunst in Zeiten der Transkulturalität: Modernistische Kunsttheorie und die Kultur der Migration«, in Dogramaci 2013b, 43–65.

Kuhlmann 2014
Jenny Kuhlmann, »Exil, Diaspora, Transmigration«, in *Aus Politik und Zeitgeschichte* 42 / 2014 (13.10.2014), 9–15, online: <http://www.bpb.de/apuz/192563/exil-diaspora-transmigration>, letzter Zugriff / last access: 1.5.2017.

Lamm 2004
Kimberly Lamm, »Seeing Feminism in Exile. The Imaginary Maps of Mona Hatoum«, in *Michigan Feminist Studies* 18 (2004), online: <http://hdl.handle.net/2027/spo.ark5583.0018.001>, letzter Zugriff / last access: 20.4.2017.

Lipphardt 2015
Anna Lipphardt, »Der Nomade als Theoriefigur, empirische Anrufung und Lifestyle-Emblem. Auf Spurensuche im Globalen Norden«, in *Aus Politik und Zeitgeschichte* 26–27 / 2015 (22.6.2015), online: <http://www.bpb.de/apuz/208257/der-nomade-als-theoriefigur-empirische-anrufung-und-lifestyle-emblem-auf-spurensuche-im-globalen-norden>, letzter Zugriff / last access: 29.4.2017.

London 2000
Mona Hatoum. The Entire World as a Foreign Land, Ausst.-Kat. / exh. cat. London, Tate Britain 23.3.–23.7.2000, hrsg. von / ed. by Edward Said, Sheena Wagstaff, London: Tate Gallery Publishing Ltd 2000.

Loreck 1994
Hanne Loreck, »Verräumlichungen. Zu Ayşe Erkmens neuen Arbeiten«, in *Texte zur Kunst* 16 (November 1994), 165–169.

Mailand 1996
Mona Hatoum. Quarters, Ausst.-Kat. / exh. cat. Mailand, Viafarini 16.10.–21.11.1996, hrsg. von / ed. by Angela Vettese, Mailand: Viafarini 1996.

Mansoor 2010
Jaleh Mansoor, »A Spectral Universality. Mona Hatoum's Biopolitics of Abstraction«, in *October* 133 (Sommer / summer 2010), 49–74.

Marchart 2008
Oliver Marchart, *Hegemonie im Kunstfeld. Die documenta-Ausstellungen dX, D11, d12 und die Politik der Biennalisierung,* Köln: Verlag der Buchhandlung Walther König 2008.

Marth 2003
Judith Marth, *Von der Performance zur Installation am Beispiel Mona Hatoums,* Diss. Universität Hamburg 2003, online: <http://ediss.sub.uni-hamburg.de/volltexte/2005/2530/>, letzter Zugriff / last access: 1.5.2016.

Matzner 1999
Florian Matzner, »Künstlerumfrage«, in *Basisarbeit,* hrsg. von / ed. by Olaf Metzel, Akademie der Künste München, München: Akademie der Künste München 1999, 176–191.

Meschede 1997
Friedrich Meschede, »Minen im Kopf. Zum Werk von Ayşe Erkmen«, in Recklinghausen 1997, 46–49.

Meschede 2005
Friedrich Meschede, »Ayşe Erkmen – ›Half of Each‹, Akademie der Künste, Pariser Platz Berlin 2005«, in *Jahresring* 52 (2005), zum Thema *Etwas von Etwas. Abstrakte Kunst,* hrsg. von / ed. by dems. / id., 160–166.

Meschede 2008
Friedrich Meschede, »)›temporary‹/=contemporary=(«, in Block 2008, 9–79.

Mexiko-Stadt 2002
Mona Hatoum, Ausst.-Kat. / exh. cat. Mexiko-Stadt, Laboratorio Arte Alameda 26.2.–21.4.2002, hrsg. vom / ed. by Laboratorio Arte Alameda, Mexiko-Stadt: Laboratorio Arte Alameda 2002.

Meyer 1999
Remix / Ayşe Erkmen, hrsg. von / ed. by Werner Meyer, Göppingen: Städtische Galerie 1999.

Micossé-Aikins 2015
Sandrine Micossé-Aikins, »»Die Kunst ist eine Tochter der Freiheit‹ – antirassistischer Kulturaktivismus zwischen Protest und Widerstand«, in *Jahrbuch der Guernica-Gesellschaft* 17 (2015), hrsg. von / ed. by Anna Greve, 155–166.

Mikdadi 2008
Salwa Mikdadi, »The States of Being in Mona Hatoum's Artwork«, in Ausst.-Kat. / exh. cat. Amman 2008, 59–73, online: <http://thekhalidshomanfoundation.org/main/activit/curentl/mona_hatoum/5.htm>, letzter Zugriff / last access: 30.9.2016.

Mönchengladbach 2004
Ayşe Erkmen – gebunden an / bound to, Ausst.-Kat. / exh. cat. Mönchengladbach, Städtisches Museum Abteiberg 20.6.–31.10.2004, hrsg. vom / ed. by Städtischen Museum Abteiberg Mönchengladbach, Mönchengladbach: Museum Abteiberg 2004.

Mohanty 1984
Chandra Talpade Mohanty, »Under Western Eyes. Feminist Scholarship and Colonial Discourses«, in *boundary* 2 12 / 3 (1984), 333–358.

Mohanty 2003
Chandra Talpade Mohanty, »Under Western Eyes Revisited: Feminist Solidarity through Anticapitalist Struggles«, in *Signs* 28 / 2 (2003), 499–535.

Morra 2007
Joanne Morra, »Daughter's Tongue«, in *Journal of Visual Culture* 6 / 1 (April 2007), 91–108, online: <http://journals.sagepub.com/doi /pdf/10.1177/1470412907075071>, letzter Zugriff / last access: 1.7.2016.

München 2011
Mona Hatoum, Ausst.-Kat. / exh. cat. München, Sammlung Goetz 21.11.2011–5.4.2012, hrsg. von / ed. by Ingvild Goetz, Rainald Schumacher, Larissa Michelberger, Ostfildern-Ruit: Hatje Cantz Verlag 2011.

Münster 1997
Skulptur. Projekte in Münster 1997, Ausst.-Kat. / exh. cat. Münster, Westfälisches Landesmuseum für Kunst und Kulturgeschichte 22.6.–28.9.1997, hrsg. von / ed. by Klaus Bußmann, Kasper König, Ostfildern-Ruit: Hatje Cantz Verlag 1997.

Münster 2007
skulpturprojektemünster07, Ausst.-Kat. / exh. cat. Münster, Westfälisches Landesmuseum für Kunst und Kulturgeschichte 17.6.–30.9.2007, hrsg. von / ed. by Brigitte Franzen, Kasper König, Carina Plath, Köln: Verlag der Buchhandlung Walther König 2007.

Münster 2017
Skulptur Projekte Münster 2017, Ausst.-Kat. Münster, *Skulptur Projekte Münster* 10.6.–1.10.2017, hrsg. von / ed. by Kasper König, Britta Peters, Marianne Wagner, Leipzig: Spector Books 2017.

Nakas 2008
Kassandra Nakas, »Vermintes Gelände. Ayşe Erkmens Arbeit mit Orten und Räumen«, in Basel 2008, 13–39.

New York 1994
Sense and Sensibility. Women Artists and Minimalism in the Nineties, Ausst.-Kat. / exh. cat. New York, The Museum of Modern Art 16.6.–11.9.1994, hrsg. von / ed. by Lynn Zelevansky, New York: The Museum of Modern Art 1994.

Ohlin 2008
Alix Ohlin, »Home and Away: The Strange Surrealism of Mona Hatoum«, in Ferrara 2008, 37–54.

Oxford 1998
Mona Hatoum. MOMA, Ausst.-Kat. / exh. cat. Oxford, Museum of Modern Art 5.4.–28.6.1998, Museum of Modern Art, Oxford: Museum of Modern Art 1998.

Panhans-Bühler 2004
Ursula Panhans-Bühler, »Involviertsein«, in Hamburg / Bonn / Stockholm 2004, 13–40.

Paris / London / Helsinki 2015
Mona Hatoum, Ausst.-Kat. / exh. cat. Paris, Musée national d'Art moderne, Centre national d'art et de culture Georges-Pompidou 24.7.–28.9.2015, London, Tate Modern 4.5.–21.8.2016, Helsinki, Nykytaiteen museo Kiasma 7.10.2016–26.2.2017, hrsg. von / ed. by Christine van Assche, Paris: Centre Pompidou 2015 (englische Fassung / English version: hrsg. von / ed. by Christine van Assche, Clarrie Wallis, London: Tate Publishing 2016).

Pejic 2008
Bojana Pejic, »Warum ist Feminismus plötzlich so sexy? Analyse einer ›Rückkehr‹ anhand dreier Ausstellungskataloge«, in *Springerin. Hefte für Gegenwartskunst* 1 (2008), 18–22.

Perrot 2016
Capucine Perrot, »Mona Hatoum, Performance Still 1985–95«, in *Performance at Tate: Into the Space of Art,* Tate Research Publication, 2016, online: <http://www.tate.org.uk/research/publications/performance-at-tate/perspectives/mona-hatoum>, letzter Zugriff / last access: 22.3.2017.

Philippi 1990 / 2006
Desa Philippi, »The Witness Beside Herself«, in *Third Text* 12 (Herbst / autumn 1990), 71–80, wieder abgedruckt / reprinted in Anastas / Brenson 2006, 120–124.

Philippi 1996
Desa Philippi, »Mona Hatoum: Some Any No Every Body«, in *Inside the Visible. An Elliptical Traverse of 20th Century Art in, of, and from the Feminine,* Ausst.-Kat. / exh. cat. Kortrijk, Béguinage of Saint-Elizabeth / Kanaal Art Foundation 16.4.1994–28.5.1995, Boston, The Institute of Contemporary Art 30.1.–12.5.1996, hrsg. von / ed. by Catherine de Zegher, Cambridge: The MIT Press 1996, 363–369.

Pichler / Ubl 2009
Wolfram Pichler, Ralph Ubl (Hrsg. / ed.), *Topologie. Falten, Knoten, Netze, Stülpungen in Kunst und Theorie,* Wien: Turia und Kant 2009.

Potts 2012
John Potts, »The Theme of Displacement in Contemporary Art«, in *E-rea. Revue électronique d'études sur le monde anglophone,* 9.2.2012, online: <https://erea.revues.org/2475?lang=en>, letzter Zugriff / last access: 26.4.2017.

Rancière 2008 / 2009
Jacques Rancière, *Der emanzipierte Zuschauer,* aus dem Französischen übersetzt von / translated from French by Richard Steurer, Wien: Passagen Verlag 2009 (Original: *Le spectateur emancipé,* Paris: La Fabrique 2008).

Rancière 2008 / 2011
Jacques Rancière, *The Emancipated Spectator,* aus dem Französischen übersetzt von / translated from French by Gregory Elliott, New York: Verso 2011.

Recklinghausen 1997
Ayşe Erkmen. I-MA-GES, Ausst.-Kat. / exh. cat. Kunsthalle Recklinghausen 4.5.–6.7.1997, hrsg. von / ed. by Ferdinand Ullrich, Köln: Wienand Verlag 1997.

Reilly 2007
Maura Reilly, »Introduction: Toward Transnational Feminisms«, in *Global Feminisms. New Directions in Contemporary Art,* Ausst.-Kat. / exh. cat. New York, Brooklyn Museum 23.3.–1.7.2007, hrsg. von / ed. by ders. / id., Linda Nochlin, New York, London: Merrel Publishers Limited 2007, 15–45.

Said 1984 / 1991
Edward Said, »Reflections on Exile« (1984), u. a. wieder abgedruckt / reprinted in *Out There: Marginalization and Contemporary Cultures,* hrsg. von / ed. by Russell Ferguson u. a. / et al., Cambridge, MA: MIT Press 1991, 357–366.

Said 2000
Edward Said, »The Art of Displacement. Mona Hatoum's Logic of Irreconcilables«, in London 2000, 7–17.

San Francisco 1996
Mona Hatoum. Current disturbance, Ausst.-Kat. / exh. cat. San Francisco, Capp Street Project 12.9.–23.11.1996, San Francisco: Capp Street Project 1996.

Santa Fe / North Adams 2001
Mona Hatoum. Domestic Disturbance, Ausst.-Kat. / exh. cat. Santa Fe, SITE 7.10.2000–14.1.2001, North Adams, MASS MoCA 18.3.–15.11.2001, hrsg. von / ed. by Laura Steward Heon, North Adams: MASS MoCA 2001.

São Paulo / Buenos Aires 2014
Mona Hatoum, Ausst.-Kat. / exh. cat. São Paulo, Estação Pinacoteca 6.12.2014–1.3.2015, Buenos Aires, Fondación Proa 28.3.–14.6.2015, hrsg. von / ed. by Chiara Bertola u.a. / et al., São Paulo: Pinacoteca do Estado 2014.

Sazzad 2008
Rehnuma Sazzad, »Hatoum, Said and Foucault: Resistance through Revealing the Power-Knowledge Nexus?«, in *Postcolonial Text* 4/3 (2008), online: <http://postcolonial.org/index.php/pct/article/view/891/791>, letzter Zugriff / last access: 1.2.2017.

Schade / Wenk 2011
Sigrid Schade, Silke Wenk, *Studien zur visuellen Kultur. Einführung in ein transdisziplinäres Forschungsfeld,* Bielefeld: transcript 2011.

Schaschke 2008
Bettina Schaschke, »Vom Schein zum Sein – Nachahmungen bei Ayşe Erkmen«, in Berlin 2008a, 169–177.

Schlenzka 2008
Jenny Schlenzka, »Mehr als man sieht / More than one sees«, in *Political / Minimal,* Ausst.-Kat. / exh. cat. Berlin, KW Institute for Contemporary Art 20.11.2008–25.1.2009, hrsg. von / ed. by Klaus Biesenbach, Nürnberg: Verlag für moderne Kunst 2008, 17–43.

Schmidt-Linsenhoff 2002
Viktoria Schmidt-Linsenhoff, »Arbeit am Stereotyp: Mona Hatoum und Gülsün Karamustafa«, in *Kunst und Politik: Jahrbuch der Guernica-Gesellschaft. Schwerpunkt: Postkolonialismus* 4 (2002), hrsg. von / ed. by Viktoria Schmidt-Linsenhoff, 219–242.

Schmidt-Linsenhoff 2005
Viktoria Schmidt-Linsenhoff, »Das koloniale Unbewusste«, in *Globalisierung / Hierarchisierung. Kulturelle Dominanz in Kunst und Kunstgeschichte,* hrsg. von / ed. by Irene Below, Beatrice von Bismarck, Marburg: Jonas Verlag 2005, 19–38.

Schmitz 2008
Britta Schmitz, »Von draußen nach drinnen, im Zickzack und vor und zurück – Unterwegs mit Ayşe Erkmens Weggefährten«, in Berlin 2008a, 13–21.

Schumacher 2011
Rainald Schumacher, »Mona Hatoum. Doppelklang – organische Arabesken und narrative Raster«, in München 2011, 20–44.

Seigworth / Gregg 2010
Gregory J. Seigworth, Melissa Gregg, »An Inventory of Shimmers«, in *The Affect Theory Reader,* hrsg. von / ed. by dens. / id., Durham, NC: Duke University Press 2010, 1–25.

Senova 2011
Başak Senova, »Ayşe Erkmen. Something connects« (Interview), in *Flash Art* 280 (Oktober / October 2011), online: <http://www.flashartonline.com/article/ayse-erkmen/>, letzter Zugriff / last access: 1.10.2016.

Smithson 2000
Robert Smithson, *Gesammelte Schriften,* aus dem Englischen übersetzt von / translated from English by Christoph Hollender, hrsg. von / ed. by Eva Schmidt, Köln: König 2000.

Söntgen 2004 / 2006
Beate Söntgen, »Interieur – das kritische Potential der Gegenwartskunst«, in Berlin 2004 / 2006, 363–375.

Spector 2016
Nancy Spector, »Dichotomies of Belonging«, in Archer 2016, 161–210.

Spinelli 1996
Claudia Spinelli, »Ich strebe eine ganzheitliche Erfahrung an. Ein Gespräch mit Mona Hatoum«, in *Kunstbulletin* 9 (September 1996), 16–22.

Spinelli 1996 / 2016
Claudia Spinelli, »Interview with Mona Hatoum«, in Archer 2016, 128–132 (Übersetzung von / translation of Spinelli 1996).

Spivak 1988
Gayatri Chakravorty Spivak, »Can the Subaltern Speak?«, in *Marxism and the Interpretation of Culture,* hrsg. von / ed. by Cary Nelson, Lawrence Grossberg, Urbana: University of Illinois Press 1988, 271–316.

St. Gallen 2003
Ayşe Erkmen. Kuckuck, Ausst.-Kat. / exh. cat. Kunstmuseum St. Gallen 1.3.–11.5.2003, hrsg. von / ed. by Konrad Bitterli, Nürnberg: Verlag für moderne Kunst 2003.

St. Gallen 2014
Mona Hatoum, Ausst.-Kat. / exh. cat. Kunstmuseum St. Gallen 7.9.2013–12.1.2014, hrsg. von / ed. by Konrad Bitterli, Nadia Veronese, Berlin: Holzwarth Publications 2014.

Steiner / Herzog 2004
Urs Steiner, Samuel Herzog, »Interview Mona Hatoum. ›Auf die Idee kommt es an!‹«, in *Neue Zürcher Zeitung,* 20.11.2004, online: <https://de.qantara.de/node/9005>, letzter Zugriff / last access: 25.2.2015 (Englisch / English: Urs Steiner, Samuel Herzog, »Interview with Mona Hatoum: The Idea is What Matters«, online: <http://montrealserai.com/_archives/2005_Volume_18/18_1/Article_4.htm>, letzter Zugriff / last access: 20.3.2017).

Stockholm 2003
Ayşe Erkmen. Tidvatten, Magasin III Stockholm Konsthall, hrsg. von / ed. by Nina Eklöf, Richard Julin, Elisabeth Millqvist, Stockholm: Magasin III 2003.

Tang 2016
Clara Tang, »Ayşe Erkmen. Fingerspitzengefühl«, in *Art Asia Pacific* 97 (März / March–April 2016), 161.

Tzelepis 2016
Elena Tzelepis, »Vulnerable Corporealities and Precarious Belongings in Mona Hatoum's Art«, in Butler / Gambetti / Sabsay 2016a, 147–166.

Üstek / Erkmen 2008
Fatoş Üstek, Ayşe Erkmen, »İlişkilendirmeler II / Relatings II« (Interview), in Block 2008, 89–112.

Ulz 2011
Melanie Ulz, »Nachrichten aus dem Black Atlantic. Das Schiff als Bedeutungsträger im Kontext von (Post-)Kolonialismus und Globalisierung«, in *FKW // Zeitschrift für Geschlechterforschung und visuelle Kultur* 51 (2011), 29–41.

Uppenkamp 2015
Bettina Uppenkamp, »Feministische Avantgarde der 1970er Jahre«, in *Lerchenfeld. Newsletter der Hochschule für Bildende Künste Hamburg* 29 (Juni / June 2015), 11.

Vancouver 2010
Mona Hatoum, Ausst.-Kat. / exh. cat. Vancouver, Rennie Collection 24.10.–28.1.2010, hrsg. von / ed. by Catherine Grenier, Vancouver: Rennie Collection 2010.

Venedig 2009
Mona Hatoum. Interior Landscape, Ausst.-Kat. / exh. cat. Venedig, Palazzo Querini Stampalia 4.6.–20.9.2009, hrsg. von / ed. by Chiara Bertola, Mailand: Charta 2009.

Venedig 2011
Plan B. »impossible short-circuits« and »serendipity« / »imkânsız kısa devreler« ve mutlu kazalar, Ausst.-Kat. / exh. cat. 54. Biennale von Venedig, Türkischer Pavillon / Turkish Pavilion 4.6.–27.11.2011, hrsg. von / ed. by Fulya Erdemci, Istanbul: MAS Matbaacılık AS 2011.

Vercoe 1997
Caroline Vercoe, »Not So Nice Colored Girls: A View of Tracey Moffatt's Nice Colored Girls«, in *Pacific Studies Journal* 20/4 (1997), 151–159.

Vogel 2014a
Sabine B. Vogel, »Die Grenzenlosigkeit der Skulptur«, in *Kunstforum. International* 229 (2014), 31–85.

Vogel 2014b
Sabine B. Vogel, »Mona Hatoum«, in *Kunstforum. International* 229 (2014), 160–163.

Volk 1998
Gregory Volk, »An der Verbindungsstelle der Dinge«, in Kassel 1998, 4–8.

Volk 2006
Gregory Volk, »Seeing through Sites: Erkmen's Altered Views«, in *Art in America* 94 (Januar / January 2006), 94–97, 151.

Volk 2008
Gregory Volk, »Karnevals-Orte«, in Berlin 2008a, 145–157.

Walker 1989
Alice Walker, *Auf der Suche nach den Gärten unserer Mütter. Beim Schreiben der Farbe Lila. Essays,* aus dem Englischen übersetzt von / translated from English by Gertraude Krueger, München: Goldmann 1989.

Wall 2010
David Wall, »Transgression, Excess, and the Violence of Looking in the Art of Kara Walker«, in *Oxford Art Journal* 33/3 (2010), 279–299.

Wenzel 2011
Anna-Lena Wenzel, *Grenzüberschreitungen in der Gegenwartskunst. Ästhetische und philosophische Positionen,* Bielefeld: transcript 2011; zugleich Diss. Universität Lüneburg 2011.

Wien 2002
Ayşe Erkmen, kein gutes Zeichen, Ausst.-Kat. / exh. cat. Wien, Secession 25.4.–23.6.2002, hrsg. von der / ed. by the Secession, Wien: Secession 2002.

Zimmermann 2007
Anja Zimmermann, »Medien und Metaphern des Schwarzweiß. Geschichte, Geschlecht und Bilderpolitik bei Kara Walker – mit einem kurzen Ausflug zu Cindy Sherman und Zwelethu Mthethwa«, in *FrauenKunstWissenschaft* 43 (Juni / June 2007), 10–21.

Biografien der Autorinnen und Autoren / Biographies of the Authors 189

Kelly Baum

Kelly Baum ist als Cynthia Hazen Polsky and Leon Polsky-Kuratorin für zeitgenössische Kunst am Metropolitan Museum of Art, New York, tätig. Sie arbeitet seit 17 Jahren als Kuratorin und hat in dieser Zeit zahlreiche Ausstellungen zur Kunst des 20. und 21. Jahrhunderts kuratiert, darunter *Carol Bove* (2006), *Nobody's Property: Art, Land, Space* (2010) und *The Body Politic: Video from The Met Collection* (2017). Im September 2017 hat sie eine große thematische Ausstellung mit dem Titel *Delirious: Art at the Limits of Reason, 1950–1980* eröffnet.

Frédéric Bußmann

Frédéric Bußmann ist seit 2011 als Kurator für Gemälde und Plastik vom 19. Jahrhundert bis zur Gegenwart am Museum der bildenden Künste Leipzig tätig. Zuvor war er von 2006 bis 2008 wissenschaftlicher Mitarbeiter am Deutschen Forum für Kunstgeschichte in Paris und von 2008 bis 2011 wissenschaftlicher Volontär und wissenschaftlicher Mitarbeiter der Bayerischen Staatsgemäldesammlungen München. Die Schwerpunkte seiner Forschungen, Ausstellungstätigkeiten und Publikationen liegen auf der bildenden Kunst vom 18. Jahrhundert bis zur Gegenwart.

Kassandra Nakas

Kassandra Nakas ist Kunsthistorikerin und lebt als Dozentin, Autorin und Kuratorin in Berlin. Nach einer Gastprofessur an der Universität der Künste Berlin unterrichtet sie derzeit an der Leuphana Universität Lüneburg und an der TU Braunschweig. Sie schreibt zu Themen der Gegenwartskunst und hat zahlreiche Ausstellungen kuratiert, unter anderem für das Berliner Künstlerprogramm des DAAD und die Staatlichen Museen zu Berlin.

Kea Wienand

Kea Wienand ist wissenschaftliche Mitarbeiterin am Institut für Kunst und visuelle Kultur der Universität Oldenburg. Nach der Promotion im Graduiertenkolleg *Identität und Differenz. Geschlechterkonstruktionen und Interkulturalität* an der Universität Trier hatte sie Lehraufträge an verschiedenen Universitäten und Kunsthochschulen inne; daneben hat sie freiberuflich als Kunstvermittlerin gearbeitet (etwa auf der *documenta 12*, 2007). Ihre Schwerpunkte in Forschung und Lehre sind Kunst und visuelle Kultur des 20. und 21. Jahrhunderts, postkoloniale Theorien, kulturwissenschaftliche Geschlechterstudien und transkulturelle Erinnerungskultur.

Elizabeth Youngman

Elizabeth Youngman ist Kunsthistorikerin und als wissenschaftliche Volontärin am Museum der bildenden Künste Leipzig tätig. Neben Ausstellungsprojekten zu zeitgenössischer Kunst hat sie eine Ausstellung mit Werken des 19. und 20. Jahrhunderts aus dem Bestand der Graphischen Sammlung des Museums kuratiert.

Kelly Baum

Kelly Baum is the Cynthia Hazen Polsky and Leon Polsky Curator of Contemporary Art at the Metropolitan Museum of Art, New York. She has been working as a curator for seventeen years, and in that time, has organized dozens of exhibitions on 20th and 21st century art, including *Carol Bove* (2006), *Nobody's Property: Art, Land, Space* (2010), and *The Body Politic: Video from The Met Collection* (2017). In September 2017, she opened a major thematic exhibition titled *Delirious: Art at the Limits of Reason, 1950–1980*.

Frédéric Bußmann

Frédéric Bußmann is curator of Painting and Sculpture from the 19th century to contemporary art at the Leipzig Museum of Fine Arts since 2011. From 2006 to 2008, he was research fellow at the German Forum for Art History in Paris and from 2008 to 2011 curatorial assistant and research fellow at the Bavarian State Painting Collections, Munich. His research, exhibition and publication activities focus on the visual arts from the 18th century to the present.

Kassandra Nakas

Kassandra Nakas is an art historian and lives and works as a lecturer, author, and curator in Berlin. She has been a visiting professor at the Berlin University of the Arts and is currently teaching at the Leuphana University of Lüneburg and the Braunschweig University of Technology. She writes about contemporary art and has curated numerous exhibitions, amongst others for the DAAD Artists-in-Berlin Programme and for the Berlin State Museums.

Kea Wienand

Kea Wienand is a research fellow at the Institute for Art and Visual Culture at the University of Oldenburg. After obtaining her doctoral degree at the graduate school *Identity and Difference. Gender Constructions and Interculturality (Identität und Differenz. Geschlechterkonstruktionen und Interkulturalität),* University of Trier, she has been lecturing at different universities and art academies and worked as a freelance art mediator (for instance at *documenta 12,* 2007). Her research and teaching interests are art and visual culture of the 20th and 21st centuries, postcolonial theory, cultural gender studies and transcultural commemorative culture.

Elizabeth Youngman

Elizabeth Youngman is an art historian and works as a curatorial assistant at the Leipzig Museum of Fine Arts. Besides exhibition projects on contemporary art, she curated an exhibition with 19th- and 20th-century works from the museum's Graphic Collection.

André Cadere
Barres de bois rond, 1971
lackiertes Holz / lacquered
wood, Museum moderner
Kunst Stiftung Ludwig Wien
⟶ 83

Judy Chicago
The Dinner Party, 1974–1979
Installation, Holz, Keramik,
Stoff, Metall, Farbe /
installation, wood, ceramic,
tissue, metal, paint,
1463×1280×91,5 cm, Brooklyn
Museum, New York (Foto /
photo: Donald Woodman)
⟶ 149

Ayşe Erkmen
Imitating Lines, 1985 / 2008
26 Stahlrohre mit Standplatten, angeschweißte Rohre,
grün lackiert, Maße variabel /
26 steel pipes with base plates
and additional welded-on
pipes, varnished in green,
dimensions variable

Ausstellungsansicht /
exhibition view, Hamburger
Bahnhof – Museum für
Gegenwart, Staatliche Museen
zu Berlin 2008
Courtesy of the artist and
Galerie Barbara Weiss, Berlin,
Barbara Gross Galerie,
München / Munich, Dirimart,
Istanbul (Foto / photo:
Jens Ziehe)
⟶ 84

Installationsansicht Museum
der bildenden Künste Leipzig /
installation view, Leipzig
Museum of Fine Arts 2017
Courtesy of the artist and the
Leipzig Museum of Fine Arts
(Foto / photo: dotgain.info)
⟶ 42

Ayşe Erkmen
Imitation / Taklit, 1987 / 2017
Installation, Ziegelsteine,
Leuchtstoffröhre, Maße varia-
bel / installation, bricks, neon
tube, dimensions variable

Installationsansicht /
installtion view, Istanbul, 1987
Courtesy of the artist and
Galerie Barbara Weiss, Berlin,
Barbara Gross Galerie,
München / Munich, Dirimart,
Istanbul (Foto / photo:
Ayşe Erkmen)
⟶ 80

Installationsansicht Museum
der bildenden Künste Leipzig /
installation view, Leipzig
Museum of Fine Arts 2017
Courtesy of the artist and the
Leipzig Museum of Fine Arts
(Foto / photo: dotgain.info)
⟶ 44

Ayşe Erkmen
Am Haus, 1994
dauerhafte Installation,
schwarzes Plexiglas / perma-
nent installation, black acrylic
glass, Berlin, Oranienstraße 18
Courtesy of the artist and
Galerie Barbara Weiss, Berlin,
Barbara Gross Galerie,
München / Munich, Dirimart,
Istanbul (Foto / photo: Jens
Ziehe)
⟶ 26

Ayşe Erkmen
Wertheim ACUU, 1995
Installationsansicht /
installation view, 4th Istanbul
Biennale 1995
Courtesy of the artist and
Galerie Barbara Weiss, Berlin,
Barbara Gross Galerie,
München / Munich, Dirimart,
Istanbul (Foto / photo:
Andreas Süß)
⟶ 22

Ayşe Erkmen
PFM-1 and others, 1997
Computeranimation in Farbe
mit Ton, auf DVD übertragen,
6 Monitore, 4 Min., Loop / computer animation in colour with
sound, transferred to DVD,
6 screens, 4 min, loop

Installationsansicht Museum
der bildenden Künste Leipzig /
installation view, Leipzig
Museum of Fine Arts 2017
Courtesy of the artist and the
Leipzig Museum of Fine Arts
(Foto / photo: dotgain.info)
⟶ 48

Ayşe Erkmen
PFM-1 and others (Detail /
detail), 1997 / 2013
90 Keramikobjekte, Maße
variabel / 90 ceramic objects,
dimensions variable,
Privatsammlung / private
collection
Courtesy of the artist (Foto /
photo: Serdar Tanyeli)
⟶ 78

Ayşe Erkmen
PFM-1 and others, 1997 / 2013
90 Keramikobjekte, Maße
variabel / 90 ceramic objects,
dimensions variable
Installationsansicht Museum
der bildenden Künste Leipzig /
installation view, Leipzig
Museum of Fine Arts 2017
Courtesy of the artist and the
Leipzig Museum of Fine Arts
(Foto / photo: dotgain.info)
⟶ 46

Ayşe Erkmen
Alkoven, 1997 / 2016
Keramikfliesen, Trocken-
bauwand, Maße variabel /
ceramic tiles, drywall,
dimensions variable

Installationsansicht /
installation view, Akademie
der Künste, Berlin 2016
Courtesy of the artist and
Galerie Barbara Weiss, Berlin,
Barbara Gross Galerie,
München / Munich, Dirimart,
Istanbul (Foto / photo:
Andreas Süß)
⟶ 78

Ayşe Erkmen
Alkoven, 1997 / 2017
Keramikfliesen, Tisch (von
UNA / Giulia Foscari) / ceramic
tiles, table (by UNA / Giulia
Foscari), 101×450×200 cm

Installationsansicht Museum
der bildenden Künste Leipzig /
installation view, Leipzig
Museum of Fine Arts 2017
Courtesy of the artist and the
Leipzig Museum of Fine Arts
(Foto / photo: dotgain.info)
⟶ 50

Ayşe Erkmen
Sculptures on the Air, 1997
Intervention zu den / interven-
tion to the *Skulptur. Projekten
in Münster* 1997
Courtesy of the artist and
Galerie Barbara Weiss, Berlin,
Barbara Gross Galerie,
München / Munich, Dirimart,
Istanbul (Foto / photo: Roman
Mensing, artdoc.de)
⟶ 74

Ayşe Erkmen
More or Less (Az Çok), 1999
Installation (vorhandener
Aufzug) / installation (existing
elevator), 565×280 cm

Installationsansicht /
installation view, Kunstmu-
seum Bonn 1999
Courtesy of the artist and
Galerie Barbara Weiss, Berlin,
Barbara Gross Galerie,
München / Munich, Dirimart,
Istanbul
⟶ 76

Ayşe Erkmen
Shipped Ships, 2001
Frankfurt am Main, *Moment*
Deutsche Bank
Courtesy of the artist and
Galerie Barbara Weiss, Berlin,
Barbara Gross Galerie,
München / Munich, Dirimart,
Istanbul (Foto / photo: Bärbel
Högner)
⟶ 28

Ayşe Erkmen
Busy Colors, 2005
Installationsansicht / installa-
tion view, SculptureCenter,
Long Island City, New York
2005
Courtesy of the artist and
Galerie Barbara Weiss, Berlin,
Barbara Gross Galerie,
München / Munich, Dirimart,
Istanbul (Foto / photo:
Oren Slor)
⟶ 31

Ayşe Erkmen
*Die Farben der Buchstaben
(5)*, 2006
ausgestanztes, farbiges
Plexiglas / die-cut, coloured
Plexiglas, 40,5×24 cm
Courtesy of the artist and
Galerie Barbara Weiss, Berlin,
Barbara Gross Galerie,
München / Munich, Dirimart,
Istanbul (Foto / photo:
Jens Ziehe)
⟶ 52

Ayşe Erkmen
*Die Farben der Buchstaben
(M)*, 2006
ausgestanztes, farbiges Plexi-
glas / die-cut, coloured Plexi-
glas, ca. / ca 45×47 cm
Courtesy of the artist and
Galerie Barbara Weiss, Berlin,
Barbara Gross Galerie,
München / Munich, Dirimart,
Istanbul
⟶ 53

Ayşe Erkmen
Netz, 2006 / 2008
Polyester-Textilband, ca.

10 000 Meter in unterschiedlichen Längen / ribbon,
polyester, ca 10,000 m in
variable dimensions

Ausstellungsansicht /
exhibition view, Hamburger
Bahnhof – Museum für Gegen-
wart, Staatliche Museen
zu Berlin 2008
Courtesy of the artist and
Galerie Barbara Weiss, Berlin,
Barbara Gross Galerie,
München / Munich, Dirimart,
Istanbul (Foto / photo:
Jens Ziehe)
⟶ 77

Installationsansicht Museum
der bildenden Künste Leipzig /
installation view, Leipzig
Museum of Fine Arts 2017
Courtesy of the artist and the
Leipzig Museum of Fine Arts
(Foto / photo: dotgain.info)
⟶ 60

Ayşe Erkmen
Jalousien, 2007
7 Jalousien, Baumwolle, Kunststoff, Maße variabel / 9 blinds,
cotton, plastic, dimensions
variable

Installationsansicht Museum
der bildenden Künste Leipzig /
installation view, Leipzig
Museum of Fine Arts 2017
Courtesy of the artist and the
Leipzig Museum of Fine Arts
(Foto / photo: dotgain.info)
⟶ 54

Ayşe Erkmen
Gemütliche Ecken, 2009
10 Aluminiumverbundplatten,
lackiert, Maße variabel / 10
aluminium composite boards,
varnished, dimensions variable

Installationsansicht /
installation view, Graz 2009
Courtesy of the artist and
Galerie Barbara Weiss, Berlin,
Barbara Gross Galerie,
München / Munich, Dirimart,
Istanbul (Foto / photo: Yashar
Dehaghani)
⟶ 88

Installationsansicht /
installation view, 2017
Courtesy of the artist and the
Leipzig Museum of Fine Arts
(Foto / photo: dotgain.info)
⟶ 100

Ayşe Erkmen
Ewig Dein, 2011
Klanginstallation, 1 Min. 11 Sek.,
Loop / sound installation, 1 min
11 s, loop

Installationsansicht Museum
der bildenden Künste Leipzig /
installation view, Leipzig
Museum of Fine Arts 2017
Courtesy of the artist and the
Leipzig Museum of Fine Arts
(Foto / photo: dotgain.info)
⟶ 96

Ayşe Erkmen
Großes grünes Pompon, 2012
Kleidungsetiketten aus Baum-
wolle, gebeizter Chrom-
ständer / clothing labels made
out of cotton, stained chrome
stand, 120×31 cm, Ø 41 cm
Courtesy of the artist and
Galerie Barbara Weiss, Berlin,
Barbara Gross Galerie,
München / Munich, Dirimart,
Istanbul (Foto / photo:
Jens Ziehe)
⟶ 58

Ayşe Erkmen
Kleines grünes Pompon, 2012
Kleidungsetiketten aus Baum-
wolle, gebeizter Chrom-
ständer / clothing labels made
out of cotton, stained chrome
stand, 100×31 cm, Ø 36 cm
Courtesy of the artist and
Galerie Barbara Weiss, Berlin,
Barbara Gross Galerie,
München / Munich, Dirimart,
Istanbul (Foto / photo:
Jens Ziehe)
⟶ 56

Ayşe Erkmen
Row-row, 2012
Metall, Farbe / metal, colour,
93×266 cm, Privatsammlung /
private collection

Installationsansicht Museum
der bildenden Künste Leipzig /
installation view, Leipzig
Museum of Fine Arts 2017
Courtesy of the artist and the
Leipzig Museum of Fine Arts
(Foto / photo: dotgain.info)
⟶ 62

Ayşe Erkmen
bangbangbang, 2013
grüne Kugel, Seil, Kran / green
ball, cable, crane, Installationsansicht / installation view,
13th Istanbul Biennale

Courtesy of the artist and
Galerie Barbara Weiss, Berlin,
Barbara Gross Galerie,
München / Munich, Dirimart,
Istanbul (Foto / photo:
Servet Dilber)
⟶ 72

Ayşe Erkmen
Bronze Acid Blue, 2014
Video in Farbe mit Ton, 4 Min.
1 Sek., Loop / colour video with
sound, 4 min 1 s, loop
Courtesy of the artist and
Galerie Barbara Weiss, Berlin,
Barbara Gross Galerie,
München / Munich, Dirimart,
Istanbul
⟶ 92

Ayşe Erkmen
Bronze Acid Green, 2014
Video in Farbe mit Ton, 3 Min.,
Loop / colour video with
sound, 3 min, loop
Courtesy of the artist and
Galerie Barbara Weiss, Berlin,
Barbara Gross Galerie,
München / Munich, Dirimart,
Istanbul
⟶ 92

Ayşe Erkmen
Bronze Acid Ochre, 2014
Video in Farbe mit Ton, 4 Min.
1 Sek., Loop / colour video with
sound, 4 min 1 s, loop
Courtesy of the artist and
Galerie Barbara Weiss, Berlin,
Barbara Gross Galerie,
München / Munich, Dirimart,
Istanbul
⟶ 92

Ayşe Erkmen
Bronze Acid Yellow, 2014
Video in Farbe mit Ton, 5 Min.,
Loop / colour video with
sound, 5 min, loop
Courtesy of the artist and
Galerie Barbara Weiss, Berlin,
Barbara Gross Galerie,
München / Munich, Dirimart,
Istanbul
⟶ 92

Ayşe Erkmen
*grass green / not the color
it is,* 2014
Bronze, Patina / bronze, patina,
30×20×10 cm

green / not the color it is, 2014
Bronze, Patina / bronze, patina,
30×20×10 cm

*light green / not the color
it is,* 2014
Bronze, Patina / bronze, patina,
30×20×10 cm

Installationsansicht Museum
der bildenden Künste Leipzig /
installation view, Leipzig
Museum of Fine Arts 2017
Courtesy of the artist and the
Leipzig Museum of Fine Arts
(Foto / photo: dotgain.info)
⟶ 64

Ayşe Erkmen
By Nature, 2015 / 2017
Installation, Porzellantier-
figuren, Plexiglasvitrine,
Maße variabel / installation,
porcelain figurines, showcase
in Plexiglass, dimensions
variable

Installationsansicht Museum
der bildenden Künste Leipzig /
installation view, Leipzig
Museum of Fine Arts 2017
Courtesy of the artist and the
Leipzig Museum of Fine Arts
(Foto / photo: dotgain.info)
⟶ 98

Ayşe Erkmen
Glassworks, 2015 / 2017
farbige Glasplatten, Strahler /
coloured glass plates, spotlights

Installationsansicht /
installation view, Cadhame
Halle Verrière, Meisenthal 2015
Courtesy of the artist and
Galerie Barbara Weiss, Berlin,
Barbara Gross Galerie,
München / Munich, Dirimart,
Istanbul
⟶ 86

Installationsansicht Museum
der bildenden Künste Leipzig /
installation view, Leipzig
Museum of Fine Arts 2017
Courtesy of the artist and
the Leipzig Museum of
Fine Arts (Foto / photo:
dotgain.info)
⟶ 90

Ayşe Erkmen
Three Eyes, 2015
Burgfelsen von Uçhisar,
Kappadokien / Uçhisar Castle,
Cappadocia
Courtesy of the artist and
Galerie Barbara Weiss, Berlin,
Barbara Gross Galerie,

München / Munich, Dirimart,
Istanbul
⟶ 71

Ayşe Erkmen
Half of, 2017
Installation, 5-teilig, Stoff,
Aluminium, Maße variabel /
installation, 5 pieces, fabric,
aluminium, dimensions
variable

Installationsansicht Museum
der bildenden Künste Leipzig /
installation view, Leipzig
Museum of Fine Arts 2017
Courtesy of the artist and the
Leipzig Museum of Fine Arts
(Foto / photo: dotgain.info)
⟶ 94

Ayşe Erkmen
On Water, 2017
Installation / installation at
Skulptur Projekte Münster 2017
Courtesy of the artist
(Foto / photo: Roman Mensing,
artdoc.de)
⟶ 24

Ayşe Erkmen
Shutters, 2017
Installation, Fensterblenden
in Bewegung / installation,
moving shutters

Installationsansicht Museum
der bildenden Künste Leipzig /
installation view, Leipzig
Museum of Fine Arts 2017
Courtesy of the artist and the
Leipzig Museum of Fine Arts
(Foto / photo: dotgain.info)
⟶ 90

Mona Hatoum
Under Siege, 1982
Live-Performance mit Kon-
struktion aus Holz und Plastik-
folie, Tonband, Eimer und
flüssigem Ton / live action
within a structure made of
wood and plastic sheeting,
sound tape, bucket and liquid
clay, aufgeführt bei / performed at *Reflections – 9
Women Artists,* Aspex Gallery,
Portsmouth
Courtesy of the Aspex Gallery,
Portsmouth (Foto / photo:
John McPherson)
⟶ 108

Mona Hatoum
So much I want to say, 1983,
Video in Schwarz-Weiß mit
Ton, 4 Min. 41 Sek. / black and
white video with sound, 4 min
41 sec
Courtesy of the artist
⟶ 32

Mona Hatoum
Changing Parts, 1984
Video in Schwarz-Weiß mit
Ton, 24 Min. / black and white
video with sound, 24 min,
Eine / A Western Front Video
Production, Vancouver
Courtesy of the artist
⟶ 126

Mona Hatoum
*Them and Us … and Other
Divisions,* 1984
Live-Performance mit schwar-
zer Kapuze, Eimer, Bürste,
roter Farbe, Zeitungen und
Drahtgeflecht, 50 Min. / live
action with black hood, bucket,
brush, red paint, newspapers
and wire mesh, 50 min, auf-
geführt beim / performed
at *2nd International Festival of
Performance,* South Hill
Park Arts Centre, Bracknell,
Berkshire
Courtesy of the artist
(Foto / photo: Robin Morley)
⟶ 109

Mona Hatoum
*Variation on Discord and
Divisions,* 1984
Live-Performance mit Kapuze,
Messer, Eimer, Scheuerbürste,
roter Farbe, Tisch, Stühlen,
Tellern, rohen Rindernieren
und Zeitungen, 40–50 Min. /
live action with hood, knife,
bucket, scrubbing brush, red
paint, table, chairs, plates, raw
beef kidneys and newspapers,
40–50 min, aufgeführt bei /
performed at The Western
Front, Vancouver
Courtesy of The Western Front,
Vancouver (Foto / photo:
Cornelia Wyngaarden)
⟶ 122

Mona Hatoum
Roadworks, 1985
Video in Farbe mit Ton,
6 Min. 45 Sek. / colour video
with sound, 6 min 45 s,
Dokumentation der Perfor-
mance für / documentation
of performance for *Roadworks,*

Brixton, London
Courtesy of the Kunstmuseum
St. Gallen (Foto / photo:
Stefan Rohner)
⟶ **107 + 128**

Mona Hatoum
Measures of Distance, 1988
Video in Farbe mit Ton, 15 Min.
35 Sek. / colour video with
sound, 15 min 35 s, Eine /
A Western Front Video
Production, Vancouver
Courtesy of the artist
⟶ **130**

Mona Hatoum
Over my dead body,
1988 / 2002
Tintenstrahldruck auf PVC mit
Ösen / ink jet on PVC with
eyelets, 204,5×305 cm
Courtesy of the Galerie Max
Hetzler, Berlin | Paris
(Foto / photo: def image)
⟶ **132**

Mona Hatoum
The Light at the End, 1989
Metallrahmen und elektrische
Heizelemente / metal frame
and electric heating elements,
166×142×5 cm

Installationsansicht /
installation view, The
Showroom, London 1989
Courtesy of the artist
(Foto / photo: Edward
Woodman)
⟶ **110**

Mona Hatoum
Light Sentence, 1992
Spinde aus galvanisiertem
Drahtgeflecht, Elektromotor
und Glühbirne / galvanised
wire mesh lockers, electric
motor and light bulb,
198×185×490 cm

Installationsansicht /
installation view, Centre
Pompidou, Paris
Courtesy of the Centre
Pompidou, Mnam-CCI /
Dist RMN-GP
(Foto / photo: Philippe Migeat)
⟶ **114**

Mona Hatoum
Keffieh, 1993–1999
menschliches Haar auf Baum-
wolltuch, Maße variabel /
human hair on cotton fabric,
dimensions variable
Courtesy of the Fondazione
Querini Stampalia, Onlus,
Venice (Foto / photo:
Agostino Osio)
⟶ **118**

Mona Hatoum
You Are Still Here, 1994
geätztes Spiegelglas und
Metallapplikationen / etched
mirrored glass and metal
fixtures, 38×29,2×0,5 cm
Courtesy of White Cube
(Foto / photo: Stephen White)
⟶ **123**

Mona Hatoum
Doormat, 1996
rostfreier Stahl und vernickelte
Pins, Leinwand und Leim /
stainless steel and nickel-
plated pins, canvas and glue,
3×71×40,5 cm
Courtesy of White Cube
(Foto / photo: Stephen White)
⟶ **114**

Mona Hatoum
Marrow, 1996
Gummi, Maße variabel /
rubber, dimensions variable
Courtesy of Alexander and
Bonin, New York
(Foto / photo: Orcutt &
Van Der Putten)
⟶ **116**

Mona Hatoum
Present Tense, 1996
Seife und Glasperlen /
soap and glass beads,
4,5×299×241 cm

Installationsansicht /
installation view, Gallery
Anadiel, Jerusalem 1996
Courtesy of the Gallery
Anadiel, Jerusalem
(Foto / photo: Issa Freij)
⟶ **119**

Mona Hatoum
Present Tense (Detail /
detail), 1996
Seife und Glasperlen /
soap and glass beads,
4,5×299×241 cm

Installationsansicht /
installation view, Gallery
Anadiel, Jerusalem 1996
Courtesy of the Gallery
Anadiel, Jerusalem (Foto /
photo: Issa Freij)
⟶ **119**

Mona Hatoum
*La grande broyeuse
(Mouli-Julienne ×17)*, 1999
Baustahl / mild steel, Haupt-
skulptur / main sculpture:
343×575×263 cm, Scheiben /
discs: 5×170×170 cm

Installationsansicht /
installation view, Museum van
Hedendaagse Kunst Antwerpen

(MUHKA) 2000
Courtesy of the MUHKA
(Foto / photo: Wim Van
Nueten)
⟶ **36**

Mona Hatoum
Untitled (passoire de J-L), 1999
Japanisches Wachspapier /
Japanese wax paper,
43,5×50 cm
Courtesy of Le Creux de
l'Enfer, Thiers
(Foto / photo: Joël Damase)
⟶ **169**

Mona Hatoum
Untitled (râpe cylindrique),
1999
Japanisches Wachspapier /
Japanese wax paper,
40×54,5 cm
Courtesy of Le Creux de
l'Enfer, Thiers
(Foto / photo: Joël Damase)
⟶ **168**

Mona Hatoum
Cube, 2006
Baustahl / mild steel,
174×174×174 cm
Courtesy of the Rennie
Collection, Vancouver
(Foto / photo: Site Photo-
graphy)
⟶ **35**

Mona Hatoum
Projection, 2006
Baumwolle, Abacá / cotton,
abaca, 89×140 cm
Courtesy of the Galerie Max
Hetzler, Berlin | Paris
(Foto / photo: Jörg von
Bruchhausen)
⟶ **121 + 160**

Mona Hatoum
Daybed, 2008
geschwärzter Stahl / black
finished steel, 31,5×219×98 cm,
Sammlung Sander / The
Sander Collection, Darmstadt

und / and

Paravent, 2008
geschwärzter Stahl / black
finished steel, 215×302×5 cm

Installationsansicht Museum
der bildenden Kunste Leipzig /
installation view, Leipzig
Museum of Fine Arts 2017
Courtesy of the artist and the
Leipzig Museum of Fine Arts
(Foto / photo: dotgain.info)
⟶ **170**

Mona Hatoum
Daybed, 2008
geschwärzter Stahl / black
finished steel, 31,5×219×98 cm,
Sammlung Sander / The
Sander Collection, Darmstadt

und / and

Paravent, 2008
geschwärzter Stahl / black
finished steel, 215×302×5 cm

Installationsansicht /
installation view, Pinacoteca
do Estado de São Paulo 2014
Courtesy of the Pinacoteca
do Estado de São Paulo
(Foto / photo: Everton
Ballardin)
⟶ **112**

Mona Hatoum
Undercurrent (red), 2008
mit Stoff verhüllte Stromkabel,
Glühbirnen und Lichtregler,
Maße variabel / cloth-covered
electrical cable, light bulbs
and dimmer unit, dimensions
variable

Installationsansicht /
installation view, Galerie
Max Hetzler, Berlin
Courtesy of the Galerie
Max Hetzler, Berlin | Paris
(Foto / photo: Jörg von
Bruchhausen)
⟶ **33**

Mona Hatoum
Hot Spot III, 2009
Edelstahl, Neonröhren /
stainless steel, neon tube,
234×223×223 cm, Sammlung
Goetz, München / Munich

Installationsansicht Museum
der bildenden Kunste Leipzig /
installation view, Leipzig Museum of Fine Arts 2017
Courtesy of the artist and the
Leipzig Museum of Fine Arts
(Foto / photo: dotgain.info)
⟶ **158**

Mona Hatoum
Impenetrable, 2009
geschwärzter Stacheldraht,
Angelschnur / black
finished steel, fishing wire,
300×300×300 cm

Installationsansicht /
installation, the Mathaf:
Arab Museum of Modern
Art, Doha 2014
Courtesy of the Mathaf: Arab
Museum of Modern Art
(Foto / photo: Markus Elblaus)
⟶ **113 + 164**

Mona Hatoum
Bunker, 2011
22 Skulpturen aus Baustahl-
rohr, Maße variabel / 22 mild
steel tubing structures, dimensions variable

Installationsansicht /
installation view, White Cube,
London 2011
Courtesy of White Cube
(Foto / photo:
Hugo Glendinning)
⟶ **117**

Mona Hatoum
Bourj A, 2011
Baustahlrohre / mild steel
tubing, 165×70×40 cm

Bourj II, 2011
Baustahlrohre / mild steel
tubing, 180×75×50 cm

Bourj III, 2011
Baustahlrohre / mild steel
tubing, 180×80×55 cm

Installationsansicht Museum
der bildenden Künste Leipzig /
installation view, Leipzig
Museum of Fine Arts 2017
Courtesy of the artist and the
Leipzig Museum of Fine Arts
(Foto / photo: dotgain.info)
⟶ **166**

Mona Hatoum
*Natura morta (medical
cabinet)*, 2012
Muranospiegelglas, Stahl,
Glas / Murano mirrored glass,
steel, glass, 61,5×54×17,5 cm
Courtesy of the Kunstmuseum
St. Gallen (Foto / photo:
Stefan Rohner)
⟶ **136**

Mona Hatoum
Cellules, 2012–2013
Baustahl, mundgeblasenes
Glas in 8 Teilen, 170 cm × Maße
variabel / mild steel, hand-
blown glass in eight parts, 170
cm × variable width and depth

Installationsansicht Museum
der bildenden Kunste Leipzig /
installation view, Leipzig
Museum of Fine Arts 2017
Courtesy of the artist and the
Leipzig Museum of Fine Arts
(Foto / photo: dotgain.info)
⟶ **174**

Mona Hatoum
Map (clear), 2015
Glasmurmeln / clear glass
marbles, je / each Ø 2 cm,
Gesamtmaße variabel / Overall
dimensions variable

Installationsansicht /
installation view, Centre
Pompidou, Paris 2015
Courtesy of the Galerie Chantal
Crousel, Paris (Foto / photo:
Florian Kleinefenn)
⟶ **121**

Mona Hatoum
*Remains of the Day
(s version)*, 2016
Drahtgeflecht und Holz, Maße
variabel / wire mesh and wood,
dimensions variable

Installationsansicht Museum
der bildenden Künste Leipzig /
installation view, Leipzig
Museum of Fine Arts 2017
Courtesy of the artist and the
Leipzig Museum of Fine Arts
(Foto / photo: dotgain.info)
⟶ **162**

Mona Hatoum
Remains of the Day, 2017
Drahtgeflecht und Holz, Maße
variabel / wire mesh and wood,
dimensions variable

Installationsansicht /
installation view, Hiroshima
City Museum of Contemporary
Art 2017
Courtesy of the Hiroshima City
Museum of Contemporary Art
(Foto / photo: Ken Kusakari)
⟶ **37**

Mona Hatoum
Quarters, 2017
Baustahl / mild steel
275×516×1515 cm

Installationsansicht Museum
der bildenden Künste Leipzig /
installation view, Leipzig
Museum of Fine Arts
Courtesy of the artist and the
Leipzig Museum of Fine Arts
(Foto / photo: dotgain.info)
⟶ **134**

Max Klinger
Beethoven, 1902
Stein (verschiedenes farbiges
Gestein), Glas, Elfenbein,
Kupfer / stones (in various
colours), glass, ivory, copper,
95×110×110 cm (ohne Thron /
without throne)

und andere Werke von / and
other works by Max Klinger
Installationsansicht Museum
der bildenden Künste Leipzig /
installation view, Leipzig
Museum of Fine Arts 2017
(Foto / photo: dotgain.info)
⟶ **87**

**Suzanne Lacy & Leslie
Labowitz**
In Mourning and in Rage, 1977
Performance / performance,
Los Angeles, Rathaus /
town hall
(Foto / photo: Marin Karras)
⟶ **146**

Gordon Matta-Clark
Conical Intersect, 1975
Schwarz-Weiß-Fotografie einer
urbanen Intervention für
die / black and white photography of an urban intervention
for the Biennale de Paris
⟶ **73**

Anny & Sibel Öztürk
Behind the Wheel, 2004
Installation, 16 Zeichnungen,
Landkarten, PKW, Textplot,
Maße variabel / installation,
16 drawings, map, car, text
plot, dimensions
variable, Galerie Vera Gliem,
Köln / Cologne (Foto / photo:
Helmut Claus)
⟶ **155**

Adrian Piper
*The Mythic Being: Cruising
White Women*, 1975
Performance / performance,
Cambridge, Massachusetts
⟶ **143**

Cindy Sherman
Untitled Film Still #2, 1977
Silbergelatineabzüge /
gelatin silver prints,
14–19,2×21,4–24,1 cm,
Museum of Modern Art,
New York
⟶ **150**

Robert Smithson
*A Nonsite (Franklin, New
Jersey)*, 1968
Bemalte Holzbehälter, Kalk-
stein, Silbergelatineabzug,
Schreibmaschinenschrift auf
Papier mit Bleistift und Präge-
buchstaben, auf Untersatz
montiert / painted wooden
bins, limestone, gelatin silver
prints and typescript on paper
with graphite and transfer
letters, and mounted on mat
board, Behälter / bins installed:
41,9×208,9×261,6 cm,
Rahmen / frame:
103,5×78,1×2,5 cm,
Blatt / sheet: 101,3×75,9 cm,
Museum of Contemporary Art
Chicago, Gift of Susan and
Lewis Manilow, 1979.2.a-g
⟶ **82**

Rosemarie Trockel
Ohne Titel, 1985
Wolle, 2 Tafeln / wool, 2 boards,
je / each 40×60 cm
⟶ **152**

Kara Walker
Slavery, Slavery!, 1997
Scherenschnitt, selbstkleben-
de Folie / silhouette, self-adhe-
sive film, 360×838 cm
Collection of Eileen and Peter
Norton, Santa Monica
(Foto / photo: Brent Sikkema)
⟶ **153**

Carrie Mae Weems
Mirror, Mirror, 1987–1988
Silbergelatinedruck / print,
gelatine process, silver,
51×41 cm, Privatsammlung /
private collection
(Foto / photo: Adam Reich)
⟶ **151**

Ayse Erkmen (Portrait)
Courtesy of the artist and
Galerie Barbara Weiss, Berlin,
Barbara Gross Galerie,
München / Munich, Dirimart,
Istanbul (Foto / photo: Serdar
Tanyeli)
⟶ **178**

Mona Hatoum (Portrait)
Courtesy the artist (Foto /
photo: Jim Rakete)
⟶ **180**

Ayşe Erkmen möchte gerne danken / would like to thank Yeşim Bakirküre, Dirimart, Istanbul, Giulia Foscari, Barbara Gross Galerie, München / Munich, Ayşe Orhun Gültekin, Ahmet Önder, Levent Özmen, Dino Steinhof, Charlotte von Uthmann und / and Galerie Barbara Weiss, Berlin.

Mona Hatoum möchte gerne danken / would like to thank Alexandra Bradley, Sophie Greig, Hannah Gruy, Sascha-Andre Hahn, Katharine Oakes, Laura Turcan, Janey Xuereb und / and Alexander and Bonin, New York, Galerie Chantal Crousel, Paris und / and White Cube.

Das Ausstellungsteam dankt zuerst Ayşe Erkmen und Mona Hatoum für die Vorbereitung und Realisierung der Ausstellung. / The exhibition team would like to thank first Ayşe Erkmen and Mona Hatoum for the preparation and realisation of the exhibition.

Wir danken auch folgenden Institutionen, die die Realisierung der Ausstellung ermöglicht haben / We thank as well the following institutions that rendered possible the realisation of the exhibition: Kulturstiftung des Bundes, Peter und Irene Ludwig Stiftung – für unkomplizierte Hilfe besonders / for her uncomplicated support especially Dr. Brigitte Franzen –, Kulturstiftung des Freistaats Sachsen, Förderer des Museums der bildenden Künste Leipzig e. V., Bundeszentrale für politische Bildung / bpb.

Besonders wollen wir White Cube für ihre Unterstützung und die Beteiligung an den Produktionskosten von *Quarters*, 2017 danken. / We thank White Cube for their support and participation in the production costs of the work *Quarters*, 2017.

Ferner danken wir folgenden Leihgebern, Museen und Galerien für ihre Unterstützung / Furthermore we thank the following lenders, museums, and galeries for their assistance: Kunsthalle Bielefeld, Galerie Chantal Crousel, Paris, Dirimart, Istanbul, GfZK Galerie für Zeitgenössische Kunst Leipzig, Sammlung Goetz, München / Munich, Galerie Barbara Gross, München / Munich, Sammlung Sander, Darmstadt, Galerie Barbara Weiss, Berlin und / and White Cube, London. Und nicht zuletzt möchten wir danken / Last not least we would like to thank: Rudaba Badakhshi und / and dem Referat für Migration und Integration der Stadt Leipzig, Bürgerverein Kolonnadenviertel e. V., Dr. Kelly Baum, Katharina Düben, Uwe Fankhänel, Frauenkultur e.V., Theresa Gnoyke, Sophie Greig, Sascha Hahn, Peter Head, Dr. Anke Hervol, Prof. Dr. Susan Kamel und den Studierenden des Studiengangs / and the students of the course Museumsmanagement und -kommunikation der Hochschule für Technik und Wirtschaft Berlin, Verena Landau und den Studierenden des Instituts für Kunstpädagogik der Universität Leipzig / and the students of the institute for art mediation at the University of Leipzig, Nick Malyon, Roman Mensing, Dr. Friedrich Meschede, Dr. Kassandra Nakas, Katharine Oakes, Lima Pfefferkorn, Friederike Plöger, Pöge-Haus e. V. mit der Evangelisch-Lutherischen Landeskirche Sachsen, Porr Deutschland GmbH, Doreen Reichel, Emma Resch, Sora Rösler, Sagart e. V., Julia Schäfer, Dr. Hans-Werner Schmidt, Audrey Staub, John-Paul Sumner, Marie Tollkühn, Ralf Urban, Dr. Kea Wienand, Janey Xuereb, ZEOK e. V. und allen Teilnehmerinnen und Teilnehmern der Projekte Stimmensammler und Newcomer / and all participants of the projects Stimmensammler and Newcomer.

Gefördert durch die /
Funded by

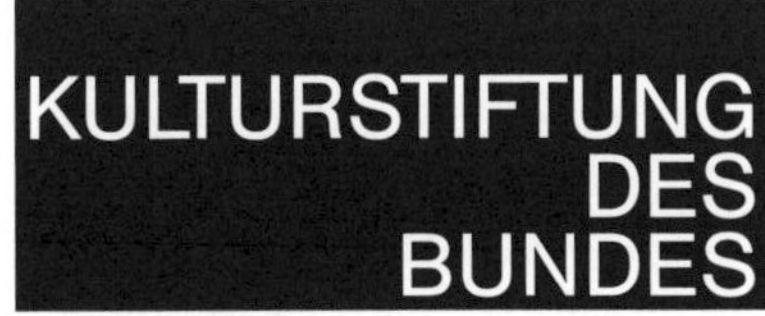

Peter und Irene
Ludwig Stiftung

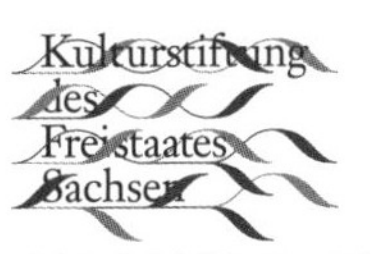 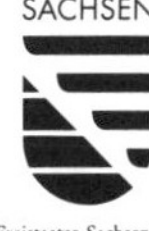

Gefördert durch die Kulturstiftung des Freistaates Sachsen.
Diese Maßnahme wird mitfinanziert durch Steuermittel auf
der Grundlage des von den Abgeordneten des Sächsischen
Landtags beschlossenen Haushaltes.

**Förderer des
Museums
der bildenden
Künste
Leipzig e.V.**

Das Vermittlungsprogramm wurde
gefördert durch / The educational
programme is funded by

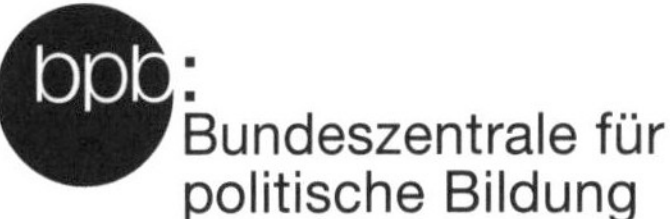
Bundeszentrale für
politische Bildung

Die Publikation erscheint anlässlich der Ausstellung /
The catalogue is published on the occasion of the exhibition
Ayşe Erkmen & Mona Hatoum. Displacements / Entortungen
im Museum der bildenden Künste Leipzig / at the Leipzig
Museum of Fine Arts, 18.11.2017–18.2.2018.

Ausstellung / Exhibition

Direktor / Director
Alfred Weidinger

Kurator / Curator
Frédéric Bußmann

Projektassistenz / Assistant
Elizabeth Youngman

Museum der bildenden Künste Leipzig

Katharinenstr. 10
04109 Leipzig
Tel. +49 341 216990
Fax +49 341 21699999
mdbk@leipzig.de
www.mdbk.de

Katalog / Catalogue

Herausgeber / Editor
Alfred Weidinger, Frédéric Bußmann

**Redaktion, Bildredaktion /
Editing, Picture Editing**
Frédéric Bußmann, Sabine Schmidt,
Elizabeth Youngman

Lektorat / Copy-editing
Peter Sondermeyer, Alexandra Bradley,
Martin Shaw

Übersetzung / Translation
Tas Skorupa, Peter Sondermeyer

Autorenkürzel / Author abbreviation
FB: Frédéric Bußmann
EY: Elizabeth Youngman

Gestaltung / Design and Layout
Ondine Pannet & David Voss,
Bureau David Voss, Leipzig

**Fotografien, Lithografie /
Photographs, Lithographs**
dotgain.info

Druck, Bindung / Print, Binding
Druckerei Kettler GmbH

Verlag / Publisher
VfmK Verlag für moderne Kunst GmbH
www.vfmk.org

ISBN 978-3-903153-79-0

Gedruckt in Deutschland /
Printed in Germany

Alle Rechte vorbehalten /
All rights reserved

**Bibliografische Information der
Deutschen Nationalbibliothek /
Bibliographic information published
by the Deutsche Nationalbibliothek**

Die Deutsche Nationalbibliothek verzeichnet diese Publikation in der Deutschen Nationalbibliografie; detaillierte bibliografische Daten sind im Internet über http://dnb.dnb.de/ abrufbar.

The Deutsche Nationalbibliothek lists this publication in the Deutsche Nationalbibliografie; detailed bibliographic data is available online at http://dnb.dnb.de/.

Vertrieb / Distribution
Europa / Europe:
LKG, www.lkg-va.de
CH: AVA, www.ava.ch
UK: Cornerhouse Publications,
www.cornerhousepublications.org
USA: D.A.P., www.artbook.com